By Fables Alone

Ars Rossica

Series Editor — David M. Bethea (University of Wisconsin – Madison)

By Fables Alone
Literature and State Ideology in Late-Eighteenth — Early-Nineteenth-Century Russia

ANDREI ZORIN

TRANSLATIONS BY
Marcus C. Levitt
with **Nicole Monnier** and **Daniel Schlaffy**

BOSTON / 2014

Library of Congress Cataloging-in-Publication Data:
A catalog record for this book as available from the Library of Congress.

The book is supported by Mikhail Prokhorov Foundation
(translation program TRANSCRIPT).

Copyright © 2014 Academic Studies Press
All rights reserved

ISBN: 978-1-61811-803-5
ISBN: 978-1-61811-357-3 (electronic)

Book design by Ivan Grave

On the cover: "Allegory of Catherine's Victory over the Turks" (1772), by Stefano Torelli

Published by Academic Studies Press in 2014
28 Montfern Avenue
Brighton, MA 02135, USA
press@academicstudiespress.com
www.academicstudiespress.com

In memory of
Genrietta Grigorievna Zorina

Contents

List of Illustrations ix
From the Author / Acknowledgements xi
Introduction: Literature and Ideology
Translated by Nicole Monnier 1

1. **Russians as Greeks:** Catherine II's "Greek Project" and
   the Russian Ode of the 1760s–70s 24

2. **The Image of the Enemy:** V. P. Petrov's "Ode on the Conclusion of
   Peace with the Ottoman Porte" and the Emergence of the Mythology
   of a Global Conspiracy against Russia 61

3. **Eden in Taurus:** The "Crimean Myth" in Russian Culture
   of the 1780s–90s 92

4. **Eden in the Tauride Palace:** Potemkin's Last Project 121

5. **The People's War:** The Time of Troubles in Russian Literature,
   1806–1807 155

6. **Enemy of the People:** M. M. Speranskii's Fall and the Mythology of
   Treason in Social and Literary Consciousness, 1809–1812 185

7. **War and Quasi Peace:** The Character and Goal of the War in 1812–1814 in
   the Interpretation of A. S. Shishkov and Archimandrite Filaret 232

8. **Holy Alliances:** V. A. Zhukovskii's Epistle "To Emperor Alexander"
   and Christian Universalism 258

9. **"Star of the East":** The Holy Alliance and European Mysticism
   Translation by Daniel Schlaffy 288

10. **The Cherished Triad:** S. S. Uvarov's Memorandum of 1832 and the
    Development of the Doctrine "Orthodoxy—Autocracy—Nationality" 325

Works Cited 359
Index 399

List of Illustrations

Figure 1   Medal commemorating the birth of Grand Prince
Konstantin Pavlovich (1779)..25

Figure 2   "Allegory of the Victory of Chesme" (1771) by Theodorus de Roode.
Tretiakov Gallery, Moscow. 51

Figure 3   "Portrait of the Grand Princes Alexander Pavlovich
and Konstantin Pavlovich" (c. 1781) by Richard Brompton.....................59

Figure 4   "A Critical Map" (1791) – an allegory of the
"balance of power."..69

Figure 5   Portrait of V. P. Petrov. 78

Figure 6   An English caricature of the Chevalier d'Éon exposing him
"as a Woman- Freemason."..89

Figure 7   "Catherine II on a Journey across Russia in 1787" (1790) by
Jean-Jacques Avril the Elder, based on a drawing by
Ferdinand de Meys. State Historical Museum, Moscow. 106

Figure 8   "View of Tauride" by V. P. Petrov (1791). Saratov State Art Museum,
Saratov. 112

Figure 9   Portrait of G. A. Potemkin-Tavricheskii by Johann-Baptist von Lampi
the Elder (c. 1790). Hermitage Museum, St. Petersburg. 123

Figure 10 and 11   Catherine II the Legislatress (1789) by F. I. Shubin. Russian
Museum, St. Petersburg. *Below* – The winter garden
of the Tauride Palace (1792) by F. D. Danilov. 132

Figure 12   First proposal for a monument to Minin and Pozharskii
(1804-1807) by I. P. Martos...158

Figure 13   Minin summons Prince Pozharskii to save the Fatherland (1800's)
by G. I. Ugriumov 168

Figure 14   Proposal for a monument to Minin and Pozharskii (1809)
by I. P. Martos 177

List of Illustrations

Figure 15 Portrait of Count M. M. Speranskii; gravure from the original
by I. A. Ivanov. 186

Figure 16 Portrait of F. V. Rostopchin. Gravure of T. Meyer
after the original by Ernst Gebauer 205

Figure 17 Portrait of Grand Princess Ekaterina Pavlovna (1810's). Gravure
by Andre Joseph Mecou after the original by Jean-Henri Benner. 218

Figure 18 Throwing French actresses out of Moscow (1812). Caricature
by A. G. Venetsianov. 227

Figure 19 Variants for a medallion commemorating the home guard
by A. N. Olenin..234

Figure 20 Portrait of A. S. Shishkov. Lithograph by P. F. Borel'
after the painting by George Dawe. 243

Figure 21 Portrait of Archimandrite Filaret (Drozdov). Gravure
by J. Brian. 249

Figure 22 Medallion commemorating the expulsion of the enemy from
Russia in 1812 by A. N. Olenin. 255

Figure 23 Prayer of Thanksgiving in Paris, 1814. Gravure by I. V. Cheskii. 267

Figure 24 Portrait of V. A. Zhukovskii. Gravure by A. A. Florov from the
original by P. F. Sokolov. 271

Figure 25 Medallion commemorating the Triple Alliance by A. N. Olenin. 280

Figure 26 Portrait of Baroness von Krüdener. Gravure by J. Pfenninger. 290

Figure 27 Mother of God (1814-1815). Icon based on a passage
from Revelations by V. L. Borovikovskii. 305

Figure 28 The manifesto of December 25, 1815. 307

Figure 29 Portrait of S. S. Uvarov. Lithograph by M. Mukhin................................327

Figure 30 Portrait of Karl Freiherr vom Stein. Sketch by S. S. Uvarov. 341

Figure 31 Monument to Ivan Susanin by V. I. Demut-Malinovskii (1838).
Drawing by V. M. Vasnetsov. 349

From the Author / Acknowledgements

This book was begun in 1993 while I was a fellow at the Russian Research Center (now the Davis Center) at Harvard University. During 1996-1998 this project was underwritten by the Research Support Scheme of the "Open Society" Institute (the Soros Fund), and in 1999 by the "Pushkinist" Program of the Moscow branch of the same Institute. The book was initially published in 2001 and the second edition from which the translation was made appeared in 2004. Last decade witnessed a lot of political changes that suggest new perspectives on the history of Russian Imperial ideology. For example, the English translation is appearing shortly after the annexation of Crimea by Russian Federation and the revival of nearly forgotten concept of Novorossia – the historical background of these developments is discussed in Chapter three. A lot of new works on the history of Russian state Ideology have also appeared. However, I decided not to make changes and additions in the text. Starting to correct it would mean either using the advantages of the hindsight to look cleverer that I really was at the end of the previous century, or writing a new book on the same topic. Neither seem an attractive option.

In 1990-s several chapters of the current book were published in the journal *Novoe Literaturnoe Obozrenie,* some were given as university lectures, public talks, and conference presentations. It is not possible to name the dozens of colleagues who have been of tremendous help with their advice, questions and criticisms, but I would nevertheless like to express gratitude to:

Mikhail Bezrodnii, Laura Engelstein, Konstantin Lappo-Danilevskii, Ekaterina Liamina, Maria Maiofis, Iurii Mann, Oleg Proskurin, Konstantin Rogov, and Andreas Schönle. Andrei Kurilkin who was the editor of the Russian edition made productive suggestions and helped preparing the bibliographical apparatus and choice of illustrations. I owe eternal gratitude to late Victor Zhivov. For the possibility to present the book to the English speaking audience I want to thank the Mikhail Prokhorov Foundation and Irina Prokhorova who in her different roles and functions supports and encourages my research for twenty years already, Kira and Igor Nemirovsky for their help and enthusiasm, Marcus Levitt for his careful and painstaking translation and Melissa Miller for meticulous editing of the English version.

I would not have been able to complete this work without the support of my family, which supported me with their unfailing support, their patience, and their impatience.

For my development both as a man and a professional I am indebted to my mother Genrietta Grigorievna Zorina (1923–1980). I dedicate this book to her memory, in my endless and hopeless desire to be worthy of her expectations.

Introduction

Literature and Ideology

Translated by
Nicole Monnier*

∞ **1** ∞

"*Habent sua fata verba* [words have their own fate], though some words have a fate more bizarre than others. The word 'ideology' sets, however, a record which is difficult to beat. Finding a common denominator to the sharply different historical uses of the term, or a transformative logic productive of its successive avatars, is a notoriously tall order," wrote the philosopher Zygmunt Bauman in his recent book (1999, 109). Ever since the late eighteenth century, when Antoine Louis Claude Destutt first put forward the idea of ideology as the science concerning the formation of ideas and human knowledge, innumerable philosophers, thinkers, historians and politicians have proposed their own definitions of this category. In his classic *Ideology and Utopia* of 1929, Karl Mannheim complained that "we do not as yet possess an adequate historical treatment of the development of the concept of ideology, to say nothing of a sociological history of the many variations in its meanings" (Mannheim 1936, 53–54).

Since then circumstances have gone to the other extreme, and one is more likely to be troubled by the superabundance of works on the subject

---

* First published in *History and Theory* 1 (40) (2001): 57-73.

(cf. the works of Larraín 1979; Kendall 1981; Thompson 1984; Ricœur 1986; Eagleton 1994; etc.; for the latest works, see Bauman's short essay "Ideology in the Postmodern World," Bauman 1999, 109–130).

The author of one of the latest of these surveys, the English Marxist Terry Eagleton, begins his book with a list of sixteen definitions of ideology taken almost at random from studies of recent years:

(a) the process of production of meanings, signs and values in social life;
(b) a body of ideas characteristic of a particular social group or class;
(c) ideas which help to legitimate a dominant political power;
(d) false ideas which help to legitimate a dominant political power;
(e) systematically distorted communications;
(f) that which offers a position for a subject;
(g) forms of thought motivated by social interests;
(h) identity thinking;
(i) socially necessary illusion;
(j) the conjuncture of discourse and power;
(k) the medium in which conscious social actors make sense of the world;
(l) action-oriented sets of beliefs;
(m) the confusion of linguistic and phenomenal reality;
(n) semiotic closure;
(o) the indispensable medium in which individuals live out their relations to a social structure;
(p) the process whereby social life is converted to a natural reality.
(Eagleton 1994, 1–2)

A significant majority of these formulations are directly or indirectly connected to Marx and Engels's *The German Ideology,* with its notion of ideology as a *camera obscura* where "men and their circumstances appear upside-down," and the "ruling ideas are nothing less than the ideal expression of the prevailing material relations ... and thus an expression of those very relations which make that class the ruling one" (Marx and Engels III, 25, 45–46). This selection of definitions not only reflects Eagleton's party affiliations, but also the actual state of scholarship. The issue of ideology has been developed most actively either within a Marxist framework, or, in the extreme case, in an attempt to get beyond it.

Interpreting ideology as a "camera obscura" left open the question of the theoretical status of Marxism itself. One possible solution was partly noted by Marxists of the start of the twentieth century, including Lenin; it was developed by Lukács in his book *History and Class Consciousness* (1922), and despite the harsh criticism of this work in the party press, was accepted by official Soviet philosophy. Reviving the Hegelian substratum of Marxism, Lukács saw in the history of class consciousness a kind of materialist analogue for the self-consciousness of the absolute spirit. Insofar as the proletariat's class interests correspond to the logic of the historical process, the contradiction between science and ideology is removed and proletariat ideology coincides with objective truth (see Lukács 1971).

Another, opposite approach sees ideology as compromised, in Engels's expression, as "false consciousness" (Marx and Engels XXXIX, 82; cf. Mannheim 1994, 66–69), contrasting this to scientific Marxist sociology. Within the Marxist tradition the most radical adherent of this view was the French philosopher Louis Althusser, who saw ideology as a type of subjectivity that could be eliminated from thought only by means of objective scientific analysis (Althusser 1971; cf. Ricœur 1984, 120–132; Eagleton 1991, 137–154). On the other hand, K. Mannheim applied the critical method worked out by Marxism to his own gnoseological premises:

> For the Marxist doctrine it is obvious that behind every theory stand aspects of vision that belong to a definite collective. This phenomenon—thought, conditioned by social and life interests—is what Marx called *ideology*.
>
> Here, as often happens during the course of political struggle, a very important discovery was made, which ... should be brought to its logical conclusion . ... First of all, it is easy to be convinced that a thinker of the socialist-communist tendency will only see elements of ideology in his opponent's thinking, while his own thinking appears to him to be free of any manifestations of ideology. From a sociological perspective there is no basis not to extend to Marxism its own discovery. (Mannheim 1994, 108)

Mannheim made a distinction between a "particular" ideology, defined as the actual "content" or programmatic component of the pronouncements made by one's political opponent, and a "total" ideology embracing the worldview of that opponent, including his categorical apparatus. Accordingly, any reference to the socially conditioned character of a "particular" ideology would more or less constitute a critical judgment, while similar reference to a "total ideology" would be considered standard scholarly practice:

> The notion of partial ideology follows from the fact that this or another interest serves to falsify and cover up the truth, [while] the notion of total ideology is based on the opinion that certain points of view, methods and aspects of observation *correspond to* certain social positions. Here too an analysis of interests is applied, not in order to reveal casual determinants but to characterize the structures of social being. (Ibid., 58)

It is precisely in terms of the latter that Mannheim worked out his concept of sociology of knowledge as a historical discipline that examines ideological practices in their social context without reference to contemporary political judgments. Yet no matter how rich and developed the procedure espoused by Mannheim for an "anti-ideological hygiene," the intellectual procedure itself does not allow one to move beyond the fatal question of the sociologist's own conditionality and the conditionality of his analysis, a question Geertz called "Mannheim's paradox."

With the inevitable logic of a boomerang, the polemical device developed by post-Marxist sociology for the criticism of its teachers only undermines its own foundations. In postwar years the inescapable question "And who are you then?" more often sounded from their liberal-leaning opponents, from sociologists and political scientists who tended to associate the concept of ideology with communistic or fascist totalitarian doctrines while viewing their own propositions as de-ideologized and grounded either in universal values or in the propositions of a positive science.[1]

The American sociologist Geertz analyzed and rejected the entire complex of Marxist and post-Marxist approaches to sociology in his article "Ideology as a Cultural System," which was included in his collection *The Interpretation of Cultures* (Geertz 1973, 193–233; Geertz 1998). Geertz

---

1 Mannheim differentiated between ideology that legitimizes the existing social order on the basis of values transcendental to it and a utopia that would destroy this order through similar values while projecting a different social construction. Working from this distinction but from the perspective of a different philosophical tradition, Paul Ricœur suggested that it was precisely the conscious acceptance of utopia that reflectively creates a pure position for the critique of ideology (see Ricœur 1984, 172). We will consider "utopian" thinking as defined by Mannheim and Ricœur as one of many varieties of the ideological.

grouped all of these various wide-ranging approaches to the analysis of ideology under the category of "interest theory": "The fundamentals of the interest theory are too well known to need review; developed to perfection of a sort by the Marxist tradition, they are now standard intellectual equipment of the man-in-the-street, who is only too aware that in political argumentation it all comes down to whose ox is gored" (Geertz 1998, 13).

In the final analysis, it is this commonsensical, man-on-the-street aspect of interest theory that constitutes at once its strength and weakness. According to Geertz:

> The battlefield image of society as a clash of interests thinly disguised as a clash of principles turns attention away from the role that ideologies play in defining (or obscuring) social categories, stabilizing (or upsetting) social norms, strengthening (or weakening) social consensus, relieving (or exacerbating) social tensions . ... The intensity of interest theory is ... but the reward of its narrowness. (Ibid., 13–14)

The emphasis within interest theory on "post-Marxist common sense" satisfies him as little as the post-Freudian cliché of "strain theory" (as Geertz calls the hypothesis according to which social conflicts within a destabilized society find their outlet in ideology).[2] In his opinion, "both interest theory and strain theory go directly from source analysis to consequence analysis without ever seriously examining ideologies as systems of interacting symbols, as patterns of inter-working meanings" (ibid., 17). It is precisely this lacuna between source and consequence that is inaccessible to traditional theoretical models of ideology and which Geertz attempts to fill with what he calls "the semiotic approach to culture" (Geertz 1973, 5, 24–30).

∽ 2 ∽

For the Russian reader this last phrase immediately conjures up very specific associations. Geertz's most famous works were written in the very same years

---

2   In the second half of the 1960s, Althusser attempted to introduce the theoretical elaborations of Freud and Lacan into the Marxist approach to ideology. According to Althusser, in serving as the basic means for the reproduction of existing industrial relations, ideology is a transhistorical phenomenon that was also located in the sphere of the "social subconscious" (see Althusser 1971). On the further development of this tradition, see Jameson 1981; Žižek 1999).

that saw the formation in the USSR of the so-called Tartu-Moscow school, a period now canonized as the Golden Age of Russian scholarship in the humanities. By 1973, when Geertz's *The Interpretation of Cultures*—a collection of essays which included in the form of an introductory chapter the first publication of "Thick Description: Towards an Interpretative Theory of Culture," a general account of the theoretical bases of his anthropology—was published, six issues of the Tartu-Moscow School's own *Studies in Symbolic Systems* [Trudy po znakovym sistemam] had already appeared.

One cannot rule out the possibility of Geertz's familiarity with the work of Lotman and his associates, translations of which had begun to appear in the West in the late 1960s; it is more likely, however, that the scholarship of the noted (although as yet not especially well-known) American anthropologist might have been in the field of vision of the Soviet semioticians. Nonetheless, there is little need to talk of any serious mutual influence. The "Geertzian" and "Lotmanesque" models of the semiotics of culture were created independently of each other and on the bases of different academic traditions—a fact that makes the points of convergence and divergence between them all the more interesting.

The anti-structuralist orientation of *The Interpretation of Cultures* is not simply transparent but clearly stated. Geertz included in *Interpretation* his 1967 review of Levi-Strauss's most important works, an essay that is at once both deeply respectful yet sharply polemical. Geertz summarizes Levi-Strauss's methodology in the following manner: "Binary opposition—that dialectical chasm between plus and minus which computer technology has rendered the lingua franca of modem science—forms the basis of savage thought as it does of language. And indeed it is this that makes them essentially variant forms of the same thing: communications systems" (ibid., 354). Steadfastly hostile to the panlinguistic quality of structural ethnography and its striving toward constants and deep structures, Geertz turns the French scholar's own scientific arsenal against its author, seeing in Levi-Strauss's anthropology a possible realization of a unitary deep structure, the "universal rationalism of the French Enlightenment."

"Like Rousseau, Levi-Strauss's search is not after all for men, whom he doesn't much care for, but for Man, with whom he is enthralled," comments Geertz (ibid., 356). Geertz himself is categorically opposed to the search for universality, instead replacing the revelation of deep structures with "thick description." In his understanding of man as a "cultural artifact" (ibid., 51), Geertz on the whole avoids generalizing uses of the term "culture," which he prefers to use in its plural form or to set it off with the article "a" or "the." In this way each of the cultures he investigates will contain within it its own anthropological dimension.

The very possibility of the construction of a single theory of culture calls forth a certain distrust; according to Geertz,

> any theoretical sharpening of one's scholarly instruments should serve for a more subtle and adequate interpretation of individual cases: coherence cannot be the major test of validity for a cultural description. Cultural systems must have a minimal degree of coherence, else we would not call them systems; and, by observation, they normally have a great deal more. But there is nothing so coherent as a paranoid's delusion or a swindler's story. The force of our interpretations cannot rest, as they are now so often made to do, on the tightness with which they hold together, or the assurance with which they are argued. (Ibid., 17–18)

It goes without saying just how distant this approach is from the scientifically minded optimism of the Tartu and Moscow semioticians, for whom Levi-Strauss remained (at least, in terms of methodology) an unshakable authority, and for whom the impulse towards a total scientific synthesis was a symbol of faith of a kind. It should be mentioned that as a whole, the philosophical anthropology of the French Enlightenment and especially that of Rousseau was especially meaningful for Lotman, who spent a lifetime studying the legacy of that epoch. It was not coincidental that at the same time that Geertz was directing his own semiotics against structuralism, the research of the Tartu-Moscow school continued to be referred to as "structural-semiotic."

However, one cannot juxtapose these two semiotic approaches without making certain important reservations. Above all, the intellectual continuum articulated in the conjunction "structural-semiotic" also contains within it, albeit somewhat indistinctly, two different methodological poles. One can (somewhat simplistically) view the evolution of Lotman himself from his *Lectures in Structural Poetics* to his study of the semiophere and his interest in the philosophical ideas of Ilya Prigogine in terms of his movement from one pole to another. Yet the immense ideological pressure to which the Tartu-Moscow school was constantly subjected placed significant limits upon the possibility of an open polemic within the school itself, and in particular, of any explicit criticism of its own views from an earlier period.

It is easy to imagine the sort of ugly gloating that would have greeted any move by Lotman or any of his close confederates to distance themselves from any of the fundamental assumptions of structuralist doctrine. Understandably, the prospect of ending up the author of the latest "monument to scientific error"[3] would block not only the writing of self-polemicizing texts, but even, to some degree, the very impulse towards self-criticism. Yet for all that one still sees clear signs of a polemic in many of the positions of the later Lotman, including his insistence that complex sign systems were fundamentally irreducible to attenuated configurations of lower-order systems.

In his attempts to overcome structuralism, Geertz turned to the categorical apparatus of hermeneutics—an approach to culture that he referred to by turns as "semiotic" or "interpretative." "The whole point of a semiotic approach to culture is ... to aid us in gaining access to the conceptual world in which our subjects live so that we can, in some extended sense of the term, converse with them" (ibid., 24). In his later book, Geertz also characterized the term "interpretative" as a euphemism for the word "hermeneutical" (Geertz 1983, 21). It is no accident that Geertz's works found such passionate support from one of the pillars of hermeneutics, Paul Ricœur, who saw in "Ideology as a Cultural System" the development of his own ideas, expressed even better than he himself had done (Ricœur 1984, 181). For Russian semioticians, Bakhtin's theory of dialogue, following a similar philosophical course, played an analogous role (see Ivanov1973; cf. Grzhibek 1995; Bethea 1996, etc.).

However, the radical nature of Geertz's break with earlier scientific paradigms should not be exaggerated. His skepticism towards excessive generalizations and scientistic utopias did not lead him to deny the principle of scientific investigation itself. He insists that the conceptual structure of cultural interpretation should underlie clearly formulated procedures of critical evaluation to the same degree that the parameters of biological observations or physical experiments do in the sciences. At the end of his

---

3   "A Monument to Scientific Error" was the title of a 1929 article by the critic Victor Shklovskii in which he renounced the errors of his Formalist beliefs. His colleagues regarded the article as an act of treason and a capitulation to ideological pressures.

theoretical introduction to *The Interpretation of Cultures* Geertz writes: "I have never been impressed by the argument that, as complete objectivity is impossible in these matters (as, of course, it is), one might as well let one's sentiments run loose. As Robert Solow has remarked, that is like saying that as a perfectly aseptic environment is impossible, one might as well conduct surgery in a sewer" (Geertz 1973, 30).

As a whole, the conception of culture proposed by Geertz is close to the formulations and definitions scattered in abundance over the pages of the collections of the Tartu-Moscow school. In his words, two of the central principles of interpretative theory are that, first: culture "is best seen not as complexes of concrete behavior patterns—customs, usages, traditions, habit clusters,… but as a set of control mechanisms—plans, recipes, rules, instructions (what computer engineers call "programs")—for the governing of behavior. The second idea is that man is precisely the animal most desperately dependent upon such extragenetic, outside-the-skin control mechanisms, such as cultural programs, for ordering his behavior" (ibid., 44). Parallel statements from Lotman's works are too many and too well-known to mention.

Many of the classic works by Lotman, Boris Uspenskii, and other scholars of the Tartu-Moscow school are closely concerned with the analysis of the semiotic mechanisms which organize various ideological systems and regulate the behavioral strategies of their bearers, be they the Decembrists, Peter the Great, or Radishchev. Sometimes such analysis is put forward as the explicit focus (see, e.g., Lotman and Uspenskii 1993), but is more often worked out in the course of circuitous argumentation. At the same time, the Tartu-Moscow school on the whole shied away from theoretical interpretations of ideology as a system of cultural norms and regulators, often replacing it with the close, albeit far from synonymous concept of "mythology." Yet the problem here was not simply one of censorship or self-censorship. In the Soviet context, the very category of ideology irredeemably belonged to a completely different discourse, the language of party propaganda, so that even to approach its study "scientifically" was psychologically problematic.

Hence for Western scholars to approach ideology from a theoretical perspective was easier in all respects. Yet even here the same inertia of philosophical tradition was powerful. It is possible that Geertz only succeeded in exploding the tradition as a result of the utterly unique combination of his personal research experience and the cultural-political reality which moved him to turn to this theme.

∞ **3** ∞

"Ideology as a Cultural System" was included in the collection *The Interpretation of Cultures*, the 1973 publication which brought its author widespread fame. However, it had first appeared nine years earlier in 1964, when it became one of the most significant responses to the processes of decolonialization just being completed at that time in the formation of sixty-six new nation-states (the number is Geertz's) which now found it necessary to build systems of nation-state self-identification almost completely from scratch.

The wave of ideological creation that seized the third world almost surpassed that seen by Europe in analogous periods of its own history: specifically, in the aftermath of the French Revolution and the First World War. Geertz, who had studied traditional cultures in such far-flung countries as Indonesia and Morocco, now found himself in a position to understand the logic of this ferment, to see in the tumultuous bloom of ideological thinking the specific processes integral to modernization:

> In polities firmly embedded in Edmund Burke's golden assemblage of "ancient opinions and rules of life," the role of ideology, in any explicit sense, is marginal. In such truly traditional political systems the participants act as (to use another Burkean phrase) men of untaught feelings; they are guided both emotionally and intellectually in their judgments and activities by unexamined prejudices, which do not leave them "hesitating in the moment of decision, skeptical, puzzled and unresolved." But when, as in the revolutionary France Burke was indicting and in fact in the shaken England from which, as perhaps his nation's greatest ideologue, he was indicting it, those hallowed opinions and rules of life come into question, the search for systematic ideological formulations, either to reinforce them or to replace them, flourishes. The function of ideology is to make an autonomous politics possible by providing the authoritative concepts that render it meaningful, the suasive images by means of which it can be sensibly grasped. It is, in fact, precisely at the point at which a political system begins to free itself from the immediate governance of received tradition, from the direct and detailed guidance of religious or philosophical canons on the one hand and from the unreflective precepts of conventional moralism on the other, that formal ideologies tend first to emerge and take hold. (Geertz 1973, 218; Geertz 1998, 24–25)

In his position of the participant-observer present during the radical mutation of the object being studied and with the reflexive experience of a man of Western civilization, which had existed almost two hundred years in conditions of fierce competition among various ideological models, Geertz was not only able to understand the genesis of ideology, but also to propose an entirely new understanding of its nature. Given this situation, the approaches of the cultural historian and the ethnographer in the field essentially become identical, and ideology inscribes itself in a series of other fundamental mechanisms of sociocultural integration. Along with "Ideology as a Cultural System," Geertz included in *The Interpretation of Cultures* his essay "Religion as a Cultural System"; the essays "Common Sense as a Cultural System," and "Art as a Cultural System" would appear in his next collection, *Local Knowledge* (1983).

At the basis of Marxist, neo-Marxist, post-Marxist, as well as anti-Marxist understandings of ideology lies a more or less articulated opposition of and comparison between ideological and scientific thought. Science is assigned the function of substantiating (if only in official Soviet philosophy) or unmasking (in almost all other philosophies) ideology's pretensions to the role of official interpreter of the past, present, and future, of verifying its premises and conclusions with its own data, as well as that of exposing the presence of ideology wherever it might hide, insofar as ideology has a habit of making itself out to be science, art, or common sense. Geertz clearly separates the two types of intellectual activity: "An ideologist is no more a poor social scientist than a social scientist is a poor ideologist. The two are—or at least they ought to be—in quite different lines of work, lines so different that little is gained and much obscured by measuring the activities of the one against the aims of the other" (Geertz 1973, 231; Geertz 1998, 33).

According to Geertz, the specificity of ideology as one of the matrices that programs behavioral strategies is the delineation of unfamiliar cultural space for human associations. The role of ideology grows sharply in conditions of instability, when more archaic orientational models reveal their full or partial unsuitability: "And it is, in turn, the attempt of ideologies to render otherwise incomprehensible social situations meaningfully, to so construe them as to make it possible to act purposefully within them, that accounts both for the ideologies' highly figurative nature and for the intensity with which, once accepted, they are held" (Geertz 1973, 220; Geertz 1998, 25).

The approach to the "figurative nature" of ideological thinking as proposed by Geertz is especially important. Of course, Geertz was not the first to address the oversaturation of ideological texts and slogans by various kinds of tropes. Generally speaking, it is impossible not to notice this fact. Even Marxism with its near-monopolization of discussion of the problems of ideology began with the metaphor of a wandering specter. Nonetheless, the figurative component of ideological concepts has been understood by scholars as a sort of rhetorical flourish, as a tool for propaganda, popularization, or deception, or as more or less effective doctrinal packaging.

Geertz thoroughly reconsiders this traditional approach to ideology and rhetoric. For him, the trope—and in the first instance, of course, metaphor—forms the very nucleus of ideological thinking, for it is precisely through the trope that ideology realizes the symbolic demarcation of social space that allows the collective and its members to make it "habitable," to make it their own. Geertz supports these observations first with an analysis of the phrase "Slave Labor Law" (the slogan raised by union activists in their battle against the famous Taft-Hartley anti-strike law), before turning to an interpretation of the initial attempts to create a national ideology in post-colonial Indonesia. Although Geertz repeatedly cautions his reader that the interpretative approach to culture is diagnostic, but not prognostic in character, his own highly pessimistic prognosis for the development of events in Indonesia proved fairly accurate. It should be remembered that Geertz's article was written before the unsuccessful communist coup in Indonesia and the ensuing butchery that took the lives of more than a half-million of the country's inhabitants.

Still, the value of Geertz's analysis is not in its concrete political judgments, but rather in its exposing of that role which "conceptual," ideological factors play in the movement of the historical process. The quality of the symbolic map drawn by ideology is determined by the degree of success with which the individual is able to orient himself by that map within the "locale" it attempts to define. The developmental paths of the collective, be it a union movement or an entire country, depend to no little degree on what kind of maps it has at its disposal. The power of an ideological metaphor, its ability to capture reality and to produce new meanings, in a very real way influences the dynamic of historical events.

4

In the late 1980s and early 90s the processes that Geertz had occasion to observe in the Third World began on the territory of the USSR and continued in the countries that were formed after its disintegration. The analysis of changing ideological metaphors proposed in "Ideology as a Cultural System" can be very productive for understanding cultural collisions that have taken place before our eyes. We will limit ourselves here to preliminary observations regarding several events of the last decade of the twentieth century in Russia.

The history of independent Russia begins with the defeat of the putsch of August 19–21, 1991. Many of the conditions of this historical drama were shaped by the logic of the country's economic development, by the clash of social forces, by institutional crisis, backstage political intrigues, the personalities of its leading participants, and so on (not to mention the morphology of the revolutionary process as studied by de Toqueville; Toqueville 1986). Nonetheless, the cultural and symbolic dimension, the system of figurative changes and substitutions that was woven into the fabric of historical events, also played a significant role (see Freidin and Bonnel 1995).

In August 1991 across several kilometers of central Moscow there was staged in accordance with the laws of high political carnival a duel of two systems, a duel repeatedly described to us in the past not only by Soviet propaganda, but by anti-Soviet propaganda as well. Throughout the entire postwar epoch, the Kremlin and the (American) White House, synecdochally representing the two "superpowers," had played the main protagonists in a skirmish destined to decide the historical fate of the entire world. Yet in a curious twist, during the events of 1991 it was the Russian White House on the Krasnopresnenskaia embankment that assumed the traditional role of its overseas older brother vis-à-vis the Kremlin. The resulting functional symbolisms proposed by each side of this drama are worth enumerating.

On the Kremlin's side were the very same attributes of power that it had demonstrated to the world throughout the Soviet period. In the first place were the tanks, useless for solving the problem that faced the putschists, but which for decades had successfully represented state power. In the second place was the use of canonized Russian music; apart from short informational reports and a pair of incomprehensible decrees, the GKChP (the so-called

State Emergency Committee formed during the coup) informed the country of its taking power by broadcasting "Swan Lake" on all TV channels.

The failure of the putsch became evident after its leaders' press conference that with lightning speed turned the trembling hands of the Soviet Union's vice president Yanaev into the symbol of the new power. The basis of this semiotic catastrophe was a profound communicative miscalculation. In notifying the country of the return to the old order, the members of the GKChP themselves used the information technologies of the glasnost' era. In the Soviet era, the organs of collective leadership that exercised real authority always acted behind closed doors. As opposed to grandiose Party Congresses and sessions of the Supreme Soviet that were for show, reports about Central Committee plenums were only read out on TV, orally, without video images, and published in newspapers without any accompanying photographs. As far as meetings of the Politburo, this kind of information had only begun to appear in 1983, after Andropov came to power.

In contrast, the defenders of the White House possessed a popularly elected president and parliament, and they clearly interpreted their own civil disobedience to the GKChP's illegal takeover by the as an act of political self-constitutionalization ("We, the people"). Minor details of the events, such as the rock concert and the distribution of free imported cigarettes only strengthened the idealized image of America as the highest embodiment of civilization, formulated in the Soviet period by the entire culture of anti-Communist protest. The three most oft-repeated sound bites of those days—"Russia," "Yeltsin," and "freedom"—served as a prototype for the synthesis of non-imperial patriotism, legality, and individualism proposed as the ideology of the new Russian state.

Two years later, from September 20 to October 4, 1993, political crisis once again spilled out into a confrontation between the same two architectural complexes. However, this time it took place against a backdrop of radically regrouped symbols and in a significantly different ideologically marked space. To begin with, the nationalist-communists who now gathered around the White House were doomed to repeat the scenario played out by their despised opponents and—even worse—to repeat to a certain degree their symbolic gesticulations. The logic of the conflict forced them to declare themselves supporters of parliamentarism and constitutional order, an assertion which was catastrophically at odds with their raised red banners, their organization of armed units, and with the expectations of their own supporters. And while at the time of the coup it was announced by one communist paper that "the White House has finally become the House of the Soviets," the rhetoric about the "defense of legal organs of power" contradicted both the appearance and actions of the defenders, who were unable to work out a convincing system of ideological metaphors.

At the same time, President Yeltsin, who had made the move into the Kremlin, appropriated Tchaikovsky from his predecessors and even, in part, their tanks, all the while preserving his earlier rhetoric of "entry into the civilized world." On September 26, the National Symphony Orchestra from Washington, D. C., under the direction of Rostropovich played the "1812 Overture" on Red Square. The number of people gathered for this twenty-five-minute concert, not including the millions who watched on television, was more than had come together for all of the meetings and demonstrations organized by both sides of the conflict combined. On the most famous of Russian squares an American orchestra played Russian music under the baton of a world-famous musician who had once been exiled from Russia by the Soviet regime. Over the heads of the communist usurpers, the new authority had attempted to present itself as the true heir of the age-old traditions of the Russian state.

In the battle of metaphors the president's side prevailed before October 5, when all of the saved-up symbolic capital was, with far-reaching political consequences, superseded by CNN's TV cliché image of "firing on the White House." Such images of civil war left an impression on Russians' consciousness and created a need for an ideology of reconciliation to which Yeltsin quickly responded, proposing that the Duma's communist majority sign an Agreement on National Reconciliation and Harmony, that subsequently gave its name to the November 7 holiday. However, the metaphors of total reconciliation were only fully realized in the framework of quite a different ideological model whose most visible and obvious expression were the celebrations of September 5–7, 1997, on the occasion of Moscow's 850-year jubilee.

As Paul Ricœur has argued, as a rule, national holidays are based on the juxtaposition of one historical epoch to another. The celebrated event is likened to an act of creation that separates the cosmos from chaos (see Ricœur 1986, 261–262). Thus, for example, the thousand-year anniversary of Russian statehood, celebrated with great pomp in 1862, and the celebration of a thousand years of Christianity in Russia in 1988 both represented a negation of pre-Varangian and pagan Rus'. In the imperial period the main state holiday was the ascension day of the reigning monarch, and it was better not to mention predecessors, especially recent ones. Of course, November 7, 1917, was felt to be the start of a new era, as was also the case for the memorable days of democratic Russia, at least at first. Religious holidays are also structured like this: those who celebrate Christmas or Easter re-experience anew the symbolic ending of the pre-Christian era. The holiday divides time into two and rejects its first half.

Choosing the date of the founding of a city as a holiday reduces this symbolic negation to a minimum. In trying *de facto* to turn the founding of the capital into the main national celebration, the organizers of the holiday did not reject any aspect of its heritage, permitting other cities and locales to exercise their own powers of myth-making. A wave of local jubilees immediately swept through Russia, especially in Petersburg which prepared an ostentatious fête on the occasion of its triennial jubilee.

In the scenario for Moscow's anniversary Russia's tragic history was unexpectedly interpreted as an endless and conflict-free succession of golden ages. Everything was wonderful under the grand princes and the tsars of Moscow who made short shrift of them, under the Petersburg emperors who rejected Muscovy, as well as under communists and under democrats. The mayor of Moscow appeared at the celebration in the costume of an ancient Russian prince. A portrait of good king Ivan the Terrible was projected on the wall of Moscow University as part of a laser show by the French composer Jean-Michel Jarre. It was as if the opening of Tseretelli's monument to Peter I during the anniversary was meant to rescind the Petersburg period of Russian history, having returned the first Russian emperor and all of his heirs to the old capital that they had abandoned.

Of course the narrative of history is thus completely washed away and history itself becomes a kind of decorative prop. Together with the newly reconstructed Cathedral of Christ the Savior, genuine historical monuments lose whatever authenticity they may have had. It turns out that it is virtually impossible to know if St. Basil's or the Kremlin have really stood on Red Square for hundreds of years or if Moscow's former mayor Luzhkov had them rebuilt together with the Iverskii Gates and the Cathedral of the Kazan Holy Mother. Of Red Square's entire ensemble it seems that for now only Lenin's Mausoleum has not been disemboweled and does not provoke questions concerning its identity. All of the other buildings look like a magnificent decoration, a stylized background for a theatrical performance which they became during the anniversary celebration.

Moscow's two central squares—Red Square, which in Soviet times served as a place for parades and as symbol of imperial might, and Manezh Square, which during perestroika became the site of huge demonstrations and a kind of symbol of the country's awakening political life—have both undergone curious functional metamorphoses. Having partitioned off Red Square with the newly-built Iverskii Gates, the city authorities blocked the way for tanks and turned it into the country's leading place for outdoor concerts. And Manezh Square was adorned with a cupola above a magnificent shopping mall. Built in an historical style, the mall differs from its New York prototype in that it does not rise above the city but is hidden underground like the stations of the Moscow Metro which once proclaimed to the world that socialism in the USSR had been mostly achieved.

The new message that the Moscow celebration announced was that Russia had joined the society of consumers, and that this was a national, imperial, Orthodox society of consumers, sanctified by the country's history and religion. Many observers during the celebrations, including the author of these lines, got the impression that the cherished idea destined to unite the nation had at last been found. Russia's future, it seemed, was as a country of neo-feudal consumerism, ruled by an alliance of apanage princes headed by Moscow's grand prince playing the role of first among equals. However, quite soon—in the fall of 1999—this ideological model and its creators suffered a crippling fall. The crisis of August 1998, the wars in the Balkans and in the Caucasus again required metaphors of a strong arm, territorial integrity, and the vertical of power.

∽ **5** ∽

Of course, the concept of the metaphorical nature of ideology propounded by Geertz is part of the general reconsideration of Aristotelian ideas on the nature and purpose of metaphor begun in the 1920s by Ernst Cassirer's *The*

Philosophy of Symbolic Forms, a discussion which has assumed a particular amplitude in the decades since "Ideology as a Cultural System" was first published. To oversimplify somewhat, this process essentially consists of overcoming the idea of the derivative nature of metaphorical as compared with literal meaning—an idea which confines the metaphorical use of language to the specific realms of linguistics, stylistics, and genre. As the influential British philosopher and linguist I. A. Richards remarked, "Throughout the history of rhetoric, metaphor has been treated as a sort of happy extra trick with words, an opportunity to exploit the accidents of their versatility, something in place occasionally but requiring unusual skill and caution. In brief, a grace or ornament or added power of language, not its constitutive form" (Richards 1990, 45).

By contrast, new theorists discerned within metaphorical thought-formation the basis of the cognitive process as well as of a person's practical activity. In his tellingly entitled work, *The Rule of Metaphor,* Paul Ricœur—a scholar who shares common ground with Geertz—also insisted upon the primacy of metaphor in language (Ricœur 1977; cf. Lakoff and Johnson 1980; Lakoff and Johnson 1987; Lakoff and Johnson 1990). Accordingly, metaphor gradually ceased to be the property mainly of poetic language, becoming an inseparable element not only of scientific and legal discourse, but also of everyday linguistic practice. Nonetheless, having lost its monopoly on the metaphor, imaginative literature acquired in return a sort of privileged scholarly status insofar as it is the realm of metaphor creation and accumulation par excellence and thus capable of serving as an ideal laboratory for investigating the mechanisms of the production of meanings.

In his own article, Geertz merely notes the direction of possible research in the field of the study of ideologies in his reference to the work of the literary theorist Kenneth Burke, *The Philosophy of Literary Forms,* then popular in the 1960s. Yet the question of the applicability of poetics to the analysis of ideology is only one (and hardly the most interesting) of the many problems arising in this connection. At the very least, the application of Geertz's ideas to the sacramental theme of the interrelations of ideology and literature offers no fewer prospects for investigation.

Understandably, Marxist aesthetics and literary scholarship have traditionally given primary significance to these very interrelations. Although we needn't return to slogan-like communist formulations culled from "Party Organization and Party Literature,"[4] it is worth recalling here William Mills Todd's exceptionally precise exposition of two authoritative contemporary representatives of this tradition in Western thought. In a work devoted to the connections between the Russian novel of the second quarter of the nineteenth century and the ideology and institutions of the aristocracy of the period, Todd writes:

> In these studies ideology appears not as a readily detachable filter between the individual and the "real" or between the text and the "real." On the contrary, it is embedded in "experience," in "common sense," in taste, in discourse, in all acts of signification. Imaginative literature works upon the ideology that presents itself to the text in language and, according to [Pierre] Macherey, wrests ideology into a new, nonideological (yet non-"scientific" in the Marxist sense) form through techniques of isolation, caricature, and figuration, thereby demystifying ideology and revealing its unacknowledged absences and contradictions. Eagleton challenges this apparent privileging of literary form, however, because it slights the persistent coherence of ideology and because, to Eagleton, ideology does not merely mystify or screen history. In his own formulation, literary form becomes not an escape from the "shame of the merely ideological," but a production of the ideological to the second power; it does to ideology what ideology does to history, makes it seem "natural." (Todd 1996, 20)

It is easy to see that for all the distinction and intellectual acuity of the two concepts, both begin with the presence of ideology and then describe how imaginative literature is able to overcome, deform, and naturalize it, or—to use official Soviet terminology—to embody and popularize it. Doubtless such a relationship between ideology and art often does exist, yet if one understands Geertz's conception of ideology as a system of metaphors, it is only one among many possible relationships.

First of all, the obverse relation between the two is also widespread. Those who possess power—politicians; authors of programmatic texts and formulas; in general, all of those who make up (in Althusser's expression) the "ideological apparatus" (Althusser 1971)—are themselves readers, or, to put it more

---

4   This was the title of an article by Lenin in which he stated that, regardless of an author's own intentions, any work of literature reflects the ideological assumptions of one or another party. Lenin's article was a required and oft-memorized text in Soviet schools and universities.

broadly, consumers of texts likewise capable of becoming imbued with and directed by the narrative and tropic models of those texts. This latter theme in particular was thoroughly explored by Iuri Lotman and his fellow semioticians in their penetrating analysis of the poetics of "literary behavior." The conversion of ideological constructions created by imaginative literature into strictly ideological rhetoric is at the very least no more difficult than the transformation of ideological clichés into poetic speech.

In this way, ideology can first appear in poems and novels only then to find itself embodied in slogans or political programs. It must be said that as far as the doctrines of oppositional politics are concerned, such a thesis appears fairly trivial: formulations like "the ideas of the Decembrists were born under the influence of the freedom-loving works of Griboedov and Pushkin" are familiar to us Russians from our earliest school days. While perfectly justified in and of itself, an analogous formulation of the question in terms, say, of the various groups who in one or another form implement practical politics, will also encounter certain difficulties. Political action inevitably runs up against resistance from the context in which it takes place, deforming its original ideological aims, which are then themselves forced to undergo adaptation. Put somewhat simplistically, one can say that the more distant the association of ideology with actual authority, the more "literary" it becomes. Yet it is precisely this ratio that allows one to reveal various further dimensions of the possible interaction between literature and the ideological arsenal of government authority.

The fact of the matter is that in the analysis of such interactions, the notorious problem of primacy and the direction of influence in general is not of paramount significance. Group and especially state ideology can exist as such as long as there is at least a minimum of consensus regarding its basic metaphors. (As we well know, with a developed apparatus of police and ideological violence an orchestrated appearance of consensus can successfully replace actual consensus, although for our present considerations this is unimportant.) The procedure for creating such a consensus requires a reasonable degree of translatability for the fundamental metaphorical constructions from the language of programmatic documents, decrees, and resolutions into the language of concrete political action, as well as the language of official rituals and mass holidays, the language of the organization of everyday life and the spatial environment and the like. As with any other translation, this takes place not without the loss of certain shades of meaning, but the general accuracy of the translation is confirmed by both the intuitions of the members of the collective as well as by specially created institutions of ideological control.

Of course, literature is just one of many possible spheres for the production of ideological metaphors. Historically, this function has often been fulfilled by theater, architecture, the organization of court, state and religious rituals and celebrations, church homiletics and many other types of human activity. In the twentieth century movies, advertisements and various genres of mass media most often play this role. That being said, the axis of ideology and literature is of particular interest because both work through an identical medium: the written word.

Poetic language is capable of constructing the necessary metaphors in their most pure form. It is for this very reason that art and especially literature acquire the potential to serve as a kind of universal depository of ideological concepts and as a measure of their practical realization. In a certain sense, ideology is capable of transforming itself into so many and such varied phenomena of social life because it possesses the "gold standard" preserved in poetic language. An old Russian saying has it that one cannot nourish a nightingale on fables alone. However, those very same nightingales use fables to nourish eagles (of both the one- and the two-headed sort!), lions, dragons, and other heraldic monstrosities, and with considerable success.

Moreover, ideological creation is most definitely a collective, albeit (the persistence of Marxist clichés notwithstanding) a far from anonymous process.[5] It doesn't matter who exactly begins this process, be it a writer, philosopher, politician, journalist, historian, or even an architect or master of ceremonies. The distribution of roles may differ completely; what is essential here is that in the course of the formation of ideological constructions, the contributions of one actor impels, completes, interprets, and misrepresents those made by other actors. And if practical politics tests poetry's practicability, then poetry returns the favor in terms of the capaciousness and expressiveness of the corresponding political metaphors.

---

5   Cf. Althusser's formula: "Human societies secrete ideology as an element or atmosphere necessary for breathing and existence" (Althusser 1969, 232).

6

The subject of this book is the history of Russian state ideology of the last third of the eighteenth through the first third of the nineteenth centuries, beginning with Catherine II's "Greek Project" and continues down to S. S. Uvarov's proposed doctrine of "Orthodoxy—Autocracy—Nationalism." Somewhat of an exception is made for the ideology of the people's body and popular war that was put forward by oppositionist literary men grouped around Admiral A. S. Shishkov that was officially adopted after he was appointed state secretary just before Napoleon's invasion of 1812.

The ten chapters offered here have been constructed in quite different ways. At the center of some are a particular work of poetry, such as an ode by V. P. Petrov or an epistle by V. A. Zhukovskii, or a group of such works, such as odes on Russian victories in the war with Turkey in 1768–1774, or the poems and tragedies written in the early nineteenth century on the theme of the Time of Troubles. Other chapters are dedicated to official and semi-official publicism—Shishkov's manifestoes, sermons by Filaret (Drozdov), Uvarov's memorandum. Two chapters concern state ceremonies and rituals—Catherine II's Crimean journey and the celebration that G. A. Potemkin staged in the Tauride Palace. Finally, two other chapters examine the cultural mechanisms of specific historical conflicts—Speranskii's fall from power and the publication of the treaty creating the Holy Alliance. Of course, these are only the main issues that are investigated and within each chapter the subjects under analysis may be similarly diverse.

This heterogeneity stems mostly from the book's basic conception. The author's goal was not to describe the regular transmission of ideological ideas from one institution to another—indeed the very existence of such regularity seems highly doubtful—but to trace the historically concrete dynamics of the working out, crystallization, and change of basic ideologems. In such an approach the ideological sphere of culture functions as a kind of reservoir of metaphors which people of various professions and types of activity both draw from and replenish.

In general, the center of our attention is on the ideological underpinnings of the Russian Empire's foreign policy: its wars and preparations for them, treaties and military projects. The great Russian reformer M. M. Speranskii once wrote that "there is not one state question ... down to tariffs" that cannot be worked out "in the spirit of the Gospel" (Speranskii 1870b, 188–189). To paraphrase, we could say that there is no sphere of state activity that does not lend itself to ideological analysis. Together with this, the sphere of foreign relations that is so closely tied to the problem of national self-consciousness and to state mythology, is most amenable for identifying and analyzing ideological symbols, whether in works of art or in practical political affairs.

Hence Catherine II's and Alexander I's active reform politics remain beyond the bounds of this study, as do Speranskii's own projects for reform that serve only as subsidiary material that helps to clarify the ideological conceptions of his political opponents. As far as Uvarov's triad is concerned, it was created after a period of war and upsets, with a view toward a long period of peaceful development for the empire, but its central goal was to define Russia's position in regard to European civilization. Paul I's short reign was left out for other reasons. This emperor, who was extremely prone to ideological creation, changed his orientation so swiftly that no productive dialogue between public opinion and artistic practice had time to develop. For this reason no consistent models significant for later periods appeared.

In the course of this work the author often confronted the following question: to what extent were the monarchs and ministers who populate these pages actually guided in their activities by ideological notions, or did these merely serve as a rhetorical cover for their true goals and interests? However, such an opposition seems artificial. Words really do have their fates and, once said, become an active factor in the historical process, whether or not the speaker was sincere. Even more important is the fact that the very posing of political goals is thoroughly ideologized, and ideas about what makes up state or national interests are subject to change and are to a great extent defined by symbolic reference points that allow people—to use Clifford Geertz's already-cited formulation—"to render otherwise incomprehensible social situations meaningfully, to so construe them as to make it possible to act purposefully within them."

In 1813 Alexander I wrote to one of his closest associates that he dreamed of making "his motherland happy, but not in the vulgar sense" (Nikolai Mikhailovich II, 7). One might say that this book represents an historical study of the actual meaning of these intentions.

CHAPTER 1

Russians as Greeks:
Catherine II's "Greek Project" and the Russian Ode of the 1760s–70s

∽ 1 ∽

Catherine II's well-known "Greek Project" is undoubtedly one of the largest, most comprehensive and ambitious foreign policy ideas that Russia's rulers have ever put forward. Like Catherine's colleagues and opponents both in Russia and abroad, modern historians tend to see it as just another of Potemkin's fantasies which the usually sober-minded empress allowed herself to be caught up in; as a manifestation of traditional imperial expansionism; as a smoke screen to hide less far-reaching but more practical intentions; or as a clear and well thought-out plan of action (see, for example, Markova 1959; Hösch 1964; Raeff 1972, Ragsdale 1988, Smilianskaia 1995, Leshchilovskaia 1998, Vinogradov 2000, and others; for the most thorough survey to date and a survey of the sources, see Hösch 1964). Authors who write about this usually limit themselves to the sphere of diplomacy and court politics, and completely ignore the symbolic dimension of the project (see Hösch 1964, 201–202). Yet for an evaluation of the project's sources as well as the historical significance of the empress's plan, this dimension may turn out to be most crucial.

Catherine laid out the "Greek Project" in comprehensive form in her letter to Emperor Joseph II of Sept. 10/21, 1782 (Arnet 1869, 143–147).

Figure 1 Medal commemorating the birth of Grand Prince Konstantin Pavlovich (1779).

Somewhat earlier, approximately in 1780, it was noted in a memorandum by A. A. Bezborodko, possibly intended for a meeting of the two emperors in Mogilev (SbRIO XXVI, 384–385). At the same time it is obvious that by Grand Prince Konstantin Pavlovich's birth in 1779 that a sufficiently well-developed outline already existed. The choice of name for the newborn and the memorial medal with classical figures and Church of St. Sophia that was minted to mark his birth testify to the empress's intentions with regard to her grandson rather clearly. As English ambassador James Harris stated, "Prince Potemkin ... is continually occupied with the idea of raising an Empire in the East; he has so far infected the empress with these sentiments, that she has been chimerical enough to christen the newborn Grand Duke, Constantine; to give him a Greek nurse, whose name was Helen; and to talk in her private society, of placing him on the throne of the Eastern Empire. In the meanwhile, she is building a town at Czarsco-Zelo, to be called Constantingorod" (Harris I, 97–98). The numerous odes on the birth of the grand prince demonstrate that, despite the secrecy that surrounded the diplomatic correspondence, the Russian public was perfectly well informed of these intentions (Ragsdale 1988, 97–98). In particular, Petrov wrote:

> … Мавксентий коим побежден,
> Защитник веры, слава Россов,

> Гроза и ужас чалмоносцев,
> Великий Константин рожден ...
> ... град, кой греками утрачен,
> От гнусна плена свободить, -
>
> (Petrov I, 164).

(The one who conquered Maxentius, / Defender of the faith, the glory of Russians, / Threat and horror of the turban-wearers, / Great Constantine is born... / ...To liberate the city from odious captivity / That was lost by the Greeks)

Apparently, the idea of the "Greek Project" originated in the mid-1770s when, after the Treaty of Kuchuk Kainarji, G. A. Potemkin gave Catherine his plan of the "Eastern System" (on which see Samoilov 1867, 1011–1016),[1] which was to replace N. I. Panin's "Northern System" in Russia's foreign policy (see Griffiths 1970). Potemkin's swift rise to power, beginning in 1774, was not only due to personal reasons but also because the ideas he put forward were in line with Catherine's strategic plans that had been worked out during the course of the Russian-Turkish War of 1768–1774.

Both contemporaries and later commentators on the "Greek Project" paid special attention to its central element, which was also the most critical and difficult to achieve: the conquest of Constantinople. However, this very idea of Catherine's and Potemkin's was not in itself new. Plans for conquering the former capital of the Eastern Roman Empire had stirred Russian tsars as early as the seventeenth century (see Kapterev 1885; Zhigarev I-II, and others). They had circulated during Peter I's Azov and Pruth campaigns and arose again under Anna Ioannovna during the Turkish campaign of 1736–1739 (see Kochubinskii 1899). In 1762 the hero of that campaign, B. K. Minikh, presented Catherine with a letter in which he called on her to fulfill Peter's will and to take Constantinople (see Hösch 1964, 181). The theme of Constantinople reverberated in Russian

---

[1] Working on a biography of Potemkin in 1814, A. N. Samoilov still considered the realization of the "Greek Project" a question of the Russian monarchs' will: "Death, having cut the life thread of this glorious man [Potemkin], put an end to (ostanovila sushestvovanie) the Ottoman Empire until the present events; but the basis of his great plan is solid even today, and Russia always has the means of implementing it" (Ibid, 1011).

journalism and social thought even later, right up to 1917, when the idea of placing a cross above St. Sophia and taking control of the straits outlived the Russian monarchy and became one of the reasons for the failure of the Provisional Government.

The special historical nature of Catherine's "Greek Project," at least if we judge by the letter to Joseph II and by public perception of the time, lies on a different plane. The empress did not at all plan to unite Constantinople with the Russian Empire, or to move its capital there. According to her project, the Second Rome was to become the center of a new Greek empire whose throne would go to Constantine only under the strict condition that he himself and his heirs would forever and in all circumstances repudiate any pretensions to the Russian crown. In this way, two neighboring powers under the scepters of the "star of the North" and the "star of the East," Alexander and Constantine, would be united (using deeply anachronistic but precisely accurate terminology) by the bonds of fraternal friendship, so to speak, while Russia would play the role (again resorting to anachronism) of elder brother.

However, more profound historical factors would have had to support the dynastic union guaranteeing this brotherhood, which in turn would have propelled a member of the Russian imperial family to the throne of the new Greek empire, thus raising the whole project above the level of just another opportunistic diplomatic game. Such a factor was the Russian Empire's religious heritage in relation to that of Constantinople. Russia had received its faith from Greek hands as a result of the marriage between a Kievan prince and the Byzantine emperor's daughter, and therefore could now act as the natural savior of the Greeks from the yoke of the infidels. This gave a new twist to the newly developing relations between Russians and Greeks, as Russia not only appeared as the savior of Greece but also as its heir, or—to continue the familial metaphor—as a daughter who was obliged to return a long-time debt to her elder and at the same time younger sibling.

Here we approach what is arguably the core of this entire ideological construction. In the "Greek Project's" system of coordinates, religious succession was equated with the cultural, as if by default. Hence Constantinople and Athens were marked as equivalent and by definition Russia's role as the single heir to the Byzantine church also made her the only indisputably legitimate heir to classical Greek culture.[2] In all aspects of the project we consistently see the mixing of Byzantine and classical motifs, including in the aforementioned celebrations on the birth of Constantine and in the program for his education.

This logical *tour de force* fundamentally changed the thinking about Russia's historical role and destiny. If it had been traditionally thought that the torch of enlightenment had gone from Greece to Rome, then taken up by Western Europe, and from there passed on to Russia, now Russia was seen to have had a direct line to Greece and therefore, had no need for intermediaries.

"The present reigning idea (and it carries away all others) is the establishing of a new Empire in the East, at Athens or Constantinople. The empress discoursed a long while with me the other day on the ancient Greeks; of their alacrity and the superiority of their genius, and the same character being still extant in the modern ones; and of the possibility of their again becoming the first people, if properly assisted and seconded," the English ambassador Harris wrote home soon after Constantine's birth (Harris I, 204). Catherine's speech reveals a highly characteristic mode of thinking. Russia was called to restore their true nature to the Greeks, to lead them back to their own origins. She may also be seen as obliged to do this, insofar as she was the legitimate heir to classical Greece by way of Byzantium, and in some sense its modern embodiment. At least in Harris's perception, Athens and Constantinople enjoy equal rights to serve as the capital of the future empire.

In an obvious way, this position led to the idea of Russia's cultural potency in Europe and to a reconsideration of her political priorities. In the early 1780s, after Catherine's meeting with Joseph II in Mogilev, negotiations began concerning an alliance between Russia and Austria. This alliance was very necessary for Catherine given her new political orientation, but at the decisive moment of signing the treaty it was almost rescinded because the Russian side raised the question of a so-called "alternative."

According to the diplomatic etiquette of the time, it was standard practice that two copies of the treaty would be signed simultaneously, and then the two sides would swap places and sign again. However, this practice did not

---

2   One may see the outline of this interpretation in Lomonosov's "Foreword on the Use of Church Books," written in the late 1750s, in which similar conclusions were drawn based on the linguistic succession from Greek to Russian (see Picchio 1992).

apply to the Holy Roman Emperor, who claimed the immutable right to sign first. Given Russia's new orientation, this did not suit Catherine in the least. As strongly as she was interested in an alliance with Austria, she could not accept its diplomatic primacy. Russia, as legitimate heir to the Eastern Roman Empire, demanded equality with the Western (see Madariaga 1959/1960).[3] A compromise that was on the whole advantageous to Catherine was finally found, but the very emergence of this conflict eloquently testifies to the enormous growth of Russian state consciousness that was unquestionably tied to the "Greek Project." According to Joseph II, during the Mogilev meeting, every time that he began to speak of Greece and Constantinople, the empress made mention of Italy and Rome (Arned III, 250). Catherine's idea was that Europe's political leadership should consist of two empires: the Viennese, heir to Rome, and that of Petersburg, heir to Constantinople.

Not even the most sophisticated imagination could fashion a figure more suited to conceive and carry out all of these hyperbolic plans than G. A. Potemkin. The English Ambassador Harris reported in his dispatches that Potemkin was little interested in Western politics but that he paid great attention to Eastern matters. Later, when the question of transferring rule of the island of Minorca in the Mediterranean to Britain was under discussion, Potemkin quickly expressed an intention to settle Greeks there (see Harris I, 203, 316; cf. Samoilov 1867, 591–592, 1010–1014, 1203–1204; Brinker 1891, 47, 59–67, et al.; on Potemkin's relations with Greeks, see Batalden 1982, 67–72; Ponomareva 1992, et al.). In an epistle to the Greek community of Enikal and Kerch, the Greek Archbishop Nikiforus called Potemkin "a true defender and patron of our people, for out of all tribes he loved Greeks most of all" (Batalden 1982, 69).

A visionary and utopian with traits of administrative genius, Potemkin—who combined in himself exalted piety, theological erudition (the schism between Eastern and Western churches was one of his favorite topics of conversation), a worshipful attitude toward classical antiquity and a passion

---

3   Madariaga suggests that Catherine's hard line on the question of the alternative was instigated by N. I. Panin, who wanted the talks to fail. This is hardly a convincing explanation. By this time Panin's influence had significantly weakened, and the empress, who knew his position perfectly well, would hardly have let him endanger such a fundamental, strategic plan had she not considered the question under discussion to be very serious.

for Greece and the Greeks—was the very person who could be inspired by the idea of Russia's gargantuan geopolitical turn toward the South. From the Baltic with its predominant orientation toward the German Protestant world, on which Peter I's politics were focused, Russia was now to be redirected toward the Black and Mediterranean Seas, to the northern Black Sea coast and the Balkans, settled with fellow Orthodox Greeks, southern Slavs, Moldavians and Wallachians—to territories that had once been united under the Byzantine scepter, and even earlier, by Alexander the Great.

Potemkin's personality very clearly dominated this entire scheme. It is all the more interesting that its basic conceptual links had been worked out during the previous five years, during the Russo-Turkish War of 1768–1774, even before the political ascent of "his most serene highness (serenissimus)."

∞ **2** ∞

V. O. Kliuchevskii himself noted that Catherine's "Greek Project" was to a great extent inspired by Voltaire's letters (Kliuchevskii 1993, 509). However, this subject has never been investigated properly. As a matter of fact, in his letters to Catherine from the time of the Russo-Turkish War of 1768–1774, Voltaire constantly addressed the theme and unfailingly urged the empress to conquer Constantinople and to revive the Greek state and learning. So it is all the more important to try to distinguish which elements of the "Greek Project" indeed stemmed from this correspondence and which might have been suggested by other sources.

On November 15, 1768, when news of the start of the war had still not reached Paris, Voltaire wrote to Catherine:

> If they make war on you, Madam, what Peter the Great once had in mind may well befall them, namely that Constantinople will become the capital of the Russian Empire. These barbarians deserve to be punished by a heroine, for the lack of respect they have hitherto had for the ladies. Clearly, people who neglect all the fine arts and who lock up women, deserve to be exterminated.
> ... I ask your Imperial Majesty's permission to come and lay myself at your feet, and to spend a few days at your court, as soon as it is set up in Constantinople; for I most earnestly believe that if ever the Turks are to be chased out of Europe, it will be by the Russians. (Catherine 1971, 20; Lentin 1974, 51–52[4])

---

4   References to Lentin indicate that the translation from the Catherine-Voltaire correspondence has been taken from his edition.

In her answering letter, the empress reported to her correspondent that before "his entry into Constantinople" she was sending him "a beautiful costume à la grecque, lined with the best furs from Siberia" (Catherine 1971, 23). This Greek-style costume made of Siberian pelts is symbolic of the Greco-Russian synthesis which would subsequently be realized in the "Greek Project." Somewhat later, informing Voltaire about the successes of A. G. Orlov's first naval expedition, which will be discussed below, Catherine developed this theme: "It depends solely on the Greeks whether Greece will be revived. I have done everything possible to adorn geographical maps with a direct connection between Corinth and Moscow" (ibid., 62).

However, Catherine's caution didn't satisfy Voltaire. Throughout their whole correspondence he scattered compliments about Russian victories and urged his correspondent not to be satisfied with partial concessions but to prosecute the war until the complete destruction of the Ottoman Empire, which for him represented an unqualified embodiment of barbarism, ignorance, and spiritual abasement. "If you follow up your victories, I think you will spread them wherever you please; and if you want peace, you will dictate it. For my part, I still want your Majesty to go to Constantinople to be crowned," Voltaire wrote to Catherine in a letter of August 28, 1770 (ibid., 67). The recognized leader of European classicism, he saw driving the Turks out of Europe as the prerequisite for its cultural renaissance, and he believed that the "Northern Semiramis"—simultaneously his patron and pupil—had to become the instrument of Providence, spreading enlightenment with her soldiers' bayonets:

> Oh Minerva of the North, oh, you, sister of Apollo,
> You will revenge Greece, driving out the unworthy,
> The enemies of the arts, persecutors of women,
> I will depart and will wait for you on the fields of
>   Marathon, -

as he wrote in his "Stanzas to the Empress of Russia Catherine II on the Occasion of the Taking of Khotin by the Russians in 1769" (Voltaire XIII, 316).

The Russo-Turkish War was thus equated to the Persian War with the Greeks, which Voltaire of course interpreted as a clash between culture and barbarism. In September 1770, he set forth before Catherine an entire program for reviving classical culture in its historical cradle:

> Those who wished setbacks upon your Majesty will be quite confounded; and why should people wish to see you disgraced when you are the avenger of Europe? I suppose these are the people who do not want Greek to be spoken; for if you were queen of Constantinople, your Majesty would very soon establish a fine Greek academy. A *Catheriniad* would be written in your honor. Many a Zeuxis and Phidias would cover the earth with statues of you; the fall of the Ottoman Empire would be celebrated in Greek; Athens would be one of your capitals; Greek would become the universal language; all the traders in the Aegean would ask your Majesty for Greek passports. ... (Ibid., 71; Lentin 1974, 86)

Two and a half years later, in February 1773, when it was already clear that the results of the war would be much more modest than both correspondents had counted on, Voltaire nevertheless returned to these ambitious plans. Not long before, Catherine had sent him translations of two of her comedies which she presented as works by an "anonymous author" (ibid., 171). Like Russian readers of Catherine's comedies, Voltaire was by no means led astray by this ploy, which it seems never seriously aimed at hiding the name of the real author from anyone. However, it gave him the opportunity of again laying out his series of geo-political theses before the empress:

> ... a rare quality indeed is that of cultivating all the arts, as you did, at a time when the entire nation was engaged in the art of war. I see that the Russians are an intelligent, a highly intelligent people; your Imperial Majesty was not made to govern fools. It is this which has always convinced me that nature destined you to rule over Greece. I keep harping on my favorite topic; this will come to pass. In ten years' time ... the Turkish Empire will be partitioned, and you will have Sophocles' *Oedipus* performed at Athens. (Ibid., 178; Lentin 1974, 148)

Voltaire's hyperbolic praise gives a very clear notion of his political and cultural priorities. He is primarily if not exclusively interested in freeing Greece from Turkish domination and in restoring the great traditions of classical culture in their original home. Russia and even her monarch—on whom Voltaire, as always, lavished the most effusive compliments—played an instrumental political role in his thinking. Envisioning Catherine as ruler of Greece, Voltaire seemed to presume her metamorphosis (at least in a cultural regard) into a true Greek; Catherine's transformation from a German princess into a Russian sovereign offered a familiar biographical precedent for such flights of fancy. "If your Majesty is going to establish your throne in Constantinople, as I hope, you will learn Greek very quickly," he wrote at the very beginning of the war, "because it is absolutely necessary to chase the Turkish language out of Europe, as well as everyone who speaks it" (ibid., 27).

Catherine responded to these sentiments with characteristic caution. At first, in August 1769, she wrote that her plans for studying the Greek language were limited to the "Greek compliment" she planned to make to Voltaire, just as two years earlier she had "learned several Tatar and Arabic phrases in Kazan, which gave great pleasure to the inhabitants of that city" (ibid., 315). However, then she probably decided not to disenchant her correspondent too strongly, and this whole passage remained in the draft. Later the empress returned to this question again, expressing greater interest in her own classical education, but also not forgetting to delicately remind her correspondent which language had to be the main focus of her attention: "I basically agree with you, that soon will come the time that I will have to go to some university to study Greek; meanwhile Homer is being translated into Russian; it's always something to make a start" (ibid., 80; she was writing about P. E. Ekimov's prose translation). Ultimately Voltaire had to agree, insofar as Catherine's position did not permit the continuation of the discussion, but his tone clearly expressed disappointment: "If the Greeks had been worthy of what you did for them, Greek would today be the universal language; but Russian could well take its place" (ibid., 169; Lentin 1974, 142).

In enticing the empress with the throne of Constantinople, giving preference to it over Moscow and Petersburg (ibid., 162), and even recalling Peter I's plans for the city (ibid., 191), Voltaire was thinking not so much about the Byzantine capital itself as much as about Athens, to which, as he wrote, he was "unalterably attached thanks to Sophocles, Euripides, [and] Menander" and to "old Anacreon, my colleague" (ibid., 139). He complained that "if you … nevertheless grant peace to Mustapha, what will my poor Greece become, what will come of that beautiful land of Demosthenes and Sophocles? I would abandon Jerusalem to the Moslems voluntarily; those barbarians were made for the land of Ezekiel, Elijah and Caiaphas. But I will always be bitterly grieved to see the

Athenian theater turned into a kitchen and the lyceum into a stable" (ibid., 123). Once in the correspondence he makes a slip and calls Constantinople "the city of that nasty Constantine" (ibid., 76). Quite clearly he was not only ignorant of and indifferent to the religious motivation of the Russian mission in Constantinople, but also openly hostile to it.

In his correspondence with the empress, the philosophe had to refrain from this kind of expression of hostility and to patiently listen to lectures on the truly Christian character of the Eastern Church and its inherent tolerance from his royal correspondent, who was not noted for her special piety. Here he could only permit himself light and respectful sarcasm: "As for me, I am faithful to the Greek church, the more so when your beautiful hands in some sense hold the censer and you may be seen as the patriarch of all the Russias" (ibid., 118). Catherine in fact more than once called herself "head of the Greek church" (ibid., 176, 193, etc.), to some extent taking up the ironic intonation of her interlocutor and to some extent just confirming the actual state of affairs. Later, responding to Catherine's words about the fact that the Greeks had "degenerated" and "love stealing more than liberty" (ibid., 78), Voltaire wrote, "My other regret is that the Greeks should be unworthy of the liberty they would have recovered, had they had the courage to assist you. I have no further desire to read Sophocles, Homer or Demosthenes. I would hate the Greek faith, if your Imperial Majesty were not head of that church" (ibid., 155; Lentin 131).

Nonetheless, in his "Ode on the Current War with Greece" Voltaire did not hide from readers that it was precisely the Greek Church that he considered most responsible for the decline of the ancient heroic spirit:

> There are no more Herculeses
> Who would follow after Minerva and Mars,
> The fearless conquerors of the Persians
> And lovers of all the arts,
> Who in both peace and war
> Gave an example to the whole earth. ...
>
> But ... under the sway of two Theodosiuses
> All of the heroes degenerated,
> And there are no more apotheoses,

> Except for those of malicious tonsured pedants ...
> And under the sway of Saint Basil
> The descendants of Achilles
> Became slaves of the Ottomans.
>
> (Voltaire XIII, 407)

Voltaire was so carried away by classical Greek models that he even wanted military action to be carried out in the antique manner. In his letters, despite his obvious lack of competence in military questions, and basing his opinion on that of some "old officer," he stubbornly and almost impudently urged Catherine to use "chariots" in her campaigns, which, in his opinion, would be particularly effective on the steppes of the Black Sea area (Catherine 1971, 28–29, 45, 48, 51–52, 71, 187, etc.) Understandably, Catherine did not find it necessary to respond to this kind of recommendation. In general, the empress had to restrain the militant enthusiasm of her interlocutor, explaining to him that they were still far from taking Constantinople (ibid., 76) and that she preferred peace to war. However, she fully shared his partiality for the Greek theme. In early 1773 when the war was winding down and it was more or less clear that the liberation of Greece would have to be put off until better times, she wrote to Voltaire, "I am now reading the works of Algarotti. He claims that all of the arts and sciences were born in Greece. Tell me, I beg of you, is this really true?" (ibid., 180).

Catherine's interest in this question is fully understandable—if the Greeks had been the fathers of the Enlightenment, then the historical significance of Russia, so closely connected to them, immeasurably rose. In an answering letter, expressing the oft-repeated hope that Count Orlov would erect himself a triumphal arch "not in icy regions but in the Istanbul hippodrome," and that Catherine would "give rise in Greece not only to Miltiades but also Phidiases,"[5] Voltaire nevertheless had to disillusion his august correspondent by stating that the Greeks owed much to ancient Egypt, to the Phoenicians, and to India (ibid., 183). This time Catherine reluctantly had to agree: "With a few words you have saved me from error: I am now convinced

---

5   Miltiades—Athenian general who led his troops to victory over the Persians at the Battle of Marathon in 490; Phidias—commonly regarded as one of the greatest sculptors of ancient Greece. (Translator's note)

that it was not in Greece that the arts were invented. Still, I am upset, because I love the Greeks in spite of all their faults" (ibid., 185).

The empress continued to be interested in the Greeks; in less than a year Potemkin's "Greek system" was destined to become state policy. Voltaire's influence on the formation of certain elements of this policy might have been significant, but would also have been of a strictly limited nature. From Voltaire Catherine might have derived her vision of a liberated Greece as a revived kingdom of antiquity, a kind of substitution of Athens for Constantinople. However, basic facets of the "Greek Project"—the notion of the complex historical succession of Greece and Russia, the link between religious and cultural succession, the utopian idea of the fraternal union of two empires based on their religious and cultural identity—were completely foreign to the French philosophe.

In connection to his ideal of enlightened absolutism, Voltaire considered the mission of the monarch to bring the light of civilization to barbarian peoples. The liberation and enlightenment of Greece was to be the acme of the royal path of the "Northern Sermiramis." "You will doubtless restore the Isthmian Games, at which the Romans assured the Greeks their liberty by a public decree; and this will be the most glorious act of your life," he wrote Catherine (ibid., 59–60; Lentin 83). Voltaire was concerned with Enlightenment and monarchs who sponsored it, but certainly not with Russia and its historical destiny. One could argue, perhaps, that from a historical and cultural point of view Catherine and Potemkin's plans belong more to the epoch of Herder than to that of the Sage of Ferney. However, the popularity of Herder's works which were published, like those of Winckelmann, in the mid-1760s, had not yet reached Russia (see Danilevskii 1980). So Catherine and Potemkin had to find inspiration in domestic sources.

∽ 3 ∽

In the fall of 1768 Turkey declared war on Russia. For the empress and her advisors the beginning of military action was somewhat unexpected and was certainly undesirable. It is not surprising, then, that their ideological interpretation of the war was somewhat belated, and that at first Catherine resorted to hallowed religious themes. The manifesto "On the beginning of war with the Ottoman Porte," signed on November 18, 1768, contained no neoclassicist motifs at all. It speaks of Turkey's interference in Polish affairs, of the arrest of the Russian envoy Obreskov in Constantinople, and about the Muslims' treachery. The empress's subjects were summoned to "war against the devious adversary and enemy of the Christian" (PSZ № 13198). Moreover, the manifesto was addressed to all strata of the empire's population, the majority of whom were not capable of appreciating classical allusions. But the authors of the first odes on the event, aimed at a far narrower audience, also focused their attention on religious themes:

> А паче просит вас туда
> Народов близкая беда,
> Соединенных нам законом,
> Они в оковах тяжких там, -

(The nearby misfortune of peoples / United with us by law / Even more calls us there / Where they are in heavy fetters)

Thus wrote M. M. Kheraskov, one of the best known poets of that time. The ideological conception of the war was not at all clear as yet to him, and for Constantinople he simply substituted not Athens, as did Voltaire, but Jerusalem:

> На вечный плач и бедство нам
> И нашим в торжество врагам
> Сии места, места священны,
> Где искупитель наш рожден,
> И гроб, чем тартар побежден,
> Иноплеменникам врученны.

(To our eternal lament and misfortune / And to the delight of our foes / These places, holy places / Where our redeemer was born, / And the grave which overcame Hell / Is in the hands of aliens.)

Additionally, Kheraskov directly juxtaposed the vain and empty achievements of classical heroes to the new crusade for the faith:

> Не для златого нам руна,
> Не для прекрасной Андромеды,

> О, Россы! предлежит война
> И представляются победы.
> Пусть древность суеты поет,
> Не гордость вас на брань зовет. (Kheraskov 1769)

([It is] not for a golden fleece, / Not for a beautiful Andromeda, / O, Russians, [that] war awaits / And victories summon. / Let the ancients sing of vanity, / It is not pride that calls you to arms.)

Then again, the very mention of peoples under the Turkish yoke and the very parallel with Greece seemed to hint at future shifts in meaning which were for now still under wraps.

In his ode on the declaration of war, Vasilii Petrov, the poet who was most influential and closest to the court and who served as the empress's reader and ode-writer, compared the countless horde of "locusts" sent "to the North" "by the devotee of Mohammed" (Petrov I, 37) not to the Persian troops attacking poor tiny Greece but to the assembly of infidels laying siege to ancient Israel. In conformity with Catherine's political views, and overall in conformity with the facts, Petrov attributed Turkey's decision to declare war to French instigation. He depicted the coming campaign as a grandiose battle between three points of the compass and the Northern kingdom:

> От Юга, Запада, Востока,
> Из Мекки и Каира врат,
> Где хвально имя лжепророка,
> Где Нил шумит, где Тигр, Ефрат,
> Уже противники России
> Стекаются ко Византии ...
> Теснятся предним над Дунаем,
> Но задним воинства их краем
> В Стамбуле движутся еще. (Ibid., 36)

(From the South, West, East, / From the gates of Mecca and Cairo, / Where the name of the false prophet is praised, / Where the Nile splashes, and the Tigris and Euphrates, / The enemies of Russia / Are already gathering toward Byzantium ... / The troops in front crowd above the Danube, / But their rear edge / Still moves in Istanbul.)

Byzantium, ancient Byzantium, that is, Constantinople, is here called Istanbul (Stambul) and is perceived as the center of the Muslim world. A half-year later, when news came of the taking of Khotin, in his ode Sergei Domashnev likened Byzantium to Mecca and Medina as Asiatic lands that were under Muslims' power and in general belonging to them:

> И бегством спасшись в Византию,
> Сколь грозно раздражать Россию
> Вещай своим потомкам в страх,
> Да зрят неверством ослепленны
> Знамена Росски водруженны
> Хотина ныне на стенах,
> Стеня по всем странам Азийским,
> Рассыпьте страх и трепет свой …
> И в Мекку идя и в Медину,
> Оплачьте черную годину
> И беззакония свои. (Domashnev 1769)

(And saving themselves by flight to Byzantium, / How dangerous to annoy Russia / Let your descendants know and fear / And let them see, blinded by infidelity, / Russia's banners unfurled / Today on Khotin's walls. / Groaning throughout Asian lands, / Spread your fear and trembling … / And going to Mecca and to Medina/ Bewail the black event / And your lawless acts.)

In another ode on the taking of Khotin, Fedor Kozel'skii compared the ancient Greeks not with Russians but with Turks:

> Афины рвали так союз,
> Спокойство мира отвергая
> И от смиренных Сиракуз
> Презорно око отвращая.
> Витийства движет там разврат
> Буян возжег Алцибиад. (Kozel'skii I, 64)

(Athens thus rent the alliance, / Rejecting the world's tranquility / And from the humble people of Syracuse / Disdainfully turned away its eye. / Debauchery there informs eloquence / The bullies were inflamed by Alcibiades.)

However, in Petrov's ode to the same event new accents appear, if tentatively and in the background. Precisely thirty years earlier, in 1739, Russian troops had taken Khotin once before. That victory had been the subject of Lomonosov's famous ode in which he described the battle as a cosmic clash between the sons of Russia "chosen for labor" and the "tribe of an outcast slave," Hagar (Lomonosov 1986, 62). A pupil of Lomonosov, Petrov used this obvious parallel to give his poem an unusually powerful Old Testament charge:

> Приникни с высоты престола,
> О Боже, на дела земли,
> Воззри, средь освященна дола
> Враги завета возлегли …
>
> Но, прелагаяй море в сушу,
> Вещает Сильный от небес:
> Я скиптр дарю, я царства рушу,
> Вся тварь полна моих чудес …
> Восстани днесь, восстань Деввора,
> Преступны грады разори …
> Не бойся, я защитник твой.
> Моей десницей чудотворной
> Казнен египтянин упорный.
>
> Восстала се, полки предводит,
> Разит преступников гоня,
> На храм Софийский се нисходит
> Дух Божий в образе огня.
> Прими, несчастна Византия,
> Тот свет от Россов, кой Россия
> Прияла прежде от тебя,
> Приимешь, узришь в нем себя.

(Come down from your throne's height, / O God, and look at matters on earth: / Amid the consecrated vale / Enemies of your testament repose … // But, turning sea into dry land / The Powerful One announces from the heavens: / I give the scepter, I destroy kingdoms, / All creation is filled with my wonders ... / Arise today, arise Deborah, / Ravage lawless cities ... / Do not fear, I am your defender. / With my miraculous right hand / The stubborn Egyptian was chastened. //It arose, led the regiments, / Smote the offenders, driving them away, / Descended to the Sophia Temple / Divine Spirit in the image of fire. / Unhappy Byzantium, accept / This light from the Russians, which Russia / Earlier accepted from you, / Take it, you will see yourself in it.)

Behind this traditional biblical rhetoric, taken to an emotional extreme, one may already see an entire complex of new motifs—Constantinople, with the Hagia Sophia as the goal of the war; Russia's returning to Byzantium the divine grace it had once been given; and the liberated country's acquisition of itself as a gift from Russia. But Petrov kept his most important conceptual innovations for the final stanza:

> С торжественныя колесницы
> Простри на юг свои зарницы ...
> Орлы твои Афин достигнут
> И вольность Греции воздвигнут,
> Там новый возгремит Пиндар
> Российския победы дар,
> Несчетны воспоют народы
> Тебя, виновницу свободы.
>
> (Petrov I, 44–49)

(From your triumphant chariot / Spread your rays to the south ... / Your eagles will reach Athens / And establish Greece's freedom, / There a new Pindar will resound / The gift of Russian victory / Countless peoples will sing out praise / For you, their liberator.)

This ode, overflowing with religious symbolism and attributes, also culminates in classical motifs. The final result of God's intervention in human events is the freedom of Greece and hymns by the new Pindar. In Petrov's next ode "On the Taking of Iassy," written in the same year of 1769, the ancient Greek coloration is even stronger:

> Воззри – несчастные народы,
> Где Пинд стоит, Олимп, Парнас,

> Лишенные драгой свободы,
> К тебе возносят взор и глас. …
>
> Спокойся днесь, геройско племя,
> И жди с терпением премен,
> Приспеет вожделенно время,
> Ваш, Греки, разрешится плен.
> Вы дух явили благодарный,
> Когда вам римлянин коварный
> Свободу мниму даровал:
> Ни пользы требуя, ни хвал,
> Вам лучшу даст Екатерина. (Ibid., 58)

(Look, unhappy peoples / Where stand the Pindus, Olympus, Parnassus, / Bereft of cherished freedom, / They turn their gaze and voice to you … // Be calm now, heroic tribe, / And await changes with patience, / The desired time will arrive / And, Greeks, your captivity will end. / You showed a grateful spirit / When the deceitful Roman / Granted you false freedom: / Without demanding service or praise / Catherine will give you better [i.e., the real thing].)

Petrov recalled the privileges that the Romans granted the Greeks during the Olympic (Isthmian) Games and juxtaposed them to the blessings that the Russian empress would give to them; this was almost a year before Voltaire made the same comparison in his letter to Catherine (see above). In his odes of the second half of 1769, the poet partly grasped and partly foresaw and anticipated the change that was about to occur in the official interpretation of the goals and idea of the war. This change was without any doubt connected to Aleksei Orlov's naval expedition.

4

The idea of equipping a naval squadron in the rear of the Turks and of encouraging the Orthodox peoples living in the Mediterranean (Greeks and Southern Slavs) to rebel—had been suggested by Catherine's then-favorite Grigorii Orlov in early November 1768, before the signing of the declaration of war. At that time his brother Aleksei Orlov wrote to him about the tasks of that kind of expedition and of the war as a whole: "If we go, then go to Constantinople and liberate all of the Orthodox and all the devout from their heavy yoke. I'll put it like Sovereign Peter I said in his document (gramota): drive those infidel Mohammedans into the sandy steppes, back to their former abode. And godliness will reign there again, and we will say glory to our omnipotent God" (Orlov 1870, 142; Barsukov 1873, 61–62; cf. Solov'ev XIV, 269–272; Petrov A. 1869, 97–106). At the beginning of 1769 Catherine reported to Aleksei Orlov that manifestoes "for the purpose of raising Christian inhabitants up in revolt" were already prepared and she recommended that he "find people who have excellent credit among the godly Greek and Orthodox peoples" (SbRIO I, 5, 14). That summer the navy left Kronstadt, circumnavigating Europe on its way to the Mediterranean Sea.

In an old monograph by V. A. Ulianitskii, it was shown that the organizers and ideologists of the expedition constantly vacillated about its purpose. If the Orlovs actually strove primarily to liberate fellow believers and to unite them under a Russian protectorate, Catherine saw in the navy's task of raising a rebellion in the enemy's rear more of a military diversion and let herself be carried away by far-reaching plans to a much lesser extent. It seems that for a long time the empress did not really believe in the naval expedition's prospects for overall success and concerned herself mainly with its narrowly military purposes. However, even the more radical plans that the Orlovs promoted bear only a faint resemblance to the future "Greek Project." Rather, they look like a continuation of Russia's traditional policy toward Constantinople, based on religious gravitation toward the capital of the Eastern Church and the desire to unite all fellow believers under its aegis. It is significant in this regard that the Greeks are only mentioned in the Orlovs' plans together with other Orthodox peoples of southern Europe (Ulianitskii 1883, 107–130; cf. Smilianskaia 1996, 88–98).

"The uprising of each people separately,... without causing the enemy significant harm (and, even worse, causing them some kind of useful diversion) which alone should be our primary goal, would only serve to open the Turks' eyes," Catherine instructed Orlov before the start of the expedition (SbIRIO I, 6), and in early 1770 when prospects for an uprising in Greece seemed rather uncertain, she encouraged him: "Despite the fact that over centuries of slavery and deceit the corrupt Greeks have betrayed their own interests, our mere naval diversion alone is sufficient to upset all of the

Turkish-held regions of Europe" (ibid., 35). Moreover, Orlov's first successes in the summer of 1770 and the diplomatic situation that seemed favorable to her gave the empress hope for more significant gains. She informed Orlov,

> To Our special and honest delight we know on good authority that all of the impartial powers of the Christian republic take justice to be on our side, and that this most general support keeps our enemies in check against their will and inclination. ... It is necessary ... that you, having united various Greek peoples under your leadership, make of them something visible as quickly as possible ... that would appear to the world as a new and complete people, and that this new body, constituted by a public act..., and thus declaring its political right to exist (politicheskoe svoe bytie), would echo throughout the entire Christian republic with this kind of message: ... That the numerous Greek peoples, by God's will subjected to the heavy yoke of Hagarene iniquity ... [have] joined together, constituting a new member of the Christian republic. ... (Ibid., 41)

The phrase "Christian republic" is repeated here three times on one page. This formula derives from a very precise source—from the idea of a confederation of Christian nations of Europe that was supposedly proposed to the French King Henry IV at the start of the seventeenth century by his minister the Duke de Sully and laid out in the last volume of his memoirs. Catherine highly esteemed both Henry and Sully. She ordered their busts from the sculptor Marie-Anne Collot, who had accompanied E. Falconet to Russia at the time of his work on the monument to Peter I (SbIRIO XVIII, 37). When Voltaire wrote to Catherine that he awaited meeting Peter the Great in heaven, she answered that for her part she dreamed of meeting Henry and Sully (Catherine 1971, 51). In this very year of 1770, a translation of Sully's ten-volume memoirs (Zapiski), which Catherine had specially ordered from the translator M. I. Verevkin, began publication in Russia.

It is significant that Sully, who was not fully sure that Russians were Christians, was skeptical about the possibility of Russia taking part in his proposed Christian republic which was to guarantee eternal peace in Europe:

> If the grand prince of Muscovy, or Russian tsar, whom writers consider an ancient Scythian ruler, refuses to participate in the common agreement which would be proposed to him in advance, then we should deal with him as with the Turkish sultan, that is, take back all of his possessions in Europe, and drive him into Asia, so that without any of our involvement (soprimeshenie) he

could continue his almost never-ending war with the Turks and Persians for as long as he wants. (Sully X, 364, 360–361)

Sully wanted to propose that Russia take its place either in the Christian republic of European states or in Asia, along with "the Turkish sultan." For Catherine, Russia's place on the global political map was certain. She had no doubt that Russia had already earned a worthy place in Europe and now herself planned to lock the sultan away in Asia and to add a "new body" to the Christian republic—Greece, restored "under Russia's protection."

However, despite its brilliant victory in the Chesme encounter, the navel expedition did not bring the desired results. In essence, the Russian forces had to abandon the Greeks to the vicissitudes of fate. Aleksei Orlov, who had made such monumental plans, tended to blame the Greeks themselves for what had happened, because in his opinion they had not shown sufficient bravery and military discipline, and had preferred plunder to a war for liberation:

> The local peoples are smooth-talking, deceptive, inconstant, impudent and cowardly, lusting after money and whatever they can get. ... Credulity and flightiness, fear at the name of the Turk—are not the last qualities of our coreligionists. ... They profess the law only with their lips, not having even a faint outline of Christian virtues in their hearts. They are possessed by servility and the yoke of Turkish rule ... as well as by crass ignorance. These are the reasons which eliminate hope of their producing some kind of well-founded armed action for their own good. (SbIRIO I, 43; Solov'ev XIV, 358–363)

The Russian navy abandoned Morea without achieving its goals. It might seem that plans for Greece's rebirth and even more so, the notion of the Greeks as descendants of ancient heroes that Voltaire constantly suggested to Catherine would have died down, if only for a time. However, in fact it was during these very years that the opposite occurred. The cultural mechanisms set in motion by the naval expedition began to function independently and hardly depended at all on immediate military and political considerations.

5

On May 16/27, 1770, Catherine notified Voltaire of the expedition's first successes. Russian sailors landed in continental Greece, joined with the rebellious Greeks, and split into eastern and northern Spartan legions. The first headed off to liberate the territory of ancient Sparta, the second moved into Arcadia. In an encounter on the Isthmus of Corinth, the commander of the Turkish garrison was captured. "Here is Greece on the point of becoming free again," concluded the empress, "but it is still very far from being that which it was. At the same time it is pleasant to hear the names of places which so filled our ears in our youth" (Ekaterina 1971, 56).

Catherine formulated the essence of the case perfectly. In the course of almost a half century, Russian culture, having assimilated European norms, had persistently dressed itself in classical attire, comparing its heroes to the ancient ones, judging its achievements by the degree of equivalence to Greek and Roman models. In the discourse of the time, the words "Sparta," "Athens," and "Arcadia" did not signify any geographical reality but rather served as a reflection of absolute perfection. Now the Russian squadron headed to this never-existent land, to the Golden Age, a habitation of gods and heroes. By the very coupling of their names with mythological toponymics, the participants in the expedition, and first of all its leaders, of course, were likened to the ancient inhabitants of these places and transformed into classical heroes.

Petrov was the first to sense the possibilities of reviving school mythology and turning it into political reality, and he began to load his odes with Hellenistic references, even while the Russian squadron stood at roadstead in Portsmouth patching up the ships that had been battered on the way from Kronstadt. The landing on the coast inspired a burst of poetic imagination. His ode "On the Victories in Morea" was just as overflowing with classical images as the Khotin ode was with biblical ones, and was just as emotionally overcharged:

> Уж взят, он [Орлов] мнит Модон, Коринф
>   предастся вскоре,
> Аркадию пленят, а я еще на море. —
> Герой! не негодуй: твой жребий не приспел.
> Тебе осталися Фессальския долины,
>   Вход черныя пучины
>   И ужас Дарданелл. ...

О коль нечаянна, коль дивна там премена!
Спартане, распустив российские знамена,
Разносят по всему Пелопонису страх.
В участие войны окрестных созывают
    И слезы проливают
    С оружием в руках.

Колико, — вопиют, — о небо, мы счастливы!
Герои наши днесь в прибывших россах живы!
Сколь кроток оных нам, коль грозен туркам вид!
Аргольцы, навпляне, к сражению устройтесь,
    Коринфяне, не бойтесь
    Во Спарте Леонид.

(Modon is already taken, thinks he [Orlov], Corinth will soon give in, / They'll capture Arcadia, but I am still at sea. / Hero! Don't rage—your lot has yet to be drawn. / The Thessalian valleys have been left for you, /The entrance to the Black Sea (chernyia puchiny) / And the terror of the Dardanelles. ... // Oh, how unexpected, how amazing the change! / The Spartans, unfurling Russian banners, / Terrify the entire Peloponnesus. / They summon the locals to join the war / And shed copious tears / With weapons in their hands. // How fortunate, they wail, are we, o heaven! / Our heroes are alive today in the Russians who have come! / How humble they are toward us, how terrible their sight to the Turks! / The inhabitants of Argos and Nauplia prepare for war, / Corinthians, do not fear—/ Leonidas is in Sparta.)

The music of Greek toponyms worked "amazing changes." Under Russian banners Spartans again became Spartans. Greece revived, for with the Russians' arrival, the Spartan heroes, with Leonidas-Orlov at their head, have come alive. Russians on this holy land turn into Greeks, in order to restore Greece at last. The arrival of the Russian navy promises a Golden Age like that described in Voltaire's letters to Catherine. Recall that the empress had asked Voltaire if the Greeks really were the fathers of the arts and sciences. For Petrov this does not raise the slightest doubt:

    Но о, отцы наук, порабощенны греки!
    Утешьтесь, паки вам златы начнутся веки.

> Достанет и до вас счастливая чредаг
> Алфейски Зрелища, умолкнувши поныне,
> В честь Екатерине
> Восставьте навсегда.
>
> По ним свои лега опять считать начните
> И имени ея начало посвятите.
> Она за подвиги вам будет мзды дарить
> Во храме вольности, покоя и отрады
> Вы образ сей Паллады
> Век должны жертвой чтить.
>
> А Ты, смиряюща неистовство тирана,
> Законодавица, победами венчанна,
> Возьми скрижаль и суд полудню возвести:
> Во область, где цвели Ликурги и Солоны,
> Пошли свои законы,
> Их будут век чести.
>
> (Petrov I, 74–77)

(But, oh, fathers of the sciences, enslaved Greeks! / Be comforted, the golden ages will begin again for you, / Your happy turn is also coming. / Alpheius' spectacles,[6] fallen silent until today / You, in honor of Catherine, / Will reestablish for all time. // You will again begin to count the years by them, / And dedicate their start to her name. / She, in reward for your deeds, will give recompense / In the temple of freedom, peace and joy; / You must do honor to the image of this Pallas / With sacrifices, for an age. // But you, who subdued the fierceness of the tyrant, / Lawgiver, crowned with victories, / Take up the tablet and announce justice to noon; / To the lands where Lycurguses and Solons flourished, / Send laws // And they will be honored forever.)

Catherine is not only named in the fully traditional way as Pallas (Athena) or Minerva, but also here becomes an Olympian goddess whose image should be the object of worship in a resurrected Greek temple—judging by the

---

6 A reference to the Olympic Games, as Olympia was located on the river Aphaieus (also: Aphaeus, Alphaois).

description, clearly a pagan one. The metaphor of repaying a debt is translated from the sphere of religion into that of lawgiving. The Russian empress is called to bring benefits with her laws (Petrov of course has in mind the *Instruction for the Commission to Create a New Law Code*) to the land of lawgiving, "the region where Lycurguses and Solons flourished."

Petrov's arch literary rival Vasilii Maikov sketches the future of Greece in the very same spirit:

> Подателей Вселенной света
> Екатерина просветит,
> Изгонит чтущих Магомета
> И паки греков утвердит.
> Науки падши там восстанут.
> Невежды гордые увянут,
> Как листвия в осенни дни.
> Не будет Греции примера;
> Одна с Россиею в ней вера,
> Законы будут с ней одни.
>
> (Maikov 1770)

(Catherine will enlighten / The bearers of light to the Universe, / Drive off those who revere Mohammed / And again establish the Greeks. / The fallen sciences will again arise, / Proud ignoramuses will fade away, / Like leaves on autumn days. / Greece will have no equal; / Of one faith with Russia, / She will now have the same laws.)

If Petrov, as the empress apparently did herself, held relatively unclear views concerning Greece's future—the Greeks might admire Catherine and her laws, either as her subjects or simply worshipping their divine perfection—for Maikov there were no doubts on this score. He did not doubt that the Golden Age would return to Greece when it successfully merged into the Russian Empire:

> Под властию Екатерины
> По всем брегам прекрасны крины
> И горды лавры возрастут.

> Польются с гор ручьи прозрачны,
> И роши и долины злачны
> Сторичный плод ей принесут. (Ibid.)

(Under Catherine's aegis / Beautiful lilies and proud laurels / Will swell on all the banks, / Transparent streams will flow from the mountains, / And the green groves and valleys / Will bear her fruit a hundredfold.)

The fierce enmity between Petrov and Maikov (see Gukovskii 1927, 143–147), who at about this time referred to his literary foe in the poem "Elisei" as a "louse" (pliugavets) (Maikov 1966, 89), behooves us to pay special attention to such convergences. The nymphs who in Maikov's ode are "strolling in the bushes, singing Russia's victory" and Parnassus that "summons the Russes to rally" are by no means perceived by the author as related to Petrov's odic practice. Arguably, Petrov voiced the change that we have been noting earlier and more powerfully than others. But in the odes celebrating Aleksei Orlov's victory in July 1770 in Chesme Bay, the spread of such imagery acquired epidemic proportions.

Catherine herself, reporting on the new victory to Voltaire, wrote, "Alexei Orlov, having defeated the enemy fleet, has burned it all to ashes in the port of Chesme, the ancient Clazomenae" (Ekaterina 1971, 74; Lentin 1974, 87). Similar rhetorical parallels appeared in Maikov's ode already cited as well as in those by Domashnev (1770) and Kheraskov (1770), that is, in the work of poets who a year or more earlier had already juxtaposed the achievements of Russian heroes to legendary classical exploits. Kheraskov even redoubled the series of historical prototypes for the recent Russian naval victories by augmenting the classical genealogy with the national, thereby equating them:

> Я вижу афинейцев новых
> У саламисских берегов;
> О! муза, вобрази Орловых,
> Гоняших целый флот врагов. …
> Я вижу, будто в древни лета
> Единоборца Пересвета,
> Биющася с его врагом. …

> Так две громады преужасны
> Слетелись в море пред собой.
>
> (Kheraskov 1770)

(I see the new Athenians / On the shores of Salamis; / Oh muse, imaging the Orlovs / Driving off a whole enemy fleet. ... / I imagine how in ancient times / Peresvet in single combat / Fighting with the foe. ... // Thus two most terrible masses / Clashed together on the sea.)

These odes were written more or less directly after the unprecedented victory, but after two years two much longer works appeared that were also dedicated to this event: Kheraskov's epic poem "The Battle of Chesme" and Pavel Potemkin's drama "The Russes in the Archipelago." By this time the Russian navy had already abandoned Morea and the expedition's failure was completely obvious, but these things had no effect at all on the general conception of either author. Furthermore, even in more balanced genres that were composed at a greater historical distance from these events, the vision of political reality that had gushed from the odes took on a consistent and formulaic character.

Figure 2 "Allegory of the Victory of Chesme" (1771) by Theodorus de Roode. Tretiakov Gallery, Moscow.

> Во славе где сиял Божественный закон
> И вера на столпах воздвигла светлый трон.
> Где храмы вознесли главы свои златые
> Курился фимиам и с ним мольбы святые
> Где муз божественных был слышен прежде глас
> Где зрелся Геликон, где древний цвел Парнас,
> В стране, исполненной бессмертных нам
>   примеров
> В отечестве богов, Ликургов и Гомеров
> Не песни сладкие вспевают музы днесь,
> Парнас травой зарос, опустошился весь.
> Герои славные в Афинах на родятся,
> Во Спарте мудрые законы не твердятся. …
> Святые здания в пустыни превращенны…
>   (Kheraskov 1961, 144)

(There where the Divine law shone in glory / And faith erected a bright throne on columns, / Where temples raised their golden heads, / And incense rose together with holy prayers, / Where the voice of the divine muses was formerly heard / Where Helicon was seen, where ancient Parnassus bloomed, / In a land filled with immortal models for us, / In the homeland of the gods, Lycurguses and Homers, / Today the muses sing no sweet songs, / Parnassus is overgrown with weeds, completely devastated. / Glorious heroes are not being born in Athens, / In Sparta no wise laws are devised. … / The holy buildings have been turned to waste…)

The relaxed and calm enumerating intonation with which the poet almost unnoticeably—with a comma—moves from religious imagery to the classical, is remarkable. At the same time, one and the same epithet is used to characterize both the one and the other. For Kheraskov the "Divine" law and the "divine" muses merge into a single semantic progression.

Then the appearance of Russian ships on Greek shores completely changes the situation:

> Там, кажется, встают Ахиллы, Мильтиады,…
> Уж храбрость вспыхнула во греческих сердцах.
> Почти умершая в неволе и цепях,…

Увидит Греция Парнас возобновленный.

(Ibid., 152)

(There, it seems, [new] Achilleses and Miltiadeses rise up,… / Bravery, that had almost died in bondage and in chains / Burst into flame in Greek hearts,… / Greece will see Parnassus revived.)

The same construction, with emphasis on the same semantic elements, is developed in Potemkin's play, too. Here Aleksei Orlov converses with the leader of the Greeks, named Bukoval, who greets the liberator, declaring to him:

Герой полночных стран, в ком греки представляют
Иракловы дела и Россов прославляют,
Дай помощь нам своей геройския руки.

(Hero of the midnight lands, in whom Greeks see / Hercules's deeds and glorify the Russes, / Give help to us with your heroic hand.)

Orlov is ready to "give help" but he is disturbed by the Greeks' own readiness to reconcile themselves with oppression, and he addresses Bukoval with a fiery reminder of the sufferings that his people endured from the Turks and with bitter reproaches:

Воспомяните вы падение Афин,
Насилие врагов, свирепство и тиранство,
Все претерпело там несчастно христианство. …

Являет все теперь чрез множество премен,
Что греческий народ геройских чувств лишен.

(You must remember the fall of Athens, / The enemies' violence, fierceness and tyranny, / There Christianity miserably endured everything. … // Now, after many changes, it becomes clear / That the Greek people is lacking in heroic feelings.)

In Orlov's monologue Christianity "endured" more than anything in Athens. He does not distinguish between Athens and the "capital city" Constantinople, whose capture by the Turks was mentioned just before. His words completely convince Bukoval, reviving the spirit of the ancient Spartans in him and his warriors:

> Надежду днесь свою имея на тебя,
> Всему, что повелишь, подвергнем мы себя.
> Ты вожделенные восставишь паки веки,
> Мы те же, государь, что были прежде Греки. ...
> Твои доброты нас и Росских войск геройство
> Одушевляют всех, дая нам прежни свойства.

(Today, placing all our hope in you, / We will subject ourselves to everything you command. / You restore those longed-for times again. / We, my lord, are the same as the Greeks were formerly. ... / Your goodness to us and the heroism of the Russian troops / Inspire us all, imparting to us our former qualities.)

The ideological basis for the "Greek Project" was thus established. Moreover, Pavel Potemkin was the cousin and close associate of the future favorite, Grigorii Potemkin, and Petrov was his old and close friend, with whom he constantly corresponded during these years when he was serving in Rumiantsev's army, and it was through Petrov that he maintained contact with the empress (see Shliapkin 1885, 398). Knowing Potemkin's literary interests, it is natural to suppose that he would have been an attentive reader of works written by people who were close to him and dedicated to events that greatly concerned him. For it was precisely Potemkin who was to transform this system of poetic metaphors into a comprehensive political program.

6

One of the curious phenomena of Russian literary life of the 1770s was the active participation of literary men of Greek origin—Grigorii Baldan, Evgenii Bulgaris, Antonii Palladoklis ("native of Mitelene," as he signed his works)—and others. The most important of these authors, Bulgaris, came to Russia in 1771. The author of a monograph on him, Stephen Batalden, directly links his invitation to the naval expedition. Among Bulgaris's first literary projects undertaken in Russia was the translation of a series of works by Voltaire on the Russo-Turkish War into Greek (see Batalden 1982, 119–120).

These poets knew Russian to various degrees; some wrote their works both in Russian and in Greek, others translated them into Russian, and also, in turn, translated works by Russian poets into their native tongue. It became usual practice to issue bilingual publications with facing Russian and Greek texts. In general, the rhetorical models that the Greek authors worked out fully coincided with those used by their Russian colleagues, although one may note several significant nuances.

In 1771 a short poem by Palladoklis appeared entitled "Verses on the Greek Clothing that Her Imperial Majesty Deigned to Wear at a Masquerade." We do not know exactly what the empress's masquerade costume was, but the author clearly compares it with that of Olympiada, the mother of Alexander the Great:

> В монархине кипя, усердие к Элладе
> В одежду облекло, что на Олимпиаде.
> Самодержавна, в ту одета, так гласит:
> В чьей одежде я хожу так облеченна.
> Той я усердствую, за ту же ополченна.
> Великий Александр, кой сел на персов троне,
> Великую, — он рек, — Екатерину зрю
> В одежде матерней. … О! Ты небес царю
> Сподобна, дай узреть ту и в моей короне,
> Так торжествующу над Мустафой строптивым,
> Как я вознес главу над Дарием кичливым.
> Как равну мне копьем и духа красотой.
>
> (Palladoklis 1771a; see the variations on these motifs in Palladoklis 1771)

(The monarch's seething zeal for the Hellenes / Has clothed her in the attire of Olimpiada; / The autocratrix, dressed thus, declares: / Who can extinguish my fervor / For the one in whose garments I go clothed / The one for whom I strive, and arm myself? / Great Alexander, who sat on the Persians' throne, / I see Great Catherine, he spake, / In mother's clothes. … Oh! You, tsar of heaven, / Let me see her also wear my crown, / As one who loves us with heartfelt purity, / Conquering obstinate Mustapha, / Just as I triumphed over arrogant Darius, / As an equal to me in spirit and lance.)

Palladoklis compares Catherine both to Alexander the Great and his mother, simultaneously depicting her as a heroine and as mother of heroes. What is more important, he finds a clear historical prototype for her military accomplishments. The parallel between Russians and Greeks almost automatically caused Russian poets to compare Turks with the Persians, the long-time enemies of ancient Greece. S. Domashnev recalled "the most glorious Battle of Marathon" and the "awesome clash of Thermopylae, where Persian strength waned" (Domashnev 1770); Kheraskov wrote that "again Xerxes has sallied forth against the ancient Athenians, but awaits the same fate on their shores" (Kheraskov 1961, 153); and Petrov drew the very same parallel:

> Остатки Перских сил где Греками разбиты.
> Там Россы, лаврами бессмертными покрыты,
> За греков с Мустафой кровавый бой вели …
> (Petrov I, 85)

(Where the remnants of Persian power were crushed by the Greeks / There the Russes [Russians], covered with immortal laurels, / Gave bloody battle against Mustapha for the Greeks…)

However, in all of these poems and in the majority of other works the comparison was to the wars the Greek republics, primarily Athens and Sparta, waged against the Persians. Combining this historical parallel with that of Alexander the Great offered a whole series of undeniable advantages. Most importantly, it put the emphasis on the military actions as aggressive and even aimed at conquest. If Leonidas and Themistocles were only defending the Greek land from invasion, Alexander was spreading classical culture into new territories. Moreover, references to Alexander the Great's empire allowed them to establish something like a line of succession between ancient Greece and Byzantium, which significantly facilitated the main logical substitution on which contemporary rhetoric was based.

And finally, the most important thing: the comparison of Russian with an empire allowed them to remove, or at least to downplay, the republican subtext that was latent in the association with ancient Greece. The Russian empress could not declare herself the historical heir to the rulers of ancient Athens, while Alexander the Great unquestionably served the role of a predecessor and model.

The same Palladoklis worked out this parallel in detail in the brochure *The Achievement of True Government* (Istinnogo gosudarstvovaniia podvig), published in 1773. Here he reviewed all of Alexander the Great's merits—he spread enlightenment into Asia, united many peoples under his aegis, was severe toward his enemies and merciful to the defeated, built cities and developed commerce, attracted to himself philosophers, natural scientists and artists, patronized art and science. The author espied all of these virtues, in an even greater degree, in Catherine. Thus he concluded this juxtaposition:

> Престань ты, древний век, пред нами величаться
> И Александровой толь славой отличаться,
> (Palladoklis 1773, 16)

(Cease, ancient age, to magnify yourself before us / And to flaunt Alexander's so great glory -)

Palladoklis crowned his discussion by shifting from Alexander the Great to Constantine the Great and a parallel between Catherine's current victories and Constantine's triumph over Maxentius. In the very same way, in his epic poem "Calliope," written after hostilities ceased, he made the Persian King Darius express joy in the kingdom of the dead that his throne had gone to Alexander. And then Otman, legendary founder of the Ottoman Empire, "pronounces Darius's words from his lips":

> Если приближился моей державе срок
> И твердо положил неумолимый рок
> Мне больше не носить короны Константина,
> Да будет в ней властна отсель Екатерина!
> (Palladoklis 1775, 72)

(If my empire nears its term / And implacable fate has firmly decreed / That I will no longer wear Constantine's crown, / Then from now on let Catherine assume its power!)

Thus—as another Greek poet, Evgenii Bulgaris, put it, also in 1775—the new Alexander was expected to drive the "Saracen tribe" (i.e., the Turks) "from Constantine's throne" and into "the barren Caucasus peaks, into the waterless Arabian wilds," and to liberate this throne for a new Constantine.

∞ 7 ∞

From the moment of his christening, the political significance of Grand Prince Konstantin Pavlovich's name was obvious to everyone. In fact the ideology of the "Greek Project" had already been implicit two years earlier in the name given to his elder brother, the future Emperor Alexander I. In principle, the tradition established over the course of many decades made it seem obvious that Paul I would be succeeded by Peter IV. Authors of odes on his first marriage addressed the grand princess:

> К тебе Россия возглашает
> Дай нам великого Петра.
>
> (Sumarokov II, 125)

(Russia summons you / Give us a great Peter.)

Or:

> … от Павловой любви
> Другого нам Петра яви.
>
> (Kheraskov 1773)

(… from Paul's love / Make another Peter appear to us.)

The name Alexander was a kind of nominative masterpiece on the part of Catherine, who was always attentive to this kind of symbolism. On the one hand, her eldest grandson's patron saint was Alexander Nevskii, the protector of St. Petersburg; thus the line of succession in relation to Peter the Great's political line was fully satisfied. On the other hand, one can clearly make out another, southern prototype for the "youth born to the purple," born "in the North." Soon after Konstantin's birth in a letter to Grimm, the empress undertook to quell rumors proliferating in Europe: "Is it permissible to interpret in this way simple names that are given at christening? One must have a disturbed imagination to find fault with this, should I have named mister A

Chapter 1: Russians as Greeks 59

Figure 3 "Portrait of the Grand Princes Alexander Pavlovich and Konstantin Pavlovich" (c. 1781) by Richard Brompton.

and mister K Nikodim or Faddei? The name-day saint of the first is located in his native city, and the second was born several days after his saint's holiday. … So it is all very simple" (SbRIO XXIII, 147). Denying the obvious, the meaning of the name Constantine, the empress made the less obvious name of his elder brother transparent. Three years later she described her lessons with her five-year-old grandson to the same correspondent: "Mister Alexander keeps demanding new reading from me. … Recently he became acquainted with Alexander the Great and asked me to introduce him in person. He was very vexed when he found out that he was already dead; he is very sorry for him" (ibid., 252). Little Alexander was required to revere Alexander the Great because he was destined to take his place.

This letter to Grimm was written at the end of 1782, when a lively correspondence was taking place between the Petersburg and Viennese courts concerning the revival of the Eastern Empire, and Potemkin was preparing to occupy the Crimea. The Russian dream of Constantinople was already firmly harnessed to the classical chariot.

CHAPTER 2

The Image of the Enemy:
V. P. Petrov's "Ode on the Conclusion of Peace with the Ottoman Porte" and the Emergence of the Mythology of a Global Conspiracy against Russia

∞ 1 ∞

The peace of Kuchuk Kainarji which concluded the Russo-Turkish War in 1774 was extremely favorable to Russia. Apart from several territorial acquisitions and tariff-free transport throughout the Bosphorus and Dardanelles, Russia received the right of remonstrance on behalf of coreligionists in the Ottoman Empire; that is, it was in essence recognized as the protector of Orthodox believers outside its borders. This provided the basis for Russia's further expansion in the northern Black Sea coast and eastern Mediterranean, whose plans acquired the status of state policy in the form of Potemkin's "Eastern System" and the "Greek Project" of Potemkin and Bezborodko.

Nonetheless, Catherine did not manage to achieve all of the goals that she and her entourage had set themselves during the most successful phases of the military campaign. First of all, despite Aleksei Orlov's naval expedition, Greece remained under Turkish control. Additionally, over the course of the war the empress's plans had encountered serious obstacles, which in turn plagued Russia's Eastern policy. Designs for Russia's military, political and diplomatic expansion into southeastern Europe came up against the stubborn resistance of many European powers which not only did not want to support Christian Russia, but also to a greater or lesser extent took Turkey's side.

V. P. Petrov undertook one of the first attempts to explain this conflict ideologically in his 1775 "Ode on the Conclusion of Peace with the Ottoman Porte." Petrov's role in working out the intellectual and cultural bases of Russian's Eastern policy was exceptionally important. While in celebrating the peace other Russian ode writers mainly stayed within the bounds of those metaphorical schemes from Petrov's odes of 1769 and 1770, Petrov himself strove further. He endeavored to comprehend the new situation in which Russia found herself after signing the peace treaty, as well as the European political structure as a whole.

In 1812 S. N. Glinka published a note in the journal *The Russian Messenger* entitled "France's Unalterable Evil Intentions Against Russia." He saw the reasons for the war that had just begun in France's age-old enmity for Russia. "As conclusive proof," he asserted, "I could simply copy out Petrov's entire 'Ode on the Conclusion of Peace with the Ottoman Porte,' composed in 1775" (Glinka 1812, 110–111). Indeed, the publicist limited his argument to citing several quotations from the ode. This rhetorical strategy is quite striking, as it involves supporting a political thesis by referencing, not historical facts or analytical calculations, but instead a thirty-year-old triumphal ode.

When Petrov's ode was created and published, Glinka was still a child. It probably attracted his attention in 1811 when a three-volume *Works* by Petrov, prepared by the poet's son Iazon Vasil'evich, came out in Petersburg. Be that as it may, here is a rare if not unique case of a poetical work's longevity in the capacity of a political treatise.

L. N. Kiseleva, who commented on Glinka's unusual reasoning, noted that in *The Russian Messenger* "almost any judgment by a Russian (of course, only a true son of the fatherland) … was given the force of an historical document" (Kiseleva 1981, 66–67). However, the ode that Glinka cites can hardly be characterized as a standard pronouncement. On the contrary, this is a work of quite extraordinary historical and cultural significance.

Even in Petrov's politically overloaded oeuvre, the 1775 ode "On the Conclusion of Peace with the Ottoman Porte" occupies a special place. The author's views are not merely embodied in a system of tropes or rhetorical figures but are also presented as a more or less consistent doctrine. Furthermore, this doctrine, it seems, first developed by Petrov, was destined to outlive the political circumstances and theoretical discussions that gave birth to it and become part of Russia's governmental life.

The news of the peace treaty found Petrov in London. He was working there as governor to G. I. Silov, who according to I. F. Martynov's likely suggestion, was the foster brother of the heir to the throne, the future Paul I (see Martynov 1979, 29–30; cf. Cross 1976; Cross 1996, 249–253; Zhukovskaia, manuscript). Soon after, Petrov and Silov received Catherine's order to return home. In his answering letter to the empress of August 24, the poet congratulated her on the successful conclusion of the war and reported that he still had not found sufficient inspiration to compose an ode on this occasion. Consequently he asked for permission to delay his departure, so as "to hold my hand with the pen nailed to the table until the thing is finished" (Obolenskii 1858, 528). Somewhat later, on September 5, Petrov's pupil addressed a similar request to Catherine (ibid., 529–530).

There is no information about Catherine's reaction to these petitions. It is known that Silov died on the way home, but the precise date of his death has not been established. I. F. Martynov found Catherine's order to repay Petrov for costs connected to Silov's funeral, dated May 7, 1776, and on this basis proposed that Silov had died six to eight weeks earlier (Martynov 1979, 30). This is far from obvious, however. Petrov could have waited any length of time for the promised repayment, and a series of his published letters supply serious basis for concluding that he was back in St. Petersburg no later than the fall of 1775 (Petrov 1841, 49–50; cf. Shliapkin 1885, 394–395). Still, it is nevertheless possible that Petrov was able to receive some extension, at least until the spring of 1775. Even if we take the reference "to hold my hand with the pen nailed to the table" as an excuse to tarry abroad, it is still clear that the ode was the result of prolonged and intensive effort, begun in London and most likely finished on his way home or when he was back in Russia. When he sent the empress a copy, Petrov was obliged to apologize for such delayed congratulations (Shliapkin 1885, 393).

Catherine had given permission for Petrov to go to England after his repeated requests. For a person interested in political problems, a stay in London during this time must have provided a unique education. The free press, accounts of parliamentary debates, the open struggle between the government and the opposition—all gave quite a different experience of high-level politics than that which Petrov had been able to glean from his proximity to the court and from his position as Catherine's reader and friend of Potemkin.

The years which the poet spent in London were unusually rich in international cataclysms. The first partition of Poland between Russia, Prussia and Austria; Gustav III's coup in Sweden and the rout of the pro-Russian party in Stockholm, which brought Russia to the brink of still another war in the North; the start of disorders in England's colonies in North America; the death of Louis XV who had ruled France for more than a half century and the change of the cabinet in Paris—all of these events instantly became the subject of violent and open debate in society, in the press, and in Parliament. The clash between the two completely different political cultures that Petrov witnessed determined much in his views and was decisively influential on the ode which brought the London period of his life to a close.

∽ 2 ∽

The "Ode on the Conclusion of Peace with the Ottoman Porte" is one of Petrov's longest triumphal odes. It contains 470 lines. At the center of our attention is the middle part that is free from the ritual glorification of the empress and contains a statement of the author's main views. A well-known fact serves as the starting point for analyzing the consequences of the recently concluded war—that Turkey had declared war against Russia in 1768, having given in to the instigation of the Parisian cabinet:

> Но где сомнительна победа,
> Тут сильного смути соседа,
> В кровавой тонет пусть реке.
> Сколь бой ни жарок и ужасен,
> Чужим уроном безопасен,
> Ты стой, и тешься вдалеке …
>
> Цветущие под солнцем Россы,
> Давно в очах его колоссы;
> Их должно сжати в общий рост.

Chapter 2: The Image of the Enemy

Падут без дружния заступы;
Чужи в полях кровавых трупы,
Прекрасен Галлу в рай помост.

(Petrov I, 98, 100)[1]

(But where victory is doubtful / Instigate a powerful neighbor / Let him drown in a river of blood. / However hot and horrible the battle, / Someone else's loss is harmless, / You just wait and take comfort from afar … // Russes [Russians] blossoming under the sun / Have long been a colossus in his eyes; / They need to be cut down to the common measure. / They'll fall without friends' relief; / Alien corpses in bloody fields, / Would be a nice bridge to paradise for the Gauls.)

There was nothing new in these Francophobe attacks. Even before the start of the war, Catherine was well-informed about the constant pressure that the head of the French cabinet and Minister of Foreign Affairs the Duc de Choiseul had applied through France's envoy in Constantinople, Vergennes, on the Turkish sultan, urging him to begin war against Russia. Choiseul calculated that war in the South would bind Catherine's hands and distract her from an aggressive policy in Poland. These calculations proved to be completely mistaken, as it was precisely the Russo-Turkish War that created the situation that ultimately led to the partition of Poland. However, in 1768 the sultan's indecisiveness and fear of a military conflict so irritated Choiseul that he decided to recall Vergennes, thinking that the new ambassador Saint-Priest would better manage this complex task. But war was declared before Saint-Priest managed to arrive in Constantinople (see Murphy 1982, 151–161; on Catherine's views on the reasons for the war, see her correspondence with Frederick II in SbRIO XX, 252–280 and passim). In his "Ode on the War with the Turks" that was published in 1769, Petrov had already written about France's role in inciting the conflict:

То жаляща меж трав змея
Да скроет зависть от Европы,

---

1 All quotations without separate references are from this edition, which reproduces the last publication of the ode during Petrov's life (Petrov 1782). Between this and the first publication (Petrov 1775) there are only a few differences that are not significant for our analysis and they will not be mentioned here.

> Она лишь будет весть подкопы
> Мощь турков, умыслы ея.
>
> (Petrov I, 35)

(Then the stinging snake in the grass, / Let it go and hide its envy from Europe, / It will only scheme / [To manipulate] the power of the Turks and [to carry out] its own designs.)

The general set of motifs remains unchanged in its overall features. As before he sees the reasons leading to war in the back-stage intrigues of a French diplomacy that was envious of Russian power and trying to stir up trouble through a third party. However, with the passing of six years the poet strove to understand France's politics on a deeper theoretical basis; now he saw its roots in the doctrine of the balance of power which then dominated European political thinking.

Eighteenth-century theoreticians of diplomacy were convinced that the system of international relations was based on the balance of power among states that would not permit any one of them to lay claim to global dominance. In his celebrated book *The Age of Louis XIV*, Voltaire had linked hopes for prolonged peace with the fear that the two halves of Europe inspired in each other. According to accepted opinion, the complex and vacillating nature of alliances and international agreements was only the external expression of this fundamental equilibrium. "Never before or since has a single idea been so clearly the organizing principle in terms of which international relations in general were seen. ... The balance was also an orthodoxy whose acceptance was now more formal and explicit than ever before ... fear and envy, institutionalized in the balance, were the necessary foundation of international relations," writes the historian of European diplomacy M. S. Anderson (1989, 163–164) on the development of eighteenth-century political thought.

In the words of an English publicist of the time, "It is a Maxim of true Policy that whensoever any prince is exalted too high ... the other princes ought to enter into League together, to pull him down, or at least to hinder him from growing greater" (ibid., 164). The Peace of Utrecht of 1713 guaranteed the separation of the Spanish and French dynasties for all time, "for the end that all care and suspicions may be removed from the minds of men and that the Peace and Tranquility of the Christian World may be ordered and stabilized in a just Balance of Power (which is the best and most solid foundation of mutual friendship and a lasting general concord)" (Wight 1968, 153). From that time references to the necessity of maintaining the balance of power began to be included in the texts of international agreements. Fenelon, who was exceptionally popular in Russia, wrote about the monarch's obligation to preserve such a balance in his exhortation to the Dauphin, the grandson of Louis XIV (see Butterfield 1968, 140).

Newtonian physics had a significant influence on the theory of the political balance of power. The equilibrium of European countries was likened to the equilibrium of planets in the solar system: "What gravity or attraction, we are told, is to the system of the universe," wrote another British political journalist, "that the balance [sic] of power is to Europe: a thing we cannot just point out to ocular inspection, and see or handle; but which is as real in its existence, and as sensible in its effects, as the weight is in scales" (Anderson 1989, 167–168). Petrov reproduced all of these arguments rather precisely:

> Везде на мочь железны крепи;
> Текла бы в бой, да держат цепи.
> Так часто яр и бурен конь,
> В бег равными зовом местами.
> Стоит востягнутый браздами
> И паром кажет внутрь огонь. ...
>
> Взаимным меж стихий упором
> Всемирный держится состав;
> Спокойство — бранью, вольность — спором,
> Крепится силой святость прав.
> Сластям здесь горесть соразмерна;
> Прекрасна роза не без терна.
> Есть гром, трясения земли.

(Everywhere there are iron constraints [krepi] on power; / It would slip into fighting if not for the chains. / Thus a steed often violent and wild / Is restrained by reins / And the fire within is turned to vapor. ... // By mutual opposition among the elements / The universal structure holds; / Tranquility – violence, freedom – quarrels, / The holiness of law is anchored by force. / Grief here is commensurate to pleasures; / A beautiful rose is not without thorns. / There is thunder, the earth shakes.)

Appeal to the doctrine of the balance of power allowed Petrov to see French intrigues as a manifestation of the general mechanisms of European politics. Moreover, the entire Old World appeared in the ode as a single political and cultural whole that was successor to the great ancient empires and inculcated with their aggressive, expansionist spirit:

> Тут мрет Ассур под гневом Кира!
> Там персов Александр секира!
> Здесь Рим готовит свет протечь
> Кровава быстротой потопа;
> По нем, кто б ждал? В ту ж мочь Европа
> Спешит Царей своих облечь.
>
> Обилуя предтеч в примерах,
> На Рим возводят очеса,
> И в малых заключенны сферах,
> Творят велики чудеса;
> Огней искусством Прометеи,
> Пременой лиц и дум Протеи;
> Сердец и счастия ловцы;
> Предосторожны, терпеливы,
> Неутомимы, прозорливы.
> Как куплю деющи пловцы.
>
> Колико строго испытуют
> Ко преможенью всякий путь…,

(There Assur is perishing from Cyrus' anger! / There Alexander is the scourge of the Persians! / Here Rome is preparing to stream across the world / With the speed of a bloody flood; / After this, who would wait? Europe hurries / To array their kings in this power. // Abundant in exemplary ancestors, / All eyes are raised to Rome, / Even enclosed in little spheres / They are creating great miracles; / Prometheus, by the art of fire, / Proteus, by changing faces and thoughts; / Fishers of hearts and fortune; / Cautious, patient, / Tireless, perspicacious. / Like sailors engaged in trade // How seriously they try / To obstruct every path ...)

Petrov's evaluation of European civilization was rather complicated, and his very approach went far beyond the bounds of eighteenth-century Russian thought. The poet took account of the many faces of the European spirit, as well as its variability, its Promethean passion for experiments and discoveries, its pathos of enrichment ("Like sailors engaged in trade"), and its desire for overseas acquisitions that would invest modern monarchs "in the power" of Roman emperors. During Petrov's years in England the European powers continued their zealous and recurrent competition for overseas colonies. The poet wrote about all of this with a characteristic alternation of admiration, horror, and distinct—albeit hidden—moral disapproval. His tone brings to mind the description of the European spirit that emerged from the pens of the Slavophiles much later.

Different countries interpreted the balance of power in their own various ways. Thus England and France both strove to avoid being just another member of this balance and fought instead for the right to arbitrate and guarantee the

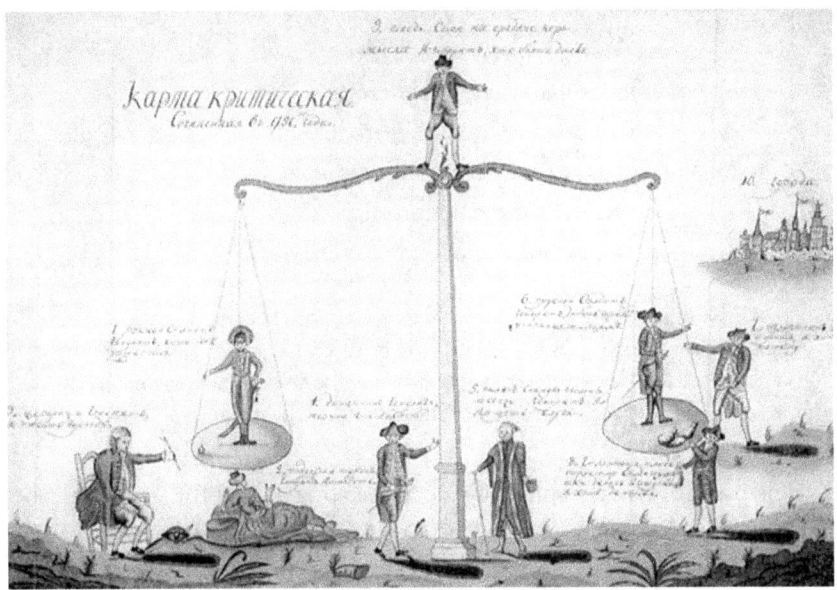

Figure 4 "A Critical Map" (1791) – an allegory of the "balance of power."

status quo. In 1774, Vergennes, the former ambassador to Constantinople and recently appointed Minister of Foreign Affairs, wrote to the new King Louis XVI about the special place of France in the European system (Murphy 1982, 218). Fifteen years earlier another minister, Cardinal Bernis, instructed one of his ambassadors: "The political goal of this monarchy has always been and will be to play the supreme role in Europe that corresponds to its ancient age, honor, and greatness, and to resist any power that would attempt to place itself above us, pretend to control us, claim undue prerogatives, or, finally, that would to try and appropriate our position in Europe" (ibid., 213).

This admonition should be seen in the context of the traditional French-English rivalry. However, in the last third of the century the main sphere in which the balance of power doctrine was applied in European—especially French—politics was the attempt to restrain Russia. After the partition of Poland and successful war against the Turks, Russia's growing power and influence was perceived as the main threat to European political equilibrium (Anderson 1989, 174–176). This is how Petrov described the situation:

> Почто сей воин безотраден?
> Другой возникнул в свет Герой;
> Так блеск чужой ему досаден;
> По нем он должен стать второй.
> Он был как кедр высок дотоле.
> Теперь он трость творений в поле;
> Не красен скиптр и шаток трон.
> Другие солнцы просияли... —

(Why is this warrior cheerless? / Another Hero has become famous; / And another's brilliance vexes him; / He has to be second after him. / Before he was tall as a cedar. / Now he is a reed of creatures in the field; / Your scepter is unattractive and your throne unstable. / Other suns have begun to shine... —)

The main aim of French diplomacy became stirring up anti-Russian sentiments in all of its contiguous lands. "We must support the Swedish king, encourage the Turks, and not allow ... the destruction of Poland," wrote the French diplomat Favier in a 1773 message to the King (Chevalier 1939, 125). In the

South France pushed Turkey toward war with Russia; in the North it played a decisive role in the anti-Russian coup that put Gustav on the Swedish throne (Gustav had arrived in Stockholm directly from Paris); and in the West, in Poland, it tried to support the centers of opposition to Petersburg, such as the defeated Barskaia Confederation (Konfederacja barska).

According to the French, opposition to Russia was meant to save Europe from Russian expansion and preserve the cherished balance of power. It is not hard to predict the Russian ode-writer's response to such ideas:

> И перст простря своей десницы
> На Росски абие границы,
> Глаголет к Мудрости Судьба:
> «Низзри, как ищут дола Князи
> Стать равны во всеобщей связи;
> Коль сила мыслей их слаба».

(And, quickly pointing its finger / At the Russians' borders, / Fate speaks to Wisdom: / "Behold, how princes of the world beneath seek a way / To become equal in universal association / When so weak is the force of their thoughts.")

∞ 3 ∞

However popular and influential the doctrine of balance of power may have been, it also had its critics. The German philosopher Johann Heinrich Gottlieb von Justi wrote about the "mutual enslavement" to which this teaching condemns states. "What streams of blood the balance of Europe, this new idol, has caused to be shed," wrote the French theoretician Réal de Curban. "For long, to avoid evils which are distant and uncertain the princes have brought upon themselves immediate and genuine ones and, in trying to avoid war, have waged it" (Anderson 1989, 176). But the most consistent critics of the idea were thinkers who proposed utopian projects for establishing "eternal peace" in Europe that were designed to replace a balance of power based on fear, jealousy and suspicion.

As discussed in the preceding chapter, one of the early and most popular versions of the idea of eternal peace was the plan to create a so-called "Christian republic." This was a confederation of the Christian peoples of Europe that had supposedly been proposed by the Duke de Sully to the French King Henry IV, as laid out in the last volume of his memoirs. For Catherine the idea of the Christian republic was a powerful propagandistic trump card (see Bartlett 1981). The political testament of this, the greatest of French monarchs, cast the support that contemporary France offered Muslim Turkey in a most unfavorable light.

Sully's idea was developed most fully in the "Project for Creating Eternal Peace in Europe" written in 1713 by Charles-Irénée Castel, abbé de Saint-Pierre. As opposed to his predecessor who entertained serious doubts about Russia's role in the new organization of Europe, Saint-Pierre looked favorably on the prospects for Russian's participation in the future confederation. He included Russia in the list of powers, explaining why, from his point of view, joining the union was in the interest of Russian monarchs, referring to the fact that "Henry IV did not deny the Tsar a place in the universal league" (Saint-Pierre 1986, 679; cf. 386, 419, etc.; cf. Souleyman 1936). Saint-Pierre actively promoted and distributed his project to monarchs and ministers, although its huge size and complex organization made it difficult for readers. In the 1750s the abbé's heirs asked J.-J. Rousseau to prepare a short rendering of the project.

This turned out to be an astute move. Rousseau wrote "An Abridgement of the Project for Eternal Peace" and "Consideration of the Project for Eternal Peace." The "Consideration," which highly assessed Saint-Pierre's idea but questioned its applicability, remained unpublished until 1781, while the "Abridgement" was published in 1761 and immediately attracted broad interest. In 1771, during the height of the Russo-Turkish War, I. F. Bogdanovich's translation of the "Abridgement" came out, pursuing the same political and propagandistic aims as the translation of Sully's memoirs. Most likely, Petrov became familiar with the "Abridgement" in the French original, but in any case, we may claim with a great degree of certainty that it was this work that served as the source for many of the ideas in his ode.

The starting point for Rousseau's thesis was the notion of European unity that we have already encountered: "All the powers of Europe form a kind of system among themselves which unites them ... by a kind of equilibrium..., which, although no one in effect tries to protect it, will not be as easy to destroy as many people think" (Rousseau 1962, I, 366).[2] In Rousseau's opinion, Euro-

---

2 We will refer to Rousseau as the author of the "Abridgement" without mentioning Saint-Pierre. As the "Consideration of the Project for Eternal Peace" attests, the major part of the opinions expressed in the "Abridgement" fully accord with those of Rousseau.

pean unity rests historically on the legacy of Rome, on the "political and civil union" that existed among the various parts of the Roman Empire:

> So great was the respect that this great body still inspired that up until the last moment those who destroyed it were honored by the titles [Rome had given them]; one sees degraded conquerors become officers of the empire. ... The old image of the Roman Empire continued to produce a kind of connection among the parts that used to compose it; and after the destruction of the empire Rome continued to dominate in a new manner. ... (Rousseau 1962, I, 367)

In support of this idea Rousseau refers to the authors of a multiplicity of works that had posed the question of whether or not the German emperor—who was called head of the Holy Roman Empire—could actually be considered "the natural sovereign of the whole world" (ibid., 367n).

In the already cited fragment Petrov reproduced these arguments with a significant degree of accuracy:

> Здесь Рим готовит свет протечь
> Кровава быстротой потопа;
> По нем, кто б ждал? В ту ж мочь Европа
> Спешит царей своих облечь.
>
> Обилуя предтеч в примерах
> На Рим возводят очеса...

(Here Rome is preparing to stream across the world / With the speed of a bloody flood; / After this, who would wait? Europe hurries / To array their kings in this power. // Abundant in exemplary ancestors, / All eyes are raised to Rome...)

According to Rousseau, this historical unity was based on the unity of the European spirit. "Add to this," he wrote,

> the special situation of Europe..., the constant coincidence of interests that the connections of blood and of commerce, of the arts, of colonies, have created among sovereigns; the multitude of rivers and the variety of their courses that make communication easy; its inhabitants' spirit of inconstancy [cf. "Proteus' changing faces and thoughts"] that makes

them travel without ceasing and to frequently journey from one to another; the invention of printing and the general taste for letters which has created a communality of learning and knowledge [cf. "With Prometheus' art of fire"]; finally, the multitude and small size of states [cf. "Even enclosed in little spheres"] which, together with the need for luxuries and the diversity of climates, make them perpetually necessary for one another. (Ibid., 368)

The equilibrium of forces that thus arose in a united Europe represented "in some respects the doing of nature. ... This equilibrium exists, and doesn't need anyone outside to preserve it or to interfere in it; and when it is briefly violated on one side, it soon restores itself on another; so that if princes that are accused of aspiring to a universal monarchy really did so aspire they would show more ambition than good sense" (ibid., 370–371). In some detail Rousseau argues that it would be impossible for any single state, or even an alliance of several powers, to establish its superiority.

Nonetheless, and this is the crux of the matter, even the impossibility of such projects and the inevitability of the balance of power that prevented their realization were insufficient to guarantee a firm and lasting peace. The successes of European Enlightenment stand in strange contradiction to the animosity that invariably rages in this part of the world:

> If on the one hand we look at the perpetual dissensions, robberies, usurpations, revolts, wars, and murders that daily afflict this respected dwelling place of sages, this shining refuge of the arts and sciences; if we consider our beautiful speeches and our horrible behavior, so much humanity in our principles and so much cruelty in our actions, a religion so mild and so bloodily intolerant, a politics so wise on paper and so harsh in practice, our leaders so beneficent and our people so miserable, our governments so moderate and wars so pitiless; we can hardly reconcile these strange contradictions; and this pretended fraternity of European peoples seems but a derisive opportunity to express their mutual animosity with irony. (Ibid., 368)

Echoing Rousseau, Petrov also writes about the impossibility of achieving the desired success and about the fact that all of the restrictions imposed by the balance of power were powerless to restrain the militarist inclination on the part of various sovereigns:

> Но сила, мати дерзновений,
> Боязнью скована всегда ль?
> Претят ли страхи преткновений
> Ей бурею нестися вдаль?
> Что не один бог мнимый мира,
> Скудельна в образе кумира
> Пал прежде, нежель в храм внесен,
> И зависть, бешенство и злоба
> Насильна не избегли гроба;
> Порок тем вовсе ль ужасен?
>
> Увы! Еще природа страждет.
> Знать, мыслей свет в Европе мал?
> Словесный дружней крови жаждет!
> Знать, зверя в лютость он ниспал.

(But is power, mother of impudence / Always fettered by fear? / Do the terrors of failure / Prevent its storm-like onward rush? / Has the fact that many false gods, / In the image of fragile idols / Have fallen before installation in the temple, / And that envy, rage and malice / Not avoided a certain grave / Thus make vice any less horrible? // Alas! Nature still suffers. / Does this mean that there is little light in Europe? / Literates thirst for their neighbors' blood! / They descend to the ferocity of beasts.)

The European Enlightenment itself, whose origins were indebted to peace, turned out to be fraught with military conflict. Petrov here recalls Lomonosov's celebrated ode of 1747 on "beloved tranquility," under whose aegis the sciences bloom, in order to contrast Lomonosov's rapture to his own skepticism:

> Науку тишины воздвигли.
> Что ж та нас реет в брань сама?
> Знать, строя ону, не достигли
> Во средоточие ума?

(Tranquility has fostered science. / Why then does it [science] lead us into battle? / Does that mean that, in establishing it, / The core of the intellect has not been achieved?)

The system of balance of power, in Rousseau's words, although indestructible, is extremely dangerous, because "action and reaction among European powers, unable to displace one another completely, keep them in a state of continual agitation; and these are always useless but always renewed, like ships on the sea which agitate its surface but can never change its level" (ibid., 372). Actually, Petrov finds a much more radical metaphor for this futile equilibrium, founded on animosity that corresponded to the cosmic scope of his political thinking:

> Как до планет и круга звездна
> Носилась мрачна нека бездна,
> Нестройством тяготевша смесь;
> Одна боролась вещь с другою;
> Так мы, борющись меж собою,
> Знать, держимся во тьме поднесь?

(As before the planets and circle of stars / A gloomy abyss was rushing about, / A disharmonious jumble, / One thing clashing with another; / Thus are we, fighting among ourselves. / Does this mean we still dwell in darkness?)

Moreover, this balance of struggle or fear itself often serves as the source of conflict as dissimilar states tend to suspect each other of dangerous intentions. As Rousseau wrote:

> In this respect the general lack of security leads to a situation in which each one, unsure that he can avoid war, tries to start it advantageously for him, when circumstances are favorable, and to forestall his neighbor, who would not fail to make use of a similar moment that favored him; thus many wars, including even wars of aggression, are [undertaken] merely out of unwarranted precaution aimed at guaranteeing one's own possessions. (Ibid.)

This idea could not help but make an impression on Petrov, who recalled that the Turkish sultan had made the decision to begin the war in 1768 after the seizure of the town of Balta by disobedient Zaporozhian Cossacks. The Russian government hurried to apologize and punish the offenders, but it was too late—the Turks had already given into the insistent urging of French diplomacy.

> Малейша тень опасных следствий
> Родит прямых источник бедствий,
> И капля буйства море слез!
> Как будут скиптры равновесны,
> Коль тьмы миров насильству тесны.
> Когда во нравах недовес?

(The least shade of threatening consequences / Becomes the source of immediate misfortunes, / And a drop of mischief breeds a sea of tears! / How can scepters be in balance / If thousands of worlds are still not enough [to prevent] violence. / When are moral habits in short supply?)

The logic of balance of power turns out to be one of war and incitement, the logic of justifying violence. Petrov, like Rousseau, is deeply convinced of its harmful, unacceptable consequences for the European order:

> Так нужно искрам злобы тлиться,
> Ковати козни и мечи;
> Рекой кровям невинным литься,
> Всему, как нудимо, течи;
> Дышать неправой нужно местью.
> Корысти жертвовати честью,
> Закон вменяти за плеву!
> Полудню нужно праться с Нордом,
> Врага зреть Россу в Турке гордом,
> Секване [Сене] злиться на Неву!

(Thus it is necessary for sparks of malice to burn, / To forge conspiracies and swords; / For innocent blood to be poured like a river, / Everyone's to be forced to flow; / To breathe unjust revenge, / To replace law with spittle! / The South must challenge the North, / The Russes see the proud Turk as their enemy, / The Seine is enraged at the Neva!)

Petrov's antimilitarist rhetoric ("Foreign corpses in bloody fields," "innocent blood poured like a river") sharply differentiates him from other eighteenth-century ode writers who were usually on the bellicose side. It is not impossible that there was influence here from Petrov's friend and patron Potemkin, whose

Figure 5 Portrait of V. P. Petrov.

repugnance for bloodshed so astonished contemporaries (on the anti-war motifs in Petrov's later ode "On the Taking of Izmail," see Bershtein 1992, 8–87).

On the whole this passage reveals how the Russian ode-writer's strategy differs from that of the French philosopher. While Rousseau, following Saint-Pierre, demonstrates the moral and political unacceptability of the balance of power doctrine, Petrov's interest is focused on those who, guided by this doctrine, want to exclude Russia from the system of European states:

> Так страж, так око мнит Царево,
> Что правит сердце в нем и ум;
> Что, яко вкруг плодами древо,

Chapter 2: The Image of the Enemy

> Отягощен тьмой новых дум.
> Угрюм, уединен, бессловен
> И как волшебник баснословен
> Сидит с орудьми в терему;
> Лишь тайной коснется пружин
> В другом текут все твари чине;
> Взгляни, Европа вся в дыму!

(Thus a guard and the tsar's eye thinks / That he guides his heart and mind; / That like a tree circled with fruit / He is weighted down with a swarm of new thoughts. / Glum, alone, silent, / And fabled like a magician / He sits in the terem with his weapons; / But when a secret spring is touched / All creatures move in different order; / Look, all Europe is up in smoke!)

The person Petrov describes here is rather puzzling. If the "secret springs" may with a certain license be interpreted as any diplomat's desire to surround himself with a veil of secrecy, then all of the other attributes with which the poet describes the gloomy figure of the tsar's advisor may apparently only be explained by reference to a completely different order of historical facts.

∽ **4** ∽

Louis XV's diplomacy possessed one striking and somewhat hard to explain feature—it was carried out through two competing institutions. Apart from the official Ministry of Foreign Affairs, the so-called "King's Secret" (le Secret du Roi) also took part in foreign policy decisions. The main feature of the "King's Secret" was that the members of French embassies in various countries that were inducted into it (sometimes the ambassadors themselves, more often officials or other, even lower-level staff members) received secret instructions, often contradicting the official ones that came from the minister. At first the coordinator of this secret correspondence was Conti, and then Tercier, the main advisor to the Minister of Foreign Affairs, and after Tercier's death in 1767, the Count de Broglie, who had been initiated into the Secret in 1752 when he had been appointed ambassador to Poland, and who soon became the inspiration and soul of this unusual structure.

That the Polish ambassador assumed this special position in the King's Secret was not by chance. In his monograph on the secret correspondence, the grand nephew of the count, the French historian A. de Broglie, wrote that "Poland was in reality the chief, almost the only, object of the secret diplomacy" (Broglie I, 4). The ambassador's job was to strengthen the pro-French party there, and first of all, to counter Russian influence. Furthermore, if the official French diplomatic position in relation to Russia oscillated between opposition, flirtation, a cautious union during the Seven Years' War and new hostility in the second half of the 1760s, the Secret's anti-Russian line that was dictated by its concentration on Polish affairs remained unchanged, even after Count Broglie's withdrawal from Poland in 1758. In May and June of 1762, after Peter III had unexpectedly taken Russia out of the Seven Years' War, having concluded a peace with Prussia, and right at the time when the coup was being prepared in St. Petersburg that would bring Grand Princess Ekaterina Alekseeva to the throne, Broglie wrote to Tercier:

> What an opportunity it will be to re-establish the affairs of the State as they were in 1756 [when the Russo-French alliance began] ... when Poland, long neglected, began to lend herself to the wish, which the King had previously manifested, that the natural liking of that nation for France should be revived! It was not without great labour that I succeeded in reanimating it. But, as for Russia, we reckoned her among the European Powers only in order to exclude her from their ranks, and to forbid her from forming so much as an idea of interfering in events. This is what we must re-establish; we must avert every opportunity of which she might avail herself to play a part in Europe; we must never enter into a treaty with her Court; but let her fall into a lethargic slumber from which she must only be aroused by the convulsions caused by internal disturbance carefully excited long in advance. By constantly stirring up these troubles, we shall prevent the Government of the Muscovites from thinking of foreign policy, and Russia will then be, in relation to ourselves, in that exact position which we should wish.

In his next letter, Broglie listed the forces that could be brought to bear against Russia:

> At present, Austria, deeply offended; to-morrow, perhaps, Prussia, who, although she makes use of Russia to gain her victories to-day, cannot wish to bring such a Power into the heart of Germany; and Turkey, including all the Tartar races, by no means the least effective instruments to employ against the Muscovites. (Broglie II, 11, 12–13)

Broglie worked out his grandiose projects (that had, by the way, the full approval of King Louis XV) while practically under house arrest in his ancestral castle (cf: "He sits in the terem with his weapons"). His oscillating periods of disfavor and exile, the last of which coincided with Petrov's time in London, did not end his connection with the king, change his role in the secret correspondence, or interrupt his influence on French politics. During his exile Broglie developed a plan for French intervention in Britain (cf. "But when a secret spring is touched ... Look, all Europe is in up in smoke!").

Broglie was not alone in his thoughts about the Tatars as a weapon against Russia. On June 28, 1762, the very day of Catherine's coup, copies of the *Social Contract*, subsequently banned, arrived in St. Petersburg (see Kopanev 2000). Here Russians could read Rousseau's gloomy prophesy concerning the fate of Russia and Europe: "The Russian Empire wants to conquer Europe—but will herself be conquered. The Tatars, her subjects or her neighbors, shall become her, and our, masters" (Rousseau 1969, 183). This opinion provoked a sharp objection from Voltaire, who thought it unlikely that "the miserable Tatar hordes, who exist in extreme degradation, would be able to subjugate an empire at once defended by two hundred thousand soldiers who rank among the best in Europe" (Wilberger 1976, 225). This debate had a rather long history. In his own works, as well as "An Abridgement of the Project for Eternal Peace," which, following Saint-Pierre, had included Russia in the system of European states, Rousseau consistently advocated anti-Russian positions.

The coincidence in views of the banned thinker and the highly-placed diplomat was not completely fortuitous. The French diplomat Claude-Carloman de Rulhière who in 1762 served in the French embassy in St. Petersburg, and who was subsequently notorious for his scandalous book on Catherine's ascension to the throne which the Russian empress used all of her influence to suppress, was a passionate follower of Rousseau. Rulhière was also a passionate Polonophile and member of the King's Secret. It was through him that in 1771, one of the leaders of the Polish Confederation, Count M. Vielgorsky, turned to Rousseau with a request to write a project for a future constitution which could save Poland from being completely swallowed up by Russia. At that time Rulhière himself on order of the minister was working on a history of the Polish problem that was intended for the heir to the French throne, Louis XVI (see Chevalier 1939, 118–125, 192–196; Madariaga 1983, 36–37). Rousseau wrote the "Considerations on the Manner of Rule in Poland" in order to help the dying country. This work was not published, but they knew of its existence in Russia from F. M. Grimm's journal the *Correspondence Littéraire* (Madariaga 1983, 36). Furthermore, even before this Grimm had also sent a copy of the "Considerations" to Catherine (Stroev 2001).

Among the other members of the King's Secret were also the former ambassador to Petersburg Baron Breteuil and Jean-Louis Favier, who had also worked in Petersburg, and who was author of a memorandum that included a proposal to create a ring of enemy nations around Russia. Breteuil, Favier and Rulhière were also connected with the abbé Chappe d'Auteroche (Chevalier 1939, 226–229), author of the famous *Voyage en Sibérie* that earned Catherine's ire, prompting her to write an entire book to refute it. Finally, the Comte de Vergennes also played an active role in the secret diplomacy; he had been ambassador to the Ottoman Porte during the Russo-Turkish War and served in Stockholm during the coup by Gustav, whom he advised to start a preventative war with Russia (Murphy 1982, 204).

Of course, neither Rousseau nor Chappe had any relationship to the inner sanctum of French diplomacy. However, to an outsider the small world of the Parisian intellectual elite in which Rulhière and Chappe read their anti-Russian works in the very same salons could seem like a secret association of philosophers and politicians, dispersing their agents in Russia, smearing her in print, and attempting to stir up trouble within and turn her Muslim neighbors against her from without.[3]

> Стремясь ко участи блаженной,
> Назначили, как царствам цвесть;
> России как изнеможенной
> Не дать главы своей возвесть.
> Стояли сто умов на страже,
> Да тьма над ней густится та же,
> Что смежных ей объемлет орд;
> Да брань ее мятет жестока,

---

3   From this perspective Catherine's suspicion of Rousseau throughout his life becomes more understandable (see Kopanev 2000).

В Европу да не возьмет втока
Подвластный ей широкий Норд.

(Striving for a blessed fate, / They decided how kingdoms should fare; / Not to allow Russia, prostrated, / To raise its head. / A hundred minds stood guard, / So that the same darkness will thicken above her [i.e., Russia] / That envelops the hordes at her borders; / That she be troubled by cruel war / So the broad North that she commands / Will not pour into Europe.)

This entire stanza seems such an exact a statement of Broglie's letter to Tercier cited above that one has to ask what Petrov could have known about the King's Secret. At the present time it is not possible to answer this question with certainty. Nevertheless we may suggest some hypotheses.

First of all, one cannot exclude the possibility that the Russian court learned about Louis XV's double diplomacy fairly early. A. Broglie reports that already at the end of 1763 the candidate for the Polish throne and former favorite of Catherine Stanisław Poniatowski turned for support over the head of the French ambassador to the envoy Hennin, possibly because he was privy to information that this "humble Hennin was an instrument of the secret policy" (Broglie II, 199). If Poniatowski had received this intelligence from Polish sources, he certainly would have shared it with Catherine, who supported him at a time when France maintained an antagonistic position against him. On the other hand, Catherine herself could have found out this crucial information through her agents and have communicated it to her protégé. Stealing, perusal and decoding of diplomatic correspondence was a fairly common occurrence then, as at other times. In this instance Poniatowski's move appears to have been calculated to neutralize France on the eve of the elections for a new king.

By 1770 not only the fact of the secret correspondence but its complete contents became known to the Austrian Minister of Foreign Affairs Kaunitz and to the Austrian ambassador in Paris, the Comte de Mercy-Argenteau. Moreover, the Austrians themselves also were unable to keep their own agents' success a secret. At the end of 1773, the secretary of the French embassy in Vienna Abbé Georgel was able to acquire decoded copies of Broglie's correspondence with Vergennes and the reports of secret agents in Stockholm and Petersburg. Among the documents which the Austrians deciphered was

Broglie's circular to participants of the secret correspondence in all capitals in which he reported that his new exile did not mean his removal from leadership of the King's Secret and that the correspondence would continue as before. To explain how he came by these documents, Georgel told a not very believable story about a stranger in a mask who sold them to him for a thousand ducats (Broglie II, 455–460).

In any case, it is clear that these documents were decoded, and that the person who supplied them to Georgel could have sold them to others as well. And in this case, these documents, or at least knowledge about their existence, could also have reached Russian diplomats. The Russian ambassador in London A. S. Musin-Pushkin and other officials at the embassy were among those with whom Petrov associated while he was in England (Cross 1996, 250). And, finally, probably the most significant fact. Just at the time of Petrov's visit to London, a grandiose scandal unfolded around the most famous and colorful participant in the secret correspondence—the Chevalier d'Éon.

Like many other diplomats initiated into the King's Secret, d'Éon began his career in the second half of the 1750s in St. Petersburg. At some time he served as courier for the secret correspondence between Elizaveta Petrovna and Louis XV. Then the Chevalier was a captain of dragoons during the Seven Years' War, after which he was assigned to London where, among his other duties, he had to prepare for a French invasion of England that Count Broglie was planning. However, here he came into sharp conflict with the ambassador, whom he charged with trying to assassinate him. In 1764 d'Éon published a scandalous book in London, in which he laid out his version of his collision with the ambassador, and in which he printed several fragments of diplomatic correspondence. D'Éon refused to obey a recall order and began to blackmail the French government, threatening to expose the King's Secret, including its plans for an intervention in England. The King was forced to compromise and to continue d'Éon's salary and his status as secret agent. On his side, the Chevalier agreed to quit the diplomatic service.

This scandal that rocked the English capitol had not yet had a chance to die down when in the early 1770s, during Petrov's sojourn in London, a new one broke. Rumors circulated throughout London, apparently set in motion by the Chevalier himself, that he was a woman. Judging by d'Éon's (none too reliable) memoirs, Princess Dashkova, who appeared in London in 1770, played some role in spreading this gossip (on d'Éon, see Broglie II, 87–182, 486–515; Kates 1995, 57–140, 175–254; Stroev 1998, 84–89, 110–115, 336–339, etc.).

The extent of social excitement that seized London on receipt of this sensational news was absolutely unimaginable. In London City they took bets on d'Éon's gender, and the money staked added up to as much as 60,000 pounds. Newspapers and boulevard sheets were full of the most diverse speculations on this issue, and at the Chevalier's house there was a constant crowd on watch. The emissary specially sent from France to find out what was going on confirmed that d'Éon was indeed a woman. On May 13, 1774, the third day after the start of Louis XVI's reign, Broglie sent him a letter with details both about the King's Secret and the strange situation with d'Éon. The young king immediately ordered that the Chevalier be recalled from England, which brought a new wave of blackmail, the most sinister threats and impossible demands for both money and status. Fearing French agents, d'Éon gave a sealed packet with secret documents to his English friend, a member of Parliament from the opposition. Paris again had to back down. D'Éon's correspondence with Broglie and the king continued from the summer of 1774 to April of 1775, when, probably after Petrov's departure from London, Beaumarchais arrived for discussions with d'Éon.

As a clever swindler, d'Éon kept the most explosive documents from exposure, holding them back as trump for extreme circumstances. Nonetheless, it is very probable that in conversations with his many English friends he could allow himself to hint at their content in one way or another. In early 1776, after he had given the documents to Beaumarchais, vague information about the King's Secret made its way into the English press (see Kates 1995, 243–246). How long they might have circulated as rumors and spoken tales is impossible to determine without special investigation of London public opinion of the time. It is curious that during the entire period d'Éon did not cease his literary activities. In 1774 his multivolume *Leisure Hours of the Chevalier d'Éon de Beaumont* was published in Amsterdam; it contained works on state administration, finances, taxation, and other similar matters.

Petrov's English acquaintances kept him adequately informed (see Cross 1976, 239–242). From late 1773 he travelled on a yacht in the capacity of

Russian teacher to one of the best-known British adventuresses, the Duchess of Kingston, who fled London after being accused of bigamy (see Cross 1977). In Rome the Pope received her. On the return trip she and Petrov visited a series of European cities, and on May 17, 1774, they set off from Geneva to Paris (see Cross 1996, 251), where Louis XVI was trying to make sense of his predecessor's strange diplomacy and forming his new cabinet. In June Vergennes, former ambassador to Constantinople and Stockholm, participant in the King's Secret and longtime enemy of Russia, was appointed Minister of Foreign Affairs. However, contrary to expectations, Vergennes's Russian policy after the liquidation of the Secret was rather cautious and ultimately led to a certain warming of French-Russian relations (see Murphy 1982, 447–454).

Let us draw some conclusions. Petrov would hardly have known details about the activity of Louis XV's secret cabinet or the identity of those initiated into the Secret. Most likely he was not familiar with the secret correspondence and may not have heard about the plan to invade England. Nevertheless we have sufficient grounds to presume that he would have known that the French king had a secret circle of advisors who directed French foreign policy, a foreign policy that was radically anti-Russian. Furthermore, from the end of the 1760s the difference in approach to Russia on the part of Broglie and the Minister of Foreign Affairs the duc de Choiseul, who carried out official policy, ceased to exist. Choiseul demanded that Vergennes draw Turkey into war with Russia with even greater persistence than Broglie. Understandably, in any discussion of behind-the-scene intrigues and policies carried out with clandestine methods, of secret sources of power and similar subjects, the lack of information only inflames the imagination. Louis XV's peculiar diplomatic creation took on hyperbolic dimensions in the Russian poet's mind.[4]

∽ **5** ∽

The tsar's secret advisor, in Petrov's words cited above, "That guides his heart and mind," is also "fabled like a magician." One is tempted to see in this description, as in the mention of Proteus who changes his "face and thoughts," a hint

---

[4] Considerable information about the King's Secret became available even during Petrov's life, as the secret correspondence of Count de Broglie was published during the French Revolution (see Roussel 1793).

at d'Éon, whose "fabled" nature and changeability exceeded all usual expectations and suggested some sort of magic. Still, it is not right to limit the meaning of Petrov's metaphors to direct historical references. As L. V. Pumpianskii put it, "the token of the classical style is … the paradoxical combination of extreme generality with equally extreme everyday concreteness" (Pumpianskii 1983, 30–31). In his ode Petrov constantly takes flight from immediate political affairs into the sphere of historiosophical generalizations. The "sorcerer" who "constructed in his mind the Labyrinth in which to entrap monsters" and dreams of having power over " the entire universe" is, of course, not d'Éon, not Broglie, and even not Louis XV. Thus after concluding a tale of the perfidious designs which "a hundred minds" are constructing against Russia, Petrov unexpectedly departs from the contemporary world into recent history:

> Се, како совещали царства,
> Когда восстал Великий Петр;
> Внезапу их расторг коварства,
> Как паутину сильный ветр.

(This is like the kingdoms' congregation / When the Great Peter arose; / He suddenly did away with all their treachery / As a strong wind does a cobweb.)

As the poet writes, Peter

> …создан был из общей персти,
> Европе чтоб глаза отверсти,
> Сколь ограничен смысл ея.

(…was created out of the common dust / To open Europe's eyes, / How limited its understanding.)

The King's Secret, setting the Turkish sultan on Russia, intent on driving her into the darkness that surrounds "the adjoining hordes," and not letting "the North" creep into Europe, turns out to be just another personification of the Old World's ancient if not eternal treachery. It was not by chance that Sully had proposed driving the Muscovite tsar "into Asia" and leaving him to fight with Turks and Persians. Here we must return to Petrov's already cited characterization of European civilization:

> И в малых заключенны сферах,
> Творят велики чудеса;
> Огней искусством Прометеи,
> Пременой лиц и дум Протеи;
> Сердец и счастия ловцы;
> Предосторожны, терпеливы.
> Неутомимы, прозорливы.
> Как куплю деющи пловцы.

(Even enclosed in little spheres; / They are creating great miracles; / Prometheus, by the art of fire, / Proteus, by changing faces and thoughts; / Fishers of hearts and fortune; / Cautious, patient, / Tireless, perspicacious. / Like sailors engaged in trade.)

We need to comment separately on the "sailors." In 1773, while Petrov was in London, an extremely bad financial crisis broke out in all European markets, connected with the British East India Company. It drew the stark attention of Parliament, society and the press to this unusual commercial undertaking that had in its control the army and navy, published laws, and without supervision ruled over a territory many times larger than that of Britain itself.

The British East India Company was only one of the institutions that were in command in the Eastern colonies. Next to this were the Dutch, Portuguese, and French; these various East India Companies fought among themselves but functioned according to the same principles. The events of 1773 forced the English government to intervene and at least to some extent to put the company under its control (see Namier 1962, 161–172; Gardner 1971). Again it would be going too far to say that Petrov had this very incident in mind, but the social resonance that the financial crisis evoked and Parliament's investigation of the company's behavior must have alerted him to the characteristic type of financial adventurist who toys with the fate of continents. That these events would not have passed unknown to Petrov is suggested by the fact that among his London acquaintances was the well-known economist and political thinker Jeremy Bentham. And even Petrov's circle of Russian friends in London, which included, for example, N. S. Mordvinov, was made up of people who were by no means foreign to these issues (see Cross 1976; Cross 1996, 249–253).

Figure 6 An English caricature of the Chevalier d'Éon exposing him "as a Woman- Freemason."

The line "Prometheus, by the art of fire" also deserves attention. At the end of 1774 when Petrov was beginning work on the ode, the so-called "fire machine"—an early model of a steam engine, a new marvel created by British technical genius—was sent from Scotland to Kronstadt. The acquisition of technology that was ordered directly by the empress (Catherine II's note on this issue was entitled "On the machine devised in England, by which water is poured out of dry docks and canals by means of fire") occupied the officials at the Russian Embassy in England, including the ambassador himself, A. S. Musin-Pushkin (see Zabarinskii 1936, 44–72).

One may compile a set of characteristics that Petrov assigns to members of the secret circle who so stubbornly and persistently intrigued against Russia. They are magi, sorcerers who "perform great miracles," magicians who invent "fiery machines." They are adventurists, "seekers of fortune" (on people of this type in this era, see Stroev 1998). They are charlatans, changing their appearance and aims, "Proteuses changing faces and thoughts." They are overwhelmed with the desire for profit, "Like sailors engaged in trade." They are, finally, "Fishers of hearts and fortune," drawing others into their nets. If we combine all of these traits into one, the cherished notion of *freemasons* comes immediately to mind. A decade earlier Catherine, composing her anti-Masonic comedies "The Deceiver" and "The Siberian Shaman," utilized the very same features.

At this time, England was the homeland and capital of European Masonry and by the time of Petrov's sojourn, had accumulated a huge mass of Masonic apologetics and anti-Masonic polemics in which the freemasons were accused of practicing black magic, of secret political plots, and of vulgar self-interest (Roberts 1972, 58–59). In the course of the second half of the eighteenth century, the Masonic movement had spread across all of Europe, bringing ever new countries into its orbit. In France, lodge members included the first leader of the King's Secret Prince Conti as well as many leading aristocrats, as well as possibly Louis XV (ibid., 49). According to M. K. Schuchard, who studied eighteenth-century European mysticism, the King's Secret was made up mostly of "Scottish Masons" (Schuchard 1992, 95). She asserts that the famous Swedish mystic and Mason Emmanuel Swedenborg, who died in 1772, had been a longtime secret agent of the King's Secret (ibid., 95–98).

It is impossible to establish what information Petrov might have had at his disposal, but he must have known of the Chevalier d'Éon's entry into the Great Lodge in London; in 1773 a caricature of d'Éon went on sale in London and Paris that mocked the Masonic membership of a person of uncertain sex (Yates 1995, 204–207). Masons played a significant role in the leadership of East-Indian companies, and filial lodges had opened in Bengal and Surinam (see Roberts 1972, 31; Jacob 1991, 177). At this time the Mason George Robison, an English mathematician and engineer who was teaching in Kronstadt, where there was an active English Masonic lodge, was trying to attract the creator of the "fiery machine" James Watt to Russia (see Cross 1971, 54–56; Zabarinskii 1936, 71–72).

Russian Masonic lodges also expanded rapidly. In 1772, one of Catherine's close advisors, I. P. Elagin, received a patent from that very same London Great Lodge to be called the Provincial Great Master of Russia. Elagin's secretary, the playwright V. I. Lukin, went to London to receive his patent (Cross 1971, 48–52). Among the Russian Masons were political enemies of Petrov's patron G. A. Potemkin, notably, N. I. Panin, and many literary foes of Petrov himself—A. P. Sumarokov, V. I. Maikov, N. I. Novikov, and others (see Vernadskii 1999, 311–312).

However, unlike England and France, Russia had almost no tradition of anti-Masonic propaganda (see Smith 1999). It seems as if Petrov was the first Russian writer who saw the spread of Masonry as a threat to Russian state interests. The balance of power and European confederation, Rousseau and Bentham, Louis XV's secret diplomacy and the East-Indian companies, the steam engine and the scandal around the Chevalier d'Éon, the free press in London and ancient Russian notions of a Holy Land surrounded by enemies on all sides—all this constituted that infernal mixture which Petrov's poetic gift transformed into a work that deserves to be part of the annals of Russian political thought.

CHAPTER 3

Eden in Taurus:

The "Crimean Myth" in Russian Culture of the 1780s–90s[1]

The "Greek Project" became a long-term strategic goal of Russian policy in the first years after the Peace of Kutchuk Kainarji. However, the course of military actions, peace talks, and the diplomatic conflict in Europe all showed Catherine and her closest advisors that the project as a whole could not be achieved without a number of intermediate stages. Undoubtedly the most important of these steps was the annexation of Crimea.

The creators of Russian foreign policy did not quickly grasp the strategic and cultural importance of Crimea. During the first Russo-Turkish War in the early 1770s, Catherine had written in a rescript to Count P. I. Panin:

> It is not Our intent at all to have this peninsula and the Tatar hordes that belong to it under our jurisdiction, but it would be desirable if they were removed from Turkish dominion and remained forever independent. Due to Crimea's position and that of those places where Tatars live outside of it, and no less due to their character, they will never be of use to Our empire, [because] no significant taxes can be collected from them. (Ekaterina 1871, 1)

---

1   Translated by Iain Fraser and Marcus Levitt, edited by Marcus Levitt.

Catherine essentially repeats the evaluation of M. L. Vorontsov as given in his report "On Little Tartary," presented to the empress in 1762 right after her ascension to the throne (see Druzhinina 1955, 65–68) and which had constituted the basis for Russia's policy toward Crimea in the 1760s.

This minimal program was realized in 1774 when the Peace of Kutchuk Kainarji detached Crimea from the Ottoman Empire and declared it a formally independent state headed by the pro-Russian Khan Shagin-Girei. However, by this time or soon thereafter, the empress's views changed radically. The annexation of Crimea was envisaged both in Potemkin's plan, according to some sources given to the empress in the mid-1770s, as well as in Bezborodko's memorandum, probably written in 1780, in which Russia's Eastern policy took final form (see Samoilov 1867, 1012; SbRIO XXVI, 385).

Crimea was annexed to Russia after complicated political maneuvers in April 1783 (on the annexation see Dubrovin 1885–1889, where the basic Russian documents are published; the "Turkish and Tatar" side is represented in Fisher 1970. On the colonization of Crimea, see Druzhinina 1959 and the survey article by Raeff 1972). In the opinion of the English ambassador James Harris, the annexation of Crimea was a peculiar type of political adventure, undertaken by Potemkin in opposition to the whole cabinet of ministers, on the outcome of which depended the continuation of his favor and influence. "If all fails," wrote Harris, "he is lost; if he achieves success he will become stronger than before" (Harris I, 516). We know that Potemkin acted on direct instructions from the empress, but his role in making the relevant decisions is not in any doubt.

The success of the Crimean campaign surpassed all expectations. In December, after about six months of political uncertainty, the annexation of the peninsula to Russia was accepted by Turkey. Thus, contrary to expectations, the matter ended without war. This very circumstance produced the greatest impression on Russian public opinion. The acquisition of such an important province without a single shot testified to Russia's power better than any victories. At the same time, it symbolically suggested the natural character of this extension of the empire.

> Процветаюша Таврида,
> Возгордись своей судьбой!

> Не облекшись громом брани,
> Не тягча перуном длани,
> Покорил тебя герой, —

(Blossoming Tauride, / Take pride in your fate! / Without the clash of arms, / Without the stress of thunder, / The hero subdued you, -)

Wrote the poet Ermil Kostrov (I, 94–95). Even earlier, in the ode "On the Acquisition of Crimea" of 1784, Derzhavin had exulted:

> Который бог, который ангел,
> Который человеков друг
> Бескровным увенчал вас лавром,
> Без брани вам трофеи дал, — (Derzhavin I, 182)

(Which god, which angel / Which friend of humanity / Crowned us with bloodless laurels, / Gave us trophies without battle.)

Later, in his "Commentaries on My Works," Derzhavin recalled that the conquest of Crimea was part of a larger-scale design. The poet provided the following extremely characteristic clarification of the line "And Konstantin is ascending": "A reference to Constantine Paleologus, the Constantinopolitan tsar, with whose death the Greek kingdom fell, and that in his place was ascending Konstantin Pavlovich, whom the empress wanted to raise to the throne, having driven the Turks from Europe, and who for this reason had been taught Greek. What grand plans! Man proposes, God disposes" (ibid., III, 604). At the start of the Alexandrine epoch when the "Commentaries" were dictated, the "Greek Project" had moved from practical politics into the realm of great fantasy, although in the mid-1780s the annexation of Crimea seemed but a prelude to even greater achievements. The author of an anonymous ode of 1784, "To Her Great Majesty Catherine II on the Acquisition of Crimea," like Derzhavin, saw in Russia's triumph the pledge of future dominion over the East:

> Поклонник буйный Алкорана
> Царем стал мудрым из тирана,
> Познал блеск истинный венца;
> И просвещен Екатериной,

Оставил, мнится, нрав звериный,
Облекся подданным в отца.

Ах, ежели во мне не ложно
Пророчество правдивых муз,
Султана убедить возможно
Избавить пленников от уз.
Пошли к нему того Героя,
Кем ханов упразднился трон [Потемкина – А.З.],
Услыша твоего витию,
Он сам оставит Византию
И выйдет из Европы вон.   (Ode 1784, 7)

(Tempestuous follower of the Alkoran / From a tyrant became a wise tsar, / Knew the true luster of a crown; / And, enlightened by Catherine, / Abandoned, it seems, his bestial ways, / Became a father to his subjects. // Oh, if the prophesy of truthful Muses / Is not false in me / It is possible to convince the sultan / To free the prisoners from their bonds. / Send that Hero to him / Who did away with the throne of the khans [i.e., Potemkin]. / Hearing your prophet / He will quit Byzantium by himself / And depart far from Europe.)

It is worth noting that on the copy of this ode that is preserved in the library of Moscow University, "Mr. Petrov" is written on the cover in an eighteenth-century hand (see SKRK II, 338). This attribution cannot be proved unconditionally, but seems highly likely, judging by the ode's poetics and phraseology. Petrov's possible authorship makes the text especially significant. In his odes the poet often expressed the cherished ideas of his patrons, and his geo-political metaphors exerted their own influence on his addressees.

∞ **2** ∞

Apart from its advantageous strategic position, Crimea possessed enormous symbolic capital for Russia. It was able at the same time to represent Christian Byzantium and classical Hellas. Above all, it was a territory colonized in the depths of antiquity by Greece and rich in ancient monuments. With the acquisition of Crimea, Russia obtained its own share of the antique inheritance, giving it the right to stand in the ranks of the civilized European nations. On the other hand, it was from the shores of the Black Sea that the start of Russian Christianity had come. "The Tauric Chersonese, the source of our Christianity and of our very humanity, is already in the embraces of her daughter. There is something mystical in this," Potemkin wrote to Catherine in August 1783, after the capture of Crimea (Ekaterina i Potemkin 1997, 180). In the Tauric Chersonese Prince Vladimir had once taken the cross and entered into matrimony with the Greek Princess Anna, laying the foundation for the heritage that was the ideological basis of the "Greek Project." Having finally reached the places where it had taken its faith and had its first acquaintance with Greek culture, Russia had now to move onward to the historical center of that faith.

Understandably, the conquest of Crimea could not help but be interpreted as the return of primordial Russian lands.

> Россия наложила руку
> На Тавр, Кавказ и Херсонес,
> И распустя в Босфоре флаги,
> Стамбулу флотами гремит, —

(Russia laid her hand / On Taurus, the Caucasus and Kherson, / And unfurling its flags in the Bosphorus, / Its fleets resound to Stanbul, -)

wrote Derzhavin (I, 182), and later in his "Explanations on My Works," he clarified that "At this very time the Caucasian hordes were brought under control and Kherson, the ancient city of Russian princes, was returned to Russia" (ibid., III, 604).

A fairly full notion of the complex of ideas underlying Russia's policy can be gleaned from Potemkin's biography. Its author was Potemkin's nephew and collaborator General A. N. Samoilov, a participant in the talks on annexing Crimea to Russia and an active figure in Potemkin's administration in Novorossiia (see, for example, Ludolf 1892, 174; Semevskii 1875, 668). The biographical value of Samoilov's work is usually rated low on account of its apologetic tone; in fact, the work crosses the line that separates biography from hagiography. However, the value of Samoilov's testimony lies elsewhere: his proximity to his uncle and benefactor as well as his complete reverence for him permit us to take the biographer's explanations as more or less reliable accounts of Potemkin's own cherished thoughts and judgments.

According to Samoilov, Potemkin

> could not without pain swallow the fact that those barbarians, enslaving the new Rome, ancient Greece ..., subjecting Greeks and other Christians to humiliating servitude, were taking pride in the destruction of Enlightenment. ... Being on the shores of the Danube, from his studies in national history he eagerly sought the places where Sviatoslav had held his victory feasts, built cities[2] ..., [and he] sought in his heart for the sanctuary of Kherson whence St. Vladimir had accepted the illumination of the Christian faith for Russia. ... (Samoilov 1867, 1010–1011)

Samoilov speaks about Potemkin's actions in Novorossiia and Crimea—founding towns and building up industry and trade. Yet his tone reaches its highest passion when it comes to the revolution in Crimean toponomy wrought by Potemkin:

> But in order the more to impress minds with the brilliance of Great Catherine's acts, to root out and extirpate all memory of the barbarians ..., the ancient names were revived in the conquered peninsula. *Crimea* was renamed Tauris (Tavrida); near the valleys where ancient Kherson stood, from the same heaps of stones near the port of Akhtiyar, Sevastopol rose; *Akhty Mechet* was called Simferopol, *Kaffa* Feodosyia, *Kozlov* Efpatoriya, *Yenikale* Pentikapium, *Taman'* Fanagoriya, and so on. ... In a word, new light shone in the ancient kingdom of Pontus under the leadership of the conqueror of Tauris, and the first unstoppable step was taken toward cleansing Europe of Mohammedans and the conquest of Istanbul.

And in a letter to Greek Archbishop Nicephorus, Potemkin even promised to "call Taganrog Sparta" (Batalden 1982, 69).

Potemkin's line of thinking as presented by Samoilov is extremely interesting. Russia was restoring to itself its own ancient holy place, and this return was accompanied by intensive Hellenization of the conquered land. Russians came into a province that had once belonged to Greece, gave it back its Greek countenance and restored their own faith and history, themselves in part

---

2   The mention of Sviatoslav on the Danube was clearly connected with the part of the "Greek Project"'s plan to create the state of Dakiia from Moldavia and Wallachia, whose crown Potemkin coveted for a while (see Madariaga 1981, 377–388).

becoming Greeks. And the Greeks, freed from slavery, would regain their national character under the Russian aegis.

> Цирцея от досады воет,
> Волшебство все ее ничто.
> Ахеян, в тварей превращенных,
> Минерва вновь творит людьми.
> Осклабясь, Пифагор дивится.
> Что зрит он преселенье душ,
> Гомер из стрекозы исходит
> И громогласным своим пеньем
> Не баснь, но истину поет, —

(Circe howls in vexation, / All her magic reduced to nothing. / The Achaeans, changed into beasts, / Minerva turns back into people. / Smiling, Pythagoras is amazed / To see the transmigration of souls, / Homer is transformed from a dragonfly / And with his thunderous singing / Chants not fables but the truth, -)

wrote Derzhavin in his ode "On the Acquisition of Crimea" (Derzhavin I, 183). The theme of the Greek renaissance in connection with Russia's plans of conquest had been relatively widespread in odes from the time of the Russo-Turkish War of 1768–1774, but Derzhavin's characteristic hyperbolic panache takes the notion to the limit. Minerva-Catherine not only turns the Greeks from slaves into heroes, but also from cattle into human beings, and her peaceful feat becomes the fulfillment of Pythagorean mysteries. Returned to his natural self, Homer can finally sing, not the fairy-tale adventures of the Trojan War, but the actual accomplishments of the Russian Athena.

The idea that the Russian Empire's expansion to the south is the fulfillment of Homer's cherished notion was not Derzhavin's invention. In 1775, in the foreword to a poem dedicated to the Peace of Kutchuk Kainarji, the Russian man of letters of Greek extraction Antonii Palladoklis also recalled Homer:

> According to Alexander the Great's phrase, Achilles was fortunate to have had Homer as chronicler of his courage. In the current war between those who are taking revenge for many peoples' stolen freedom and those who

stole it ..., Homer could rightly be called happy if he were resurrected today, for he would find here many Agamemnons, Achilleses, Ajaxes, Diomedeses and Odysseuses, who distinguish themselves heroically under Pallada's leadership. ... His loud and sweet-sounding song would be drowned out by the eternally thundering victorious glory of Her Imperial Majesty's arms, which the *Epoch of Kherson* and the noise of the waves separating the Azov and Black Seas ... proclaim. (Palladoklis 1775, n. p.)

In 1787, during Catherine's Crimean tour, Ermil Kostrov's verse translation of the *Iliad* was published. In dedicating the work to the empress, Kostrov in particular wrote:

> Он (Гомер. — А. З.) в песнех сладостных
>   витийственным искусством
> Еще в свой мрачною покрытый мглою век
> О славе дней твоих, владычица, предрек!
> Живая кисть его, Минерву описуя,
> И щит ее и шлем очам изобразуя,
> Явила в истине россиян божество
> И храбра севера над югом торжество.
>   (Kostrov 1972, 157)

(In delightful songs with eloquent art / In an age still obscured by gloomy haze / He [Homer] foretold the glory of your days, sovereign! / His living brush, depicting Minerva, / And presenting her shield and helmet to our eyes, / Revealed in truth the Russians' deity / And the triumph of the brave north over the south.)

Despite geographical reality, the Greeks' victory over the Trojans became a victory of north over south, that is, the prototype of the wars Russian commanders were waging against the Turks:

> Под сению твоих бесчисленных эгидов
> Ахиллов зрели мы, Аяксов, Диомидов,
> Со именем небес, со именем твоим
> Стремивши молнию в Стамбул и буйный Крим. ...
> Взвивающийся твой над Геллеспонтом флаг
> Есть ужас варварам, источник грекам благ.

> Почий Гомер, почий средь лавра и оливы,
> Сколь вымыслы твои приятны, справедливы!
> О россах истинно предчувствие твое,
> В Екатерине зрим его событие. (Ibid.)

(In the shade of your numberless aegises / We saw Achilleses, Ajaxes, Diomedeses, / With the heavens' name, with your name / Striving like lightning toward Stambul and unbridled Crimea. ... / Your defiant flag above the Hellespont / Is a horror to barbarians, source of good for Greeks. // Homer, resting in peace among laurel and olive, / How pleasant, how just are your inventions! / Your true premonition about the Russes / We see as fact in Catherine.)

The connection between Russian expansion to the South and the Trojan War evidently became a commonplace at the time of the Turkish campaign of 1768–1772. The plot of Kheraskov's epic poems, which by their generic nature were designed to become the basis for national myth, is comprised of the siege of a city that hides a cherished beauty within. Moreover, if in the "Rossiada" (1779) the city turned out to be Kazan, besieged by Ivan the Terrible, in his second epic poem written in the first half of the 1780s, Kheraskov finds a more adequate focus for Russia's geographic, political, and erotic gravitation. In Tauric Chersonese Prince Vladimir needs to acquire both the Christian faith and a Greek princess:

> В уме его Херсон и греческа княжна.
> Одно рождает в нем несытый гнев отмщенья.
> Другое — нежные любови ощущенья.
>   (Kheraskov 1785, 174)

(In his mind are Kherson and the Greek princess. / The one inspires insatiable anger of revenge, / The other – sensations of tender love.)

Faith, like the bride, is won in Tauris by force, and in the end –

> Соединился князь со греческой княжной.
> Запечатлелся ад священною печатью,
> И озарилася Россия благодатью.

(The prince was united with the Greek princess. / Hell was sealed with a holy seal, / And Russia was illumined with grace.)

Chapter 3: Eden in Taurus

> Предрек уже тогда, предрек мятежный Тавр,
> Что в недрах сокрывал Екатерины лавр,
> Который обовьет Российскую корону
> И будет от срацин оградою Херсону.
> (Op. cit., 242, 232)

(Even then rebellious Taurus [i.e., the mountain] foretold / That in its depths it was hiding Catherine's laurel, / That will wind round the Russian crown / And protect Kherson from the Saracens.)

Kheraskov's epic was begun approximately in 1779, when the "Rossiada" was completed, and came out in 1785. It seems natural to suppose that the last cantos of the poem, in which the Kherson campaign is described, were composed in 1783–1784, when the annexation of Crimea occurred.

As mentioned, Catherine considered the choice of names for her grandsons with exceptional care. It is indicative that the daughter born to Pavel Petrovich and Maria Fedorovna in 1784 was named Elena (Helen). Of course, the name was suggested first of all by Byzantine history (see Ruban 1784), but insofar as Greek Christianity and the classics were very closely connected in the consciousness of people of the time, the Homeric connotations of the newborn grand princess's name could not have been absent. Indeed, in a letter to Grimm, Catherine admitted that she had given her granddaughter her name, and referred to her as "the beautiful Helen" (SbRIO XXIII, 326).

In his "Ode on the Acquisition of Crimea" Derzhavin used blank verse, which was extremely rare for him, specifically connecting this innovation with the poem's classical coloration. When sending the ode to the journal *Collocutor of Lovers of the Russian Word* (*Sobesednik liubitelei rossiiskogo slova*), he wrote in the accompanying letter: "It is not unknown that the ancients wrote their poetry without rhyme, which even the most recent authors have imitated and still imitate. This ode was written as an experiment—will it seem to our respected public that this work (sei obraz) is in our poetic language, and should it be continued…"? (Derzhavin I, 182). Derzhavin was not alone in the attempt to Hellenize Russian poetry; even earlier, since 1775, Petrov had experimented with forms of the Pindaric ode (see Gasparov 1984, 99; Bershtein 1992, 83–84). His odes to Potemkin of 1777 and 1778 came out in 1780–81 in bilingual editions. The facing translation in Greek was done by G. Baldani, and in an ode of 1782 Derzhavin tried—for the first time in Russia, it seems—to precisely reproduce the form of ancient Greek choral lyrics complete with strophes, antistrophes, and epodes.

∞ 3 ∞

After the conquest of Crimea, Catherine and Potemkin started to erect the new Hellas. Immediately after the Peace of Kutchuk Kainarji, the new towns of Kherson and Slaviansk were founded in the new territories (SbRIO XXVII, 50–51). The meaning of these towns' names is quite evident. Kherson was to recall the Tauric Chersonese, and Slaviansk, the legendary city of the ancient Russians near Novgorod. "With this name we are also renewing those most famous designations that Russian history conserves from the depth of antiquity, that our people is of one stock and is a direct offshoot of the ancient Slavs, and that Kherson was the source of Christianity for Russia, where after Prince Vladimir took baptism the light of the divine faith and true religion shone and became established in Russia," wrote Catherine in an *ukase* of September 9, 1775, on the creation of the Eparchy of Kherson and Slaviansk (PSZ №14366). The Eparchy was given an exceptionally high status and Eugenius Bulgaris, one of the leading figures of the Greek Enlightenment who had moved to Russia some years earlier, was appointed as its archbishop. The simultaneous foundation of fortresses with Greek and Slavic names was to symbolize the unity of the Christian peoples on the border with Turkey.

Several years later Potemkin wrote to Eugenius to request that he write a history of Novorossiia:

> As you combine in yourself knowledge of various ages, you are our Hesiod, Strabo and Chrysostom. Take on the task of writing an historical description of our region, what it was in ancient times, when from time immemorial there were marvelous men and prolific cities—Olbia, Melitopol, the islands of Achilles's journey. ... Borysthenes [ancient Greek name for the Dniepr], home to the ancient Rosses' fleets, was not named this for nothing; its shores recall the shining path of Andrei the First-Called who preached salvation to our fathers. (Potemkin 1879, 19)

Of the two cities planned by Catherine, Slaviansk was in fact not built, whereas Kherson was to see furious development.

In that same year of 1775, the College for the Foreign Orthodox was founded in Petersburg, essentially to educate Greek youth, and in 1779 it was transferred to Kherson (PSZ № 15658; see Arsh 1970, 134–135). In the second half of the 1770s, massive resettlement of foreigners to the new Russian lands was taking place, many from Crimea, which was still under the power of the Khans. Petrov wrote in an ode to Potemkin in 1778 (I, 180–181):

> Не совершается ль
> Пророчествие мира?
> Херсонски жители,
> Единой веры чада
> Не все ль, оставя юг,
> На север к нам грядете?
>
> Весь двинулся Херсон,
> Конца ему не видно,…
> Молдавец, Армянин,
> Индеянин иль Еллин,
> Иль черный Ефиоп
> Под коим бы кто небом
> На свет не произшел
> Мать всем Екатерина. …
>
> Со всей земли племен
> Слыви усыновитель.
> Чужих растенья стран
> Преносятся на север.
> Языки чужды ты
> Преображай во Россов, —

(Is not the world's prophecy / Coming true? / The inhabitants of Kherson, / Children of one faith, / Will you not all, forsaking the south, / Come to us in the north? // All Kherson has taken off, / There's no limit to it,… / Moldavian, Armenian, / Indian or Hellene, / Or black Ethiopian / Under whatever native sky / They were born / Catherine is mother to all. … // Be known as adoptive parent / Of all tribes on earth, / Plants from alien lands / Are transplanted to the north. / You, transform these alien peoples / Into Rosses, -)

Of course, the picture Petrov drew was not as much a depiction of Potemkin's actual colonization activities as an odic metaphor of world domination. In actuality, Potemkin did found various Greek, Armenian, Moldavian, Albanian and Serbian settlements. As far as Ethiopians are concerned, the poet might have had in mind General Hannibal, who served in Novorossiia. As for the "Indians," we have no information of them in Russian service of the time. However, turning diverse nationalities into one whole was the mission of empire, now formulated anew and on fresh ideological foundations in the Black Sea littoral.

In an ode of 1782 to Potemkin, Petrov's main focus was again the ethnic variety of Potemkin's settlements, where "even foreign peoples from distant countries of the world" found refuge:

> ... тамо Азиатец
> И солнцем осмуглевший Афр,
> Климатов разных европеец,
> Герой, пустынник, селянин
> Без маск очам твоим предстанет
> В единой храмине увидит
> Восток и запад, норд и юг,...
> Черты их лиц, одежды нравы,
> Языки их И веры разны.
> Но угоститель всех — один. ... (Ibid., 18–19)

(... there an Asiatic / And an African, swarthy from the sun, / Europeans of various climes, / A hero, a hermit, a villager / Will appear before your eyes, without disguise, / And see in a single dwelling / East and west, north and south,... / Their facial features, clothes and customs, / Languages and faiths all different, / But the host of all—is one. ...)

Potemkin's desire to settle the land entrusted to him of Novorossiia with immigrants from other countries became a symbol of the future unity of the peoples of the Russian Empire's new provinces. The Tower of Babel is overcome as all peoples merge, completing the circle of universal civilization under Russia's aegis.

Competition with Peter and Petersburg, and the Baltic territory as a whole, permeates all of Potemkin's activity. It was no accident that Samoilov called his political doctrine "the Eastern System," which was clearly juxtaposed to N. I. Panin's "Northern System" that saw Russia's natural place among northern European states (see Griffiths 1970). Furthermore, with the change in the political situation in the 1780s, the prospects for speedy accomplishment of the "Greek Project" were becoming increasingly dim and were put off indefinitely. Correspondingly, the theme of Crimea ceased to be subordinate to that of Constantinople and took on increasing autonomy.

"Petersburg, established on the Baltic, is the northern capital of Russia," wrote Potemkin to Catherine in 1783. "The middle one is Moscow, and Kherson of Akhtiar will be the southern capital of my Sovereign. Let them see which ruler has made the better choice" (Ekaterina i Potemkin 1997, 172). In another letter written the same day, he cheerfully asked the empress to "look on this place as one where the glory is yours originally (tvoia original'naia) and you will not have to share it with your predecessors; here you will not follow in the footsteps of anyone else" (ibid., 173). Samoilov wrote that Potemkin "to the glory of his empress strove to bring about in the South what Peter the Great had accomplished in the North" (Samoilov 1867, 1203). However, the point evidently concerned something bigger—the global reorientation of all Russian politics, culture and self-awareness.

Of course, this program was initiated and supported by the empress herself. "How can that hamlet (Ochakov, still under Turkish control— A. Z.) dare raise its nose against the young colossus of Kherson?," she wrote to Potemkin. "Peter I, who subjugated nature in his Baltic enterprises and constructions, faced greater obstacles than we at Kherson. But had he not initiated them, we would have been deprived of many of the capacities we needed for Kherson itself" (Ekaterina I Potemkin 1997, 153). From this perspective, Peter, with his enterprises on the Baltic littoral, merely served as a predecessor to Catherine and Potemkin. But all these statements were made in private correspondence, known only to its participants. The symbolic demonstration of the chosen course was to be Catherine's trip to Crimea in the first half of 1787.

4

The route and timing of this journey were worked out with extreme care. Catherine was to leave St. Petersburg immediately after the New Year's festivities; travel through the winter provinces of Great Russia; pass the end of the winter and the first half of spring in Kiev, in lands ruled by the hero of the Russo-Turkish War of 1768–1774, Field-Marshal Rumiantsev; enter Potemkin's possessions in Novorossiia in early May, and spend the last two weeks of the month in Crimea. The movement of the royal suite southward coincided with the spring revival of nature. In Kherson itself, the empress and the foreign ambassadors accompanying her were to meet with the new ally of Russia—the Austrian Emperor Joseph II, travelling under the name of Count Falkenstein (for an analysis of the Crimean myth as interpreted by Catherine's European travel companions, see Wolff 1994, 126–141).

An important component of the journey, linking it with the "Greek Project," was to be the presence in the empress's suite of grand princes Alexander and Constantine, on which Catherine insisted despite the

Figure 7 "Catherine II on a Journey across Russia in 1787" (1790) by Jean-Jacques Avril the Elder, based on a drawing by Ferdinand de Meys. State Historical Museum, Moscow.

stubborn opposition of their parents, Tsarevich Pavel Petrovich and his wife Maria Fedorovna. But the measles one of her grandsons had caught forced Catherine to drop this idea. It was precisely in Crimea, on May 21, in the presence of the ambassadors and Count Falkenstein, that the feast of St. Helena and Constantine was to be celebrated (see, e.g., SbRIO XXIII, 411); this was meant to confirm Russia's succession in relation to the Eastern Roman Empire.

Still more significant than the itinerary was the program for Catherine's journey. A. M. Panchenko's article "Potemkin Villages as a Cultural Myth" was the first to describe this program as a kind of symbolic text (Panchenko 1983). In analyzing Potemkin's mythology, the researcher directed his attention to military and state themes: the navy, the army, and civilization, leaving a whole series of crucial historical and cultural associations without explanation. Thus, Panchenko interprets the famous episode with the squad of Amazons as a "manifestation of the capricious willfulness Potemkin was famous for" (ibid., 96; on the "Amazon regiment," see Dusi 1844). In fact, the parade of exotic, partially clad "armed women" marching before the two emperors introduced the theme of the Scythians into the journey's array of associations.

Paragraphs 110–117 of Book IV of Herodotus's *Histories* tell of warlike women who entered into marriage with the Scythians, bringing into the world the Scythian tribe of Savromaty (Sarmatians). Further, the ancient Scythians had not only once been inhabitants of the northern Black Sea coast, but were also counted in official eighteenth-century historiography as among the forebears of the Slavs. In that very year, 1787, Catherine's *Notes on Russian History* had appeared. Here already was a clear orientation toward the new ethnic conditions that arose in the conquered territories; thus the empress asserted that the Greeks had called the Scythians "Slavs, Sarmatians and Tartars" (Ekaterina VIII, 12). Catherine describes the life of the Scythian tribes with evident sympathy, projecting onto it the conception of the Russian national character that she was formulating in those years:

> Darius, the Persian emperor, they had chased off with disdain. Cyrus with his whole army could not prevail against the Scythians. ... The Scythians were never subject to the Romans. Only Alexander of Macedon had success against the Scythians and made an alliance with them. ... The northern Scythians had the same language as the Slavs. ... They had their

> own absolute rulers (samovlastnye gosudari). The Scythians could not tolerate other nations being called older. They admired friendship and virtue, loved the fearless, despised wealth, raised cattle, dressed in the same clothes winter and summer. They were always on horseback, their best weapon their pride; they gave judgment reasoning with common sense, as they had no written law, and severely punished vice. The bravery and justice of the Scythians were praised by neighboring peoples. ... Their women rode out to war with the men. (Ibid., 20–22)[3]

Having such a genealogy was of course flattering, but the empire that had conquered Crimea was heir not just to Scythians and Slavs who were "more inclined to military service than to the arts and sciences" (Ekaterina VIII, 12), but also to the Greeks. Not coincidentally, the Amazon regiment itself was made up of Greek women from Novorossiia. The "historical presentation" written by the empress in 1787, "The Beginning of Oleg's Reign," pointedly shows the conclusion of an alliance between the warlike Slavic tribes and Christian Byzantium (on the political connotations of the work, see Cross 1990; Maiofis 1996). In the finale of this play, Prince Oleg and Emperor Leo of Constantinople together watch Olympic competitions and a performance of Euripides's "Alcestis" to the music of choirs singing passages from Lomonosov's odes.

Catherine's interest in Euripides at the time deserves special attention, since during her stay in Crimea his tragedy "Iphigenia in Taurus" had become sharply topical. Already in the 1784 ode "To Her Great Majesty Catherine II on the Acquisition of Crimea," it stated that

> Так ты теперь Херсона страж.
> Так Ифигения в Тавриде
> И гроб сея царицы наш? (Oda 1784)

(So you are now the guardian of Kherson, / So is the grave of this queen, / Iphigenia in Taurus, ours?)

---

3 It was probably in Catherine's history that the parallel "Russians—Scythians"—so forcefully projected by Blok a century and a half later—was first articulated. It played a special role during the 1812 invasion, when certain elements of the Russian military strategy (dividing the troops into two armies, retreating deep into the country, destroying supplies, partisan attacks on the enemy, etc.) were directly associated with the Scythians' war against Darius as described by Herodotus (on the so-called "Scythian plan" of attack, drawn up by M. A. Barklay de Tolly, see Tartakovskii 1996).

According to the main versions of the myth, Iphigenia, who fled Taurus to Attica together with Orestes and Pilades, was buried in her native land. But for the Russian poet, Iphigenia's grave becomes a variant of the Holy Sepulcher, and the conquest of Crimea the equivalent of the Crusades.

The most important events of Russia's Eastern politics took place in parallel to the growing European popularity of the myth of Iphigenia. On 18 May (European style), 1779, ten days after the birth of Grand Prince Konstantin Pavlovich, Glück's opera "Iphigenia in Taurus," with libretto by the French poet N.-F. Guillard, was performed in Paris to great success. The premiere of the German version of "Iphigenia" was held on December 31, 1781, in Vienna. Present were the heir to the Russian throne Pavel Petrovich, his wife, and her brother, Prince Eugene of Württemberg, who had earlier, incidentally, attended the premiere of Glück's "Alceste." The royal guests were so struck by the music that they paid a visit to the aged composer, which caused a sensation in the city (see Kroll 1964, vi-vii). Pavel's journey to Vienna, literally forced on him by his mother, was meant to indicate Russia's turn towards an alliance with Austria, a necessary condition for eastward expansion.

In late 1783 "Iphigenia" was revived in Vienna by the command of Emperor Joseph II, a gesture possibly hinting at a welcome for his ally Russia, whose annexation of Tauris had only just become a legal fact. And finally, in 1787, virtually overlapping with Catherine's journey to Crimea, though by pure coincidence, the most famous interpretation of the myth was published—Goethe's *Iphigenia in Taurus* (on the eighteenth-century Western European projection of the myth of Iphegenia onto Crimea, see Wolff 1994, 138).

Not long before Catherine's journey she wrote to Prince de Ligne, a French officer and wit in Austrian service at the Russian court: "I shall be taking your associates to a country where, they say, Iphigenia once dwelled. The mere name of that land arouses the imagination, so there is no sort of fancy that might not be set free on account of my journey to Tauris and my stay there" (SbRIO XXVII, 378–379). Catherine did not miss the chance here to recall Potemkin's taste for all things Greek: "I do not really know if my governor-general will appreciate your critical remark about Homer, because he was dissatisfied with me because I thought that the Count of Stolberg made an excellent translation of that poet into German" (ibid.). Criticism of the German translation of Homer at this moment, when a Russian translation was about to appear, also implicitly suggested a special connection between Russians and Greeks.[4]

The empress not only reminded de Ligne about Iphigenia in her letter, but even gave him an estate "on the shores of the Black Sea, in the very spot where according to tradition there stood the temple in which Queen Iphigenia was priestess" (Ségur 1907, 193). One of the most enlightened people in Europe was to be given a place in a little corner of Tauris settled by Tatars, where once an envoy of enlightened Greece had ruled the minds and souls of barbarian peoples, being at the same time their captive. As can be seen from his letters, de Ligne highly valued this gift (Ligne 1989, 505–506, 510; cf. Waegemans 1992).

For Catherine, Iphigeneia's fate may have resonated with a strange similarity to her own. She, like Euripides's heroine, was given in sacrifice by her singular destiny and thrown into ruling a people that must inevitably have seemed to her barbarous, and whose peculiar sort of prisoner she also found herself. Be that as it may, she felt the time had come to realize old dreams and to restore ancient Greece. But since Constantinople was still beyond reach, she planned to do so on the territories she already controlled. The cornerstone of that revival was to be laid during the empress's journey—the city of Ekaterinoslav (literally, "Glory to Catherine"), intended to become the capital of Novorossiia, and possibly of the whole empire.

According to the plan for the new city, its shops were designed to "resemble the Propylaea or palace square (predvor'e) in Athens, with a stock

---

4   A. M. Panchenko is hardly correct when he juxtaposes Potemkin's "Novorossiia Project" to Bezborodko's "Greek Project" (Panchenko 1983, 95). The assertion widely encountered in historical studies that the "Greek Project" was chiefly connected with Bezborodko's activities (e.g., Markova 1958; Raeff 1972, 201, etc.) is contradicted by Bezborodko's own testimony that at the moment his diplomatic career started the empress was already fully caught up in this idea: "From the first moment I understood that the sovereign's intentions in regard to the Greek monarchy were serious, and I fully appreciated that this project was worthy of a great spirit, and moreover, that of course it could be carried out" (SbRIO XXVI, 444). The "Greek" and "Crimean" projects were part of one larger conception, and for all of the mutual bad feelings between Potemkin and Bezborodko they worked on both projects toward a single end. "The idea of Crimea was our common one," wrote Bezborodko in his "Autobiographical Note" (Ibid). Moreover, in both projects Potemkin took the role of ideologist, while Bezborodko had to prepare the necessary documents for Catherine. "A cane, led by a broad intellect," wrote the well-informed Derzhavin in an ode to Crimea, and explained that this referred to "The pen of Count Bezborodko, led by Prince Potemkin's ideas" (Derzhavin III, 603).

exchange and theater;" the governor's palaces were to be designed "in accordance with the taste of Roman and Greek buildings." The town was also to accommodate a university and a music academy (see Ekaterina i Potemkin 1997, 209). However, Ekaterinoslav, while evidently intended to combine Rome and Athens, was yet to be built, while in a few years Kherson had already managed to grow at a speed that astonished even the none too sympathetic observers from politically hostile France (see Ségur 1907, 243; Ludolf 1892, 172). Concerning Kherson, Count Ludolf reported that "evidently the empress intends to devote all her attention to this city," and predicted without hesitation that "the buildings to be erected in Ekaterinoslav will be magnificent" (ibid., 173, 177).

> Катись свозь новы, Днепр, Афины,...
> Цвети Темпейской рай долины, -

(Flow, Dnieper, through the new Athens, / Blossom, paradise of Tempe's Vale, -)

wrote V. Petrov about Kherson in an ode of 1777, later translated into Greek (Petrov I, 159). A land finally restoring its Russian and Christian nature becomes the prototype for the coming earthly paradise.

∽ 5 ∽

Themes of paradise seem to be an unavoidable attribute of imperial utopias; it is worth recalling how obstinately Peter went on calling his beloved marshes in Ingermanland Paradise (Paradiz), but of course the nature in Novorossiia and especially Crimea was literally begging for such an interpretation. Almost immediately after the annexation of Crimea, Potemkin's estate near the Baidar Gates began to be called the Vale of Tempe. In 1789 Ségur, in a letter to Potemkin, exulted over "the commerce brought to Kherson by a fleet built in Sevastopol in two years, as if by a miracle. ... Your Vale of Tempe, your Ekaterinoslav, where in two years you built more monuments than other capitals in two centuries" (Potemkin 1875, 232).

The empress's entire journey to Novorossiia and Crimea played out under the sign of the Paradise topos. One can follow how these themes develop in Catherine's letters to Ia. A. Bruce:

April 30. from Kremenchug:

> The governor's house ... is in a handsome oak grove and regular fruit orchard, with all the trees and even the oaks spreading, and it is as warm here as July in Russia. All in all, since we journeyed into the Ekaterinoslav area the air and all things and people have changed their appearance, and everything seems more alive.

May 4, on the road from Kremenchug to Kherson:

> I consider the climate here the best in the empire, here without exception all fruit trees grow in the open air, and I have never in my life seen pear trees the size of the biggest and thickest oak, and the air is the most pleasant.

May 14, from Kherson:

> Kherson may be considered among the finest of our cities. This child promises much: where they plant, everything grows, where they plough, there is abundance. The buildings are all stone, we have not yet felt the heat, all are healthy, the people here have no sick appearance and everything is in motion, there are many people and they come from all lands, though for the most part from the South.

We can note in the last quotation that the rapid increase of stone buildings and the variety of people who settled in the area are described here as fruit of the

Figure 8 "View of Tauride" by V. P. Petrov (1791).
Saratov State Art Museum, Saratov.

powerful local nature, bringing forth both vegetation and people in incredible abundance and variety.

Catherine's final judgment may be found in a letter of May 16, also from Kherson: "I am very happy to have seen it all with my own eyes, … this land is an earthly paradise" (Ekaterina 1889, 21–25). Catherine even took part herself in cultivating paradisiacal gardens, planting an apricot tree in Kherson which took extraordinarily well and lived at least until 1840 (Pelino 1844, 607). The memoirs of A. I. Mikhailovski-Danilevskii tell of his visit to Kherson with Emperor Alexander I in 1818: "The sovereign took us into the garden near the dining room, and stopped at a large apricot tree. Touched, he looked at it silently for a long time. Not knowing why he thus stood, we were also silent. Finally he said, 'This tree was planted by the empress Catherine. She hoped to found the capital of Southern Russia in Kherson, and she often told me of these intentions of hers'" (Shil'der IV, 100).

Taurus was to serve as the apotheosis of these paradisiacal gardens. A year before her journey, the empress wrote to I. G. Zimmermann that she saw the cultivation of "gardens and especially botanical gardens" as "one of the most important objectives in Tauris" (SbRIO XXVI, 360). Prince K.-G. Nassau-Siegen, in Catherine's retinue, wrote from Crimea that "the orchards of this place can give the impression of the gardens of paradise" (Timoshchuk 1893, 297). One can get an idea of Potemkin's typical flair when arranging this paradise from a contract he concluded with the gardener I. Blank, obliging him to plant "all kinds of trees … such as olives, figs, sweet and bitter oranges, various kinds of lemon, bergamot and others … 1000 almond trees, 2000 silk trees and 500 peach trees for sowing every year and 200 walnuts every two or three years" (Potemkin 1875, 254; cf Schönle 2001).

Accordingly, literary works connected with the annexation of Crimea also reflect the paradise theme and motifs of the transfiguration of nature. Derzhavin begins his Crimean ode (I, 182):

> Летит и воздух озаряет,
> Как вешне утро тихий понт!
> Летит, и от его улыбки
> Живая радость по лугам,
> По рощам и полям лиется, —

(It flies and lights up the air, / Like a spring morning [lights up] the quiet sea! / It flies, and from its smile / Living joy pours through the meadows, / Groves and fields, -)

In letters and statements from the empress in those months there is continual comparison of the false Petersburg paradise with the real Crimean one. "We talked of the balmy air and the warmth of the climate," noted Khrapovitskii in his diary on May 4, recording his conversation with the empress. "A pity Petersburg was not built here, because passing through these places you imagine the times of Vladimir I" (Khrapovitskii 1874, 34).[5] Prince Vladimir's name did not come up by accident. In 1782, just on the eve of the conquest of Crimea, the Order of St. Vladimir was founded, and during the journey south a ship christened the "Vladimir" had its launch ceremony (Khrapovitskii 1874, 35).

The idea of a competition between the new lands and Peter's Baltic conquests was given fuller development in Catherine's letter to P. D. Eropkin from Bakhchisarai on May 20:

> Those who belittled the acquisition of this land know very little about the value of things: not only will Kherson and Taurus pay for themselves in time, but one may hope that if Petersburg yields one eighth of the empire's revenue the aforementioned places will surpass those barren places with their fruits. ... I still recall that no one liked that area [St. Petersburg], and this [Crimea] truly is incomparably better. (Ekaterina 1808, 259)[6]

On June 8, already on the return journey, Catherine expressed her highest approval of Potemkin's labors and bestowed on him the honorary title of Prince of Taurus (Kniaz' Tavricheskii). Evidently, the question of Russia's future geopolitical orientation was basically clear to her. And her contemporaries understood that.

The celebration of the twenty-fifth anniversary of Catherine's ascension to the Russian throne in Moscow on June 28 served as a kind of culmination of the trip. As he had a quarter century earlier, M. M. Kheraskov took part in arranging an ideologically significant celebration, writing the scenario for a performance

---

5   On reverence for Vladimir as a kind of substitute for the already traditional cult of Peter the Great, see Rasmussen 1978.
6   The question whether Peter's choice for the place of his capital was voluntary or connected with military failures in the south was of wide interest in the nineteenth century (see Ospovat 1994).

of "Happy Moscow" (Shchastlivaia Moskva). According to this libretto, four Geniuses appeared before the public, representing the four corners of the earth, each telling why he was glorified in the Russian Empire. Last to appear was the "Genius of the South," who solemnly proclaimed:

> Celebrate your good fortune, blessed Geniuses! You are truly happy, yet it may be I have some advantage over you; everything you glory in individually I combine in my southern domains: abundance is my fortune, fat flocks pasture in my fields, salubrious air invigorates my inhabitants, I fly amid fragrant flowers, I rejoice! And I taste the sweetest fruits in my woods: but most important of all, a whole realm has come under my sway again, a kingdom flowing with milk and honey. (Kheraskov 1787, 11)

It should be recalled how persistently throughout the century Russia had been called "the North" and "the septentrional power" (polnoshchnaia, "midnight"), while the Turks were "sons of the South" (poludnia, "midday"), if one is to appreciate how radical this rhetoric was. The appearance of Taurus within the bounds of the Empire, "a kingdom flowing with milk and honey," promised to fundamentally alter Russia's national self-perception and cultural geography. Yet none of these transformations was to be fully realized. The second Russo-Turkish War, starting two months after Catherine's return, delayed the development of the southern provinces, and Potemkin's death in 1791 dealt her plans an irreparable blow. In 1796 the empress herself also died, and all of the southern projects were shelved forever, although they remained in Russian culture as an intention, a lost possibility, a latent—but for that all the stronger—realm of attraction.

∞ 6 ∞

In 1798 S. S. Bobrov's descriptive poem "Taurus" (Tavrida) was published in Nikolaev. It was dedicated to N. S. Mordvinov. Both the place of publication and the dedication were profoundly significant. During Catherine's journey Mordvinov had received the rank of counter-admiral and his fortunes were closely connected to the Crimean peninsula. Despite complications in their personal relations at the end of Potemkin's life, Mordvinov was his true intellectual heir (see Ospovat 1994, 481). After Potemkin's death, it was to Mordvinov that Petrov directed his muse, and the poet's ode to him was one of the first publications by the Nikolaev typography. Throughout the 1790s Mordvinov occupied himself with improvements to Nikolaev, a city whose position seemed to him more fitting as a "second Athens" than Kherson or Ekaterinoslav (Ikonnikov 1873, 70). By 1798 Mordvinov was out of favor with Paul I, who did not care much either for his mother's projects or for her disciples.

Bobrov's "Taurus" is for the most part a description of nature in Crimea. But at the time, any story about Crimean flora was full of tense political meaning:

> Ах! — Тамо рай за ним сияет,…
> Блаженное жилище Флоры,
> Блистающий престол Помоны, —
> В прекрасном Афинее Темпе …
>   под висящими плодами
> *Черешней, вишней, слив и груш;*
> На коих дикий *виноград*,
> Объемля ветви до вершин
> И их приятный взор сугубя
> Своим сиянием багровым.
> Растут без попеченья сами
>
>   (Bobrov 1798, 57–60;)

(Oh! There paradise shines behind it,… / The blessed dwelling of Flora, / The sparkling throne of Pomona,—/ In the beautiful Vale of Tempe … / under hanging fruits / *Cherries, plums and pears*; / On which wild *grapes*, / Entwining branches to the top / Intensifying the pleasant sight / With their purple glow, / Grow by themselves without tending.)

However, this paradisiacal garden has its history, and Bobrov tells of Iphegenia who suffered from the coarse manners of the Sarmatians and Scythians; about the enlightenment brought to the peninsula by the Greeks; about Vladimir's baptism; and about the Muslim conquest of Crimea. According to Bobrov, this conquest led not only to political but to so-to-speak biological degradation:

> Природа резвая дотоле
> На сих горах, на сих лугах
> Оцепенела, побледнела

> Под мрачной сению луны …
> О сколь ужасна перемена
> Тогда была во дни их буйства,
> Тогда ни виноград, ни смоква,
> Ни персики, ни абрикосы
> Природных вкусов не имели. (Ibid., 136–137)

(Henceforth spirited nature / In these hills, in these meadows / Grew frozen, became pale / In the gloomy shade of the moon … / Oh, what a horrible change / Was then, in the days of that mayhem. / Then neither grapes nor figs, / Neither pears nor apricots / Had their natural flavors.)

This interpretation of Crimea's evolution fully corresponds to Mordvinov's views as he expressed them in "An Opinion Related to Crimea" of 1802: "Crimea went into decline as soon as Christians were sent out of the hilly region and Tatars took over their gardens and homes" (Mordvinov 1901, 211). Only the return of the peninsula to the protection of the Christian monarchs of Russia can lead to a revival of the Crimean paradise. Taurus not only takes its place in the Russian Empire, it becomes the jewel in the crown of European civilization. With Crimea's unification with Russia, history completes its logical circle and a Golden Age begins:

> Но если б росски Геркулесы,
> Одушевленные Минервой,
> Ступая на сии хребты.
> Здесь лики водворили муз
> И преселили в мирны сени
> Столетни опыты Европы
> На помощь медленной природе.
> Тогда бы гордый Чатыр-даг
> Меонией прекрасной был бы.
> Салгир чистейшей Иппокреной,
> Тогда исполнился бы тот
> Период славный просвещенья,
> О коем бесподобный Петр
> Пророчески провозвещал.

> Тогда бы музы совершили
> Столь дивно царствие свое
> И *эллиптический* свой путь
> Скончали там, где начинали.
> Из знойного исшед Египта
> В Элладу на брега Эгейски
> И поселясь при гордом Тибре,
> Тамизе, Таге и Секване,
> Дунае, Рене и Неве
> Обратный путь бы восприяли
> И возвратилися в источник.
> Тогда бы новые Омиры,
> Сократы мудры и Платоны
> На горизонт наук взошли
> И потекли бы как светила
> По новому порядку лет. (Bobrov 1798, 163–164)

(But if Russian Herculeses, / Animated by Minerva, / Stepping on these crests, / Established here the assembly of muses / And brought to this peaceful abode / Europe's experience of centuries / To help sluggish nature, / Then prideful Chatyr-dag / Would be beautiful Maeonia / And the Salgir [River] the purest Hippocrene, / Then the period of glorious enlightenment, / About which matchless Peter / Prophetically proclaimed / Would be fulfilled, / And then the muses would marvelously / Complete their kingdom / And their *elliptical* path / Would end there where it began, / Departing sultry Egypt / To Hellas, to the Aegean shores / And settling near the proud Tiber, / Tamiz, Tar, Sequana, / Danube, Rhine, Neva / Would perceive the way back / And return to their source. / Then new Homers, / Wise Socrateses and Platos / Would rise to the horizon of learning / And would stream like a luminary / On the new order of the ages.)

Peter's prophesy that Bobrov mentions was based on the words he said to the ambassador from Hanover, K. Weber, that became widely known in Russia:

> Historians suppose that the cradle of all knowledge was in Greece, from where (due to the vicissitudes of time) it was driven out, and moved to Italy, and then also spread throughout all of the European lands. ... The movement of knowledge indicated above I compare to the circulation of blood in the human body, and it seems to me that with time they will quit their

current dwelling in England, France and Germany, spend a few centuries in our country and then return again to their true fatherland—to Greece. (Weber 1872, 1074–1075)

Bobrov makes substantial corrections to these prophesies. The Muses, as a matter of fact, have no reason to leave Russia and return home to Greece, because the Russians are in a certain (mainly religious) sense Greek themselves, and they have acquired their own Greece in Taurus. From this perspective there is no reason to fight for Constantinople, because the reborn Tauric Chersonese becomes the perfect embodiment of Constantinople.

∽ **7** ∽

The academician Pallas, travelling in Crimea in the 1790s, described the ruins of Chersonese, which in his opinion were located in Quarantine Bay (Karantinnaia bukhta) very near Sevastopol (Pallas 1883, 56). Precisely two centuries later Russia and Ukraine contended over the bay for its part of the Black Sea fleet. On the long list of lands that fell away from Russia in 1991, Crimea remains almost the only loss that it seems still troubles Russian social consciousness.

Explanations for Russians' sharp nostalgia usually boil down either to the mundane "now we have nowhere to vacation" or to the militaristic "Sevastopol—a city of Russian glory." Nevertheless, Crimea is still more accessible for holiday visits than Abkhaziia, ravaged by war, or even the Baltic, places that were just as popular with Soviet vacationers. As far as "Russian glory" goes, Sevastopol of course cannot compete with, say, Poltava. Still, these other places do not evoke emotions anything like those that Crimea does. One may suggest that behind these explanations lies a deeper one, deeper and for that reason less reflected on, that possessing Crimea constitutes the crown of Russia's historical mission, its civilizing task. It is worth contemplating how these cultural and symbolic concepts—literally, those "of the times of the Ochakovs and the conquest of Crimea"—come to life in the consciousness of Russians today.

Without pretending to an exhaustive answer to the extremely complex issue of the mechanisms that "retranslate" cultural memory, we make so bold as to put forward one suggestion. The decisive factor in preserving the memory of Potemkin's projects in mass consciousness, in our opinion, is the architectural design of Crimean sanatoriums and Pioneer camps. The world of white houses by the sea, gravel paths among laurel bushes, alleys of Cyprus trees with plaster vases and statues, buglers in crimson kerchiefs at morning line-up, vacationers strolling in light-colored pajamas—this was our ancient Greece, our paradise, even though it may have been cleansed from excessive ethnic diversity by the father of the peoples after the war. But it was accessible—available through a tourist group from the trade-union or via a directive from the Pioneer organization for a citizen of the empire. Here he or she could rest peacefully, for on guard (na reide) atop the waves was the Black Sea fleet of the Red Banner, with sailors in white and blue uniforms and rimless caps for whom girls in far-off villages were pining. Precisely in such things do the everyday and militaristic interpretations of Crimea's allure for Russians become indistinguishable.

Vladimir Papernyi's book *Culture Two* describes the sharp and the climactically unexplained "warming" of Soviet, and especially Muscovite, architecture in the 1930s, at the height of totalitarianism. Architects seem to have ceased to notice the winter, worrying only about coolness, moisture, greenery. In Papernyi's words, "cultural sensation of the world seemed to slip southward by several dozen degrees, from sixty degrees latitude to at least those of the Mediterranean" (Papernyi 1996, 171). It is hard to say if these were the latitudes of the Mediterranean or of the Black Sea, but in any case it is clear that Catherine and Potemkin's dream did come to pass, if only strangely and temporarily. Constantinople was never attained, although the empire turned to the South and the midday genius transformed "happy Moscow" into "a kingdom flowing with milk and honey."

CHAPTER 4

Eden in the Tauride Palace:
Potemkin's Last Project

∽ **1** ∽

Semen Bobrov's long poem in which the conquest of Crimea is interpreted not as a stage in the "Greek Project" but as the symbolic apotheosis of Russian expansion in the south was only published after Catherine II's death. The late empress would hardly have approved of this kind of revision of her cherished plans. Until her last days the empress remained convinced both of their feasibility and of their benefit for Russia (see Ragsdale 1988). At the same time her notion of how long it might take to realize them fluctuated, depending on changes in the political situation. One of these changes occurred during 1789. On January 26, after having ordered that triumphal gates be built for Potemkin in Tsarskoe Selo, Catherine commanded that they be inscribed with the line from Petrov's ode "On the Taking of Khotin": "You will descend to the Temple of Sophia amid applause." While giving these instructions, the empress commented that "He [Potemkin] will be in Tsargrad [i.e., Constantinople] this year" (Khrapovitskii 1874, 245). However, on October 10 of the same year she made quite a different prediction: "On the Greeks: they can be revived. Constantine is a good boy; in thirty years he will go from Sevastopol' to

Tsargrad. Now we are breaking the horns [i.e., Ottoman power] and then it will be easier for him to smash them" (ibid., 312).

Thus the time frame for realizing the "Greek Project" grew from one to thirty years, clearly far beyond the time the empress could aspire to rule. This change might have been caused by a variety of circumstances—the not very auspicious course of the Turkish and Swedish wars, the start of the Revolution in France, and the revived hostility of European powers toward Russia's expansionist plans. But the main factor was apparently the danger that Catherine perceived in the events transpiring in Poland. In the words of S. M. Solov'ev, "the Eastern question lost its importance for a while [and] then Polish question took first place" (Solov'ev 1863, 251).

In the second half of the 1780s, Poland, which it seemed had completely vanished from the European stage due to the partitions and to inner strife, suddenly acquired political existence once again. At the opening of the Sejm in late 1788, the patriotic party that demanded the replacement of the archaic aristocratic system with a more effective governmental system, as well as political and social reforms and the creation of a national army, acquired enormous influence. The leaders considered the only solution to be an alliance with Prussia. The Sejm demanded the withdrawal of Russian troops from Poland and prohibited Russia from using Polish territory for communicating with the army fighting the Turks.

Russia, which was waging war on two fronts, had to accept these demands. In May 1789 the occupying Russian garrison was ordered to leave Poland, where it had been quartered for a quarter of a century. Before concluding peace with the Turks and Swedes, Catherine strove to avoid yet another open armed conflict. Nevertheless, it was clear to her that the empire would be acquiring yet another hostile neighbor on her western border, and one which at any moment might demand a review of the results of the partition (see Lord 1915, 92–111). Russian diplomacy had to work out a new course that would take into account the newly changed power alignments. This task also demanded a fundamental ideological reorientation.

The new points of reference for Russian politics were again outlined by Potemkin. However, his significant loss of influence on the empress and then his sudden death evidently prevented the official and conclusive formulation of his ideas. Still, Potemkin's exceptionally interesting projects defined the

Chapter 4: Eden in the Tauride Palace

Figure 9 Portrait of G. A. Potemkin-Tavricheskii by Johann-Baptist von Lampi the Elder (c. 1790). Hermitage Museum, St. Petersburg.

symbolism of the celebration that he organized for the empress in the Tauride Palace on April 28, 1791.

Richard Wortman dedicated several pages of his study *Scenarios of Power: Myth and Ceremony in the Russian Monarchy* to Potemkin's celebration (Wortman 1994, 143–146). His analysis centers on the extremely detailed "Description of the Celebration in the House of Prince Potemkin" by Gavriil Derzhavin. Wortman comments that the personal intonations characteristic of Derzhavin only became usual for ceremonial texts in the nineteenth century (ibid., 143; for an analysis of the philosophical and cosmological ideas reflected in the celebration, both in the Tauride Palace's architecture and in Derzhavin's "Description," see Pogosian 1997). This "personal slant" of Derzhavin's "Description" might be connected with the fact that Potemkin's celebration, despite its scale, characteristic of the prince, and despite the participation of the royal family, was not, strictly speaking, official. Its extent and program were clearly marked as belonging to a faithful subject of the great sovereign, one who was offering her a tribute of love and thankfulness for her unparalleled beneficence. On the other hand, the pretext for the celebration was an event of utter state importance—a great victory of Russian arms. "The lord of all-powerful Rome ... could not have created a bigger house or have presented greater magnificence for his celebration. It seemed that all the wealth of Asia and all the art of Europe were combined to adorn the temple of celebrations for the Great Catherine. There is hardly [another] private person [living] today who has such a vast building as his dwelling place," wrote Derzhavin (I, 391, note). In 1808, when editing the "Description" for the fourth volume of his works, the poet changed this phrase to: "There is hardly [another] ruler [living] today. ..." It was precisely the opposition and connection between "private person" and "ruler" that constituted the main tension in the celebration's meaning.

By celebrating the taking of Izmail in his own home, Potemkin was declaring himself the single party responsible for the victory. Suvorov, the one who had been in direct command of the assault, had been sent off to inspect the Swedish border. "The prince [Potemkin] urged mistrust of the Swedish king," Catherine's secretary Khrapovitskii wrote in his diary. "They say that this was to keep Suvorov away from the celebration and from displaying the captured pashas" (Khrapovitskii 1874, 362; cf. Ekaterina i Potemkin 1997, 455).[1] However, Potemkin's initiative also had another possibly even more

---

1   V. S. Lopatin, who has done much to clarify the true facts of Potemkin's biography, falls into excessive apologetics for his hero when he asserts that Suvorov's departure from Petersburg was not connected with Potemkin's desire to exclude his renowned subordinate from the celebration but due to military necessity (see Lopatin 1992, 230–231). There was no such crucial necessity that would have prevented delaying Suvorov's departure for three days, and furthermore, there was nothing to keep Potemkin from mentioning Suvorov's role in storming Izmail during the celebration.

Chapter 4: Eden in the Tauride Palace

important aspect. The "privatizing" of the celebrations allowed their organizer to affirm not only his version of the Izmail triumph but also of Russian politics as a whole in the minds of the empress and of elite Petersburg society.

Potemkin sent Catherine his first dispatch about the taking of Izmail on December 18, 1790, and on January 11 he began to lobby for permission to return to Petersburg (Ekaterina i Potemkin 1997, 444, 447). But His Serene Highness (as Potemkin came to be called) could not wait, and two days later informed her that he was going to inspect shipbuilding on the Dnieper "so that once I receive your permission I shall already be that much farther along on the way to Petersburg, and shall thus shorten my journey" (ibid., 449; Catherine 2004, 378[2]). However, Potemkin did not leave Iassy and continued to bombard Catherine with pathetic requests that he be allowed to come. Having received permission to leave the theater of military action as long as his departure would not harm the start of peace negotiations, the prince set off for the capital, where he arrived on February 28 (Khrapovitskii 1874, 358). According to contemporary memoirs, reports concerning Platon Zubov, Catherine's latest favorite, and his increasing influence on the empress were what hastened his arrival in Petersburg. As Derzhavin recalled, Potemkin, "on leaving the army told his retinue that he was unwell and was going to Petersburg *to pull some teeth* [zuby dergat', i.e., to remove Zubov]" (Derzhavin IV, 617).

Despite the recent successes in the Turkish War and the already signed peace with Sweden, Russia's political position in the winter and spring of 1791 was far from satisfactory. She was threatened with an incalculably more powerful coalition. The English fleet was preparing to sail to the Baltic, Prussia had declared a mobilization, and in Poland anti-Russian sentiments were growing. Many of Catherine's closest advisors tried to convince her to yield to this pressure and accept unfavorable conditions in the peace with Turkey. Potemkin, who was well-informed about the true condition of the army and who did not believe in the possibility of "recruits battling Englishmen" (Khrapovitskii 1874, 361), added his voice to this chorus. While still in the South, he advised her to cede territorial acquisitions in Moldavia to Poland, open talks with Prussia, and to "stroke" England by enticing her with profitable

---

2   References to Catherine 2004 indicate that the translations of the Catherine-Potemkin correspondence have been taken from this edition.

trade agreements (Ekaterina i Potemkin 1997, 402, 442–43). After arriving in Petersburg, he used all of his influence to force Catherine "to correspond with the Prussian king," and together with Chancellor Bezborodko he also compiled a "memorandum to prevent war" (Khrapovitskii 1874, 359, 361).

Catherine, however, was able to withstand both domestic and foreign pressure. As Robert Lord writes, Catherine "won a complete victory, perhaps the most brilliant of her reign, thanks to her own splendid courage and constancy" (Lord 1915, 190). Finally, due to strong opposition to war with Russia that was deftly boosted by Russian diplomacy, the English government backed down from its ultimatum and agreed to accept conditions for peace that were much more acceptable to Catherine, and these were quickly approved by the Turks as well (see ibid., 153–191; Madariaga 1981, 416–421; and others). "A courier with the news that England apparently … will not begin war" arrived in Petersburg on April 30, two days after the celebration in Potemkin's residence (Khrapovitskii 1874, 362).

It was in these extremely dramatic personal and political conditions that Potemkin anxiously prepared for the celebration. The completion of the construction of the house, the outfitting the park and space in front of the palace, the digging of canals, the interior decoration of the space being prepared for theater and ballet—all took place under the direct supervision of His Serene Highness over the course of two months following his arrival in Petersburg. The celebration was originally planned for Catherine's birthday, April 21, which in 1791 fell on St. Thomas Monday, the second Monday after Easter. But even Potemkin's organizational genius could not overcome all obstacles, and it was necessary to put it off for a week. Nonetheless, by April 28 all preparations had been completed.

In the words of Ia. K. Grot, this "festival, whose unprecedented magnificence was supposed to eclipse all earlier celebrations of this type" was conceived by His Serene Highness as "the final word to prove to the empress that no one could compare with him in his devotion to her" (Derzhavin I, 378). However, for all of Potemkin's love for luxury and for hyperbolically rich ceremonies, he could hardly have counted on blinding Catherine with it. His goal was to once again snatch the political initiative away from the new favorite and to show that he was capable as before of dreaming up and carrying out the most grandiose undertakings. Of course, he could share the main idea of these undertakings in his correspondence with the empress as well as in personal conversations. At the same time, a celebration could do away with the suggestion of his projects' immediate diplomatic or court jockeying and reveal their fundamental ideological dimension. Potemkin's conception of Russia's state mission was to acquire visual and graphic embodiment. Considering the fact that His Serene Highness died less than six months later, one could say that the celebration of April 28 represented his last political testament.

∾ **2** ∾

Potemkin's rise in the mid-1770s was connected with his "Eastern System," on which basis Catherine II's "Greek Project" took shape. In order to impress the empress just as strongly with his new conceptions, he had to propose ideas that were qualitatively different from his former project yet retaining definite continuity with it.

In 1779, on the occasion of the birth of Grand Prince Konstantin Pavlovich, Potemkin had staged a celebration in honor of Catherine at his dacha in Ozerki. This was wholly staged in the spirit of stylized antiquity characteristic of "Greek Project" imagery. Ia. K. Grot described it on the basis of V. P. Petrov's description:

> The place where supper was prepared represented a cave in the Caucasus Mountains (i.e., one of the territories that had been entrusted to the host); the cave was decorated with myrtle and laurel trees, among which roses and other flowers were entwined; a stream that rushed down from the top of the mountain and crashed into cliffs cooled the air. During supper, which was arranged according to ancient customs, to the sounds of an organ a chorus sang stanzas composed in the *Hellenogreek* language in honor of the glorious visitor; Petrov, who enjoyed Potemkin's special patronage, translated them into Russian. (Derzhavin I, 379)

The role that Potemkin had played in the "Greek Project" created a persistent reputation among contemporaries and affected the perception of all his plans and actions. In his ode "On the Taking of Izmail" written in early 1791, Derhavin addressed the European powers who were trying to intercede on behalf of Turkey. His admonitions were fully in keeping with Catherine's long-time dreams of a resurrected Greece and a renewed Christian republic that had once been prophesized by Henry IV and M. de Sully:

> <...> Росс рожден судьбою
> От варварских хранить вас [европейцев] уз,
> Темиров попирать ногою,
> Блюсть ваших от Омаров муз,[3]
> Отмстить крестовые походы,
> Очистить Иордански воды,
> Священный гроб освободить,
> Афинам возвратить Афину,
> Град Константинов Константину
> И мир Афету[4] водворить.
>
> Афету мир? - о труд избранный,
> Достойнейший его детей,
> Великими людьми желанный!

(Ross [the Russian] is born by fate / To preserve you [Europeans] from barbarian bonds, / To trample the Tamerlanes underfoot, / To protect your muses from Omar, / To avenge the crusades, / To purify Jordan's waters, / To liberate the Holy Sepulchre, / To return Athena to Athens, / The city of Constantine to Konstantin / And to establish peace for Japeth. // Peace for Japeth? O chosen mission / Which is most worthy of his children, / Desired by great men!)

Later, while compiling the "Explanations" to his own works, Derzhavin indicated that "the city of Athens should be returned to the goddess Minerva, by which is understood Catherine," and "Constantinople should be subject to the rule of Grand Prince Konstantin Pavlovich." He also clarifies that "Henry IV and other great men wanted to establish peace in Europe" (ibid., 357). At approximately this time a Russian translation appeared of *The Peace of Europe... or A Project for Universal Conciliation* by Ange Goudar, completed "in the encampment near Ochakov in 1788" (SKRK I, 262, № 1662).

Somewhat unexpectedly for a military ode, but fully foreseeable given the political situation at the beginning of 1791, when everyone was nervously expecting an attack by England and Prussia, "On the Taking of Izmail"

---

[3] Caliph Omar (or Umar) (579–644), who led a Muslim army to conquer Alexandria, reportedly had its famous library burned in 642.

[4] Noah's son Japeth, commonly believed to be the father of the Europeans.

Chapter 4: Eden in the Tauride Palace

culminates with an apotheosis of universal peace in which victorious Russia occupies its worthy place.

When he received the order to describe Potemkin's celebration, Derzhavin in general interpreted it in this key. "In surprise one seems to find oneself in flourishing Greece," he wrote, "where the odeum, lyceum, stages, exedras and theaters from various cities and places gathered in this building have been restored to life" (ibid., 390). The basic cluster of metaphors associated with the "Greek Project" again appeared in the choruses that he wrote for the occasion. Fourteen years earlier Catherine had not been able to take her grandsons on the Crimean journey; now their presence at the celebration seemed to sanctify the ideas that had been connected with them:

> Кто Александр великий.
> Кто будет Константин,...
> Тот громы к персам несть.
> Сей вновь построит Рим. (Ibid., 402)

(Who is Alexander the Great, / Who will be Constantine,... / This one will take thunder to the Persians / That one will again build Rome.)

The subject here is the capital of the Eastern Roman Empire—Constantinople. The mythology of resurrected Greece was also the mythology of the earthly paradise that Potemkin was still trying to recreate in his Tauride and "New Russian" territories. Now the task was to reproduce this theoretical Edenic Greece in the Tauride Palace. It was no accident that, when presenting the palace to Potemkin, Catherine wrote that she was giving him "an earthly paradise, as you call this dacha that you requested of me" (Ekaterina i Potemkin 1997, 436; Pogosian 1997, 459–460).

The celebration in classical taste that Potemkin had arranged twelve years earlier in Ozerki took place in late June, while the celebration of the taking of Izmail—at the end of April (in New Style, early July and May, respectively). Considering St. Petersburg's climate, the difference is quite substantial. In the words of one memoirist, "for the whole day" of the celebration "it was raining and the cold was appreciable" (Kir'iak 1867, 679–680; on Kir'iak as memoirist, see Fomenko 1999). Of course, it was much harder and more costly to imitate lush southern nature in the "cold, partly rainy, partly snowy" Baltic spring (ibid.) than in the middle of summer, but this also emphasized the creative, transformative will of the celebration's organizer and demiurge.

Derzhavin (I, 409) exclaimed:

> The highest possible palms, with their stately, regular stalks wrapped to the very tops with what looked like stars, burn like flaming columns. Aromatic groves with trees laden with bitter oranges, oranges and lemons; green, dark red and yellow grapes, hanging by their stems in flaming clusters, and in the shadows along black flowerbeds, lilies and tulips, pineapples and other fruits whose colorful blaze offers the astonished gaze indescribable variety and wonder. ...

T. Kir'iak, describing the celebration in a private letter, left a more prosaic interpretation of this spectacle:

> The garden consists of several knolls, thickly planted with lemon, bitter orange and other similar trees, of which several have fruit; but on the majority of trees there were fruits fabricated from glass, for example plums, cherries, and grapes of various colors of which whole clusters were also made of glass, like lanterns. From among the flowerbeds rise imitation cedars the tops of which, covered with leaves, support the ceiling; without them, judging by the size of the building, it seems like it would not hold. The pathways, whose sides were covered with turf, also attracted the eye. All of them were covered with pineapples, water-melons and other melons that were of a natural color, shape and size. Their leaves and stems were made of tin, and the fruit of glass; all of the fruits had a fire inside. (Kir'iak 1867, 687)

It is obvious that neither Potemkin, who ordered all of these imitation fruits, nor Derzhavin, who praised them, had any idea of deceiving anyone. The point was to symbolically transform the space, to create a kind of theatrical decoration that would let the guests feel like participants in a mythological performance (see the analogous interpretation of the so-called "Potemkin villages" in Panchenko 1983). The southern plants decorating this winter garden testified that the opulent land that had produced these fruits was also part of imperial space. In the words of another memoirist, "the abundance and taste reigned everywhere, and the fruits that one saw in the winter garden made of glass appeared on the tables in their natural form, in great profusion" (Derzhavin I, 416; for the full texts of memoirs published in 1808 by the Hamburg journal *Minerva*, see Potemkin 1852; Potemkin 1991). Derzhavin, who in one of the poems that went into the "Description" described the celebratory feast as a joint production of the various parts of boundless Russia, reserved a special line for "the sweet fruits" of Taurus, the land Potemkin had won for the empire (Derzhavin I, 417).

Apropos, the living plants and trees that were abundantly planted in the garden required a special controlled climate. The air was heated by stoves "of which the winter garden required no small number" and which were "hidden behind a proliferation of mirrors that were of one size and of extraordinary cost" (Derzhavin I, 388, note). The incredible number of mirrors that all who wrote about the celebration noted not only hid the practical necessities but also contributed to the illusion of amplified space. "A facing colonnade separates the garden from the gallery, whose ornaments are the more brilliant because a great number of them are made up of mirrors. At both ends of this colonnade great mirrors adorned with greenery and flowers were placed between the last two pillars. They made it seem three times longer," wrote Kir'iak (1867, 685). With the help of this pattern of infinite reflections that multiplied the light of 140,000 lamps and 20,000 wax candles (Derzhavin I, 408, note), the garden and palace were symbolically expanded to represent the universe.[5]

According to Kir'iak, the main hall of the festivities represented

> some kind of temple. To lend magnificence to this temple and its entryway, in the last week the prince gave the order to place two huge columns painted to look like red marble in front of the aforementioned gates. This was done with a kind of creative flair. … The temple or pantheon itself is in the shape of a square with cut corners, but there are only two main walls, on the right and left hand, while the other sides are taken up by columns holding up small choruses with a vault. (Kir'iak 1867, 682–683)

The entrance to the hall recalled "the royal gates in the big court church" (ibid.).

The motifs of a classical temple were again exploited and intensified in the center of the festivities' conceptual space: "In the garden facing the very center of the gallery was erected a kind of altar on eight columns of more than an arshin [c. 28 inches] in diameter and as tall as the columns in the gallery. On top was a cupola, and the floor was of grey marble. In the middle of this altar, on a pedestal of red marble, stood a full-sized image of Catherine, carved

---

5 On the metaphor of the garden as the universe, see Pogosian 1997, 456–471; on the mirrored grotto and mirrored pyramid and the optical effects they created, see Kir'iak 1867, 687–688.

Figure 10 and 11 Catherine II the Legislatress (1789) by F. I. Shubin. Russian Museum, St. Petersburg. *Below* – The winter garden of the Tauride Palace (1792) by F. D. Danilov.

out of the purest white marble, in the guise of a goddess and in long Roman robes" (ibid., 686).

In the more expressive if less clear description by Derzhavin, a guest at the celebration "imperceptibly approaches a round altar raised on steps and surrounded by eight columns that support its dome. Around it are fixed jasper chalices on stands, and above hang lamps and chains of flowers, and wreaths; on a pedestal of porphyry amid the columns shines the image of a goddess of pure marble and with a golden inscription, the one through whose generosity this home was built" (Derzhavin I, 286).

During the first Russo-Turkish War, Petrov had written that the liberated Greeks "in a temple of freedom, peace and joy ... should honor the image of this Athena [Pallada, i.e., Pallas] for an age" (Petrov I, 77), and Voltaire had predicted that "Phidases and Zeuxises" would cover Hellas with images of Catherine II (Ekaterina 1971, 71). Twenty years later, in the absence of a liberated Hellas, a temple of peace and joy was put up in the northern capital, and the image of Athena for the altar—in the place of the Greeks Zeuxis and Phidias—was fashioned by the sculptor from Archangel, Fedot Ivanovich Shubin.

∽ **3** ∽

Caught up in the circle of classical associations that he knew so well, Derzhavin touched on other symbolic aspects of the celebration, although with less detail. Nevertheless it is these aspects that lent the entire event its distinctive conceptual dynamics.[6] The celebration, which began with the appearance of the royal family, was opened with a quadrille "composed of twenty-four pairs of the most famous and most beautiful women, young ladies and young men" (Derzhavin I, 395). According to Derzhavin, "they were dressed in white clothing" (ibid.). Kir'iak writes that "the cavaliers were clothed in Spanish dress, the ladies in Greek" (Kir'iak 1867, 691). The quadrille began with a "Polish dance" to whose melody Derzhavin wrote his celebrated chorus "Thunder of Victory Resound" (Derzhavin I, 395–398). Then this "march became a Greek (dance)" that "lasted less than a quarter of an hour," after which "the theatrical performance began" (Kir'iak 1867, 692).

After the performance the dancing was renewed, and an elegant quadrille choreographed by the famous ballet-master Charles Le Pique was succeeded by "dances to Little Russian and Russian folksongs (prostym pesniam), in which one followed another"; Derzhavin adds that "Since those who love their fatherland love their own folk singing more than the foreign, it was very satisfying to see the monarch's approval of this entertainment" (Derzhavin I, 412). Potemkin also organized a similar amusement for his guests in a distant part of the garden

---

6   We do not touch here on the whole circle of "Orientalist" imagery that is very important for understanding both this celebration as well as the "poetics" of Potemkin's behavior, but which is not directly relevant to the current discussion (see Pogosian 1997, 459–462).

where "many sailors and rowers, richly dressed" were to perform rowing songs out on the ponds; but as Kir'iak notes, "the bad weather did not permit this" (Kir'iak 1867, 694).

Derzhavin explains the changeover to folk music with exclusively patriotic considerations, but it is characteristic that in the first place he lists "Little Russian"(Ukrainian) songs. It is natural to assume that this type of song was sung most often. Moreover, Derzhavin included in his "Description" an example of Little Russian song lyrics, "Na berezhku u stavka" (On the Shore by the Pond) (Derzhavin I, 413). According to Ia. K. Grot, "one may find this Little Russian song in I. Gur'ianov's 'Songbook' (part IV, Moscow, 1835, p. 114), where it is listed under the title 'A Cossack Rewarded [by a Kiss] for Saving a Girl from Drowning'" (Derzhavin I, 413).[7]

It is not fully clear if this was the same song that Kir'iak had in mind when he wrote that "after the departure [of the empress] they sang, with all of the instruments [as accompaniment], a certain Little Russian song that was the favorite of the prince [Potemkin] and now of the whole city" (Kir'iak 1867, 694). In any case, there is no doubt that the Ukrainian element was significant in the structure of the celebration. The movement from classical to folk motifs, especially Ukrainian ones, had in part already been prefigured by the earlier theatrical performance.

"The curtain opened," wrote Derzhavin. "The stage and place of action was illuminated by a radiant sun, in the midst of which shone Catherine II's monogram in green laurels. Dancers representing male and female peasants performed. Raising their hands to this noble luminary, they demonstrated their most heartfelt feelings with their movements" (Derzhavin I, 405). The performance's further presentations clearly demonstrated the main reason for their gratitude.

According to a contemporary account published in the Hamburg journal, the first comedy performed at Potemkin's celebration was called "Les faux amants" (The False Lovers). There is no such play listed in the bibliography of

---

7   In the article "On Russian Folk Singing," published about the same time, Derzhavin's close friend N. A. L'vov made a clear distinction between Great and Little Russian songs: "The character of Little Russian songs and melodies are quite different from the Russian: there is more melody in them than in our dancing songs; but I do not know of any Little Russian choral (armonicheskaia) song that could equal our 'drawn-out' (protiazhnye) songs" (L'vov 1994, 314).

eighteenth-century French plays, but there is one called "Le faux amant" (The False Lover). Its full title is "The Servant-Aristocrat, Or the False Lover, or Pride Punished," and belongs to the pen of Madame A.-L.-B. Beaunoir; it was first staged in Paris in 1776 (see Brenner 1947, 175, № 3538). Unfortunately, we have not been able to locate a copy of this play, but there is another work whose performance at the celebration can be established with complete certainly.

The author of the play "Le Marchand de Smyrne" (The Smyrna Merchant) was the famous French playwright and aphorist Nicolas Chamfort. Written in 1770, it had been performed in the Comédie Français, enjoyed great success and provoked sharp criticism from Grimm and La Harpe (Arnaud 1992, 50–51; Teppe 1950, 100–101). The main feature of the comedy was its radically anti-feudal and egalitarian pathos. In fact, much later, Chamfort, who had become one of the most popular publicists of the French Revolution, was accused during the Jacobin terror of sympathy for aristocrats, and in his justification he cited this very play. He wrote:

> Chamfort—an aristocrat!—those who know me would burst out laughing. ... Aristocrat! One whose love for equality was always the reigning passion, an inborn, unconquerable and automatic instinct! One who more than twenty years ago brought "The Smyrna Merchant" to the theater, which even today is often performed on stage and in which nobles and aristocrats of any kind are sold cheap, because they are worth nothing. (Arnaud 1992, 246).

For all of the excessive rhetoric of these declarations, made under compulsion, Chamfort's essential point is true (and literally so). The plot of his comedy is quite uncomplicated. The noble Turk Hassan, whose freedom had once been purchased by an anonymous altruistic Frenchman, takes an oath to buy a Christian out of slavery once every year. In fulfilling his oath, by chance he buys out his benefactor Dorval, whose ship had been captured and who had been sold into slavery together with his companions. On the same day, Hassan's equally noble wife buys the freedom of a Christian woman who unexpectedly turns out to be Dorval's beloved. Hassan, touched, purchases all of Dorval's companions in misfortune and gives them their freedom, and together they all celebrate the union of the newly liberated lovers.

At the center of the play is the scene of the slaves being sold by the merchant Kaled. The price for which the greedy slave trader sells his goods paradoxically reflects the actual worth of each person. A German baron, a Spanish hidalgo, a jurist from Padua, and learned connoisseur of genealogy are all worth nothing because they are incapable of genuine labor. On the other hand, the servant "able to work, till the land, and … [who] is no nobleman" is truly worth good money. The moralist Hassan cannot believe that among Europeans there exist "such people who do not study anything, relying on their natural right to lead their lives in idleness at the cost of their near ones" (Chamfort 1789, 43).[8]

It would be very tempting, especially in view of the possible connection to the title of Madame Beaunoir's comedy, to see the choice of repertoire for the celebration as the "upstart" Potemkin's challenge to the aristocratic conceit of his more pedigreed rivals at court. However, such a suggestion must only be put forward with great caution, insofar as it is quite unclear what exactly the audience saw on the stage that had been set up in the palace.

An anonymous memoirist from the journal *Minerva* calls "The Smyrna Merchant" a "comedy" (see Derzhavin I, 404, note), while Derzhavin speaks of it as a ballet and only remarks on the scene when the slaves are sold. It is not impossible that this is not a slip. As early as 1771 the German composer Georg Joseph Vogler had written an operetta of the same name based on Chamfort's play, which was "in the popular Italian style with brilliant arias, two bravura arias, a duet and trio" (Schafhäutl 1979, 14). One of the overtures to the operetta earned very broad popularity and was often sung separately.

It is doubtful that Derzhavin would have confused a ballet with an operetta, but it is possible that at the celebration it was not Volger's complete work that was performed, but only a balletic divertissement. However, here we encounter another contradiction. In *Minerva* the performance is described as consisting of "two French comedies and two ballets" (Derzhavin I, 404, note), whereas Derzhavin's "Description"—depending on how we qualify "The

---

8   The history of "The Smyrna Merchant"'s reception in Russia is unique and very interesting. The first reworked version of the play appeared almost immediately after the original's appearance, in 1771, under the title "Good Deeds Gain Hearts" (Blagodeianiia priobretaiut serdtsa). V. S. Sopikov ascribes this translation to A. S. Shishkov. Then in 1780 a comedy entitled "The Smyrna Merchant" (Smirinskoi kupets), translated by V. V. Lazarev, appeared in the journal *Chto-nibud'* (*Something*). Finally, in 1789, another anonymous translation with the title "A Good Deed Returned" (Vozvrashchennoe blagodeianie) was published by the University Typography (see SKRK I, 106, № 591; III, 484, № 591; I, 172, № 1045; III, 485, № 1045; Pukhov 1999, 183–184). We do not discuss these texts here insofar as at the Potemkin celebration the comedy was presumably performed in French.

Smyrna Merchant"—notes two ballets and one comedy or two comedies and one ballet. The contradiction disappears only if we count Chamfort's play twice and suggest that the performance of the comedy ended with the ballet, for which the impressive scene of the slave market was chosen.

The interpretation that Derzhavin gives to the story of the "Smyrna merchant who trades in slaves of all nationalities" is unambiguous:

> To the honor of Russian arms there was not one of our fellow Russians who was taken prisoner by this venal barbarian [in the play]. What a change in our political situation! Has it been so long since Ukraine and its lower reaches were subjected to the incessant raids of predatory hoards? Was it so long ago? Oh, how pleasant is the recollection of past misfortunes when they have passed by like a horrible dream! Now we take pleasure in a most joyous celebration of our well-being. Oh, posterity! Know that all of this is the creation of Catherine's spirit. (Ibid., 405–406)

Thus the ballet that demonstrated the peasants' gratitude to the "radiant sun," as well as Chamfort's comedy (independent of the question what the select public saw), were taken to glorify the joint achievement of Potemkin and Catherine—freeing the southern territories of the empire from Turkish overlordship and the threat of Tatar raids. Four years earlier, during the empress's journey to Crimea, the Ukrainian element had been virtually absent in the symbolic presentations that Potemkin staged. At that time he was more interested in the possibilities of a Greco-Scythian synthesis. Now focus had shifted precisely to "Ukraine and its lower reaches," that is, the territories where Cossack troops had been settled.

We do not know whether the balletic peasants who thanked the empress were dressed in a conventionally idyllic way or in folk—Russian or Ukrainian—costumes; Derzhavin does not say, and the more observant but less eloquent Kir'iak did not attend the performance (Kir'iak 1867, 692). He did, however, notice the uniforms of the "extremely huge footmen" (gaiduki) who served the guests during the feast who were dressed "in Polish or Greek" dress (ibid., 693). Like the characters in others of Potemkin's masquerades, these footmen lead us to the very center of the political problem that was occupying Potemkin.

4

Potemkin's position on the Polish question is almost impossible to untangle. During the whole of this period he proposed various, sometimes mutually exclusive, plans of action, and with his characteristic energy and decisiveness quickly set about to realize them. Moreover, if some of his ideas succeeded one another, he would undertake other steps in opposite directions, as if wanting to have responses at the ready for any contingency.

In 1787–1788 Potemkin's main idea was to conclude a Russian-Polish alliance under which a significant part of the Polish forces would merge into the Russian army, then fighting Turkey under his command. In return Russia would make financial subsidies available to Poland and agree to several important government reforms there. Potemkin simultaneously held negotiations with the reform-minded King Stanisław Poniatowski and with leaders of the aristocratic opposition, such as Hetman F. Branicki, who saw dependence on Russia precisely as a guarantee against any kind of change. Most likely, in maintaining contacts with both sides Potemkin saw a way to preserve his future freedom of action. At the same time, this policy indicates that Poland's internal problems seemed of little importance to him compared with the possibility of uniting military forces and having Polish forces under his command.

One may get a general notion of the way Potemkin saw the Russian-Polish union from two notes he wrote to Catherine (Ekaterina 1874, 269–280). These memoranda are undated, but according to their content probably relate to the same period. Still, we do not have enough basis for a firm dating, insofar as Potemkin kept producing many plans of this type from 1787 practically until his death. Potemkin proposed beginning by forming Polish national brigades on whose basis a pro-Russian confederation could arise. Potemkin had attempted to realize this idea already at the time of Catherine's journey south in the spring of 1787 (see Lord 1915, 515). In a letter to Catherine of December 25, he recalled his achievement in creating the alliance with Austria and emphasized that his current proposals were a continuation of the same policy:

> You deign to mention that the alliance with the [Austrian] emperor is my doing. This proceeded from my zeal. It was from this as well that the Polish alliance in Kiev also sprang. ... You may see what sort of alliance this would have been from the plan enclosed herewith. They would already have been fighting for us by now, and would have been helpful, for the harder we come down on the enemy, the easier we'll achieve our goal. My counsel always proceeded from fervor. If I am out of place, then, of course in the future I'll only speak on those matters that have been entrusted to me. (Ekaterina i Potemkin 1997, 257–258; Catherine 2004, 215)

The tone of this letter indicates that Potemkin knew that his plans were not supported by Catherine, who was extremely skeptical toward the Poles and the utility of an alliance with them. However, he continued to insist, arguing that he could and must head a Polish national armed force. He wrote on February 5:

> How good it would be, matushka, if we could quickly come to a decision about the Poles. And so, to entice the entire nation, they must be promised parts of the Turkish lands, for without this it cannot be done. When you deign to approve new brigades for their nation's army, order that the one given to Count Branicki be attached to my army. What marvelous people and, one might say, horsemen. It is a pity that you are not favorably disposed to giving me command, if not over the cavalry of the entire nation, then at least over one brigade. I'm as much a Pole as they are. I would do much good. (Ibid., 265; cf. 260, 268; on the plan for a "people's militia," put together by Branicki, probably with Potemkin's participation, see Ekaterina 1874, 274–280; Catherine 2004, 230)

As V. S. Lopatin justly remarks, "by calling himself a Pole, Potemkin is referring to his descent from Smolensk *szlachta*" (i.e., Polish gentry) (Ekaterina i Potemkin 1997, 807). Of course, in emphasizing the Polish element of his genealogy so hyper-bolically, Potemkin did not cease to think of himself as Great Russian. Most likely, he meant that he could play the role of a link between the two peoples, the more so since the above-named Count Branicki was married to one of his nieces.

Potemkin bought up estates in Poland with tremendous eagerness and became one of the largest landholders in the republic, which gave him the right to vote in the Sejm and the status of a Polish magnate. In the already-cited letter of December 25, he wrote that he had purchased Liubomirskii's estate in Poland, "since by becoming its proprietor this conferred upon me the right to participate in their affairs and in the military command" (ibid., 257; on Potemkin's Polish properties, see Lord 1915, 514–515; Catherine 2004, 215).

Catherine was not at all convinced by her correspondent's argument. Partially following Potemkin's urgings, at the same time she wrote that: "… Benefits may be promised; [but] if we oblige the Poles like this and they stay true to us, this will be the first instance of fidelity in their history. … Accepting them into the army and putting them in positions of responsibility should be under [your] personal supervision, because among them reign frivolity, a lack of discipline, and the spirit of revolt" (Ekaterina i Potemkin 1997, 271). Potemkin tried to object: "As far as discipline," he wrote, "matushka, be assured that I am telling you the truth: in their military institutions it is observed even to the point of pedantry. On the personal level they have people of exceptional courage and no few outstanding people in the other services" (ibid., 274).

He was not, however, able to convince the empress. The project for an agreement did not contain any substantive concessions to Poland and could not put a stop to the growing anti-Russian feeling. "Things are bad in Poland, which, of course, they wouldn't be had my plan been followed," Potemkin wrote to Catherine at the end of 1788, after the opening of the Sejm. "But so be it" (ibid., 327; cf. 334–335; Catherine 2004, 271).

The lack of success in this undertaking moved Potemkin to act in other directions with increased ardor. Presuming, as before, that "a national army necessarily demands expanding the militia" (ibid., 340), that is, creating a civilian home force, he transferred his main hopes from the Polish cavalry onto the Cossack troops. Potemkin had actively concerned himself with forming Cossack units ever since the start of the Russo-Turkish War (see ibid., 258, 266, 329, 341, 353, and ff; for more detail, see Petrov A. I, 125–129). Potemkin needed these forces on the Turkish front but also made plans for them of a completely different kind. At the end of 1789 he sent the empress "a plan concerning Poland" (Ekaterina i Potemkin 1997, 381). Excerpts from this plan were recently published by V. S. Lopatin. Potemkin wrote:

> On Poland. It would be good if it were not divided, but if it is, it would be better to destroy it completely, [because] its neighbors have already closed in. In this case the evil will be less if there were no mediators between us, because it would be more difficult for them to start a war with us than act by intrigues, instigating a third party against us, thus making it hard for us without losing either people or property. And so—leave Poland only the kingdom of Mazowieckie + a bit of Lithuania. If the first Prussian King took it, this would be even more useful, [because] then we would be able to involve the *tsesartsy*. ...[9]

In Potemkin's words, the inhabitants of the Polish republic's Eastern voivodeships (voevodstva) desired

> to renew their former condition when they were under their own hetmans; now they all insist that they need to be the way they were, awaiting assistance

---

[9] This refers to Austrians (Translator's note).

from Russia. This matter can be accomplished very easily. For my leadership of the Cossacks name me Hetman of the Cossack troops of Ekaterinoslav province. (Ibid., 893)

Potemkin thus planned to become hetman of Eastern Poland, which was inhabited by a significant number of Orthodox Ukrainians.

As we know, Potemkin's propositions somewhat troubled Catherine. "Naming you Hetman of the troops of the Ekaterinoslav province is not difficult," she responded, "and drawing up a rescript on this won't take long. But one thing holds me back from signing such a document, and this I entrust to your own judgment: won't the use of this title in Poland provoke the untimely attention of the Sejm and cause alarm that will harm our cause?" (ibid., 387). It is possible that this response to his ideas led Potemkin to conclude that the empress herself or his enemies at court interpreted his desire to receive the hetman's mace as a manifestation of his excessive and far-reaching ambitions. In his answer, Potemkin counters not only what Catherine said but the arguments his imperial interlocutor had woven in between the lines:

> This will increase both the Poles' troubles and fear. An unexpected weapon always startles the enemy. The plan will be secret. It will be made known at the right time, and its name should not give anything away. I am not seeking anything for myself with this; if your benefit did not demand it, would I adopt this position, which is more ridiculous than distinguished? It's a means to achieve our goal, however, and there is one thing I can say: however we resolve matters, we cannot give up Poland. Thus, it must, of course, be weakened or, better, destroyed. (Ibid., 394; translation adapted from Catherine 2004, 330)

Catherine accepted Potemkin's conclusions. "Pray toil away, Sir Grand Hetman," she wrote to him indulgently. "You are a most intelligent, good and loyal man, and as for us, we love and honor you" (ibid., 396; Catherine, 332). The *ukase* naming Potemkin Great Hetman of the Imperial Ekaterinoslav and Black Sea Cossack forces was signed on January 10, 1790, and was quickly disseminated by Potemkin to all of the affected territories (ibid., 901–902). It is hard to say to what degree Potemkin really considered the new title "more ridiculous than distinguished." At least he deemed it important to appear in a quickly tailored hetman's uniform, in which dress he long remained in the memory of contemporaries and posterity (Engel'gart

1997, 82–83). It was in this costume, incidentally, that he appeared in the pages of Gogol's story "The Night Before Christmas" (Gogol' I, 235).

Potemkin's plans to incite a rebellion of Ukrainian residents of Poland and, with the help of Cossack troops, to incorporate Poland's Eastern regions into his hetmanate date to the end of 1789. But as Robert Howard Lord perceptively suggested, they had probably existed even earlier when Potemkin formed the Cossack units and bought up Polish land (Lord 1915, 516). An indirect but important confirmation of this may be found in Derzhavin's humorous poem "To Fortune" (Na Schastie), written in the spring of 1789, precisely during Potemkin's first arrival to Petersburg from the south. In this poem Derzhavin allegorically depicted the situation in the then present-day Europe, exhibiting how well-informed he was about all of the nuances of Russian diplomacy. In the opinion of Ia. K. Grot, the poet's sources of information could have been both Catherine's secretary, his old acquaintance A. V. Khrapovitskii, as well as his very close friend N. A. L'vov, who served under Chancellor Bezborodko (see Derzhavin I, 247). When listing Fortune's various acts, which in the poem emblematize Catherine and Russian politics as a whole, Derzhavin in particular wrote that Fortune "swells the Uke in Warsaw" (*khokhol v Varshave razduvaet*).[10] The meaning of the line becomes transparent if we compare it to Derzhavin's self-commentary on the line "I v'etsia lokonom khokhol" (and the Uke's hair is curled) from the same poem. Derzhavin explains that "khokhol" stands for Bezborodko and other Ukrainians "who happily played exalted roles" (ibid., 255).

Insisting on the union with Poland, at the same time Potemkin—"just in case"—prepared to unleash a civil war there. In the very same way, while actively putting forward plans for an intervention by the Cossacks and the partitioning of the kingdom, he kept in reserve a variant of the plan for a Russian-Polish union. "My behavior in Ukraine attracts all of the Poles," he wrote to the empress in March 1790 (Ekaterina i Potemkin 1997, 401), and six months later he assured her that "the majority" of the Polish nation "is inclined towards us" and that only the "Prussian" Sejm was an obstacle to this natural inclination. At the very end of the year, already having sent Suvorov to storm Izmail, he again

---

10 "Khokhol" is a pejorative Russian term for a Ukrainian and refers to the tuft of hair it was customary to leave after having one's head shaved. (Translator's note)

insistently urged Catherine to gain the Poles' sympathy by promising them Moldavia (ibid., 442, 443; Catherine 2004, 361).

The question naturally arises: what was the relationship between these mutually exclusive projects? Can one uncover a single strategic plan in them? In other words, did Potemkin change his vision of Russia's political goals for opportunistic reasons, or was it a question of finding the best way of implementing these goals? Many contemporaries and later historians have presumed that Potemkin's motives were mostly of a personal nature, and that he was trying to create an independent power base for himself in Poland in case of Catherine's death (and in view of the heir Pavel Petrovich's well-known hatred for him). In 1787 the English emissary Fitzherbert wrote to London that "Perhaps Prince Potemkin will make a *Tertium quid*[11] out of his newly-purchased lands in Poland that will be independent of both Russia and Poland" (Khrapovitskii 1874, 28). Discussions about Potemkin's similar hopes during the last year of his life are repeated in reminiscences of such varied people as the Polish aristocrat M. Oginski (I, 148) and Potemkin's relative L. N. Engel'gart (1997, 95).[12] According to Engel'gart, rumors of Potemkin's plans began with his forming the regiment of the Great Hetman's Mace (*Bulava*, Polish *Bulawa*) which was so well equipped that, in essence, it comprised an entire army: "Some supposed that he wanted to become king of Moldavia and Walachia, others— that he wanted to declare himself an independent hetman, and still others thought that he wanted to be king of Poland" (ibid., 94–95).

Potemkin of course knew of these rumors and rejected them with indignation. "Do you really suspect me? It is forgivable for a weak king to think that I want his place. As for me—the devil take them. And it's a sin if they think I act out of any interests except those of the state," he wrote to Bezborodko (Ekaterina i Potemkin 1997, 920). Of course one must take any declarations of this sort, especially coming from such a major and experienced politician, with a large dose of caution. Still, Potemkin's words deserve a certain amount of trust. As the historian A. N. Fateev emphasized (without knowing of this letter), "there is no basis whatsoever ... to speak of Potemkin's secret

---

11 "Third thing," i.e., a third element that changes an equation or formula. (Translator's note.)
12 For a survey of the sources and literature on this question, see Lord 1915, 512–515. Lord misinterprets the cited passage from Khrapovitskii's diary and attributes the argument taken from a perlustrated letter of the English emissary to Catherine.

intention to wear the crown of the Piasts. Potemkin bought up Polish land and received the status of a Polish noble in the Sejm. [But] he was hardly so simple-minded as to think that he could get along without Catherine, and he did not ignore the interests of his country. ... [Furthermore,] the king of Poland could only be a Catholic, and Potemkin did not resemble an apostate" (Fateev n.d., 90).

However, if we suppose that the issue was not about the Piasts' crown but instead concerned hetmanship over the territory of Ukrainian lands in Poland and a series of south-western provinces of the Russian Empire, then that would change the equation. Potemkin himself wrote to Catherine about similar intentions, and consequently had a basis to hope that she would go along with them. Moreover, given the political structure of Poland at the time, with the constantly changing map of confederations and re-confederations, this kind of hetmanship would have had significant independence. This interpretation helps us understand the idea behind the somewhat strange testimony of Potemkin's niece Countess Branicka, who said that the prince intended "to rule all of the Cossacks, to unite with the Polish army and declare himself king of Poland" (Lord 1915, 513).

In formulating this kind of plan, Potemkin certainly displayed characteristic ambition, but he definitely believed that he was acting in Russia's highest state interests. In a possible complex union of Russia and Poland, the Ukrainian Cossacks that were under Potemkin's control would have played a central role, geographically and politically. The proposed structure distinctly recalled the one that was to have arisen as the result of enacting the "Greek Project," which had foreseen the creation of the kingdom of Dacia between the resurrected Greek and Russian Empires; moreover, its throne at one time had also been earmarked for Potemkin (see Madariaga 1981, 377–388). Now the prince came forward with a new initiative in which he was allotted an even greater role.

If the basis for the "Greek Project" or "Eastern System" that Potemkin advocated as an alternative to Panin's "Northern System" had been the religious unification of Russia, Greece, and the Danube princedoms, from which it was proposed to create Dacia, the new project (which by analogy one could call the "Western System") made its basis the fraternal unity of the Slavic peoples. Its living embodiment was the figure of His Serene Highness, who combined in himself a Polish magnate, a Ukrainian hetman, and the closest associate (according to some, the secret husband[13]) of the Russian sovereign.

∞ **5** ∞

Throughout Potemkin's career the bard for his victories, celebrations, and undertakings had always been Petrov. But this time Potemkin turned to Derzhavin, which as Grot rightly noted, "is easily explained by the latter's poetic fame at the time" (Derzhavin I, 407). It was during these years that Derzhavin began to be welcomed at court, and his ode "On the Taking of Izmail" found favor with the empress, who upon meeting the poet said, "I did not know until now that your trumpet is just as loud as your lyre is pleasant" (ibid., IV, 614). This response established the singer of "Felitsa"'s status as an official poet and confirmed his universal popularity on the part the reading public, which had never been especially well-disposed toward Petrov.

I. I. Dmitriev, who became close to Derzhavin at this time, later recalled the somewhat jealous attitude toward the older poet that characterized Derzhavin's circle of friends: "His [Petrov's] odes were then greatly respected at court and among many literary folk; but the public hardly knew him, only by hearsay, and Derzhavin and the poets around him, while they didn't deny Petrov's lyric talent, emphasized the harshness of his verses rather than their rich ideas, exalted feelings or force of intellect" (Dmitriev 1986, 302).

Taking up Potemkin's request, Derzhavin felt the need to rely on Petrov's precedent. In any case, he copied out by hand the ode that Petrov had written for Potemkin's masquerade in Ozerki in 1779, and also sketched out one of the choruses for the Izmail celebration on the other side of the paper (Derzhavin I, 407). In truth, the task set before Derzhavin was both unfamiliar and complex. While he may have had significantly greater general recognition than Petrov,

---

13   V. S. Lopatin, offering substantial arguments in favor of the old version of Catherine's secret marriage with Potemkin, calls him her "husband and co-ruler" (Ekaterina i Potemkin 1997, 531, 540 and passim). Earlier, A. N. Fateev used the same terms in his Prague reports (n.d., 34–46). But even if we agree to the first label, one cannot concur that Potemkin was ever "co-ruler" with Catherine. Of course the empress trusted him and valued his talents, but neither according to her ideas, her character nor her political style did she have any need for co-rulers, and she would not have tolerated them at her side. And indeed the material so scrupulously gathered by Lopatin leaves no doubts on this score. In his letters Potemkin proposes, petitions, insists, and begs, but it is Catherine alone who makes all of the decisions, and at times she acts in ways that were not at all pleasing to her correspondent.

and probably a more powerful poetic gift, he did not possess the solid education nor was he such a deep and independent political thinker as his predecessor. And most importantly, he did not have the decades of close communion with Potemkin that Petrov had behind him. In his "Lament on the Demise of Potemkin," Petrov wrote of the "debates" (pren'ia) he had had with the prince "about Providence and fate, about death and being, about the course of the whole world" (Petrov II, 111; cf. Kochetkova 1999, 425–428).

It is not surprising, then, that the fuller reflection of Potemkin's late ideas may be found not in Derzhavin's "Description," which was still fully oriented on the "Greek Project"[14] that was already familiar to the author, but rather in Petrov's odes, written both during the prince's last years of life as well as after his death. Petrov's ode "On the Taking of Ochakov" is made up of a monologue by the allegorical Dnieper River which is celebrating the liberation of its estuary from Turkish domination:

> Я сам подвержен был несчастью,
> Мой желтый брег судьбины властью
> Постыдной сделан был межой;
> Поитель Россов, друг их славе,
> Я с радостью в их тек державе,
> Неволей кончил век в чужой.
> Но ныне вполне я восставлен,
> О Россы, силой ваших рук.
> От поношения избавлен
> И нестерпимых сердцу мук.

(I myself experienced misfortune: / By force of fate my yellow shore / Was made a shameful boundary; / Provider of water to Rosses, friend of their glory, / I joyfully flowed through their land, / [But] was forced to finish my course in an alien one. / But today I am fully restored, / Oh. Rosses, by the strength of your hands, / Saved from abuse / And from intolerable torments to the heart.)

---

14 As is well known, the "Description" aroused Potemkin's ire. After reading it, wrote Derzhavin, "he ran out of his bedroom in a fury … and galloped off God knows where" (Derzhavin IV, 619–620). Derzhavin, his contemporaries (see Dmitriev 1896, 299) and biographers (see Grot 1997, 397–398; Khodasevich, 1988, 169–170) all gave different explanations for his anger. With necessary caution, one may add to their various hypotheses the suggestion that, at least in part, Potemkin may have been unhappy that Derzhavin did not fully understand his thoughts and intentions.

This stanza describes the transfer of the Dnieper estuary from Turkish to Russian control. With the capture of Ochakov, located in this estuary, the process was completed. However, for a long time the Dnieper still served as the Russian border, or in Petrov's words, as a "shameful boundary," not only with Turkey but also with Poland.

Petrov celebrated the final transformation of the Dnieper into a river fully within Russia in 1793 in the ode "On the Integration of Polish Regions into Russia," written after the Second Partition of Poland, which he interpreted as the fulfillment of the cherished hopes of his late friend Potemkin. Catherine did not want large-scale celebrations on the occasion of the Second Partition. In the foreword to the first edition of the ode, Petrov notes that "concerning this event, however salvific, no service was held, no salutes fired from cannons," and he is overcome by doubts whether it is necessary "to load ideas with poetic thunder in describing a matter that was completed without any noise," and whether it would please the empress "to broadcast everywhere with amplification that which is evidently considered of little importance." The poet was freed from this doubt by the appearance "of the Dnieper, a grandiose god with a wreath on his head, in triumphal garments, holding a long scroll in his hands on which the villages, cities and peoples through which he flows were depicted." As Petrov writes, "the quality or weakness of the song which I sang [i.e., wrote] rests with the Dnieper—I did not take part in [writing] it and only copied it down" (Petrov 1793, n.p.). Like the Ochakov ode, this poem is structured as an apotheosis of the Dnieper which is celebrating its complete liberation:

> Услышав Днепр веленье рока,
> Дабы, сколь логом ни далек,
> Он весь от моря до истока
> Во области Российской тек,
> Чело венками увивает,
> Пресветлу ризу надевает
> И должную воздав хвалу
> Великой Севера Богине,
> Его веселия причине,
> Восходит спешно на скалу.

(The Dnieper, having heard fate's command, / That however long or remote its channel / From sea to source, he will flow / In the Russian realm; / He drapes his forehead in wreaths, / Dons most bright garments / And, giving deserved praise / To the Great Goddess of the North, / Due to his joyfulness / He hurriedly mounts a crag.)

The final reference is probably to Smolensk, Potemkin's native city, located in the upper reaches of the Dnieper. Downriver lies Ekaterinoslav, the city founded by His Serene Highness as Russia's southern capital. It was also along the Dnieper that Catherine had begun her journey to Crimea in 1787, which was the high point of Potemkin's career and recognition of his achievements as the creator of a new state. Celebrating the annexation to the empire of the last regions bordering the Dnieper, Petrov recalls the empress's river cruise that heralded the Dnieper's future position in the heart of the country and transformed its banks into an earthly paradise:

> Каков величествен в вершине,
> Коль славен в устии моем,
> Таков теперь в моей средине
> Я живо движусь телом всем.
> Весь с матерью, нет части сирой,
> Весь красной оттенен порфирой;
> Со дня как Боги принесли
> На брег Тя мой, сладчайша Мати,
> Предзнак грядушей благодати
> На ней оливы проросли.

(How majestic at the source, / How glorious in my estuary, / So too am I in my center; / I move vigorously with my entire body. / All within my mother[land], no orphaned part, / All tinted with beautiful porphyry; / Since the day the Gods brought / You to my shore, sweetest Mother, / Olives have grown all over it, / A sign of future plenty.)

It was precisely the Dnieper, uniting the Great Russians, Little Russians and Poles that in Petrov's rhetoric symbolizes the Russian Empire and that can therefore prophesy about the future Slavic brotherhood, in which Russia is destined to play the leading role:

> Приидет некогда то время,
>
> Днепр если может то проречь,
>
> В котором все славянско племя
>
> В честь Норда препояшет меч.
>
> Росс будет телеси главою,
>
> Тронув свой род побед молвою,
>
> Он каждый в рассеяньи член,
>
> Собрав в едино, совокупит
>
> И тверд родствами гордо вступит
>
> Меж всех в подсолнечной колен.

(The time will come one day / If the Dnieper can foretell it / On which the entire Slavic tribe / Will gird on sword in honor of the North. / Ross will be the body's head / Rousing its clan by news of victories, / Every dispersed member / He will gather into one, he will unite / And will proudly take his place, strong with his kin, / Amid all of the tribes in the universe.)

This panslavic utopia of the future unification of Slavs around Russia reserves a special place for Poland which became part of the Russian Empire earlier than the other peoples of one blood:

> Но вам, наперсники России,
>
> Поляки, первородства честь;
>
> Вы дни предупредили сии,
>
> Вам должно прежде всех расцвесть.
>
> Став с Россом вы в одном составе,
>
> Участвуйте днесь первы в славе,
>
> В блаженстве имени его.

(But to you, confidants of Russia, / Poles, the honor of primogeniture; / You anticipated these days, / [So] you should blossom before the rest. / Having become one entity with Russia, / Enjoy your glory first today, / In the happiness of its name.)

In his summons to Polish-Russian fraternity Petrov achieves truly ecstatic inspiration:

> Причастники усыновленья,
> Того же ветви древеси,
> Язык свят, люди обновленья!
> Которым небо, небеси
> И мира таинства открыты,
> И подвиги презнамениты,
> И счастья храм, где славы трон,
> Поклоньшися Екатерине,
> Присутствующей в нем Богине,
> Не выходите тщетно вон. (Petrov II, 138–151)

(Adopted sons of Russia, / Branches of one tree, / Holy language, people of renewal! / To whom the sky and heavens / And world's secrets are revealed, / And outstanding deeds, / And the temple of happiness, where the throne of glory / Bows to Catherine, / And to the Goddess present there; / Do not go forth in vain.)

∞ 6 ∞

The reality of the Second Partition of Poland had nothing in common with these dreams. Even earlier Catherine had received Potemkin's ideas with great caution. She did not approve of a Polish-Russian union, or in any case did not think that Russia should make any concessions because she didn't trust the Poles. Fearing the Cossacks' anarchy, she thought that Potemkin's Ukrainian plan could only be set in motion if Prussia and Poland attacked Russia. She did not see particular advantage in the planned partition because she did not want to allow the strengthening of Russia's worst enemy, whom she believed to be the Prussian king. Apparently, she considered the best variant to be the restoration of the status quo of 1788; if Poland remained a weak and anarchic republic incapable of influencing European politics, Russia would continue to exert unimpeded influence. However, developing events made such a reversion to the past impossible.

On the day after the celebration in the Tauride Palace, a courier from the Russian envoy in Warsaw, Ia. I. Bulgakov, arrived in Petersburg to report that a revolution had taken place there on May 3 (New Style) (AGS I, 851). This revolution was completely unacceptable to Catherine, both because as a result of the political changes the Polish patriotic party that was inimical to

Russia had triumphed and because the empress saw this as the French revolutionary infection coming dangerously close to the Russian border (Madariaga 1981, 420–424). In May and July Catherine wrote two rescripts for Potemkin, who was preparing to go south, regarding the plan of proposed action. In the first of them she sanctioned his projects in principle, while modifying the order and conditions of their realization. Catherine tasked Potemkin with "bringing the nation around to our side" with promises "of helping to unite Moldavia to Poland ... insisting [that it will only happen] at a convenient opportunity." At the same time, they both knew that such a "convenient opportunity" would not occur insofar as Russian diplomacy had already rejected the demand that Turkey yield Moldavia. In precisely the same way, His Serene Highness's planned Cossack invasion and the uprising of the Orthodox population of Eastern Poland were supposed to take place only after war with Prussia, Poland, and possibly England, began. In the opinion of some historians, the phrasing of Catherine's refusal was meant to soothe Potemkin's pride, since by the time of Catherine's writing the rescript she already knew that war had been completely taken off the agenda (see Lord 1915, 247; cf. Łojek 1970, 580–581).[15]

The second rescript considered preparation of a confederation of pro-Russian Polish aristocrats who would oppose the decisions taken by the Sejm. Such a confederation would have to turn to Catherine for help in restoring the old constitution, whose guarantor during the First Partition had been Russia. In the extreme version of events, Catherine considered a new partition possible (cf. Ekaterina 1874, 246–258, 281–289).

As the empress had assumed, Russian intervention in Poland began right after signing the peace with Turkey in May, 1792. This occurred at the summons of the so-called Targovitskii Confederation, whose formation Potemkin had begun in Iassy and Bezborodko had continued after Potemkin's death. However, the role of the Targovitsians was purely formal.

---

15 According to J. Łojek, there were arguments in Catherine's circle about whether it would be preferable to accept the results of the May 3 revolution, that Catherine herself experienced major vacillations on this question, and that it was only the traitorous indecision of the Polish leaders, and first of all that of King Stanisław-Augustus, that drove her to intervention (cf. Łojek 1986, 172–182). Unfortunately, there are no documents that support this hypothesis, including those first published by the historian himself.

Guaranteeing Catherine a pretext for invasion, after that they basically followed along in the rear of the advancing Russian army. And of course, all military actions were carried out by regular Russian troops; Potemkin's ideas about national Polish brigades and Cossack units that Catherine had refused to sanction had been buried with him.

As for the role in Russian policy on the part of loyal Polish magnates, the makers of the Targovitskii Confederation were simply and cruelly deceived. Having promised them the revival of the former szlachta freemen, Catherine conducted negotiations behind their backs about a new partition with Prussia and Austria (Lord 1915, 271–282; Madariaga 1981, 427–440). In a rescript to Ia. E. Sivers of December 22, 1792, the empress formulated her position on the Polish question with extreme clarity:

> We do not concern ourselves so much with this mighty event as much as with the disposition of the current destructive French doctrine that [has spread] so far that in Warsaw have sprung up clubs like those of the Jacobins where this despicable teaching is blatantly preached and from which it could easily spread to all parts of Poland, and consequently also touch the borders of its neighbors. ... By past experience and according to the current disposition of things and minds in Poland, that is, according to the inconstancy and capriciousness of this people, by its proven maliciousness and hatred toward ours, and especially due to the propensity they have shown for the depravity and brutalities of the French, we will never have in them either a tranquil or a safe neighbor unless we lead them into utter impotence and debility. (Solov'ev 1863, 303–304; cf. Bulgakov 1792)

The uprising led by Tadeusz Kosciusko and the Third Partition that followed, which erased Poland from the map of Europe, strengthened just this kind of interpretation of events (Madariaga 1981, 441–454; Lord 1924/1925).

Petrov's ode that was written on this occasion no longer contained eloquent hopes for Slavic brotherhood. Rather, the final elimination of Poland is figured here as necessary to eradicate the influence of revolutionary France, which was menacing the entire world. Precisely twenty years after the ode on the Kutchuk Kainarji peace, Petrov intensified his earlier framework, but the role of conductors of evil French schemes was now played by Poles and not Turks:

> Подобья сущие детей
> Им лестны новые затеи.
> И были б только чародей,
> Они есть жертва их сетей. ...
>
> В чудовищей преобразились,
> Секванским (парижским. — A. Z.)
>   духом заразились.

(Like absolute children / New capers flatter them. / And if there only was a sorcerer / They'd be victim to his traps ... // They have been turned into monsters, / They've been infected with the Sequana [i.e., Parisian] spirit.)

This revolutionary spirit that came from France and seized Poland is depicted as a worldwide catastrophe that threatens altars, thrones, people's personal safety, and ultimately, the existence of the universe:

> Поправ священные права,
> Грозят срыгь храмы и расхитить,
> Чужим имуществом насытить
> Их алчны руки, рты, чрева.
>
> Грозят во все края достигнуть,
> Царей с престолов низложить,
> Восстать на Твердь, Творца в ней сдвигнуть
> И в век законом уложить.
> Чтоб все на свете были равны;
> Все наглы, хищны, зверонравны.
> Когда не так: весь дол трясти,
> Поделать пропасти ужасны,
> И, кои с ними несогласны.
> Живых во аде погрести.
>   (Petrov II, 165–167)

(Having trampled sacred rights / They threaten to plunder and raze temples, / To glut their greedy arms, mouths, bellies / On others' property. // They threaten to reach all lands / To depose tsars from their thrones, / Rise up against Creation, displace its Creator / And to establish a law forever / That everyone on earth is equal; / They are all rude, predatory, beast-like. / And if not, shake up the entire world, / Create horrible pits / And in this hell bury alive / Those who don't agree with them.)

The only force able to avert this fatal threat to the whole world order turns out to be Russia who, dependent on the historical experience and mystical support of its heroes, had already once, at the start of the seventeenth century, brought the Sarmatian hydra to heel:

> Блеснул, как новьх луч светил.
> На мгле, несомой от Эфира,
> Великолепный Михаил [Романов]
> Спускается, и с ним Пожарской,
> Восстановитель власти царской,
> Простерт взор долу обоих;
> И Минин (зри, небесны круги
> Не знатность ставят, но заслуги),
> И Минин смотрит из-за них. (Ibid., 171)

(In the mist brought by the Ether, / Magnificent Mikhail [Romanov] / Shone forth like a ray from new luminaries; / He descends, together with him Pozharskii, / Restorer of tsarist power. / The gaze of both extends to earth; / And Minin (look, the heavenly circles / Value not celebrity but merits) / And Minin looks out from behind them.)[16]

Again, ideological intuition did not fail the aging poet. The inventory of metaphors that Petrov left behind was to be actively exploited by Russian politicians and publicists of the next, nineteenth, century.

---

16 Prince Dmitrii Pozharskii and the merchant Kuz'ma Minin were heroes of the Time of Troubles who rallied the Russians against the Polish invaders and helped establish the Romanov dynasty (Translator's note).

CHAPTER 5

The People's War:

The Time of Troubles in Russian Literature, 1806–1807

∽ 1 ∾

The Second and Third Partitions of Poland turned the Russian public's attention to the stories connected to the end of the Time of Troubles—Minin and Pozharskii's militia, the liberation of Moscow, and the election of Mikhail Fedorovich Romanov as tsar. After just over ten years, during the short period that separated the Austerlitz defeat from the Peace of Tilsit, these figures and events occupied the central place in the nation's historical pantheon. In 1806 Derzhavin wrote the "historical presentation" entitled "Pozharskii" that was published two years later, and in 1807 one after another there appeared the poems by S. N. Glinka "Pozharskii and Minin," S. A. Shirinskii-Shikhmatov's "Pozharskii, Minin, Germogen [Hermogenes], or Russia Saved" as well as M. V. Kriukovskii's tragedy "Pozharskii." At the same time the very young A. S. Strudza began writing the tragedy "Rzhevskii," which was dedicated to the same events and remained unfinished and unpublished (RO IRLI F. 288, op. 1, № 13; cf. Gukovskii 1995, 165–166).

In 1807 a competition to design a monument to Minin and Pozharskii was announced, which resulted in I. P. Martos's celebrated work. The choice from among the many proposals that were entered was made by the Sardinian Ambassador Joseph de Maistre. In 1808 he reported to his king:

> His Imperial Highness deemed it proper to order a monument to be erected out of bronze or marble in honor of Prince Pozharskii and a certain butcher by the name of Minin, who in the first years of the seventeenth century saved Russia in miraculous fashion from the foreign yoke. A large number of plans for this monument were located at the house of Princess Kurakina, the wife of Prince Aleksei who was the minister of internal affairs. One fine morning the princess, at whose house I had supped the previous evening, sent me a huge bundle of these plans, requesting my opinion of them in a note. I immediately guessed where this request came from and who would be given my answer, but I didn't let on. After carefully reviewing the plans, I sent the princess my response, basically supported by quite serious reasons, but in a manner written for ladies. Soon after this there was a dinner for fifty at Count Stroganov's on his name day. The old count, president of the Academy of Arts, said to us after dinner: "Gentlemen, His Imperial Majesty considered it proper to erect a monument. He was presented with a multitude of projects. Here is the one he preferred and has just presented to me to have carried out." Thus His Majesty wants it known de perpetuam rei memoriam [for posterity] that his minister decided the choice of monument to Minin and Pozharskii, those celebrated heroes whose name I just learned this year. (Maistre 1871, 117–118)

The first sketches for Martos's monument, exhibited at the Academy of Arts, were discussed on the pages of the *Journal of Fine Arts* (*Zhurnal iziashchnykh iskusstv*) (see Koshanskii 1807; cf. Kovalenskaia 1938, 57–62)[1] and in the separately published "Panegyrical Speech on Prince Pozharskii and Kuz'ma Minin" by V. M. Severgin. Simultaneously the Academy of Arts asked its students in the class on historical drawing to address the following theme for their yearly project: "Pozharskii's praiseworthy deed when he arose from his sick bed and rushed with the citizens of Moscow who had come to him to give aid to the capital city that was being threatened by the enemy" (Petrov 1864, 493).

Of course these heroic pages of Russian history had attracted writers before this—it's enough to mention M. M. Kheraskov's tragedy "Moscow Liberated," written in 1798, or Derzhavin's idea for a long poem called "Pozharskii" that Ia. K. Grot dates to the 1780s (Derzhavin III, 469). And in the post-Tilsit years

---

[1] In N. N. Kovalenskaia's opinion, one of the sources for Martos's conception of the monument was an article by S. S. Bobrov of 1806.

S. N. Glinka published the "national drama" "Minin" (1809), and P. Iu. L'vov, the historical narratives "Pozharskii and Minin" (1810) and "The Election of Mikhail Fedorovich Romanov as Tsar" (1812). In 1811 S. A. Dekhtiarev's oratorio "Minin and Pozharskii" with libretto by N. P. Gorchakov was performed with great success; characteristically, the libretto was taken to a large degree from Shirinskii-Shikhmatov's poem. But it was in 1806–1807 that the events of two hundred years earlier were canonized. The liberation of Moscow from the Poles and the ascension of the Romanov dynasty began to be perceived as the key moments in Russian national history. Throughout the eighteenth century a similar role had been exclusively assigned to Peter's reign.

In the first half of the 1830s Minin and Pozharskii's Moscow campaign and the Zemskii sobor (Assembly of the Land) of 1613 were definitively canonized as the mythological beginning of the Russian state. The continuity of the new state ideology with the material of 1806 was indicated by the fact that the newly built Alexandrinskii Theater opened in 1832 with a performance of Kriukovskii's "Pozharskii" (Kriukovskii 1964, 603). It was only later that the ideological baton of the long deceased playwright passed on to Mikhail Glinka's "A Life for the Tsar" and Nestor Kukol'nik's "The All-Mighty Hand Saved the Fatherland" (see Kisileva 1997). At the heart of the new official interpretation of the Time of Troubles lay the historical parallel with 1812, made explicit in the titles of M. N. Zagoskin's first two novels: *Iurii Miloslavskii, or the Russians in 1612* and *Roslavlev, or the Russians in 1812*.[2] Moreover, contemporaries could easily perceive the parallel between the July 1830 Revolution in France and the Polish rebellion of November of the same year. It is all the more interesting that even before Napoleon's invasion of Russia, the interpretive models that took on official status in the 1830s had already been worked out in a literary atmosphere notably inimical to the state political course of the time.

In one way or another, virtually all of the authors of the works listed above were connected with A. S. Shishkov's circle. The old Derzhavin and the young Shikhmatov were the leading poets of this circle, and Sergei Glinka was close to him ideologically (Al'tshuller 1984; Kisileva 1981). Shishkov promoted the novice playwright Kriukovskii as an alternative for V. A. Ozerov. In the words of

---

2 According to D. Rebekkini's calculations, plots concerning the invasion of 1812 and the Time of Troubles predominated in the corpus of historical novels in the 1830s (see Rebekkini 1998, 421).

Figure 12 First proposal for a monument to Minin and Pozharskii (1804-1807) by I. P. Martos.

Nikolai Grech, "on Aleksandr Semenovich's advice [Kriukovskii] changed and corrected a lot in his new, just finished tragedy, and through his mediation became known" to the Director of Imperial Theaters A. L. Naryshkin (Grech 1930, 282).

The reasons for such a burst of interest in historical thematics are obvious, and were also well understood by readers and writers of those years. S. P. Zhikharev, for example, connected the ecstatic reaction given to the plays by Ozerov and Kriukovskii to the current political situation and the anti-Napoleonic campaign of 1806–1807. He predicted beforehand that Kriukovskii's tragedy would "have great success on stage because almost all of the verses for Prince Pozharskii's role relate to current patriotic circumstances and to the patriotic feelings of the people" (Zhikharev 1955, 410; cf. Bochkarev 1959 and others). Indeed, the defeat of Austerlitz only increased hatred for Napoleon in Russian society. It also served to heighten the bellicose mood which was essential to Alexander I at the time; the emperor had already begun preparing for a new war, and thus needed justficiation for refusing to ratify the peace agreement of July

1806, that had been signed by his envoy P. Ia. Ubri (see Dubrovin 1895; Zharinov 1911). Still, the choice of this one particular episode from out of all of Russia's rich military history requires explanation.

∾ 2 ∾

In the consciousness of Russian society there existed a distinct metonymic connection between France and Poland based on their geographical position *vis–à–vis* Russia, their common religion, as well as political and historical factors. France most actively opposed Russia's involvement with Poland and the disturbances in Warsaw of 1791 and 1794 were perceived in Russia as the spread of the French revolutionary spirit.

The Orthodox Church played a huge role in the ideological justification for the campaign of 1806–1807. In the Synod's announcement concerning the start of war of November 30, 1806, that was read aloud in all churches, Napoleon was accused of apostasy from Christianity, idolatry, and a desire "to throw down Christ's Church"; thus the nascent campaign took on the character of a religious war "against this enemy of Church and Fatherland" (Shil'der I, 354–356). Alexander's *ukase* of the same day explained and advertised the purpose of the Synod's announcement. Entitled "On the Formation and Development of Temporary Universal Guards or Militias (Militsii)," the emperor's *ukase* appealed to all estates, summoning them "to manifest zealous love, a courageous spirit, and true passion for the Fatherland's glory. The people, only moved and enflamed by such feelings," the manifesto affirmed, "can make the universal guard an impenetrable bulwark against the enemy's forces, no matter how strong they may be" (PSZ № 22374).

Careful observers quickly threw doubt on the purely military effectiveness of this measure. From among "people of all conditions whom I know very well," I. V. Lopukhin wrote to the emperor, "there is no one, except those guided by personal selfishness or frivolity who does not find the establishment of the militia burdensome and able to upset the general economy and especially the peace of peasant life" (Lopukhin 1990, 169). In a few years Karamzin repeated the same ideas in his "Note on Ancient and Modern Russia": "There is no doubt that the noble sons of the Fatherland were ready then for magnanimous sacrifices, but the general ardor soon cooled; they saw that the government wanted the impossible; trust in it weakened, and the people who had read the

Manifesto for the first time with tears in their eyes began to laugh at the pitiful militia!" (Karamzin 1991, 64–65).

According to the rather widely shared opinion, a small draft of recruits would have brought the army much greater benefit (Dubrovin 1895, № 4, 237–239). Ideological and political goals, however, carried more weight with Alexander as he sought to transcend barriers of class and politics in his efforts to mobilize the country for battle with the enemy. Despite the emperor's efforts, dialogue with the lower classes remained the prerogative of the Synod. The Imperial manifesto was primarily aimed at the nobility, which during Alexander's five year rule had already developed a certain caution toward initiatives and projects issuing from the throne.

In part, the manifesto declared, "In such difficult circumstances We turn to the distinguished estate of the noble gentry of Our empire with complete confidence in your service and loyalty on the field of battle and the supreme sacrifice of life and property, which have provided the basis for Russia's greatness" (PSZ № 22374). Count F. V. Rostopchin responded from Moscow, "This celebrated estate, inspired by the spirit of Minin and Pozharskii, sacrifices everything for the fatherland and only prides itself in the title of Russian"; he further expressed satisfaction that the emperor had "finally" recognized the gentry "as the unequalled mainstay of the throne" (Rostopchin 1892, 418).

Because the goal of national unity seemed more a distant hope than a plausible reality, the necessity for emotional gestures was felt all the more strongly. In the same letter, Rostopchin told Alexander: "All of this enthusiasm, the actions and mobilization, heretofore unheard of, will turn to nothing in a moment if rumors of alleged emancipation inspires the people to procure it by annihilating the gentry, which is the single aim of the common folk in all of its uprisings and disturbances, and to which it is striving even more impatiently after the French example."

Annoyed, Alexander rejected the idea that he was devaluing the gentry: "… I don't know why you say that I *finally* began to recognize its support of the throne, because I have never ceased regarding it as such"; and he decisively rejected the supposition about possible uprisings (Alexander 1902, 634). But however sharp the emperor's reaction to these unsolicited warnings, he himself was deeply worried by the country's current mood.

"Banish thoughts about any evil undertakings, do not be blinded by the insidious delusions of refractory, perverted people, leading to temporary or permanent ruin," stated the Synod's announcement (Shil'der II, 355–356). Simultaneously with the manifesto creating militias, the Senate issued the *ukase* "On the Expulsion of All French Citizens from Russia." Those who wanted to stay either had to take an oath of Russian citizenship or, if they were in certain special categories for which there were exceptions, they had to swear that they had no connection to France (PSZ № 22371). These special allowances seriously frightened Rostopchin, who asserted that

> the measures taken to expel foreign scum from the empire,... instead of benefit have produced an extraordinary evil: for out of forty people hardly even one would choose to leave a land where every foreigner finds both respect and riches. The oath of citizenship inspired by fear and self-interest provokes Frenchmen to harm Russia, which they do by influencing the whole class of servants, who are already waiting for Bonaparte so as to gain their freedom. Sovereign! Cure Russia of this infection. (Rostopchin 1892. 419).

To prepare the country for the encounter with the enemy it was necessary to cleanse it completely of foreign pollution. Rumors about the coming liberation that Napoleon promised to the lower classes were actively circulating in Petersburg (Dubrovin 1895, № 6, 24–25).

Public opinion of that time saw an even greater danger in the Poles who, in the atmosphere of pre-war hysteria, were perceived as a fifth column within the empire. Together with rumors about liberation of the serfs, predictions about the future restoration of Poland also circulated in society (ibid.). These fears were fed by the exultation with which Napoleon was met in Warsaw, the pro-Napoleon proclamations of Polish patriots, and, most disturbing, discontent in Russia's newly acquired Polish provinces (see Zavadskii 1993, 164–167). "Rumors reach me that in the Russian provinces that formerly belonged to Poland hostile attitudes are revealing themselves," wrote the Minister of Foreign Affairs A. Ia. Budberg (Bogdanovich II, appendix, 20), while the journal *The Messenger of Europe* also asserted that it was specifically "the Poles [who] gave Napoleon the title of invincible" (Zimnii pokhod 1807, 45).

Anti-Polish attitudes had taken root in Russian society since the partitions and the rebellions of the 1790s. These ideas formed part of the plainly ideological notions that P. Iu. L'vov had formulated three years earlier, writing of "the ancient envier of the Russian kingdom, the eternal hater of Moscow, power-hungry Poland, which always seeks to harm us" (L'vov 1810, 42–43). Under these circumstances it was particularly alarming that Prince Adam Czartoryski, who had only recently quit the post of Minister of Foreign Affairs, remained one of the notable members of the emperor's inner coterie.

"Prince Adam Czartoryski who ran foreign affairs ... became hated by all," F. F. Vigel later recalled. "In the middle classes they bluntly called him a traitor, and his secret joy at events that were unfavorable to us did not escape the eyes of the highest public. At that time the emperor still valued Russia's opinion, which loudly called for him to remove the traitor, and at the end of the summer Czartoryski was forced to leave the ministry" (Vigel' II, 206). For Czartoryski himself neither his reputation nor the reasons for it were any secret: "One circumstance that concerned Emperor Alexander was the constant censure and criticism directed toward him. This was because of my presence at his side and my appointment to a high post. ... A Pole who had the emperor's complete trust and who was privy to all of his affairs was a phenomenon insulting to Russian society's deep-seated prejudices" (Chartorizhskii I, 310–313).

However, in this ferocious rejection there was one thing that gave the prince pause: "They [the Russians] suspected me of secret sympathy for France, of wanting to draw Alexander into relations with Bonaparte and to make him subservient to him, under the spell of his genius, so to speak" (ibid., 313). Such suspicions did not have the slightest basis in reality. Czartoryski's foreign policy was predicated on confrontation with the French emperor. In Alexander's retinue he unquestionably belonged to the "hawks," both because of his general political convictions and due to his Polish predilections (Grimstead 1969, 104–156; Zavadskii 1993, 61–136). He himself later wrote that he was "far from the thought" of "inclining Russian politics toward a close connection with Napoleon," insofar as it was obvious to him that "any agreement between these states would be ruinous for Polish interests" (Chartoryzhskii I, 322). It was not by chance that it was the news of the minister's retirement, as many supposed, that moved the envoy P. Ia. Urbi to sign the unfavorable peace treaty that Alexander subsequently rejected (Nikolai Mikhailovich 1903, 393).

Nevertheless, these subtle political considerations could not shake the course of public opinion. Those who were in the know about Czartoryski's

Chapter 5: The People's War

position gave it an even more sinister explanation. The Bavarian envoy Ol'ri denounced him, asserting that after the battle of Austerlitz, "they spoke everywhere and in public places only about the fact that that Prince Czartoryski had agreed to this war because he had foreseen that the Russians' defeat would lead Napoleon's army into his fatherland, that he didn't doubt that the conqueror would raise the standard of rebellion there and force the Sejm to accept Prince Czartoryski as king, supporting his selection with his victorious army" (Ol'ri 1917, 464). The stubborn correlation of France and Poland presumed that a Pole who found himself near the Russian throne would invariably have Bonapartist sympathies.

∾ 3 ∾

To understand the conceptual parallel that literary figures of the Shishkov circle drew between the events of the early seventeenth and early nineteenth centuries, it is essential to examine the sources of their notions about the people and national unity more closely. The key role in our analysis becomes the influence of Rousseau's philosophy on the political views of the older archaists. This question runs up against obvious difficulties. For literary people who were more or less oriented on Shishkov's program, the intellectual legacy of Rousseau—not only the committed democrat, apostle of natural religion, and prophet of the French Revolution, but also as a thinker who had a persistent and profound enmity toward Russia—was, understandably, not only not acceptable but positively abhorrent. In their writings we almost never find direct references to the Genevan thinker. At the same time, the thinking of Russian traditionalists of the late eighteenth-early nineteenth century had been formed within the powerful magnetic field of Rousseauist doctrines (on the influence of Rousseau's ideas on the linguistic conceptions of the so-called "elder archaists," see Lotman 1992; Lotman 1969; Lotman i Uspenskii 1996, 345, 353, 405; Kisileva 1981; Kisileva 1983).

From the start Russian readers' interest in *The Social Contract* or *Emile* was inseparable from the harsh and one-sided assessment that the intellectual leader of enlightened Europe had given of Russia's historical development: "Russians will never be really civilized, because it was civilized too soon. Peter['s] … first wish was to make Germans or Englishmen, when he ought to have been making Russians. … In this fashion too a French teacher turns out a pupil to be an infant prodigy, and for the rest of his life to be nothing whatsoever" (Rousseau 1969, 183; translation from Rousseau 1979, 198–199). This judgment could not be accepted by Rousseau's Russian admirers, the more so since it was pronounced at a time when the unanimous cult of Peter was still at its zenith and when Russians' rights to a worthy place among European nations were upheld by the authoritative Montesquieu, who had written that "Peter I, in imparting European customs and manners to a European people achieved success with an ease that he didn't expect" (Montesquieu 1955, 418). Nonetheless, Rousseau's notion of the Russians' lack of national character ("caractère national"), which he had emphasized as a defining weakness of the Russian state in his "Project for a Corsican Constitution" (Rousseau 1969, 268), was taken in Russia to some extent as appropriate criticism of the court, although with each successive decade Russian readers grew more responsive to his assessment.

When the author of *The Social Contract* compared Peter to "a French teacher" (un précepteur françois) he was doubtless alluding to contemporary French teaching practices that he had condemned in *Emile* that same year. The issue had to do with French teachers for French pupils, and the word "French" functioned as a synonym for "bad." At the same time, for a Russian audience that was already used to being characterized—not without some irritation—as pupils of "enlightened Europe," Rousseau's analogy suggested a foreigner teaching a *Russian* pupil, and the same word—"French"—here signified "alien."

"Everything that is our own becomes bad and despised in our eyes. The French teach us everything: how to walk, how to stand, how to bow, how to sing, how to speak, and even how to blow our noses and to cough," declared Shishkov in his "Treatise on Old and New Style" (Shishkov II, 14). His close associate E. Stankevich despaired that "foreigners take charge of Russian children at their birth, foreigners supervise their childhood and direct their youth. ... From the capital to the farthest settlements you will find foreigners everywhere, rearing, educating, guiding our gentry" (Stankevich I, 18). Moreover, for these authors the problem was not only about the bad quality of foreign teachers. In Shishkov's words, "the most honest and well-intentioned of them cannot teach me to know my country and love my people" (Shishkov IV, 180). It is difficult not to see in these demands an echo of that patriotic education that the preceptor gives Emile.

This focus on pedagogical problems was not unique to any particular circle of thinkers—all Europe was drawn into discussions of education. But the idea of national education that depended on the traditional forms of folk life—customs, holidays, games, songs—clearly signaled Rousseauian roots, although it was subsequently developed most fully by late eighteenth and early nineteenth-century German pedagogical thought (see König 1954). From the Russian perspective it was significant that Rousseau had discussed this issue in an especially broad and in-depth fashion in the "Considerations on the Form of Rule in Poland." This work, written after the First Partition of Poland and dedicated to the way Poles could preserve their national being in face of the Russian threat, became—in the words of Jean Starobinski—"Jean-Jacques's political testament" (Starobinski 1962, 32). Rousseau's anti-Russian sentiments reached their culmination here, and this kind of work by the famous philosopher could not have failed to provoke the liveliest interest in Russia, although references to it, understandably, were absolutely out of the question.

In "Considerations," the chapter "Education" that opens with the phrase "This section is important" (Rousseau 1969, 465) precedes such sections as "On the King," "The Administration," "The Military System," and so on. The political existence of Poland was coming to an end, but according to Rousseau, the task for the country was to preserve itself by supporting its national cultural identity. "You cannot stop the Russians from swallowing you up, but at least arrange it so that they will not be able to digest you. ... If you can succeed in preventing even one Pole from becoming a Russian, I tell you that Russia will never succeed in subjugating Poland to itself. ... It is precisely education that gives souls their national form. ... A child, opening its eyes, should see the fatherland and until death should see nothing but the fatherland. ... At twenty years of age a Pole should not be a person, he should be a Pole. ... Their educators should all be Poles" (Rousseau III, 959–960; Rousseau 1969, 465–466).

Still, Rousseau's ideas about the fundamental principles of national education were significantly different from those of the nationally-oriented Russian thinkers of the early nineteenth century. While for Shishkov and his supporters the basis was language, Rousseau had not paid special attention to this. Judging by the "Treatise on the Origin and Bases of Inequality" and the "Essay on the Origin of Languages," Rousseau did not consider language part of the cultural tradition, relating it rather to the realm of natural phenomena. Moreover, in developing his political doctrine, Rousseau doubtlessly oriented himself primarily on the Republic of Geneva, and the linguistic situation in Switzerland did not lend itself to considering language a factor of national originality. But even for Poland the issue of language did not play any significant role in Rousseau's recommendations.

Yet even here the Russians' conceptions reveal their distinctly Rousseauian source. Shishkov's attempts in the "Treatise on Old and New Style" to demonstrate the national nature of word creation and to crowd out French borrowings with the help of neologisms that he thought up with Slavonic roots were clearly derived from German sources, especially J. H. Campe's *Dictionary of Improvements and the Germanization of Our Language* that had been published in Braunschweig in 1798 (Campe 1798). Shishkov translated Campe's works for children and followed his work with interest (see Campe I-II; cf. Zemskova 2000), and the German pedagogue's almost religious adulation of Rousseau is well known. Among other things, Campe initiated and provided commentaries for a translation of *Emile* into German (see Mournier 1979, 126–130, 286–298).

Shishkov followed Campe's logic. Evidently having in mind Germany's divided political situation, as well as the ideas of German nationalists about the existence of an ideal Germany everywhere that the German language was spoken, Shishkov asserted, "It has been proven by experiments that bringing regions together will not create a perfect unity of body and soul if their languages are different, and that, to the contrary, regions that are divided and separated from each other, if they have one language, will preserve their secret unanimity" (Shishkov IV, 184). The rhetoric of "a single body and soul" clearly reveals the notion of the people as a moral personality (in Rousseau's phrase, "personne morale"), endowed with one will, which strives to be embodied in a single state organism.

Evstafii Stankevich, discussing how Russia should treat the subjugated Poles and Swedes who had once threatened its existence (in the context of a discussion concerning the Finnish provinces won from Sweden) wrote, "We should put all our efforts into destroying not their cities and towns, but their dialects" (Stankevich II, 18). Rousseau, instructing the Poles how not to be "digested" by its powerful neighbor, advised them to put down roots into the soil of their native traditions. Stankevich recommended that his government pull them out from that soil, precisely in order to digest them into the single body of the Russian Empire.

Rousseau had spoken of the necessity for national education primarily in relation to small and politically weak states—Poland, Corsica, and his native Republic of Geneva. Starobinski even saw in this a projection of the author's own biographical problems: "By strange coincidence, the Poland of 1772 for which Rousseau was writing a law project offers a rather accurate image of Jean-Jacques himself, surrounded, besieged, persecuted by real and imagined enemies and pursuers" (Starobinski 1962, 98–99). The interest in this problem on the part of Rousseau's German admirers is also understandable: for divided Germany the consolidation of national traditions via education became the pledge of future political unification.

Russia, it would seem, was in a completely different position, but the sense of the state organization's precarity and the fragility of its very existence were also familiar. The reason for this sad state of affairs, in full agreement with Rousseau's conceptions, had to do with ignoring national traditions and customs:

> If they start entertaining us with alien customs, foreign games, foreign rites, foreign language, charming and seducing our imagination, then despite all rules, despite all good intentions and dispositions the prime basis of love of the fatherland—the spirit of national pride—will begin to decrease. ... If one people attacks another with flame and sword in their hands, where does the latter find the strength to repel this horrible storm cloud, this lightning bolt, if it does not come from love for the fatherland and national pride? ... From this it is clear that it is not only weapons and the power of one people that can be dangerous for another—a covert attempt to entice minds, to charm hearts and to shake their love for their land and pride in their name is a means more dependable than swords and cannons,—

wrote Shishkov in his "Treatise on Love for the Fatherland," which he read at a ceremonial meeting of the "Colloquy of Lovers of the Russian Word" a few months before Napoleon's army crossed the Neiman (Shishkov IV, 170–171).

The logic of this construction is completely transparent. Foreign teachers inculcate Russian youth with fondness for foreign languages and the customs of foreign countries, due to which young Russians lose their national pride and become incapable of withstanding a military challenge. The effeminizing and weakening influence of French civilization turns out to be especially dangerous. Recall that later on in the passage from *The Social Contract* cited

Figure 13 Minin summons Prince Pozharskii to save the Fatherland (1800's) by G. I. Ugriumov.

earlier Rousseau says that Russia, in losing its national character, like those European countries that had once lost theirs, would fall prey to the Tatars.

This Rousseauian national-cultural isolationism provoked sharp criticism from D. I. Khvostov: "Speaking of education, the author rejects foreign teachers, but how can the country become enlightened?... What can enrich the language of the people if it shuns the productions of foreign countries? In places, [Shishkov's treatise] is written well and effectively, but while it might be suitable for the age of Mikhail Romanov it is not for his descendants" (Khvostov 1938, 378). Khvostov's mention of the times of Mikhail Romanov was not accidental. Shishov found examples of genuine love for the fatherland in classical times, selecting parallels to them from Russian history. He wanted to show his audience that Russians were no less capable of patriotic feelings than the heroes of Greece and Rome, and in far greater measure than modern Europeans. At the same time, of his four examples, three were from the Time of Troubles when Russia was threatened by Polish domination.

Shishkov chose this era for his historical excursuses because he saw an analogy to his day. In his opinion, Russia was in danger of being conquered by

Napoleon, and he believed that only a patriotic upsurge like the one led by Minin and Pozharskii would be able to save the country from certain destruction. In essence, the leader of the "Colloquy" reproduced a model that had been formulated several years earlier by his comrades and ideological allies.

∞ **4** ∞

The history of Moscow's liberation in 1612 could not have been a more appropriate ideological reference point for Russia in her current state. More than anything else, it gave Russia, badly defeated at Austerlitz, some necessary historical perspective. Once humiliated and almost subjugated by the Poles, Russia now ruled over that hostile people. Shikhmatov began a poem with this juxtaposition between her past misfortunes and her current greatness. More than that, Shikhmatov has Patriarch Germogen reveal the future, prophetically exclaiming:

> Отверзлись очи мне душевны,
> Я вижу таинства времен…
> Забудь Россия дни плачевны;
> Царица ты земных племен.
> Врагов бесчестья полны лицы,
> Потухли бранныя зари,
> Почиют царства и цари
> Под сению твоей десницы
> Сармация твоя раба.
> (Shirinskii-Shikhmatov 1971, 368)[3]

(My inner eyes have opened, / I see the secrets of the ages… / Russia, forget these tearful days; / You are tsaritsa of the tribes of earth. / Your enemies'

---

3 Cf. in Strudza:

> Но в будущем, я зрю, народ сей заблужденный,
> Каратель и тиран, к славянам приобщенный,
> Под скиптром русским мир и счастие вкусит.
> (RO IRLI, f. 288, op. 1, № 13, l. 27)

(But in the future, I see, this prodigal people [the Poles], / Punisher and tyrant, attached to the Slavs, / Will enjoy peace and happiness under Russia's scepter.)

faces are full of dishonor, / The violent suns have set, / Kings and kingdoms repose / In the shade of your right hand / Sarmatia is your slave...)

Of course, the contrast between, say, the Tatar yoke and the conquest of Kazan could in principle have supplied the author with the same set of associations. However, these were "affairs of days long past" (Pushkin), whereas the final defeat of Poland could still be recalled by the majority of the reading and writing public, which made the historical allusions more alive and relevant. It is not by accident that a play about Pozharskii was put forward to counter Ozerov's "Dimitrii Donskoi," filled with the pathos of gentry honor and individual freedom (see Gordin 1910) and unacceptable to Shishkov's group, (for Shishkov's response to the play, see Sidorova 1952). Moreover the story of a people's militia marching on Moscow could serve as an ideal analogy—both for a creating a militia and also for the role that the Orthodox Church played in the action.

The entire first canto (out of three) of Shirinskii-Shikhmatov's poem "Pozharskii, Minin, Germogen, or Russian Saved" describes a prayer by Patriarch Germogen, who is imprisoned in the Chudov Monastery; miraculously, the prayer reaches Nizhnii Novgorod and spurs Minin to gather a militia. In the plays by Derzhavin and Kriukovskii, the outcome of the siege of Moscow and culminating moment is the patriarch's summons to the troops. In both plays, especially Derzhavin's, the "cellarer of the Trinity Lavra" Avraamii (Palitsyn) plays no small role (Derzhavin IV, 132). Glinka's poem begins with Minin reading a letter from Avraamii. The words of the spiritual pastors move the people to rise up for the sake of their liberation, for the war must first of all be waged to protect the faith. Shikhmatov exclaims at the start of his poem:

> Раскол латин душеотравный
> Уже — о, нестерпимо зло —
> На гибель веры православной
> Возносит гордое чело, —
> (Shirinskii-Shikhmatov 1807, 19)

(The soul-destroying Latin schism / Is already—oh, unbearable evil— / Raising its proud brow / To destroy the Orthodox faith.)

The very titles that Shikhmatov and Glinka gave their poems indicate the most important mythologems that the current political situation demanded. The formula "Pozharskii, Minin, Germogen, or Russian Saved" emblematized the unification of all classes in the name of a lofty goal, and the formula "Pozharskii and Minin, or Russians' Sacrifices"—the enthusiastic character of that unification, the surge of sacrifice that the Supreme manifesto had demanded of all subjects.

"It seems that nature produced one closer to the throne and the other closer to huts on purpose so that, guided by the wisdom of all of the estates, it could act with greater strength for the general good," wrote Severgin (1807, 16) of the heroes in a sketch of Martos's monument. If Ozerov in "Dimitrii Donskoi" or Kheraskov in "Moscow Liberated" (which was also dedicated to the events of 1612–1613, but written in the eighteenth century) depicted national unity as an alliance of princes, all of the above-named authors describe the history of the *people's* rising. Of course, within the people estate divisions remain,[4] but the general spiritual outpouring brings them together as one. Shikhmatov compares Pozharskii's troops to a Siberian river that absorbs innumerable streams:

> Текут в него со всех градов,
> Преславны жаждущи трудов
> Отечества нелестны чады.
> (Shirinskii-Shikhmatov 1971, 366)

(Honest progeny of the fatherland / Flow into it from all cities, / Thirsting for labors, most glorious.)

Such an image of the birth of the people is directly connected with the basic metaphor of a sacrifice on the altar of the fatherland, which was perfectly expressed in Minin's anthologized summons to the people of Nizhnii Novgorod to give their last for the salvation of Moscow. Sacrificing one's most valuable and cherished property in the name of the general good not only had pragmatic material importance, but also symbolized the voluntary rejection of the private and personal, liberating oneself from everything that did not belong to the single national body.

---

4   Thus Glinka's Minin refuses to be leader of the militia, triumphantly declaring:

> Я б изменил себе, Отечеству и вам, принявши сан военный. (Glinka 1807, 9)

(I would betray myself, the Fatherland and you if I took on military rank.)

> Дадим себя, как Россам сродно
> Отечеству и вере в дань.
> Все силы, все стяжанье наше
> Слием для подвига сего, —
>
> (Shirinskii-Shikhmatov 1807, 22)

(We will give ourselves, as is characteristic of Rosses / As tribute to the fatherland and our faith. / All our strength, all our earnings / We give for this deed—)

declares Minin in Shikhmatov's poem.

The Synod's announcement, made known on November 30, 1806, admonished the flock "to sacrifice with gratitude those goods to the Fatherland for which we are obliged to the Fatherland" (Shil'der II, 357). Orientation on the same historical model may also be divined in a diary description of the success of the first subscription lists, noted by Zhikharev on January 4: "Our grandees of old families and eminent clergy showed a praiseworthy example, and after them followed and continue to follow people of other conditions, all of them vying with one another to give as much as they can manage for the Fatherland; some lay their very last [penny] on the altar" (Zhikharev 1955, 311).

The censors gave permission to publish "Pozharskii and Minin, or Russians' Sacrifices" on January 31, 1807, and Shishkov read "Pozharskii, Minin, Germogen, or Russian Saved" at a literary evening at Derzhavin's on February 10 (ibid., 358–359). Weeks earlier Zhikharev had spoken of the latter poem as "a recent work" (ibid., 351). Most likely, in producing Minin's speech that occupied significant space in the poems, both authors were directly responding to the Synod's announcement. In any case, there is no doubt of the similarity of the mobilization strategies that the poets and the church administration had created for the fight against the fearsome new enemy.

This type of national mobilization strategy is apparently unthinkable without the mythologems of conspiracy and treason. The image of the people as a single organism, a single will into which a multitude of individual wills merge together, presupposes a preliminary purge of filth and infection without which neither the great act of self-renunciation nor victory in the eschatological battle with evil are possible. Preparing for war with Napoleon, in whom they saw a sinister fruit of revolutionary France, the conservative Russian literary figures reproduced the logic of the Jacobins with their incessant search for enemies who defied the "volonté générale," embodied in the Convention. Or rather, both of these groups reproduced the logic of Rousseau's *Social Contract*.

In Severgin's words, "however strong an external enemy,… conflicts within the state are the worst antagonist" (Severgin 1807, 18). Derzhavin and Kriukovskii and Glinka in his "fatherland drama" "Minin" written two years later, as well as Strudza in "Rzhevskii," all reserved a key role in the drama for the intrigues of Zarutskii the Cossack hetman and the last companion of Marina Mniszech, a power-hungry villain who was trying to clear his way to the Russian throne by treason and by a secret deal with the Poles. In contrast, in Kheraskov's "Moscow Liberated" Zarutskii does not figure at all. The authors of these plays were hardly all spontaneously aiming at Czartoryski, but the system of ideological coordinates, in which they were setting up the figure of a foreigner who by the will of fate became the leader's comrade and prepared to enter into secret relations with the enemy for selfish reasons and to destroy the fatherland, turns out to have been absolutely necessary.

Derzhavin and Kriukovskii perceive the Cossack Zarutskii as not fully Russian, which in part motivates his treason. "As if a Russian would betray," Derzhavin's Marina Mniszech tells the traitor Zarutskii apropos of the vacillating Trubetskoi (Dezhavin IV, 155), and Kriukovskii calls Zarutskii "a Ukrainian hetman" (Kriukovskii 1964, 274). An additional circumstance leading to the hetman's ruin is his connection to the Pole Marina Mniszech, who names him heir to the Polish puppet Otrep'ev. Apart from this, Derzhavin also has Pozharskii fall in love with Marina and heroically overcome his passion in the name of the fatherland.[5] For many years to come the figure of a Polish woman became a symbol of danger and seduction in Russian literature.

---

5   It is tempting to see this as a hint at Alexander's mistress Maria Antonovna Naryshkina, born Princess Chetvertinskaia, who was Polish by birth. It was just in 1806 that their relationship became open, as the Bavarian emissary Ol'ri reported (see Bray 1902, 119). However, it is apparently necessary to reject this hypothesis. In the drafts of the poem "Pozharskii" which Ia. K. Grot dates to the 1780's, Pozharskii is in love with a fictional Polish woman named Kleonisa (see Derzhavin III, 368–372). This is probably the case of a literary stereotype whose function was to increase the conflict between love and duty. On the other hand, not all of Grot's datings are irreproachable, so this problem may require further study.

However, Poland's subversive activity is by no means limited to Marina Mniszech's charms. Poles "try to introduce dangerous innovation to the Russian land," and

> Желая в воинстве раздоры поселить,
> … кабалу в России разрешают
> И вольности мечтой сограждан обольщают.
>   (Derzhavin IV, 273)[6]

(Hoping to sow discord in the army, / … they [would] destroy slavery in Russia / And try to seduce their fellow citizens with the dream of freedom.)

This internal menace threatened the foundations of the state and the very existence of Russia, which was destined to endure by depending solely on national unity and traditions. At the same time the writers of the Shishkov camp were by no means deaf to the dangerous parallels between their own constructions and the rhetoric of their sworn enemies; they strove to prevent the sinister features of "les enfants de la patrie" from showing through their own idealized image of the "sons of the fatherland."

In the beginning of the seventeenth century, the Poles ended up in Moscow as a result of decisions by the Boyar Duma that had sworn allegiance to Władysław. However, this historical episode from the Time of Troubles was only mentioned vaguely in the works we have discussed. Those behind the oath of allegiance to the Polish heir had not been jettisoned from the national body even after the liberation of Moscow but, on the contrary, played a leading role in the state administration. None of the writers describing these events in the early nineteenth century wanted to undermine national unity by casting doubt on the loyalty of the best-born families in the state. The foreigner Zarutskii was a much better fit for the role of traitor. Even more indicative, however, was another quasi-historical episode.

---

6   We will not dwell in detail on this circle of allusions since they have been exhaustively analyzed by Mark Al'tshuller (1984, 157–166). It seems that the researcher somewhat exaggerates, however, seeing in the just cited lines a hint at the five-year-old attempt by Alexander's advisors on the Secret Committee to abolish serfdom. Fears of the spread of revolutionary ideas among the lower classes which were discussed in the last section provided a fully adequate historical context for these lines.

∞ 5 ∞

In all of the works we have discussed, the election of Mikhail Fedorovich as tsar that established the Romanov dynasty serves as the conceptual culmination of the described events. It is almost always Pozharskii who poignantly and magnanimously refuses the crown offered to him and initiates the election. In Derzhavin the people first express their preference for autocracy over the power of the Boyar Duma, exclaiming "No need for boyars, long live the tsar," and then, together with the Duma, proclaim that "Pozharskii's our man (Pozharskii nam liub)" (Derzhavin IV, 187–188). In Kruiukovskii the "leader of Smolensk" offers the crown to Pozharskii in the name of the army (Kriukovskii 1964, 273). But Shakhmatov paints the most expressive picture:

> Но что? Се возникает глас,
> Подобный шуму вод спокойных:
> Пожарский первый из достойных!
> То будет царь, кто царство спас!…
>
> Духовный лик и сонм бояр,
> Несущи угвари державных,
> Величество богов земных,
> Грядут — и вся Россия в них —
> К свершителю деяний славных.
>
> Взложи сияющий венец;
> Одеян красотою царской,
> На царский фон воссядь, Пожарской!
> Воссядь — и будь царем сердец!
>   (Shirinskii-Shikhmatov 1971, 378–380)

(But what is this? A voice is heard / Like the sound of calm waters: / Pozharskii is first among the worthy! / Let he be tsar who saved the kingdom (tsarstvo)! … // The clergy and the assembly of boyars / Carrying the symbols of state, / The majesty of earthly gods, / Will come—and all of Russia with them— / To the one who achieved glorious deeds. // Bestow the shining crown; / Arrayed in royal beauty, / Mount the royal throne, Pozharskii! / Mount it—and be tsar of our hearts!)

In his poem Shikhmatov tried quite seriously to follow historical events faithfully. Derzhavin and Kriukovskii, in consonance with the laws of dramatic genres, introduced many fictional characters into their plays, although a certain historical verisimilitude was also important for them. Derzhavin endowed his "heroic presentation" with a foreword in which he indicated what was fiction and what was taken from historical sources. He definitely included the episode of offering the crown to Prince Pozharskii in his list of historically authentic events. However, neither the documents that had been published by the time nor the known manuscripts nor any historical works contained anything similar.[7] Here, for example, is how I. I. Golikov described the country's gratitude to Pozharskii:

> After offering their most ardent prayers to the Lord, all eyes and thoughts were directed to those responsible for their happiness, Prince Dmitrii Mikhailovich Pozharskii and Koz'ma Minin. Recognizing them as the instrument of God's grace, they so to speak poured out their hearts to them which were overflowing with the most lively gratitude, called them their benefactors and saviors, and as testimony of this all the government ranks unanimously resolved to grant the prince the honor of Boyar-hood and to present him with a patent signed by the hand of boyars from all over the state and by distinguished clergymen, which was then also affirmed by Mikhail Fedorovich. (Golikov II, 336; cf. Mankiev 1770; Novyi letopisets 1792).

The discussion here concerns an award that was certainly a very high honor, but nevertheless far from the tsar's crown.

Clearly, Derzhavin felt a bit awkward about this episode. While referring in all other cases (and with full reason) to "the 'Core of Russian History' (Iadro Rossiiskoi istorii) and other chronicles," here he limited himself to the vague suggestion "as some foreign writers and all circumstances confirm" (Derzhavin IV, 131). The reference to "all circumstances" indicates that the anonymous "foreign writers" are no more than a figure of speech. But whatever his sources, the source for all of the other writers, mostly likely, was Derzhavin himself.

---

7   In Prince Obolenskii's chronicle Pozharskii is actually named among the active participants in Mikhail's election (see Platonov 1913, 411), but there is not a word about his candidacy for the throne. On the contrary, the only evidence of this kind is the assertion of the nobleman Sumin—which was most likely a slander and most likely not known to the literary men of the early nineteenth century—that Pozharskii attempted to be crowned in Moscow and that he had offered him 20,000 rubles for this (see Zabelin 1848, 85).

In Pavel L'vov's historical narrative *Pozharskii and Minin* that came out in 1810, he follows Golikov's version, at times literally, but deviating from it, however, on the question of Pozharskii's voluntary refusal of the throne. To this episode the author supplies the following commentary:

> Our chronicles are silent about Prince Pozharskii's praiseworthy refusal, perhaps because in those times virtue was no surprise and virtue's frequent victories did not attract special attention but were considered the essential duty of an honest person and a God-fearing Christian, but word of this that was passed down from generation to generation, from mouth to mouth,… has reached us. … This legend was proclaimed in the song of one of our illustrious Skalds. With delight I accept this legend as a truth that should not be doubted, for I strongly believe that such an extraordinary event could take place in Russia since there was a Pozharskii and because such unparalleled greatness of soul was not foreign to him. (L'vov 1810, 175–176)

By "the song of a Skald," L'vov had in mind not Derzhavin's play that had been published two years earlier and that had had no success, but his celebrated ode

Figure 14 Proposal for a monument to Minin and Pozharskii (1809) by I. P. Martos.

"On the Perfidy of the French Rebellion and In Honor of Prince Pozharskii." In this ode, among other things Derzhavin wrote about his beloved historical hero:

> Не вняв к себе народа клику,
> Избрал достойного владыку
> И над собою воцарил;
> Который быв покорен воле
> Избранного собой царя.
> Не возроптал и в низкой доле,
> Его веления творя. ...
> Царя творец и раб послушный,
> Не ты ль, герой великодушный,
> Пожарский, муж великий мой.
>   (Derzhavin I, 23–231)

(Not accepting the people's adulation for himself, / He elected a worthy sovereign / And made him tsar over himself; / He submitted to the will / Of the tsar he chose. / He did not grumble over his humble role / Carrying out his commands. ... / Obedient slave and maker of tsars, / Is this not you, magnanimous hero, / Pozharskii, my great man.)

In 1789, when Derzhavin wrote this ode, he did not worry much about the correlation of the legend he was presenting to the facts and documents. Now, in an era of growing interest in native history, when he himself had accused Ozerov's "Dimitrii Donskoi" of violating "historical faithfulness" (vernost') (see Zhikharev 1955, 331), the poet was obliged to support the legend he had once created by references to doubtful sources and incomprehensible "circumstances."

However, there does exist a text that reflects this precise version of historical events. This is an historical folk song first published by P. V. Kireevskii in 1868:

> Как и взговорют бояре — воеводы московские:
> «Выбираем мы себе в цари
> Из бояр боярина славного —
> Князя Дмитрия Пожарского сына!»

> Как и взоворит к боярам Пожарский князь:
> «Ох вы, гой еси, бояре — воеводы московские!
> Не достоин я такой почести от вас,
> Не могу принять я от вас царства Московского.
> Уж скажу же вам, бояре — воеводы московские:
> Уж мы выберем себе в православные цари
> Из славного, из богатого дому Романова
> Михаила сына Федоровича». (Putilov 1966, 95)

(So say the boyars, voevodas of Moscow: / "We are choosing a tsar for ourselves / A renowned boyar from the boyars / Prince Dmitrii, son of Pozharskii!" / So says Prince Pozharskii to the boyars: / "Hail to you, voevodas of Moscow! / I do not deserve such honor from you, / I cannot accept the kingdom of Moscow from you. / But I will say to you, voevodas of Moscow, / Let us choose an Orthodox tsar for ourselves / From the splendid, rich house of Romanov, / Mikhail Fedorovich.")

It is possible that this song, recorded many years later from a seventy-year-old woman in the village of Slobod of the Borovskii region, Kaluga province (ibid., 345)[8] might have served as Derzhavin's source. The poet had an interest in folklore (see, for example, Al'tshuller 1984, 285–291), and the song tradition may have influenced his depiction of Marina Miniszech in "Pozharskii" as a sorceress and magician (see Putilov 1966, 30, 36; Adrianova-Peretts I, 373). Still, another possibility is more likely. In the same ode, "On the Perfidy of the French Rebellion," Derzhavin mentions Belisarius, who he describes elsewhere as "the very greatest military commander … of the Greek Emperor Justinian; he conquered Carthage,… the Goths, Syracusans, Palermo, Naples and many other cities and peoples; he refused the crown the Goths offered him. …" Belisarius is also mentioned in this context in the ode "The Waterfall" (see Derzhavin I, 320; III, 520).

---

8   Cf. the characteristic note on this song by the author of an academy history of Russian folklore: "Pozharskii is a national hero, and therefore the song, contradicting history, presents an episode relating that a council of boyars and voevodas decided to pick Pozharskii to be tsar, but he allegedly refused the throne for himself, proposing that they elect Mikhail Romanov. In this way the memory of the struggle among various candidacies for the Russian throne was reconstituted in folklore" (Adrianova-Peretts I, 376; cf. Busanov 1992, 112–113).

The historical Belisarius was well-known in Russia thanks to J.-F. Marmontel's novel that Catherine, together with her travelling companions, had translated in 1767 during their trip down the Volga (ibid., III, 239). By the time "Pozharskii" was written, five editions of the Russian translation of *Belisarius* had already been published (SKRK II, 218–219). Most likely, Derzhavin made use of the very traditional scheme of likening Russian heroes to those of antiquity and modeled the legend of Pozharskii's renunciation of the throne on Belisarius. Of course, both Marmontel and the folksong might simultaneously have served as sources for the relevant place in the ode; their combination could only have lightened the poet's task. It also seems possible that the early nineteenth-century works about Pozharskii might themselves have led to this folksong. Such a pattern is not unusual.

In any case, the Pozharskii of the ode "On the Perfidy of the French Rebellion" is a model of Stoic virtue of a classical cast. In the drafts for the poem "Pozharskii," when the hero makes his oath to Mikhail, "he declares that he is going into seclusion, but that if his arm or advice are ever needed for the fatherland, he is always ready to serve" (Derzhavin III, 373). In the first decade of the nineteenth century, this self-effacing act took on quite other features. In Kheraskov's "Moscow Liberated," Pozharskii's speech summoning of Mikhail to the throne only serves as the compositional completion of an already essentially finished tragedy (see Kheraskov 1961, 371). In sharp contrast, for authors writing on this theme in 1806–1807, the corresponding monologue becomes the crux of the work's message. In Derzhavin the hero refuses the "holy porphyry" of the tsars, saying: "Only one heir by blood / Can give them tranquility and return us to peace" (Derzhavin IV, 190). In Kriukovskii he exclaims: "Tsars are ordained for us by God" (Kriukovskii 1964, 283). In Shikhmatov the corresponding episode reaches an emotional and conceptual peak:

> … возник земный Эдем
> Для россов из земного ада;
> И я — о, из наград награда.
> Сподобился быть их вождем.
>
> Господь возводит на престолы,
> Владеть оправдывает он;

Вотще чрез пагубы, крамолы
Теснятся хищники на трон.
Пусть высоты достигнут звездной.
На землю наведут боязнь, -
Приспеет медленная казнь,
Восторгнет их рукой железной
И свергнет в тартар от небес.
И я — дерзнув ступить на царство,
В себе вместил бы их коварство,
Их студ достойно бы понес.
    (Shirinskii-Shikhmatov 1971, 383)

(… an earthly Eden / Arose for Rosses out of an earthly hell; / And I—oh, reward of rewards, / Was honored to be their leader. // The Lord raises [kings] to the throne, / He justifies their rule; / While through destruction and treachery / Predators crowd up to the throne. / Let them reach the starry heavens / And make the whole world scared of them: / A slow punishment will ripen, / Rip them out with an iron hand / And send them down from the heavens into Tartarus. / And I, having dared to tread this path / Would embody their perfidy myself / And would have been worthy of their shame.)

The poet places before his hero the choice between an absolute moral triumph and a just as absolute catastrophe, between heaven and hell. The leader, creating "an earthly Eden" for his people, turns out—if he takes the throne—to be like a "predator" who strives for power through destruction and treachery and who is destined to be thrown down to Tartarus. Ethical maximalism on this scale and the degree of anxiety becomes comprehensible if we take into consideration that Shikhmatov and the other writers of the time projected Pozharskii's final apotheosis onto the fate of Napoleon.

    General Bonaparte had been able to put an end to the chaos of revolution, pacify civil tensions and raise France to an unprecedented pinnacle of power. In this context the imperial crown could be seen as a reward for obvious and extraordinary services to the fatherland. However, it is precisely here that an abyss of moral bankruptcy lurks. It was no accident that Napoleon's coronation preceded the execution of the Duke of Enghien that shocked Russian society (see Dubrovin 1895, № 2, 204–208). In contrast, it is precisely Pozharskii's decision to refuse supreme power, passing the throne on to its legitimate owner, that comprises his triumph:

> Велик, велик ты незабвенно
> Кровавых множеством побед!
>
> Но сей победою бескровной
> Ты всех героев победил. ...
>
> Вещайте, славные народы!
> Сыны всех лет, всех стран, всех вер:
> Блеснул ли где в прошедши годы
> Подобной доблести пример?
> Ему совместника в вас нет;
> Един Пожарский во вселенной!
>   (Shirinskii-Shikhmatov 1971, 383)

(Great [man], you are unforgettably great / For your many bloody victories! // But with this bloodless victory / You [Pozharskii] have conquered all other heroes. ... // Be it known, glorious peoples! / Sons of all times, countries, faiths: / Has there shone anywhere in past years / Any such example of valor? ... / You have no equal for him; / There is only one Pozharskii in the universe!)

Golikov's story of Mikhail Romanov's election speaks of the earlier "disagreement and disturbance in thought that was like fierce ocean waves during storm winds" (Golikov II, 343). Only after the name of the future tsar is mentioned by "the voice of God" does the disquiet turn into general consensus. In contrast, Shikhmatov compares the voice of the people inviting Pozharskii to rule to "the sound of calm waters." This is Rousseau's general will (volonté générale) that was so dear to writers of national-conservative orientation. Only this time the general will, despite Rousseau's assertions (Rousseau 1969, 170–171), was in error, for it did not rely on divine blessing and national tradition. "The first among the worthy" may not inherit the throne.

The election of Mikhail Romanov was also weighted with such providentialist significance because it was precisely this inheritance that would—according to authors of Shishkov's circle—ultimately guarantee Alexander's victory over Napoleon, despite his human weaknesses and dangerous mistakes. "And the one who stole the throne will fall to dust before the tsar"—with this line spoken by Pozharskii, Kriukovskii's tragedy came to a close

(1964, 284). The play's premiere was performed with thunderous success in Petersburg on May 22, 1807 (see Zhikharev 1955, 543–546). Ten days were left before the defeat at Friedland and a month until the Peace of Tilsit.

∽ 6 ∽

The second war with Napoleon of 1806–1807 strongly energized the national-conservative opposition. Its ideologues sensed that the national mobilization created favorable possibilities for going on the political attack. It was just at this time that regular literary readings began at Shishkov's and Derzhavin's; these meetings would a few years later develop into the "Colloquy of Lovers of the Russian Word" (Al'tshuller 1984, 48–9). The works written during these months by writers of the circle presented an entire range of ideological metaphors from which to build a new mythology of the origins of Russian statehood, to find historical analogies for current events, and to rearrange the figures in the national pantheon. By 1807 the contours of the new state ideology were basically defined. Evidently, even the emperor himself was thinking over the prospects for allying with his former intellectual foes.

In Derzhavin's memoirs it says that, "in 1806 and at the beginning of 1807, at the time when the French went into Prussia," he wrote to the emperor

> two notes about measures to subdue the impudence of the French and to defend Russia from an attack by Bonaparte, ... about which he[9] spoke to Him in person, asking permission to compose a project for which he had already collected his thoughts and sketched out a plan; it only needed some corrections from the War College and other places concerning the troops' dress, the fortresses, weapons and similar things. The Sovereign accepted this proposal with favor, wanted to summon him to meet, but, having gone in March to the army near Friedland and then returning from there, he changed his former gracious behavior and no longer greeted him and didn't speak to him. (Derzhavin VI, 828)

We should not doubt that it was not respect for the aging poet's gifts as a commander that caused Alexander to demonstrate his previous favor to Derzhavin, whom three years earlier he had scandalously fired from service.

---

9   In his memoirs, Derzhavin often referred to himself in the third person.

However, the development of events brought Derzhavin, Shishkov and their adherents bitter disillusionment. As was stated in the *Political Journal*, "In the year 1807 from the Sarmatian land, irrigated with floods of blood, *sprouted an olive tree of friendship* which, quickly rising, embraced France and Russia with its branches" (Istoricheskaia kartina 1808, 83). Instead of the purging of foreign scum and a battle to the death, there followed the Tilsit peace, Speranskii's rise, and a new round of reformist activism. Nonetheless, the ideological elaborations that did not suit the state during these years were again called into action in 1812 when, on the threshold of the approaching war, Shishkov was appointed State Secretary and Rostopchin Moscow's governor-general.

CHAPTER 6

Enemy of the People:
M. M. Speranskii's Fall and the Mythology of Treason in Social and Literary Consciousness, 1809–1812

∾ 1 ∾

Shishkov and his supporters' new summons to power was preceded by the sensational dismissal of M. M. Speranskii. On March 17, 1812, Alexander I had sent for his state secretary and, after a highly emotional audience that lasted many hours, accompanied by dramatic effects and His Majesty's tears, he relieved him of all of his duties. That evening Speranskii was sent under guard to Nizhnii Novgorod. Russian history is rich in instances of the sudden fall of yesterday's all-powerful favorites; nevertheless the disgrace of the emperor's closest advisor and "right hand" produced a deafening impression on contemporaries. F. F. Vigel' wrote in his memoirs that "the news of his [Speranskii's] exile still remains a puzzle for us and even posterity probably will not figure it out. In Russian legend it will remain like the history of the Iron Mask in France" (Vigel' IV, 34). Speranskii's first biographer M. A. Korf, who knew him personally during the last years of his life, agreed with this assessment (Korf II, 27).

There are not many documents at our disposal that would allow us to judge what happened behind the closed doors of the emperor's study. They consist of the following: Speranskii's letters to Alexander justifying himself, the

Figure 15 Portrait of Count M. M. Speranskii; gravure from the original by I. A. Ivanov.

story he told F. P. Lubianovskii, which the latter passed on in his *Memoirs* (Lubianovskii 1872, 227–229), and several fragmentary and contradictory statements by the emperor (for the most complete collection of the documentary evidence, see Shil'der III, 31–52, 366–371, 487–532; see also Korf 1902; Bychkov 202–203; for an almost exhaustive bibliography of the question, see Raeff 1957, 202–203). The extremely detailed *Memoirs* of Ia. I. Sanglen (Sanglen 1883), the head of the secret department of the Ministry of Police and an active participant in the unfolding intrigue against Speranskii, are unreliable, and for all of their unique value must be used with caution.

These memoirs were written more than thirty years after the fact, as well as after the death of Speranskii, who had ended his life a respected official. At first Sanglen refused to share his notes with Speranskii's biographer Korf, pleading his obligations to Alexander, from which only the reigning emperor could free him. Korf, intrigued, attempted to procure the necessary permission from the emperor, but Nicholas I, who had an extreme antipathy toward Sanglen, wouldn't hear of it. Nevertheless, Sanglen, apparently wanting to justify himself, flooded Korf with his papers.

Understandably, Sanglen's constant attempts to separate himself from those who took part in the intrigue and to demonstrate his extraordinary perspicacity and present himself as a "knight without fear and beyond reproach" do not deserve the slightest trust. Such efforts boldly contradict both his immediate superiors and eminent courtiers and even the emperor himself. However, his bare account of the charges that Speranskii's enemies brought against him augments other known sources and does not contradict them in any way. The well-informed Nikolai Grech writes of secret conversations between Alexander and Sanglen (Grech 1930, 512), and in his diaries L. I. Golenishchev-Kutuzov asserted that after the state secretary's exile Sanglen told him that "Speranskii's crime is treason." He further noted that Sanglen was "in some kind of ecstatic rage" (Bychkov 1902, 18).

This "ecstatic rage" on the part of a humble bureaucrat who had been admitted to the highest circle of power amply explains his unusual ability to recall all of the details of what turned out to be the acme of his career. For this reason he was so eager to explain everything for posterity, presenting his own role in as attractive a light as possible. Of course, Alexander, who to put it mildly was not apt to excessive candor, was least likely to reveal his cherished thoughts to Sanglen. Most probably, he repeated the main charges that came in the denunciations he had received, testing them against Sanglen's responses and formulating a version of events that was most favorable to himself.

Of all the above-mentioned sources, Speranskii's letter sent to the emperor from Perm on February 4, 1813, is the most significant. Known to Korf only in a corrupt and incomplete copy, the genuine text was found and published by N. K. Shil'der (III, 515–527). The letter is credible in at least in one respect. Trying to justify himself, Speranskii lists all possible accusations against himself in maximum detail, both those he heard from the emperor as well as those about which he could only guess. "I do not know with precision what was imputed to me in the secret denunciations," he wrote. "From the words which Your Highness was pleased to tell me at our parting I can only conclude that there were three main points of accusation: 1) that I tried to disrupt the state through financial dealings; 2) to make the government hated by means of taxation; 3) my opinions about the government" (ibid., 521–522). On the first two counts Speranskii noted that, while he was running the country's financial system, state income had more than doubled, and that raising taxes—unavoidable for a state burdened with a huge budget deficit and preparing for war—can never be a popular measure. These conclusions not only seem indisputable but obvious; it is impossible to imagine that Alexander would not have known of them earlier. Consequently, these charges were a rhetorical cover for Alexander's true motives. The emperor evidently did not make much effort to hide this from Speranskii, insofar as on parting he said to him that "in any other, less urgent situation, he would have taken a year or two to closely review and verify" the information he had received (ibid., 515).

Therefore, besides refutation of the stated charges, Speranskii also had to respond to others that might have remained unexpressed. The most threatening was the suspicion, widespread in society, and allegedly confirmed by his disgrace, that he was acting in the interests of France. Speranskii later wrote in a letter to Alexander:

> This cruel prejudice concerning my ties with France, confirmed by the fact of my banishment, now comprises the main accusation, and, I may say, the *single stain* on my reputation, among the people. You alone, Gracious Sir, and your sense of justice, have it in your power to remove this. I make bold to say affirmatively: in eternal truth before God you are obliged, Sir, to do this. ... The finances, taxes, new laws—all public affairs for which I had the happiness to be your executor—will all be justified with time; but how can I justify myself when everything is hidden and must be kept secret? (ibid., 523)

The issue in these dramatic lines concerns the fact that for several years Speranskii's responsibilities included carrying on a secret correspondence with Talleyrand which his agent in Paris, K. V. Nessel'rode, had managed to establish. This correspondence went on outside usual diplomatic channels, and neither Chancellor Rumiantsev nor the Russian ambassador to France A. B. Kurakin knew of its existence (Nikolai Mikhailovich I, 83). Speranskii's real misstep in the service that he describes in this letter was connected to this relationship with Talleyrand. To wit, his wrongdoing was: the unsanctioned reading of materials perlustrated from foreign diplomatic correspondence (see Shil'der III, 53–68). However, this trifling overextension of his almost unlimited authority as state secretary could not have been the reason for his firing, for at the time of their fatal audience Alexander knew nothing about it. Speranskii himself sent Alexander the relevant documents, together with an accompanying letter on the night after his fall. The emperor subsequently showed this admission to the Minister of Justice I. I. Dmitriev as evidence of Speranskii's guilt, as "his impudence swelled to the point that he wanted to share in state secrets" (Dmitriev 1986, 346). Paradoxically, Speranskii's behavior that was aimed at modifying the pro-France direction of official diplomacy could be seen by poorly-informed parties as an indication of his special sympathy for France. Still, Alexander, who had placed this responsibility on his state secretary, could not help knowing the true nature of events. "My enemies may question my political rules," Speranskii wrote in his letter from Perm, "and could have imagined that I had sympathy for the French system, but Your Highness could not have harbored any doubts" (Shil'der III, 524).

Nine months earlier Speranskii had sent the emperor his first letter of self-justification from Nizhnii Novgorod. It was much shorter than the letter from Perm and does not contain an analysis of the charges against him. Nonetheless, one may find a suggestion of what the disgraced favorite considered the reason for his fall. "The first and single source of everything" (ibid., 44) is named here as the plan for state reforms that he was preparing. In the letter from Perm he recalled that he had put together his plans for legal reform at the emperor's request and in close cooperation with him. He also noted that they were approved by other statesmen and were only aimed at perfecting the system of government administration; in no way did they limit the prerogatives of monarchial power (on Speranskii's political ideas of this period, see Dovnar-Zapol'skii 1905; Raeff 1957; Predtechenskii 1957; Kaliagin 1973; Morozov 1999, etc.).

According to Sanglen's testimony, Alexander told him of his displeasure with Speranskii's reformist ideas and on the very day of the final audience had even declared to him that Speranskii "was trying to undermine autocracy" (Sanglen 1883, № 2, 178; cf. Shil'der III, 8). However, even if we take this testimony on faith, this kind of formulation was most likely an excuse for firing the state secretary, rather than the emperor's sincere opinion. If in conversations with Sanglen, Dmitriev and the rector of Derpt University, G.-F. Parrot, Alexander mentioned treason, with people who were closer to him—A. N. Golitsyn, N. N. Novosil'tsev, and K. V. Nessel'rode—he made it known that he did not believe in Speranskii's guilt. In his characteristic style he said completely different things to different people. In particular, he mentioned to Novosil'tsev that Speranskii was not a traitor and was only guilty before him personally, "having paid for my trust with the blackest, most horrible ingratitude" (Shil'der III, 493; Nikolai Mikhailovich I, 105). In N. K. Shil'der's opinion, it was precisely unguarded skeptical statements about the emperor that were the real reason for the state secretary's downfall, and everything that happened on March 17, 1812, was "the settling of personal accounts by an insulted, vengeful heart" (ibid., 50).

M. P. Pogodin was of a similar opinion, noting that the disgraced favorite was never fully rehabilitated. The emperor did not show Speranskii the same good graces as before. For many years Alexander kept him far from Petersburg on various pretexts, and when they did meet, they avoided talk of the past (Pogodin 1871, 1146–1149). However, knowing Alexander's vengefulness and his penchant for melodramatic effects, it is difficult to doubt that either he would never have forgiven Speranskii his disdainful words or that he would have arranged a ritual of forgiveness in a way he saw fit. On the other hand, it is always unpleasant to look someone in the eyes whom you have cruelly and unjustly harmed. One can say without irony that the fact that Speranskii was nevertheless returned to state service, and did not end his days in exile, is to the emperor's great credit.

Practically all references to Speranskii's critical statements about the emperor ultimately lead back to the denunciations of him. These often contained very improbable information (see Shil'der III, 35). We will cite one example. Speranskii's famous alleged evaluation of Alexander—"Everything that he does, he does half way. ... He is too weak to rule and too strong to be ruled"—we know through three connecting links. Sanglen recorded in his memoirs that the statement came from the emperor, who had heard it from the Minister of Police Balashov, who had been assigned to watch over the state secretary. From the four people who might have made the statement, Speranskii seems the least likely. According to Sanglen, when he had heard the emperor's account of the episode he quickly expressed his doubts: "Speranskii is a clever man, so how would he have said this, and on first acquaintance with whom—with the Minister of Police, and to be so frank with him? Moreover, this phrase was said before about Louis XV—it is a repetition" (Sanglen 1883, № 1, 23–24). Even if Alexander had really been so open with this middle-rank official, it seems almost impossible to imagine that Sanglen would have allowed himself to contradict the emperor. More likely, he assigned himself this response that had just begged to be made only in retrospect. In any case his reaction is hard to gainsay. Speranskii's career had begun at the very bottom and before serving at court he had had to spend time in close association with several important officials. The milieu in which he had to make his way did not dispose one to ingenuousness. Moreover, Speranskii knew that he was surrounded by a solid wall of malevolence and denunciations, and indeed because of this he had applied for retirement several months earlier, which Alexander did not accept. In such circumstances it would have been hard to imagine such suicidal and senseless openness from him.[1]

In the Perm letter Speranskii tried to explain to the emperor the source of the rumors about his "personal opinions." "How, they will ask, did the same message come from various people? Because these various people were in fact one body, and *the soul belonging to this body was the same that seemed to everyone and still seems an outsider*" (Shil'der III, 523). As Shil'der notes, next to this passage "in the original on the side is written in pencil, *apparently* in Emperor Alexander's hand, 'NB'" (ibid.). In the opinion of M. A. Korf, the person referred to is the emperor's sister, Grand Princess Ekaterina Pavlovna (Korf 1902, 475). The validity of this guess is supported by the fact that Speranskii, as mentioned, considered the main reason for his fall the plan for state reforms, and a French translation of it, by the emperor's order, had been given to Ekaterina Pavlovna's husband, the prince of Oldenburg (Shil'der III, 44). Many contemporaries were also of this opinion. Rostopchin, who was closely connected to the grand princely couple, later recalled that people attributed Speranskii's fall to "GPK i Pr.O" (Grand Princess Katerina and Prince Oldenburg) (Rostopchin 1992, 246).[2]

According to F. Gauenshil'd, who was close to Speranskii, the state secretary attributed his fall primarily to Prince A. N. Golitsyn (Gauenshil'd 1902, 261). However, he discussed this question with Speranskii ten years after the

---

1   N. K. Shil'der cites a revolutionary statement also allegedly made by Speranskii (III, 35), taken from a denunciation made almost twenty years later to Nicholas I, that suggests total paranoia (see Shil'der 1898/1899).
2   The initial "K" in the text instead of the more correct "E" is, of course, the result of a careless translation of the French "C" for "Catherine."

fact, by which time the latter might have changed his opinion. Moreover, Speranskii would hardly have expressed his suspicions about a member of the royal family to anyone except the emperor himself. Furthermore, by that time the grand princess was no longer living.

Ekaterina Pavlovna may have played an instrumental role in the campaign to bring down the state secretary, but Speranskii did not know, or did not want to know, that directly behind the backs of the informers and provocateurs who surrounded him stood the emperor himself.[3] It was Alexander who ordered the Minister of Police A. D. Balashov and Baron G. Armfel'dt to collect compromising information on Speranskii and simultaneously asked Balashov's subordinate Sanglen to keep an eye on his boss. "We acted like telegraphs whose wires were in the emperor's hands," noted Sanglen. This statement can raise no doubts (Sanglen 1883, № 3, 394).

In light of the above we may make a careful suggestion concerning one of the murkiest details of the whole intrigue. As we know, Balashov and Armfel'dt made a proposal to Speranskii to form a triumvirate with them that would have taken the government administration into their hands. Speranskii unequivocally refused, but did not report on this conversation to Alexander right away (Shil'der III, 529). Furthermore, he had some kind of meeting planned with Balashov which he missed; the note of apology that he sent the Minister of Police was later used against him. Traditionally, this unconsidered step has been explained by Speranskii's fastidiousness (see, for example, Lubianovskii 1872, 230; Shil'der III, 37–38 and passim). However, if we allow that Speranskii had understood the provocatory nature of this proposal, which would have been completely natural, but that he mistakenly assumed that the grand princess was behind it, then he might have thought that before entering into battle with such a powerful opponent he would need to prepare and collect more information first. For this reason he might not have wanted to break off all relations with Balashov immediately.

---

3   V. A. Tomsinov describes the logic of this process somewhat differently: "The web of intrigue against Speranskii, huge in scope, took hold of Alexander and pulled him along to a denouement he had not planned. And he, instead of resisting, suddenly went along submissively, at first passively, trailing along the others, but then gradually found his legs and went off on his own, overtook the ones who had been dragging him along, and himself drew them forward to the place to which they had just recently been drawing him" (Tomsinov 1991, 196).

At times, in discussing the reasons for Speranskii's disgrace, Alexander preferred to describe himself as a victim of circumstances. "Last night they took Speranskii from me," he told Golitsyn on March 18, and then on the next day declared to Nessel'rode that "only current circumstances could have snatched this victim of public opinion away from me" (Shil'der III, 48). Of course, the emperor was not being completely sincere. The entire initiative for removing the state secretary belonged exclusively to him. Nevertheless, there was also a bit of truth in these complaints.

Speranskii's departure and Shishkov's appointment in his place was one of those symbolic gestures for which Alexander had an extraordinary flair. These changes in personnel signaled the end of the Tilsit era, when the figure of the priest's son Speranskii, brought to the foot of the throne after Alexander's meeting with Napoleon in Erfurt, emblematized not only the pro-Bonapartist political course, but also Speranskii's readiness to control the autocrat without reckoning with the public. Now, on the threshold of a mortal conflict, the emperor turned to face his subjects directly. According to one of Speranskii's last accounts, Alexander said to him, "You have powerful enemies, public opinion demands your dismissal, and only on this basis do they agree to give us the money we need, and I have Napoleon and an inevitable war on my hands" (Bychkov 1902, 11). It isn't clear if Speranskii was repeating words actually spoken at his audience with Alexander, or if this simply reflects his retrospective interpretation of the tsar's motives. It is hard to say what money is being discussed, whether military subsidies were to come from England or future popular offerings. Nevertheless, the underlying political situation shows through almost transparently. "Was Alexander really convinced of the justice of the accusations and suspicions that he voiced to Speranskii or was this was only a mask to convince him, or perhaps, himself, only an excuse to rid himself at any cost, without evident due process, of a person to whom he himself had given too much influence?" asked Korf. "Most probably, the latter" (ibid., 10).

This explanation leaves one significant question unanswered. To demonstrate a change in political policy the retirement and new appointment were sufficient; that is, such a decision did not require any additional explanations on Alexander's part. Thus, the complex intrigue he set into motion and the wild accusations levelled against a close advisor seem excessive. Speranskii himself, without much success, tried to figure out why his enemies needed to annihilate him and not merely remove him from office (Shil'der III, 529–532). At the same time several participants in the intrigue managed to penetrate the emperor's motives, or, what is far less probable, to infect him with their own ideas. Sanglen cites a conversation that he allegedly had with Armfel't on the eve of Speranskii's dismissal. "'You know,' said Armfel'dt, 'whether he is guilty or not, he has to be sacrificed; this is necessary to bind the people to the head of the state for the sake of the war which must be national.'" "This conversation," comments Sanglen, "revealed the secret to me that Speranskii had been inexorably marked for sacrifice, which under the pretext of betrayal and hatred would unite all estates and inspire everyone with patriotism in the current war" (Sanglen 1883, № 3, 377).

This conversation so struck Sanglen that he considered it necessary to revisit it: "The Sovereign, forced by the pressure of political circumstances to fight a war against Napoleon on his own soil, wanted to find something which, awakening patriotism, would unite all estates around him. To achieve this it was necessary to fabricate a case of treason against the state and fatherland. The public, rightly or wrongly, had long ago proclaimed throughout Russia that [Speranskii] was a traitor anyway. Who would make a better choice [of victim] than he?" (ibid., 394). We repeat that the low reliability of Sanglen's memoirs does not prove who precisely expressed this point of view. Still, the constellation of ideas and images he describes so expressively—"sacrifice," "treason," "general hatred," "unity of the people," "patriotism," "national war," etc.— unquestionably helped to color the entire course of events.

∽ **2** ∽

At the very end of the Perm letter, Speranskii names still another possible reason for his disgrace. He mentions it in passing, clearly feeling awkward that he had to touch on slander that was so obviously ridiculous to his addressee as well: "Is it really necessary, most gracious sir, for me to defend myself against those accusations that my enemies have spread about my morals and connections with Martinists, Illuminati, and so on? My papers clearly show that I never had any ties to them; in general I have tried to have my own opinions and to never believe anyone else blindly" (Shil'der III, 526). Speranskii had long known about such rumors but never took them seriously, and apparently did not believe that the emperor, well-informed about his activities, could have any doubts on this score. Five years later, in a letter to his friend A. A. Stolypin, Speranskii, who by that time had become the governor of Penza, gave such rumors—involving completely different people this time—an unambiguous characterization: "How little enlightenment there is yet in Petersburg! From your letter I see that they still believe in Martinists and Illuminati there. Old wives' tales with which one can only frighten children!" (Speranskii 1870, 1152).

However, the derisive tone of these responses hardly corresponded to the actual state of affairs. In reality the issue had to do with a well-developed complex of cultural and historical stereotypes that played a large role not only in the personal fate of the state secretary, but in the fates of Russia and Europe as well. The notion that a powerful secret conspiracy moves historical events has deep roots in human history. In the eighteenth century this explanatory practice acquired broad popularity (see Roberts 1972; Pipes 1997). Enlightenment philosophers saw the cause of the victory of ignorance and prejudice as the age-old conspiracy of churchmen with the powers-that-be. Conservative thinkers, on the contrary, saw a similar conspiracy on the part of the Enlighteners themselves. Masonic lodges had spread widely in the first half of the eighteenth century, first in Britain and then across Europe, and they served as the material embodiment of evil behind-the-scenes intrigues (see, for example, Deforneau 1965; on the spread of Masonry, see Le Forestier 1970; Roberts 1972, 17–145; Piatigorskii 1997, 37–232, etc.; on the origins of Masonry, see Stevenson 1988).

With its constantly advertised cult of secrecy, Masonry was an ideal object for the mythology of universal conspiracies.[4] In comparably free and tolerant England, Masonic lodges recalled secret clubs and touted moral self-perfection and philanthropy as their programmatic goals, while in continental Europe they were more often seen as secret political societies or religious sects. On top of the three degrees adopted by English lodges, French and German Masonry constructed very elaborate systems of distinction that sharply complicated the ritual of initiation. They also enlarged the official Masonic genealogy by making connections with the medieval order of the Templars and with ancient esoteric

---

4   On the constant and persistent propaganda of its own profound secrecy as one of the fundamental phenomenological paradoxes of Masonry, see Piatigorskii 1997, xiii–xiv, 76–77 and passim.

cults. Occult and mystical movements asserted a strong influence on Masonry. The most important of these movements are Rosicrucianism, which focused on alchemical and para-medical research, and Martinism, a philosophical movement concerning "regeneration" or the reunion of the initiate's soul with the spirit world to which it had earlier belonged (see Wyatt I-II; Le Forestier 1970; Roberts 1972, 101–117; Macintosh 1992, etc.).[5] On the other hand, the order of Illuminati, a secret society founded in 1776 in Bavaria by a professor at Ingolstadt University, Adam Weishaupt, also played a role in the development of the lodges. The Illuminati promoted radical political reforms, partly of an egalitarian-socialist type (see Le Forestier 1974; for a representative collection of documents on the order's history, see Dälmen 1977; cf. Roberts 1972, 118–145). At first the order was not connected with Masonry, but at the start of the 1780s its leaders began to join Masonic lodges to make use of their popularity to spread their ideas. The prohibition of the Illuminati by the Bavarian authorities in 1785 and the publication of the order's secret documents that had fallen into the hands of the police created a real panic. This was true both among the Masons, who suddenly understood that they had been used as weapons in a dangerous game, and also among their traditional adversaries.

Weishaupt and the Illuminati came to serve as a symbolic marker of cosmic conspiracy in European public opinion. "The shadow of the disbanded order became a phantom that took on horrifying reality for weak minds," wrote the historian of the order, René Le Forestier (1974, 613; cf. Pipes 1997, 62–66). The diverse, conflicted and internally contradictory phenomenon that Masony represented in the late eighteenth century[6] became for many outside observers a menacing monolith, in which political radicalism and occult interests seemed parts of a single plan. Moreover, elitism and hierarchy merged in

---

5   The term "Martinism" apparently derived from the name of the originator of the doctrine of regeneration, Martinesa de Pasquale, but was often connected to the name of his follower, Louis-Claude de St. Martin, one of the most popular mystic authors of the eighteenth century (see, for example, Roberts 1972, 103–104). On the origins of Rosicrucianism and its relationship to early Masonry, see Yates 1999.

6   "On the one hand Masonry promoted the doctrine that all men are brothers, united by a common devotion to a 'Great Architect of the Universe' in defiance of religious dogmatism and sectarianism. On the other hand it taught that there is an ancient wisdom, handed down by initiates and embodied in secret rites and symbols and accessible only to those who have reached the appropriate grade," wrote the British historian Christopher Macintosh (1992, 40).

their imagination into a deeply conspiratorial organization whose members acted via numerous and often uninitiated disciples. With the outbreak of the French Revolution, all of these mythologems acquired universal recognition. The lightning-fast destruction of this thousand-year-old monarchy and the quick spread of the revolutionary avalanche outside of France seemed to confirm the conspirators' enormous power. Already by the start of the 1790s, a series of tracts and pamphlets appeared that tried to prove that everything that had happened was the handiwork of world-wide Masonry (see Roberts 1972, 146–202). By the end of the century several studies appeared in which these ideas received full and systematic presentation: *Memoirs Illustrating the History of Jacobinism* by Abbé Barruel in French, John Robison's *Proofs of a Conspiracy Against All the Religions and Governments of Europe* in English, and J. A. Starck's *The Triumph of Philosophy in the Eighteenth Century* in German (see Barruel I-IV; Robison 1797; Stark 1803). Despite the somewhat later date of Stark's book, it was mostly written at the same time as the two others, and a significant part of it had been printed in the journal *Eudaimonia* that was published in various German cities from 1795–1798 (see Droz 1961, 313–339).

For all of the common premises and goals of the authors, who to some extent worked together, in many ways they took different positions. Robison and Stark were themselves active Masons and strove to unmask the dangerous and menacing tendencies of some groups in order to defend others as well-intentioned and benign toward society. At the same time, the zealous Jesuit Barruel was a principled opponent of Masonry as such. He was ready to admit that many Masons did not pursue dangerous goals; but he explained this by arguing that many were ignorant of the criminal designs of the leaders of other, secret lodges. "I ask honest Masons once again not to think that they are being accused of wanting to carry out a similar revolution," Barruel wrote. "When I will touch on that article of their laws, I will relate how many noble and virtuous souls did not suspect the true idea of Masonry—they saw in it only a philanthropic society and the kind of fraternity that all sensitive souls would want to make universal" (Barruel II, 263; cf. 257–259; on Barruel, see Roberts 1972, 193–202; Riquet 1973; Shaepper-Wimmer 1985).

In Barruel's opinion the French Revolution was the result of a triple conspiracy consisting of "sophists of atheism," "sophists of rebellion," and "sophists of anarchy." The first wanted to overthrow the Church, the second, the monarchy, while the third dreamed of destroying all social institutions. "The Jacobin conspiracy," wrote Barruel, "was nothing other than an association, a coalition of the triple sect, a triple conspiracy which ripened long before the revolution, and to this day still ripens, to destroy the altar, throne, and all of society" (Barruel I, xvii). The conspiracy of "sophists of atheism" originated in the union of three figures: Voltaire, d'Alembert, and Frederick the Great; the conspiracy of "sophists of rebellion" was formulated in the lodges of Freemasons; and finally, the center of the "sophists of anarchy" was the order of Illuminati headed by Adam Weishaupt, who under Barruel's pen took on the typical features of the devil's representative on earth. The three conspiracies that Barruel defined may be correlated to the three parts of the triple formula "liberty, equality, fraternity." A person who has been enlightened by the philosophical teaching of the encyclopedists becomes free of religious dogmas with which church doctrines limited him; then adherents of the new philosophy join in unions whose goal is bringing down the monarchy and establishing equal rights; and the result of the destruction of the basis for any state system is the abolition of the state as such. A utopia of universal brotherhood then follows in its place. Barruel suggested that "the whole secret of Masonry consists in these phrases—equality and freedom; all people are equal; all people are brothers" (ibid., II, 261).

On the one hand, Barruel connected the category of brotherhood with the secret rituals of Masonic lodges, and on the other, with the Illuminati's cosmopolitanism, which did not recognize national boundaries. Here is how Barruel reconstituted the logic of the Illuminati:

> At the moment when people constituted nations they ceased recognizing each other as human beings. *Nationalism* or *love of the folk* took the place of general love. ... And so it became a virtue to extend the borders of your empire at the cost of those who are not under your power. It became permissible to despise foreigners, to deceive and insult them. *This virtue is called patriotism.* ... Lessen, eradicate this love for the fatherland and people will again learn to recognize and love one another as human beings. (Ibid., III, 172–173)

Exposing the Masons, Barruel latched on to both the Masons and Rosicrucians' speculation regarding the ancient derivation of their rituals. In his opinion, "specialist initiates in Masonry itself have not erred when they named the Templars among their predecessors" (ibid., II, 387). He saw the roots of Masonic symbols and organization in the order of Templars and in the heretical medieval sects of the Cathars and Albigensians; ultimately, he traced the Freemasons' teaching to Mani, the founder of Manichaeism (see ibid., 387–412). Before the reader's eyes arose a unified picture of the horrible activity of this anti-Christian, anti-state and anti-social sect that from prehistoric times had united all enemies of order, from adepts of the occult sciences to eighteenth-century enlighteners. In this construction, the French Revolution functioned as the culmination of this destruction and a step on the conspirators' path to world domination.

Memoirs Illustrating the History of Jacobinism gained recognition all over Europe and was quickly translated into English and German, and subsequently into most other European languages. On the one hand, Barruel offered the most unified and detailed version of the theory of world-wide conspiracy, and on the other, one that was the simplest and most internally consistent. In the words of the French historian Daniel Mornet, "all of nineteenth-century anti-Masonic programs have Barruel's book as their source" (Mornet 1967, 362; cf. Roberts 1972).

To the twenty-first century reader, Barruel's picture of a world-wide conspiracy certainly seems familiar. But for it to be complete one important figure is still needed—the Jew. This addition was made almost immediately. In 1806 Barruel received a letter from Florence from a certain Captain Simonini, whose identity neither the abbé nor later historians were able to establish. Expressing delight with *Memoirs Illustrating the History of Jacobinism,* Simonini complained that Barruel had not described the decisive role of the Jews in the entire conspiracy from Mani to the French Revolution (see Shaepper-Wimmer 1985, 251–252, 402–406). The letter was published for the first time only in 1878, but its contents nonetheless quickly became known to a wide public. Barruel himself found it easy to believe Simonini—in one of the notes to the German translation of his book he had already expressed similar views (see Pipes 1997, 216). At first he even planned to publish a new work on this subject, but then rejected this idea. According to some accounts, he feared causing a mass extermination of Jews, and thus he limited himself to circulating suitable warnings only among his correspondents, especially officials of law enforcement and the church. As the German historian Johannes Rogalla von Bieberstein indicated, this material made it to Alexander I through Joseph de Maistre, who believed it (see Bieberstein 1976, 627). Indeed, Alexander referred to the Neapolitan Carbonari as "one of Satan's synagogues" (Nikolai Mikhailovich I, 546). In the archive of N. K. Shil'der, who had access to the emperor's papers, there is a copy of Simonini's letter to Barruel, probably made by the historian himself (Pièce trouvée parmis les papiers de feu de P. Barruel jésuite, auteur d'une Mémoire pour server à l'histoire de jacobinisme, OR RNB, Kart. 20, № 10).

A conspiracy of such strength and menace demanded ample means with which to combat it. The immediate and obvious solution was to liquidate all secret societies that not only posed an implicit threat to traditional absolutist regimes but also challenged the basis of the fledgling national consciousness. The newly-forming national body was seen as an organic whole that did not permit ancillary developments that were hidden from public sight. In *The Social Contract* Rousseau had emphasized that in popular sovereignty private associations were inadmissible because they contradict "the general will" (Rousseau 1969, 171).[7] However, such a prohibition was insufficiently reliable, insofar as, on the one hand, it could not guarantee that conspiracies would not arise, and, on the other, it deprived defenders of the existing order of a powerful and effective weapon that the conspirators themselves could make use of. In Barruel's opinion, the Illuminati "were delighted with the laws and practices of the Jesuits, who under a united leadership were able to rouse so many people scattered around the world to act in the name of a single goal, and they tried to imitate their methods, *furthering diametrically opposite views*" (Barruel III, 11).[8] Both Barruel himself and Joseph de Maistre, who seconded him on this question, were convinced that the expulsion of the Jesuit order from European countries had been orchestrated by the Masons as a way to free their hands. "One celebrated French revolutionary said that the revolution would have been impossible if that order had existed, and indeed, nothing could be more just," de Maistre wrote to Victor Emmanuel in 1811 (Maistre XII, 73).

Therefore, in the milieu that had created and supported the mythology of a satanic world-wide conspiracy, the idea constantly arose of a secret association of the powers for good. If for some people the Jesuits could serve as an example of such a "righteous conspiracy," others put forward the notion of "a

---

7   On the basis of completely different material, Jean Starobinski demonstrated that the struggle for "transparency" was Rousseau's fundamental life-long obsession (see Starobinski 1971).
8   According to Barruel, the words in italics are taken from Mirabeau's *The Prussian Monarchy*.

brotherhood of philosophers," who armed themselves "in the name of the truth," opposing the "anti-Christian fraternity," as Barruel wrote to Starck (see Droz 1961; Shaepper-Wimmer 1985, 387). In the Masonic and Rosicrucian milieu they tried to oppose the Illuminati threat with a unification of true Christians, inspired by the desire for genuine heavenly enlightenment (Epstein 1966, 84–111). Here dangerous aspects of Masonry were often connected with the Jesuit's penetration into their lodges and orders (see Roberts 1972, 138–141, 180, etc.).

Such an adoption of the enemy's weapons, of course, was a two-edged sword. In the political battles of the nineteenth century, Barruel's book served as not only a warning against conspiratorial groups but also as a textbook for conspiracy. The colossal destructive power with which Barruel credited the Illuminati was extraordinarily attractive for many revolutionary organizations of the new era and, in particular, increased the attractiveness of Masonic symbols and attributes. The mythology of world-wide conspiracy, conclusively formulated by the end of the eighteenth century, substantially contributed to the growth of a multitude of local conspiracies that marked the start of the nineteenth century (see Roberts 1972, 203–246; Pipes 1997, 76–80; on the Decembrists' interest in Barruel, see Landa 1975, 251–306, 366; Rogov 1997, 115–117). Prerevolutionary Europe entered the age of secret political societies head first.

∞ **3** ∞

The history of the image of Masons in Russia, as Douglas Smith has shown, mostly followed the European model (Smith 1999, 136–175). However, in the Russian interpretation anti-Masonic mythology almost immediately merged with traditional ideas about secret conspiracies against Russia that were spun beyond its borders. Almost from the advent of Masonic lodges, a significant number of texts appeared in which the Mason was depicted, on the one hand, as Satan's servant, and on the other, as an incorrigible Francophile who followed the prescriptions of hostile France. One of the poems that reflected these notions, the anonymous "Psalm Exposing the Freemasons," was even included in Kurganov's *Pis'movnik* (*Letter-Writing Manual*), thus testifying to the popularity of this text and guaranteeing its broad dissemination (Kurganov 1769, 325; cf. Martynov 1988, 439; Smith 1999, 140–142).

In the 1780s the most significant anti-Masonic polemics were the comedies and publicistic works by Catherine II. These depicted Masons as charlatans and deceivers who ensnared unsuspecting citizens in their intrigues (see Semeka 1902). But the ironic and scornful tone of the empress's printed comments on the secret societies only functioned to mask her profound anxiety over them. According to the stories of Metropolitan Platon as recorded by F. P. Lubianskii, after her return to Moscow from Crimea in 1787, Catherine was apt to see "omens" of her funeral "at the instigation of the Martinists" everywhere: in the sand that was sprinkled on the streets, in the dark grey paint of the street light poles, and even in the body type of certain Muscovite clergymen. "They will bury me here," she said to Platon, "your preacher must be a dark Martinist: look at him, skin and bones, all dried out" (Liubianovskii 1872, 187–188). At that moment Catherine was worried about connections between the Moscow Masons and Prussia, as well as their attempts to make contact with the heir to the throne, Pavel Petrovich (see Vernadskii 1999; Zapadov 1976, 46–48, etc.). The Masons, whom the empress did not distinguish from the Martinists, which she hated, again appeared simultaneously as sorcerers devoted to black magic and agents of foreign powers. In these years Catherine was moving from polemics and restrictions to unqualified repression. At approximately the same time there were widespread rumors in Russian society that the Jacobins and Masons planned to poison the empress (Turgenev 1887, 88). Much later in Rostopchin's "Notes on the Martinists" he wrote that the Martinists "drew lots for who should stab the empress and the lot fell to Lopukhin" (Rostopchin 1875, 77; cf. Smith 1999, 166–167). For their part, the Masons did not dispute the reality of this conspiracy but instead tried to emphasize their own innocence, referring to some unknown Illuminati as the perpetrators (Barskov 1915, 200–203).

The rebirth of Russian Masonry in the first years of Alexander's reign inevitably stimulated the revival of traditional phobias. Characteristically, fear of the Masonic menace grew especially strong in 1806–1807, during the conflict with France. It was just at this time that Russian versions of the two most well-known books on the world-wide conspiracy came out: two simultaneous editions of Barruel and a paraphrase of Robison (see Barruel 1805 / 1809 I-XII; Barruel 1806 / 1808 I-IV; Robison 1806). At that time the popular lodge "People of God" or "The New Israel" was closed and its founder, Tadeusz Grabianka, a

Polish count and follower of the radical Avignon system "of Masonry in a Catholic spirit" (Lubianovskii 1872, 214), was arrested and locked away in the fortress (see Longinov 1860; Pypin 1997, 323–332; Serkov 2000, 59–62). Several members of this lodge also suffered: A. F. Labzin's journal "Messenger of Zion" was banned and F. P. Lubianovskii was almost exiled to Yakutsk for his translation of J. H. Jung-Stilling's mystical book *Longing for the Homeland* (see Lubianovskii 1872, 214–216; cf. Bakunina 1967, 280, 311).

Stilling himself, who corresponded with Russian Masons during these years, also cautioned them against "the great society … of the enemy of Our Lord and his kingdom … in which Voltaire was the first member." The main role in this evil society was played by Weishaupt and the Illuminati, who had as their goal "a universal republic, the extermination of earthly rulers or enslaving them by the Illuminati, and the complete destruction of the Christian faith" (letter to I. V. Lopukhin of September 16/27, 1804, in Vinitskii 1998, 297–298; on the letter's circulation in Masonic lodges, see ibid., 28). Of course, in distinction from Barruel, the Protestant Stilling did not see the Jesuits as the bulwark against the satanic criminal plotters but the activities of the Hernhutter sect. He believed that in apocalyptic times the Hernhutters were destined to acquire their promised land in "Asiatic Solima," located in "Crimea, the Volga steppes and Astrakhan" and under the wing of the "Eagle," that is, Alexander I. "Let us all pray together," Stilling wrote, " and may the Lord preserve this great and good Sovereign and those around him from Illuminism which is especially strong today" (ibid.).

On the threshold of the coming war, the Committee for Preserving the General Safety was created on January 13, 1807. The first point of the secret "Regulations of the Committee" contained a very clear indication of the empire's main threat:

> The perfidious government of France, trying to achieve its ruinous goal of world-wide destruction and disorganization, among other things, as is well known, patronizes the remnants of secret societies spread through all lands under the names *Illuminati, Martinists,* and other similar ones, and through this has secret collaborators in all European countries—not including those noxious people whom they openly send and support for this end—who in a collateral way so to speak assist the French government, and by means of whom it succeeds brilliantly in its evil plans. (Shil'der II, 365; Ivanov 1997, 83–87).

The author of the "Regulations" and, probably, the initiator of the committee, was one of the "young friends" of the emperor, N. N. Novosil'tsev. On March 5 of the same year, 1807, he wrote to Alexander, "Our chancelleries are full of 'Martinists,' 'Israelites' [a reference to "The New Israel"], 'Illuminati' and scoundrels of all shades, and at home it teems with French and Jacobins of all nations" (Nikolai Mikhailovich 1999, 280).[9] However, the attack on the Masons did not go very far at this time, and only those who were connected with Grabianka's lodge were subject to persecution. The anti-French direction of Russian foreign policy did not last long, either. In June 1807, the Tilsit peace was signed. In the autumn of 1808 there followed the Erfurt meeting between Alexander and Napoleon, which firmly placed the Russian-French alliance at the center of the new political alignment in Europe. It was after his return from Erfurt that Speranskii became the emperor's confidante and right-hand man.

∽ 4 ∽

The circumstances of Speranskii's rise turned him into a kind of symbol of the unpopular pro-French policy. Rumors of the unprecedented praise that Napoleon had bestowed on the new favorite, as well as his constant meetings with the French ambassador, Armand de Caulaincourt (see Tomsinov 1991, 126, 188–189), did not work in his favor. When it became clear that it was Speranskii who was to be the soul and prime mover of the far-reaching and poorly-understood reforms, his image took on clear-cut and familiar contours in contemporaries' eyes. In December 1809 Joseph de Maistre, referring to "well-informed people," reported to his king that "in the emperor's cabinet [Speranskii] fulfills … the orders of that widespread sect that is trying to destroy monarchies [expédter les Souverainetés]" (Maistre 1995, 132; Maistre XI, 385). De Maistre did not name the leaders of this "sect," but there was no need for this. In all of the courts of Europe everyone would have understood perfectly well whom he had in mind.

In 1812 Speranskii's subordinate in the Commission to Compile a New Law Code G. A. Rozenkampf accused him of "treason to the state and Illuminism" (Korf II, 31). At the same time a denunciation sent to Alexander and

---

9   It is not impossible that Novosil'tsev was himself a Mason. In T. A. Bakunina's dictionary of Russian Masons his name is listed with a question mark (Bakunina 1967, 373).

Figure 16 Portrait of F. V. Rostopchin. Gravure of T. Meyer after the original by Ernst Gebauer

signed "Count Rostopchin and Muscovites"—but possibly coming from the old freethinker Fedor Karzhavin (ibid., 10)[10]—said that Speranskii, "under the guise of patriotism wanted to act against the person" of the emperor, " to provoke all estates to anger and incite the people to pronounce a great and terrible demand." The author of the letter also claimed to know "the place where Napoleon's correspondence with the exposed participants in the conspiracy is kept" (Rostopchin 1905, 413). In ascribing his own fantasies to Rostopchin, whose views were well-known to the public, the author of the denunciation only partly sinned against the truth. By this time Rostopchin had already sent Alexander his "Note on Martinists" through Grand Princess Ekaterina Pavlovna, in which he listed those who, in his opinion, were active in secret societies. Furthermore, this number "are all more or less devoted to Speranskii, who while not belonging to any sect in his heart (and perhaps not even to any religion), makes use of their services for conducting business and keeps them

---

10 People from whom copies of the denunciation had been confiscated told the commission about the authorship of Karzhavin, who had died in March of 1812. Of course, evidence obtained this way must be treated with extreme caution.

dependent on himself." Behind the back of Speranskii, who was manipulating the Martinists, loomed an even more menacing figure. At the end of the memorandum, Rostopchin wrote:

> I am sure that Napoleon, who is directing everything toward the achievement of his goals, patronizes him, and at some time he will find strong support in that society which is just as much worthy of scorn as it is dangerous. Then people will see, but too late, that their ideas are not chimeras, but reality; that they do not mean to be the butt of ridicule but to go down in history, and that this sect is nothing other than the hidden enemy of governments and states. (Rostopchin 1875, 80–81)

Rostopchin substantiated the connection between contemporary Martinists and Napoleon with the fact that the Martinists of Catherine's era had acted "on the instructions of Bavarian Illuminati, whose letter to Novikov was apprehended in the post" (ibid., 76–77). This confiscated letter from the Illuminati to Novikov, it seemed, was echoed in Alexander's words as recorded by Sanglen: "I think that it would not be difficult to take possession of the Illuminati's correspondence with their leader Weishaupt; Balashov says that Speranskii is the Illuminati's regent (*regent*)." According to Sanglen, "the sovereign began laughing" when voicing this tirade; he then told the memoirist that Speranskii had his own lodge, and that "in Arnfel'dt's opinion, it's a lodge of Illuminati" (Sanglen 1883, № 1, 33). The specific rank in the order of Illuminati that the Minister of Police Balashov and the emperor attributed to Speranskii is worthy of attention. According to Barruel a regent is the highest, eighth degree for an Illuminant who is not yet initiated into the great mysteries. Above regents stand the Magi or People-kings, and above them the Areopagites, the supreme council of the order headed by Weishaupt (Barruel III, 213–288), who after the dispersal of the movement lived uninterruptedly in the city of Gotha on a modest pension and spent his time writing verbose treatises defending his earlier activities.[11]

---

11 It is worth citing the description of Weishaupt's personality by the historian of Illuminism, René de Forestier: "Weishaupt was neither an evil genius nor a benefactor of mankind, but a common university dean. ... He was a typical pedagogue of his time in his bookish knowledge, his proud self-satisfaction, his doctrinaire and pedantic tone, authoritarian spirit, and his complete ignorance of real life. He saw people and society only through books and was convinced that a person who had read the most well-known works that had been written since antiquity would possess holistic understanding and be able to resolve all of the problems that confront the human race" (Le Forestier 1974, 555).

The traditional Polish component was also not forgotten. After Tilsit, Adam Czartoryski, the main agent of Polish influence at Alexander's court, no longer played a substantive role in Russian politics and his mythological function was transferred to Speranskii. In the above-cited denunciation that was attributed to Karzhavin, it said that Speranskii got the emperor to agree to introduce taxes to support the Polish army (Rostopchin 1905, 413). The same rumors circulated even in circles closest to the main players in this historical drama. According to A. A. Loginov's story, "A. S. Shishkov brought news to Count Pavel Aleksandrovich Stroganov's house in the presence of Speranskii's underlings A. N. Olenin and A. I. Turgenev. 'He was tempted by a trifle,' said Shishkov, stating as reliable fact that Speranskii had been bought off by Napoleon to betray Russia in return for the promise of the Polish crown" (Bychkov 1902, 32).

As noted in the last chapter, Shishkov was a main figure in the struggle against Czartoryski (see Al'tshuller 1984, 28), who belonged to one of the oldest Polish families and who might have received the crown in a restored Poland. On the other hand, Speranskii, the son of a provincial Orthodox clergyman, could in no way have been considered a possible candidate for the Polish throne. This did not deter Shishkov, who was totally caught up in the logic of the myth, nor, apparently, did it bother his interlocutors. Moreover, by his character Shishkov was least of all given to cynical slander. Unquestionably, he seriously believed these accusations.

According to the testimony of a contemporary, these rumors eventually reached Speranskii himself. "In Perm they let it slip out that he had betrayed the fatherland not for money, but for the Polish crown. 'Thank God,' he said, crossing himself. They are starting to think better of me—after all, it is more excusable to be seduced by a crown!'" (Bychkov, "Prebyvanie" 1902, 239).

Eighty years after these events, the historian P. I. Bartenev published a story he had heard from Count Stroganov, a story from the Polish Marshal (regional marshal of the nobility) Liubetskii about how Balashov had asked him for information on the state of public opinion in the Polish provinces. Liubetskii showed him a note that had already been prepared for Napoleon that was "allegedly signed '*your faithful Speranskii*.' Having seen this note, Balashov did not conceal his satisfaction," and several days later Speranskii was exiled to Nizhnii Novgorod. "Of course," added Bartenev, "the note that Liubetskii procured was counterfeit" (Bartenev 1892, 79). Needless to say, this whole narrative was completely absurd, starting with the fact that a note with this kind of content could not have existed. Still, one can recognize a living echo of the rumors that surrounded Speranskii's disgrace.

Actually, money did figure in Speranskii's crisis. In the denunciation attributed to Karzhavin, it said that Speranskii had been "drawn away from loyalty to the fatherland" by means of "gold and diamonds given him through the French ambassador" (Rostopchin 1905, 414). In the first weeks of exile when Speranskii was especially suffering from his lack of money, waiting in vain for the salary that was owed him, his close friend P. G. Masal'skii, who was acting in his name, wrote to him with vexation about the fantastic rumors of his unprecedented riches—"several millions held in an English bank," "700,000 in silver, sent to Kiev for contracts," dozens of homes, and so on (Speranskii 1862, 17; cf. Tomsinov 1991, 187–188). The idea of "Kievan contracts" most likely derived from Balashov, and the emperor spoke with Sanglen about them (there the sum mentioned was 80,000; Sanglen 1883, № 1, 39–41). Massal'skii was especially disturbed by the participation in these conversations of people whom he had considered Speranskii's well-wishers, in particular Count Kochubei, who knew the disgraced favorite well and had helped advance his career (Speranskii 1862, 14).

In Derzhavin's *Memoirs* (*Zapiski*) is an episode relating to an earlier period, but written down during the war years. The poet recalled his struggle at the start of Alexander's reign to defend Russia's interests against Polish and Jewish influence at court. The leader of the former was Czartoryski, of the latter—Speranskii, "who was completely devoted to the Jews (zhidy) through the well-known tax-farmer Perets" and who "was publicly suspected of avarice ... in his connection to Perets" (Derzhavin VI, 801, 805). Czartoryski and Speranskii turned out to be parallel, and consequently interchangeable, representatives of two dangerous nations that were hostile to Russia.

Even such a seemingly irrelevant element of the myth as black magic came into play. Balashov told Sanglen that

> having arrived at Speranskii's the previous evening at seven o'clock he was gripped with horror. In the vestibule a tallow candle was burning dimly, and in the second large room as well, and from here he was led into his study where two wax candles were burning out and the fire in the fireplace was

going out. Upon entering the study he felt the floor under his feet shaking as if it were on springs, and on the shelves instead of books stood phials.

Seeing Balashov, Speranskii "quickly closed" an ancient book that he had been reading (Sanglen 1883, № 1, 23–24).

The image of a traitor at the foot of the throne plotting unheard-of misfortunes for the fatherland, the agent of dark forces, a sorcerer, a French spy in the pay of the Jews and counting on the Polish throne, took its final form. "Near him it seemed to me that all of the time I smelled sulfur and could see bluish flames of the underworld in his pale blue eyes," wrote F. F. Vigel' (II, 10). Of all the traditional components of the image of Masons and Illuminati, the state secretary, it seems, only lacked sex and alcohol addictions. In Rostopchin's "Note on Martinists," for example, I. V. Lopukhin is labeled "a drunkard given to debauchery and unnatural vices" (Rostopchin 1875, 80), but Speranskii escaped this kind of accusation. Vigel', who hated him, wrote of the "immorality of his rules (although not of his behavior)" (Vigel' II, 9). This was hardly due to the state secretary's ascetic lifestyle. More likely, early nineteenth-century Russian society was insufficiently puritanical to consider these kinds of moral lapses significant attributes of so menacing a personage.

∞ **5** ∞

The set of ideologems that clustered around Speranskii had been formed before his rise. The new favorite simply filled a functional niche that had developed after the members of the Secret Committee—especially Czartoryski—had departed the political scene. However, Speranskii came to play this role in a much more powerful and credible way than any of his predecessors. A significant factor in the crystallization of these notions was the fact that the emperor who had raised the unknown son of a priest to the heights of power, as well as Speranskii himself, were both in thrall to the very same mythology.

The striking lack of correspondence between Speranskii's power and influence, on the one hand, and his official duties, on the other, was nothing new. Favorites always found themselves at the center of public attention, yet acted more or less off-stage. But in the Alexandrine epoch this familiar phenomenon of political culture took on rather unusual forms. Alexander's "young friends" had formed a closed circle that was called upon to play the role of a kind of shadow cabinet and to make fundamental decisions behind the backs of official office-holders. It was not without reason that the members of the Secret Committee jokingly called it the Committee of Public Salvation, thereby likening it to a Jacobin club (see Lotman and Uspenskii 1996, 502). In 1808–1811 Speranskii fulfilled the function of the entire Secret Committee as far as internal affairs were concerned. In foreign policy he became one of the leading participants of an analogous, unofficial coterie that likewise substituted for state institutions.

> The advisor to the Russian ambassador in Paris Nessel'rode writes to the state secretary, bypassing Prince Kurakin [i.e., the official emissary]. R. A. Koshelev conducts a direct correspondence with the Russian ambassador in Vienna, Count Shtakel'berg and the Austrian chargé d'affairs [poverennyi] St. Julien, again, bypassing the chancellor [N. P. Rumiantsev], and Koshelev reports on it all directly to the emperor. A special procedure, but it is Emperor Alexander's approach,

wrote Grand Prince Nikolai Mikhailovich, the publisher of many Russian diplomatic documents (Nikolai Mikhailovich I, 83; cf. Shil'der III, 53–54; Sirotkin 1966, 178). We know from Speranskii's Perm letter that it was he who initiated this secret correspondence (Shil'der III, 524). It closely recalled— down to using code names for governmental figures (see Nikolai Mikhailovich I, 101)—Louis XV's "King's Secret," which as we have seen had a reputation in Russia as the center of an anti-Russian Masonic conspiracy. It is not clear to what extent Speranskii and Alexander consciously oriented themselves toward this very familiar model. It is of course impossible to exclude a simple coincidence, but it is fully credible that they would have set up their anti-French conspiracy using means that had been tried and tested in Paris. It is worth noting that apart from Speranskii, the soul of Alexander's "Imperial Secret" was the well-known Mason R. A. Koshelev.

Despite Rostopchin's and Vigel''s assertions on Speranskii's atheism (see Rostopchin 1875, 80; Vigel' II, 9), for his entire life he remained a profoundly religious person and a thinker of a clearly articulated mystical tendency (see Kadetov 1889; El'chaninov 1906, etc.). Already in 1804 he counted the experienced mystic I. V. Lopukhin as a mentor, and in his turn he had familiarized his friend Archbishop Feofilakt (Rusanov) with mystical works by Eckartshausen, Fénelon, and Madame Guyon (see Lopukhin 1870; Speranskii, "Pis'mo" 1870;

Bychkov 1872; cf. Korf 1867, 444–454; Speranskii, "Pis'ma" 1870). Later, Speranskii willingly shared his exceptional knowledge in this area with the emperor. He wrote in the Perm letter,

> When Your Highness desired to have information about this kind of subject and in particular about their mystical side, I was ready to dedicate all of the fruits of my own searchings and meditations to you with pleasure. These talks were the more pleasant for me, the more I could see that your feelings were commensurate with their subject. (Shil'der III, 526)

However, the strong interest in mysticism by no means meant necessary participation in Masonic societies. We have no information concerning Speranskii's affiliation with any lodges before 1811.[12] In 1822, after the closing of all Masonic lodges in Russia, Speranskii wrote in a statement that he had taken no part in secret societies but that in 1810, as a member of a state committee for investigating Masonic affairs, he was "taken into Fessler's lodge with the government's knowledge and visited it two times" (Bakunina 1967, 503; cf. Serkov 2000, 90). At the time of this testimony Speranskii had just returned to Petersburg after a year and a half of exile and prolonged service in the provinces. His position was very uncertain, and he understood that his every word, especially on such a sensitive question, could attract very close scrutiny. All aspects of his biography were well-known to the emperor and could easily be verified, so it is hard to imagine that in this situation he would have given any false testimony. It is a different matter that in many respects he changed the emphasis.

In the memoirs of Baron F. Gauenshil'd, Speranskii's close colleague of those years, it tells of the "plans to reform the clergy" that inspired the state secretary and of the "extremely strange" means by which he wanted to implement them:

> The proposal was to found a Masonic lodge with branches throughout the Russian Empire which the most capable religious figures of all conditions would be required to join. *Religious* brothers would have to write articles on well-known humanitarian questions, write sermons, etc., and these papers

---

12 The evidence that Speranskii visited Grabianka's lodge (see, e.g., Sokolovskaia 1915, 176, etc.) is only documented by Magnitskii's denunciation (see Bakunina 1967, 509). In general, both pro- and anti-Masonic historians have striven, albeit for opposing reasons, to increase the number of celebrated and influential people who took part in lodges, often borrowing unreliable information from one another.

would be taken to the main lodge so that the first master of the great lodge would review them (this honor was offered to me), according to whose recommendations the most worthy would receive promotions in the union of Masonic lodges and in the state. But since the many already existing lodges will by no means agree with this project and pursue completely different goals (actually they did not have any goals), Speranskii offered two *ukases* for the emperor's signature. With one of them the emperor ordered the Minister of Popular Enlightenment Count Aleksei Razumovskii to temporarily close all lodges in the empire and to demand of the masters of the chair [copies of the texts of] their various rituals. This *ukase* was signed by the emperor and was quickly carried out; the second ordered heads of lodges to either accept new rituals for Masonic lodges compiled by Speranskii (at that time not completely worked out) or to close them. The emperor promised to sign this *ukase*, but this was not done.

Although I was only twenty-five years old at that time, I felt that this project was totally impractical and that it would create an even more unfavorable impression because it too closely recalled that of Weishaupt. (Gauenshil'd 1902, 253–254)

In these memoirs written many years after the fact, there are minor inaccuracies. Thus the order of the Minister of Police given to the leaders of the lodges did not involve temporary closure but only a temporary halt in accepting new members (Pypin 1997, 335–336). However, on the whole Gauenshil'd correctly described the course of events. The well-known Masonic reformer I. Fessler was invited to Russia to work out the new unified ritual, and Speranskii obtained a position for him as professor of Hebrew and philosophy at the Alexander Nevskii Academy. This appointment was likely part of his plan to orient the future lodge towards clergymen.

According to the testimony of Mason K. P. Rennenkampf, he translated the ritual from German to French for Speranskii's initiation (Pypin 1900, 310). This circumstance, by the way, serves as indirect confirmation of the fact that until this time Speranskii had not taken part in Masonry. According to Masonic rules, a brother once accepted into any lodge did not require a second initiation. As A. I. Serkov indicates, "in June 1810 M. M. Speranskii first opened the session of his Great Lodge, and at the start of September the emperor ordered that the acts of all Masonic systems be collected and a committee be created to review the M. M. Speranskii-I. A. Fessler plan" (Serkov 2000, 74; cf. Pypin 1900, 303–310; Sokolovskaia 1915, 174–179).

Later, however, the project came to a standstill. Alexander refused to give the lodge official status, and then he simply had it closed. Fessler was forced to retire and leave Petersburg (Gauenshil'd 1902, 255).

In trying to reform Masonry, Fessler "demanded that the brothers accept the ancient English system with some changes" (Pypin 1997, 243; on Fessler see Barton 1969; Gordin 1999, 173–180). He proposed simplifying the ritual and rejecting occult research and the higher ranks, which he thought should be transformed from practical gradations into an object of historical study. In the words of G. Florovskii, "he thought that the task of a true Mason was creating a new type of citizenship, reeducating citizens for the impending Age of Astraea" (Florovskii 1937, 140). Undoubtedly, it was these very ideas that attracted Speranskii.

The strategic goals that Speranskii pursued in planning such a simultaneously secret and official lodge and their relation to his attempts to "transform the clergy" become comprehensible if we set them in the general context of his reform activities. It was just at this time that Speranskii began a reform of the government administration on a colossal scale (see Raeff 1957; Chibiriaev 1989, etc.). Naturally, he could not fail to consider the people who would be destined to take up responsibilities in the reformed system. The aim of forming a cohort of educated government servitors of all ranks also dictated the *ukase* on exams that were to accompany elevation to the first noble rank. It also created the Lycée at Tsarskoe Selo, an elite educational institution where children of the high nobility were to be prepared for state service. But Speranskii naturally saw the estate he came from himself as the main reserve for staffing the bureaucracy (on Speranskii's activity in organizing religious education itself, see Chistovich 1894; on his educational projects as a whole, see Raeff 1957, 57–63; Tomsinov 1991, 133–135). The issue concerned a consistent system for selecting the most talented representatives of the clergy, first of all, students from religious educational institutions. The selected persons were to be connected to one another by the bonds of mystical brotherhood, united by a single center and under government supervision. In the words of the celebrated German statesman G.-F. Stein, Speranskii "believed in the revival of the world by means of secret societies" (Pertz III, 57). Stein arrived in Petersburg later and knew this whole story second hand, but his discussion basically coincides with what we know from other sources.

To Gauenshil'd Speranskii's project "too closely recalled that of Weishaupt." However, both Speranskii and the memoirist himself took their understanding of the Iluminati's activities primarily from Barruel and similar works of this kind. Moreover, as has been noted, Barruel asserted that the Illuminati "were delighted with the laws and practices of the Jesuits ... and they tried to imitate their methods, *furthering diametrically opposite views*" (Barruel III, 11). The organization that Speranskii conceived, with its official character and orientation towards the clergy, appeared as something midway between a traditional Masonic lodge and the order of Jesuits. Joseph de Maistre, who suspected Speranskii of fulfilling the commands of "the vast sect," wrote that he had publicly "lauded the Jesuits and their system of education" (Maistre 1995, 132; Maistre XI, 385). In spite of his presumptions, Speranskii was probably completely sincere. He most likely valued the organizational practice and pedagogical system of the Jesuits and wanted to use elements of their experience for his own ends. Analogously, organizing a centralized Masonic lodge in Russia could, in his view, have averted the spread of Illuminist tendencies. It seems that Speranskii was not alone in this idea—later the diary of the painter B. L. Borovikovskii echoed rumors circulating in Petersburg that "Prince Golitsyn and Filaret would like to create a new Christian social order (soslovie) in opposition to the Masons" (Nikolai Mikhailovich I, 202).

Be that as it may, this project, like others of Speranskii's reformist plans, reflected the position of Alexander, who saw a definite danger in Masonic lodges and wanted either to place them under unconditional state control or to counter their influence via other secret societies that would realize his own purposes. In 1810–1811 he corresponded with Koshelev on these issues and sent him the intercepted creed of the Italian Illuminati (ibid., II, 55). At that time the panicky emperor asked his sister Grand Princess Ekaterina Pavlovna not to write anything to him about the Martinists by regular post but to send her letters only via courier (Nikolai Mikhailovich 1910, 60). He told Sanglen that it was essential "that there be no secret lodges from the government" and ordered that all of the protocols of Masonic meetings be presented to him (Sanglen 1883, № 1, 33, 42).

This was connected to the creation in 1810 of a committee to review Masonic documents, one of whose members was Speranskii (see Sokolovskaia 1915, 178–179; Serkov 2000, 74–75). It seems that A. N. Pypin was the first to draw attention to the fact that this initiative that had earlier been considered "the private affair of Speranskii, Rozenkampf and Fessler [actually] had official underpinning" (Pypin 1997, 341). He also published a letter to the emperor from an unknown party proposing "to establish Masonry in its original purity." The total coincidence of the proposals contained in this letter with what Gauenshil'd wrote causes us to conclude that if it was not directly written by Speranskii, then it at least developed his ideas:

> I considered it my duty to present to Y[our] H[ighness] several thoughts regarding those wise measures which Y[our] H[ighness] proposes to use for establishing Masonry. They seem to me to guarantee the success of Your intentions.
>
> 1. It should eliminate the increase of rotten habits, establishing healthy morals founded on the solid basis of religion.
> 2. It should prevent the introduction of any other society founded on harmful principles, and thus develop a kind of constant but unnoticeable surveillance . ...
>
> After the organization of this order will be established and purified in this way, it will be necessary to form a center of unification in some place or other to which all of the institutions of this type that could be formed within the empire will come together. ... Any other lodge in the empire not established by this mother-lodge must not be tolerated. (Ibid., 333–335)

However much Speranskii's projects corresponded to the monarch's own profound aspirations, they were doomed to fail. Gauenshil'd was correct when he called them "totally impractical" and also "strange and suspicious" (Gauenshil'd 1902, 254). Apart from the fact that a mystical fraternity of this type was the fruit of Abbé Barruel and his allies' poetic fancy and could hardly have been put into practice, the attempt to organize it would have inevitably come up against opposition from diverse and very influential circles.

Perhaps the first to sound the alarm was Joseph de Maistre. All of Speranskii's reform activity prompted a strong negative reaction from him. Already in 1809 he had responded to rumors of the new favorite's constitutional projects with his "Essay on the Principles that Produce Political Constitutions," in which he sharply criticized the very idea of a written constitution as the basis for national jurisprudence. However, it was precisely the state secretary's educational projects that most deeply affected the Jesuits' direct interests in Russia, insofar as in the first decade of the nineteenth century schools for the high Russian aristocracy were to a significant degree under their control (see Flinn 1970; Edwards 1977). Practically all of de Maistre's publicistic activity in 1810–1811 was directly leveled against Speranskii. In June and July of 1810 he wrote "Five Letters on National Education," addressed to the newly appointed Minister of National Public Enlightenment Count A. G. Razumovskii; in March 1811, "Observations on the Curricular Plan Proposed for the Nevskii Seminary by Professor Fessler"; in September 1811, "Note on the Freedom of National Education" to the ober-prokuror of the Synod and intimate friend of Alexander, Prince Golitsyn. In December 1811, this cycle was finalized with "Four Fragments on Russia" which were directly intended for the emperor. The fourth fragment, "On Illuminism," was dedicated to various secret societies and mystical movements and the degree of danger each represented (Maistre VIII, 157–360; cf. Triomphe 1968; Fateev 1940).

No less harsh was the reaction of Orthodox hierarchs on whom had been foisted a Mason and defrocked Catholic monk who had become Lutheran in the capacity of overseer of future pastors. Even Speranskii's friend Archbishop Feofilakt (Rusanov), who owed him his church career, came into conflict with him (Chistovich 1894, 29–62). And to top it all the Masons were indignant over the proposal that they conduct their lodges according to Fessler's reformist plans or have to close them (see, e.g., Pypin 1997, 339–348). Furthermore, the state officials who were to put these plans into effect—in particular, Minister of Popular Enlightenment Razumovskii and Minister of Police Balaskov—were themselves Masons (see Bakunina 1967, 42, 435–436; Serkov 2000, 74).

Even without leading to any practical results, this unusual initiative could not help but provoke dissatisfaction. In 1811, requesting that Alexander limit his expanding circle of activities, Speranskii enumerated the rumors that were going around about him in society: "In the course of one year I was in turn a Martinist, an advocate of the Masons, a defender of freedom, foe of slavery, and, finally, a confirmed Illuminatus. ... I know that most of them [his accusers] do not themselves believe this nonsense, but, concealing their own obsessions under the guise of public utility, they try to adorn their personal animosity with the label of state animosity" (SbRIO XXI, 460). There was no need for alternating criticisms—the accusations Speranskii lists formed a single and fully integral image. But it is hard to doubt that the unsuccessful initiative to create a centralized Masonic lodge greatly fostered notions of a "confirmed Illuminatus" in public opinion. Against the background of the growing anti-Illuminati hysteria and spy mania on the threshold of war, the myth of a conspirator near the throne took on a necessary wholeness. The state secretary's first major defeat became the prelude to his coming downfall.

∞ 6 ∞

Speranskii considered his fall the result of intrigues on the part of some "secret committee" whose mainspring was Grand Princess Ekaterina Pavlovna (Shil'der III, 259). This understanding was predicated on the very same fundamental ideologems of conspiracies and secret societies that guided his political opponents. At the same time the grand princess did not hide her enmity toward the state secretary (see Lubianovskii 1872, 261; Semevskii 1911/1912, 224–225). It was she who instigated the creation of the two main publicistic works that were directed against Speranskii—Rostopchin's "Notes on the Martinists" and N. M. Karamzin's "Memoir on Ancient and Modern Russia"—and she who passed them on to Alexander (see Rostopchin 1876; cf. Semevskii 1911/1912, 231; Pipes 1959, 69–75; Martin 1997, 93–103).[13] Russian society of the time might possibly not know about one or another of the grand princess's statements, or, indeed, about the documents that the emperor received through her intermediacy (on the pre-publication history of Karamzin's work see Tartakovskii 1997, 181–189). But it is incontrovertible that Ekaterina Pavlovna's opposition to both the Tilsit agenda and to the reformist plans connected with Speranskii's name was rather widely known and made her unusually popular (see Vries de Gunsburg 1941, 26–29). In their reports foreign diplomats even recorded discussions about the possibility of her replacing Alexander on the throne with some frequency (see Martin 1997, 200).

---

13 Karamzin clearly went far beyond criticism of Speranskii's proposed reforms, offering what was in essence one of the first holistic conceptions of Russian history. Nonetheless, the initial polemical direction of the "Memoir" that was revealed by its first investigators (see Korf I, 132–144, 161–165; Pypin 1900, 214–260) seems rather obvious. In our opinion, Iu. M. Lotman's attempted revision of this perspective (1997) does not have sufficient basis.

Figure 17 Portrait of Grand Princess Ekaterina Pavlovna (1810's). Gravure by Andre Joseph Mecou after the original by Jean-Henri Benner.

Ekaterina Pavlovna's betrothal to the prince of Oldenburg announced at the start of 1809 gave rise to great patriotic enthusiasm. During 1807–1808 Napoleon had unofficially raised the question of seeking the grand princess's hand in marriage. Her quickly organized betrothal to the prince was not only an expression of Ekaterina Pavlovna's deep antipathy and that of her mother, the widowed Empress Maria Fedorovna, toward the ruler of France who was not born of the purple, but also in essence a first affront to the new ally (see Vries de Gunsburg 1941, 34–41). Already in late November 1808 de Maistre had reported on Ekaterina Pavlovna's coming wedding to the prince of Oldenburg and expressed his satisfaction over it:

> This marriage, unequal in some respects, is nevertheless sagacious and worthy of the grand princess who is just as sagacious as she is charming. Most of all, any princess in a family that enjoys Bonaparte's horrible friendship should hurry to marry even somewhat below her level, because who knows what kind of ideas will enter that singular head. ... Nothing can compare with the goodness and grace of my lady the grand princess. If I were

an artist I would send you a depiction of her gaze and you would see how much virtue and intelligence nature bestowed on her. (Maistre XI, 163–164; Maistre 1995, 111)

In 1807 Derzhavin began to write an "Epistle to Grand Princess Ekaterina Pavlovna on the Patronage of the Native Word"[14] that remained unfinished. The epistle was probably meant as an official greeting from the literary circle formed that year, which had begun to meet in the poet's home and thereafter grew into the "Colloquy of Lovers of the Russian Word." The poet called the young grand princess a "connoisseur (iskusnitsa) of the language of her people." This exaggerated praise nevertheless reflected the young grand princess's real interest in her native tongue, so rare in the court milieu and so important for Shishkov's literary coterie. As Ekaterina Pavlovna's letters to Karamzin demonstrate, she wrote in Russian only with great difficulty, but displayed a strong desire to master that skill (see Ekaterina Pavlovna 1888, 43–56). In the capacity of "colleague" and "interlocutor" of the great empress, who had borne the same name (soimennoi) as the addressee of the epistle, Derzhavin summoned Ekaterina Pavlovna to heed "the voice of your homeland's lyre" and serve as "champion (predstatel'nitsa) … of the Russian word before the throne" (Derzhavin III, 527–528).

As Mark Al'tshuller has shown, Napoleon's courtship of Ekaterina Pavlovna became the background for the allusions in Derzhavin's tragedy "Eupraxia" (Evpraksiia), written in 1808–1809 (Al'tshuller 1984, 160–164). This tragedy, based on the "Tale of the Destruction of Riazan by Batu," relates how the Tatar khan demands that Eupraxia, wife of Fedor, prince of Riazan, come to him in his camp. The battle that follows Fedor's refusal ends with his death and Eupraxia's suicide. In order to arouse the audience's patriotic feelings, Derzhavin ended the tragedy with still one more battle in which Batu is defeated by troops from Moscow. The reason for this deviation from the source is revealed in the tragedy's "Foreword":

---

14 The dating was made by Ia. K. Grot, first publisher of the "Epistle," who based it on a mention in a letter from Evgenii Bolkhovitinov to Derzhavin in that year (Derzhavin III, 527). However, insofar as the poet calls her "Grand Princess" (*velikaia kniaginia* and not *kniazhna*) in the title it is obvious that he also returned to the work after her wedding.

> Insofar as they [our Russian forebears] did not betray either their faith or their fatherland, their misfortune gives us an image worthy of emulation, sowing in the souls of later generations the courage with which in subsequent years they destroyed Batu's kingdom. ... But if our forebears had betrayed the faith and if their love for the fatherland and loyalty to their sovereigns had grown cold, then Russia would long ago have ceased to be Russia. We conclude with Solomon's saying: There is nothing new under the sun. (Derzhavin IV, 298)

The final phrase unequivocally ties the historical episode depicted by the poet to contemporary events. The marriage of Ekaterina Pavlovna to the prince of Oldenburg prompted a burst of jubilation from Derzhavin, and he sang of their wedding in the ecstatic poem "Hebe" in which he wrote:

> О изящна добродетель,
> О Великий образ жен,
> Кто, быть могши сам владетель,
> Но став волей унижен,
> Явил выше царской власти
> Дух отечеству служить. ...
> Сим одним Екатерина,
> Именем своим одним
> Ты повергла исполина
> Росса ко стопам твоим. (Ibid., III, 2–3)

(Oh refined virtue, / Oh Great image of women, / Which, able to be sovereign itself, / Was voluntarily humbled / And showed that the spirit of serving the fatherland / Was higher than tsarist power. ... / By this alone, Ekaterina, / By your name alone / You brought the giant, / Russia, to your feet.)

The issue in these deliberately vague lines concerns the grand princess's opportunity to become the spouse of the mightiest of earthly monarchs, whom the new bride, in Derzhavin's view, had rejected in favor of patriotic duty. The next year the poet dedicated the poem "Procession of the Russian Amphitrite Along the Volkhov" to the same couple, and in it he again connected his hopes for Russian letters to the grand princess.

Derzhavin was not alone in setting his hopes on Ekaterina Pavlovna. In the public consciousness of those years, the personality of the grand princess was subjected to the very same process of intensive mythologization as the figure of the state secretary, albeit in reverse. The beautiful and decisive sister of the sovereign who symbolically bore the name of her great-grandmother and who was selflessly fighting for Russia's interests was set against that of the dangerous intriguer and conspirator who, in his position near the throne, was trying to carry out the orders of the country's most malicious enemy.

Many tragedies written in 1808–1809 reproduce the very same collision. The state is faced with an immeasurably stronger enemy whose arrogant lord proposes a shameful peace. In such a situation and in view of the obvious inequality of forces, the negative characters propose to accept humiliation, while the noble heroes demand to take the field and, against all odds, finally triumph. Besides the already mentioned "Eupraxia," this scheme repeats in "Mikhail, Prince of Chernigov" by S. N. Glinka (1808); L. N. Nevakhovich's "The Souliotes, or Spartans of the Eighteenth Century" (1809); A. A. Shakhovskoi's "Deborah" (1809); and a series of other plays. In earlier plays by Derzhavin and Glinka the main villain was Batu, and the Russian princes who at first are ready to shamefully capitulate finally see the way to repentance and redemption. In contrast, in Nevakhovich's and Shakhovskoi's plays, written after Speranskii's elevation, the enemy leader is moved off stage and first place is taken by the figure of a traitor who craves destroying the motherland out of vengeful ambition.

Both Heber (Khaber) in "Deborah" and Palaska in "The Souliotes" turn out not only to be fainthearted tools of the enemy's will but also central movers in ominous intrigues undertaken out of hatred for their native land and its tsars, and who have personal power as their goal. When Heber exclaims:

> Что можем сделать мы?
> Врагов несметна сила
> Подавит смертью нас и истребит вконец, -

(What can we do? / The enemies' endless power / Will crush and finally exterminate us,)

- he is moved not by error and not even by cowardice but by a secret pact with the enemy. Even without knowledge of his treason, Deborah answers him:

> Что можем сделать мы, великий мой отец
> То миру доказал. Иль силою единой
> Сисар мог завладеть обширной Палестиной?
> Иль воины его храбрей израильтян?
> Нет, не оружие, а лесть, раздор, обман,
> Служащие его намереньям жестоким,
> Израиль, поразя унынием глубоким,
> Сисару предали…

(What can we do? My great father / Showed the world what. Or was it by force alone / [That] Sisera [Sisar] was able to take charge of vast Palestine? / Or are his [the enemy's] troops braver than the Israelites? / No, it is not weapons but flattery, discord, deception / Serving his cruel intentions, / That betrayed Israel, struck by profound dejection, / to Sisera. …)

By twist of fate both traitors turn out to be royal advisers. "Your friendship will help me bear the heavy burden of rule," the young tsar of Israel Lavidon tells Heber (ibid., 464). Both traitors also enter into secret negotiations with agents of the monstrous enemy. Naturally, both Heber and Palaska abhor the people and traditions of their native land in equal measure. "The Souliotes are used to go into some kind of incomprehensible ecstasy from the word *fatherland*. Let me call this but the fruit of prejudices"—Palaska thus paraphrases Barruel's description of the Illuminati's views. "… In the enlightened countries of Europe even people who triumphantly declare that they find no sense in the word *fatherland* and call themselves citizens of the whole world are tolerated. Tell me, what will the Souliotes lose if Ali Pasha will rule them?" (Nevakhovich 1809, 56). It is precisely the converted Jew Nevakhovich who is disposed to explain Palaska's treason by his alien ethnicity. "Souliote blood did not flow in this monster—his father was a foreigner," Amaseka, the wife of the Souliote leader, tells the people (ibid., 93).

In both plays the decisive role in the victory over the terrible enemy is played by a woman who not only inspires courage in her brave but doubting spouse, but also appears herself on the field of battle at the critical moment. It is hard not to see in the elevation of Deborah and Amaseka into the limelight a reflection of the providential role that the writers of this circle assigned to Ekaterina Pavlovna. Similarly, the prototypical basis for both villains is rather obvious. But it would still be premature to assert that the authors of these plays are directly trying to charge the new favorite with treason. The time for such accusations was still ahead. The heart of the matter lies elsewhere.

The tragedies of 1808–1809 became one of the main manifestations of the ideologem of conspiracy as applied to the concrete political circumstances and statesmen of the day. At the same time, the metaphorical correlations in social consciousness not only reflected historical collisions in their own peculiar ways but also foreshadowed, and, to some extent, even created them. Thus the image of women-warriors, heirs to Catherine the Great, most likely stimulated the feverish activity that the grand princess displayed in 1812 when forming a people's militia. "The sovereign still knows nothing, but … the idea of creating special regiments belongs to the count [Rostopchin] and to me," Ekaterina Pavlovna wrote to V. P. Obolenskii at the start of the war, "and it came into being because Count Rostopchin was in Moscow" (Ekaterina Pavlovna 1888, 22). As events demonstrated, Rostopchin was not such a wholehearted supporter of this idea. "The great project is being created despite the count's resistance," we read in a letter of June 7 to the same addressee. "… Not two weeks will pass before Moscow shows its city head that he does not know her. Let this all be between us. I am happy that a good enterprise is being carried out, and it doesn't matter by whom" (ibid., 24).

Speranskii also felt the pressure of his mythological role. In his letter of self-justification, declaring that he had no relationship to secret societies or menacing intrigues, Speranskii exclaimed, "Most Merciful Sovereign! In the unseen presence of God the Seer of Hearts, I make so bold as to ask: is this how a gloomy power seeker who hates his sovereign and desires that be become hateful to others behaves, gives advice, acts and speaks?" (Shil'der III, 526).

In the tragedies, the villains are preordained for suicide by the canons of the genre. "I accept the damnation of the people from all sides," declares Heber and stabs himself (Shakhovskoi 1964, 511); then an abyss opens up under him and he tumbles into hell. In Nevakhovich Paluska throws himself down a precipice. The land will not accept a traitor, and he must literally disappear from the face of the earth before the triumphant people can unite to celebrate victory. In was in this key that the majority of contemporaries perceived Speranskii's expulsion.

V. I. Bakunina described the event in eschatological terms:

> God showed his mercy to us, again turned to us, and our enemies fell. Crime unheard of in Russia, treachery and betrayal, is unmasked. ... One must only conclude that Speranskii meant to betray the fatherland and sovereign to our enemy. They say that at the same time he wanted to inflame rebellion in all regions of Russia, to give freedom to the peasants and to give them weapons to wipe out the gentry. A monster who did not rise due to his valor wanted to use the sovereign's trust to destroy him. ... On the 19th this became completely public and the news was met with delight; people visited each other to offer congratulations, gave thanks and glory to the Lord Savior and praise to the still unnamed son of the fatherland who uncovered the treason. ... No one, however, was surprised by the treachery; they had long assumed it from all of the new regulations. (Bakunina 1885, 393)

There is much that is indicative in this statement. There was general agreement about the character of Speranskii's crime, despite the fact that no official announcement had been made about it; conviction of his unprecedented secret power and ability "to inflame rebellion in all regions of Russia"; prayers of thanks; the sense that no such betrayal had ever occurred in Rus'; as well as the use of the word "monster" (izverg), which in Russian suggests something expelled from the national body. A. Ia. Bulgakov also called Speranskii a monster, recording in his diary that "a conspiracy has been uncovered in Petersburg whose goal was to turn Russia over to the French" (Bulgakov 1867, 1367–1368). As Vigel' later recalled, Speranskii's disgrace "was celebrated as the first victory over the French" (Vigel' IV, 33). The calculations of those who had instigated his downfall were fully validated. The expulsion of the hated "monster" gave rise to a remarkable wave of patriotic exaltation.

∽ 7 ∽

Alexander's complaints that his "right hand" had been taken away and was a "sacrifice" he had to make to public opinion should probably be understood in as literal a way as possible. It was not for nothing that Minin and Pozharskii's militia, one of whose initiators had called for risking wives and children in the name of the country's liberation, became the prototype for the war Russia was expecting. Thus Speranskii's exile could be interpreted simultaneously as a sacrifice from two perspectives. On the one hand, the sovereign as the first son of the fatherland put what was most valuable to him—his plans for reform—on the sacrificial altar, and on the other, the ritual slaughter of a traitor became a symbolic pledge of national unity.[15] It is not surprising that while the emperor himself considered the sacrifice that he had made almost excessive, the majority of his subjects thought it insufficient.

According to Vigel's memoirs, everyone "was surprised ... and dissatisfied. How could they not execute this criminal, traitor to the state, betrayer, and be satisfied with sending him away from the capital and removing him from office?" (Vigel' IV, 33). Varvara Bakunina noted in her diary that "in society all right-thinking people ... were not happy with this leniency, calling it indulgence" (Bakunina 1885, 395). Even such a far from bloodthirsty person as Karamzin, according to a contemporary witness, said that "he thinks this should end with the scaffold" (Bychkov 1902, 34). Whatever the precise meaning of the words "should end" (doit finir)—the historian's moral opinion or his prediction of the future—his judgment was extremely indicative.

However, the scaffold seemed appropriate and the inevitable conclusion only for the small and very Europeanized elite. A bit lower on the social ladder, quite different measures were discussed. In his pamphlet on Speranskii, G. P. Ermolov, a distant relative of the famous general, wrote as if he were addressing the exile: "Scorned everywhere and by all estates who are ready to tear you to pieces and to rid the earth of even your dust—here is the reward for the lawlessness and evildoing you prepared for Russia, and an even greater punishment awaits you ahead as a monster who wanted to destroy everything pleasing to Him" (Ermolov 1895, 24). Formulas like "tear to pieces" and "rid the earth of your dust" were not mere rhetorical clichés. Speranskii was taken into his exile in Nizhnii Novgorod without going through Moscow, where rumors circulated that as soon as he and Magnitskii (who was being exiled with him) "will be brought into Moscow they will be torn apart by the people" (Bestuzhev-Riumin 1859, 72). Word came to Vigel' that in Nizhnii Novgorod Speranskii "was almost murdered by an enraged rabble" (Vigel' IV, 34). It is hard to say to what degree such aggressive intentions toward the fallen favorite were really widespread among the lower levels of society. We know that in exile Speranskii spent much time taking walks and in the company of the simple folk and apparently did not find this particularly dangerous (see Bychkov,

---

15 We are not considering the archaic roots of such ritual sacrifice, although it is possible that such an approach to the given material might yield interesting results (see Girard 2000).

"Prebyvanie" 1902). All of the testimony that we have concerning the universal hatred for Speranskii comes from the noble milieu, which was in this way articulating its notions about the people and the forms in which national unity was (or should be) manifested.

Later, in his "Memoir on 1812," Rostopchin—with a bit of ingenuous cynicism—referred to the campaign against Speranskii as a "dark intrigue" and asserted that he "was one of the most astonished when ... [he] learned of his exile" (Rostopchin 1992, 245–246). "Unfortunately," he wrote, "... Speranskii was reputed a criminal, a betrayer of his tsar and fatherland, and people of a humble estate substituted his name for that of Mazepa, which is their epithet for a traitor" (ibid., 246). The very notions that Rostopchin had actively helped formulate and propagate he now attributed to the ignorance of "people of a humble estate."

This maneuver was quite characteristic of Rostopchin. In the second half of August 1812, not long before the Battle of Borodino, he arrested more than forty French residents of Moscow (see Popov 1875, № 10, 132–133), put them on a wooden barge and in the presence of a huge crowd sent them downstream, which he accompanied with the following highly expressive farewell speech:

> French people! Russia gave you shelter but you did not cease thinking up evil against her. To avoid bloodshed, not to besmirch the pages of our history, and not to imitate the satanic frenzy of your revolutionaries, the government is forced to send you away. You will live on the banks of the Volga among peaceful people who are true to their oaths, who scorn you too much to do you harm. For some time you will quit Europe and go off into Asia. Cease being scoundrels [mauvais sujets] and become good people, and, whatever you were up to until now, turn from Frenchmen into good Russian citizens; be calm and humble or await even greater punishment. (Ibid., 130–131)

In his memoirs, Rostopchin wrote that he did this "having received proof of the degree to which the people were agitated, ... in order to calm them and to diminish their fury" (Rostopchin 1992, 290). However, even such a likeminded admirer as Sergei Glinka asserted that there was no danger of mob law: "I lived with the people in the streets, on the squares, at the markets, everywhere in Moscow and in the environs, and I declare by the living God that no kind of furious hatred disturbed Russia's sons" (Glinka 1836, 42; cf.

Figure 18 Throwing French actresses out of Moscow (1812). Caricature by A. G. Venetsianov.

Popov 1875, № 10, 130–133). No matter which memoirist gauged the temper of the Muscovites more accurately, it is incontrovertible that Rostopchin was carrying out his own longstanding plan. We will recall that already in 1806 during recruitment for the people's militia, he had demanded that Alexander exile all of the French from Moscow without exception (Rostopchin 1892, 419).

In the same way, for his entire tenure as Moscow governor-general Rostopchin persecuted the Martinists with unflagging energy. He wrote to the emperor about the intrigues of the Martinists and Illuminati on the second day after his appointment and the closer that Napoleon's army came to Moscow, the more time and effort he spent on the internal enemy (see Popov 1875, № 8, 277; Kizivetter 1915, 158, 160–170). After having sent the director of the post office F. P. Kliucharev out of Moscow to Voronezh, Rostopchin wrote to Alexander that this was on his part "the single means to prevent the Martinists' plans, which have been already brought to the point of threatening Russia with misfortune, and you—the fate of Louis XVI. In time you will see, Sovereign, that this horrible sect gained your favor with the help of those who themselves belonged to it" (Kizivetter 1915, 166).[16] In the context of the "Notes on Martinists" that he had earlier given to the emperor, the last phrase of this tirade plainly took aim at Speranskii.

Even in exile the disgraced favorite did not give Rostopchin peace, and he wrote to Alexander that "from the first to the last in all of Russia he is considered a traitor," and warned the emperor of the deadly menace emanating from the outcast (Rostopchin 1892, 428–435). In August 1812, he again and without the emperor's sanction wrote an order to the governor-general of Nizhnii Novgorod to send Speranskii to Moscow (Bychkov, "Prebyvanie" 1902). The demand to bring a state criminal to a city to which enemy forces were approaching seems puzzling, to say the least. The single possible explanation of Rostopchin's strange behavior comes from Korf: "But here the question arises, and it is here that we see its importance, with what goal did Rostopchin dare to take such a step so far exceeding his prerogatives? Doubtless, with only one [purpose] … to sacrifice the man the people hated to their aroused passions, as he did with the unfortunate Vereshchagin" (ibid., 234; cf. Kizivetter 1915, 184).

The Vereshchagin episode, described repeatedly from first, second, and third-hand accounts by shocked contemporaries and analyzed in detail in the historical literature (for a collection of documents, see Dmitriev 1998, 546, 556–559; cf. Popov 1875, № 8, 287–291; Kizivetter 1915, 115–121), is very familiar from Tolstoy's *War and Peace*. For the issues discussed in the current book, Rostopchin's own explanations for this horrible act present the main interest. In a report preserved by M. A. Dmitriev from Rostopchin to his uncle, the Minister of Justice I. I. Dmitriev, on October 13, 1812, it says, "As concerns Vereshchagin, just before the entry of our enemies into Moscow I handed this traitor and state criminal over to the people crowding around him who saw in him the voice of Napoleon and prophet of their misfortunes and made him a

---

16 A. N. Popov and S. P. Mel'gunov are inclined to explain Rostopchin's hysterical hatred for Martinists in part by his connection to the Jesuits, whom he supported through his wife who had converted to Catholicism (see Popov 1875, № 8, 275–278; Mel'gunov 1923, 134). It seems as if such an approach accords with the interpretive practices described in this book. At the same time it is probable that his wife's conversion to Catholicism that made Rostopchin's position rather vulnerable might have stimulated his interest in the widespread mythology of conspiracies and secret societies, and also to some extent may have fostered his swift transformation from a proponent of pro-French policies to a militant Francophobe.

sacrifice to their righteous wrath" (Dmitirev 1998, 99). Ten years later Rostopchin related another version of these events in his memoirs:

> I ordered that the merchant's son Vereshchagin, author of Napoleonic proclamations, be taken from prison and brought to me, as well as a certain French fencing teacher by name of Mouton. ... Addressing the former, I began to reproach him for a crime so much more vile because he alone out of the entire population of Moscow wanted to betray his fatherland; I told him that he had been sentenced to death by the Senate and that he had to suffer for it—and I ordered two subordinate officers of my convoy to kill him with their sabers. He fell without saying a single word.
> Then, turning to Mouton, who, expecting the same fate, was saying prayers, I said to him: "I grant you life; return to your own and tell them that the scoundrel whom I just punished was the only Russian to betray his fatherland." (Rostopchin 1992, 313)

Let us consider the contradiction between these two accounts. On the heels of recent events and before the end of the war, Rostopchin presents himself as instrument of popular anger, and ten years later—as the executor of a legal sentence. (Actually the Senate sentenced Vereshchagin not to death but to hard labor.) However, the symbolic dimension of the event is clear in both descriptions. From the huge mass of the people Rostopchin isolates a single traitor on whom guilt for the national tragedy is placed. The especially metaphorical and theatricalized character of this fixation on one criminal becomes particularly visible if we take into consideration that, during the investigation of the Vereshchagin affair, Rostopchin tried to expose an extensive Masonic conspiracy behind the back of the unfortunate merchant's son (see Shchukin VIII, 44–77).

The expulsion of the traitor from the national body becomes fearsome news for the enemy about the solidarity the people have acquired; the need to inform them of this news saves the life of the fencing master Mouton. Let us recall that in front of Rostopchin's home had gathered a crowd of people who had been summoned in his posters to form a fearsome people's militia to repulse the enemy. In his accounts Rostopchin splits the story of the punishment he carried out into two parts. In one the people play the role of executioner, in the other it is the subordinate officers from his convoy. In the words of M. A. Dmitriev, Rostopchin pointed Vereshchagin out to the people, of whom many had gathered, and, calling him a traitor, he ordered a police dragoon to stab him; the dragoon did not obey immediately, but when ordered a second time took out his saber and struck him a blow. The surname of this dragoon was Burdaev. Then they threw Vershchagin off of the steps to the people who tore him to pieces and dragged him through the streets. (Dmitriev 1998, 98–99)

All of the memoirists sketch a roughly similar picture; only the ballet master A. P. Glushkovskii asserted that "Rostopchin's orderly Pozharskii delivered the first blow to Vereshchagin's head with a broadsword, and not Burdaev" (Glushkovskii 1940, 96). This difference indirectly supports Rostopchin's later account that he gave the order to hew the man to *two* subordinates. If Glushkovskii's information is true,[17] then the inevitable historical analogy that arises is most probably no accident. The governor-general, occupied with forming the Moscow militia, which he and his cohort constantly and persistently projected onto the Nizhnii Novgorod militia of 1611–1612, could not have helped but notice the famous surname of his orderly. Shoving him onto the stage of history at this dramatic moment Rostopchin, consciously or not, elevated his self-motivated action to the level of emulating the heroic national past.

Leo Tolstoy depicted Vereshchagin's killing as a desperately cowardly step that Rostopchin committed in order to distract the enraged crowd and slip away unnoticed. This version provoked P. A. Viazemskii's determined protest. Seconding the opinion of Varnhagen von Ense, who knew Rostopchin, he wrote that "Rostopchin made Vereshchagin a sacrifice in order to *increase the people's indignation,* and at the same time gave Napoleon and the French as it were a foretaste of the bitterness with which they would be greeted in *hospitable* Moscow" (Viazemskii VII, 212; cf. Varnhagen von Ense 1859). D. N. Sverbeev (1871, 520) also wrote about the fact that Rostopchin "might have been ... the criminal murderer of Vereshchagin, but he could not be and was not a killer out of cowardice."

However, Tolstoy's critic Viazemskii also presumed that the commander of Moscow "handed Vereshchagin over to the people as a sacrifice" "at a moment of great sorrow, great frustration," and that there was "nothing premeditated,

---

17 I. F. Zhukov writes that the second man who carried out the punishment was A. G. Gavrilov (Zhukov 1866, 255).

nothing planned" in his action (Viazemskii VII, 212). Still, the entire scenario of the tragedy was invented by Rostopchin beforehand. Of course, there was nothing accidental about the fact that Vereshchagin and Mouton had been left in jail while all of the other prisoners had been taken away three days before the fatal event; according to Rostopchin's later testimony, "they forgot to send them off with the 730 [other] criminals" (Rostopchin 1992, 312).

To a certain degree the only chance factor was the person of Vereshchagin, who by the will of fate ended up at the center of events and who substituted for a much larger-scale figure who had already been singled out long before by public opinion for the role of the main traitor and conspirator. But it was precisely the basic interchangeability of the sacrifice that serves as the clearest proof that on the streets of Moscow, a monumental ideological ritual was played out: an incarnation of the myth of the people's body.

∞ 8 ∞

The Vereshchagin incident aroused His Majesty's dissatisfaction. "His execution was not needed, and especially should not have been carried out this way," Alexander wrote to Rostopchin on November 6, 1812. "It would have been better to hang or shoot him," the emperor added with his characteristic humanism (Shil'der 1893, 184). In the opinion of many contemporaries, this act of vengeance was the reason for the sovereign's negative disposition toward Rostopchin.

We are not fated to know whether Alexander felt that the bloody farce that played out in front of the governor-general's house was a parody of the sophisticated sacrifice he himself had offered almost six months before in the name of uniting the nation around the throne. In any case, having returned to Russia from vanquished Paris, he hastened to send Rostopchin into retirement. The *ukase* on removing him from office was signed on August 30, 1814. On the next day, August 31, the emperor permitted Speranskii to leave his place of exile. The people's war was over.

CHAPTER 7

War and Quasi Peace:

The Character and Goal of the War in 1812–1814 in the Interpretation of A. S. Shishkov and Archimandrite Filaret

∽ **1** ∽

By sending Speranskii away in this manner, Alexander attracted enormous public attention to the office of state secretary. The next important symbolic step was the appointment of a successor to the disgraced favorite. On March 22, 1812, the emperor summoned A. S. Shishkov to an audience. Frightened "by the removal of Speranskii and the retirement of Mordvinov,… and, finally, by the sovereign emperor's clear disfavor" toward him, Shishkov prepared for the worst, but things did not turn out that way (Shishkov 1870, 120). "I have read your treatise on love for the fatherland," said Alexander. "With such feelings, you can be useful to it. It seems as if we cannot avoid war with the French; we need to carry out a levy of troops; I would like you to write the manifesto about it" (ibid., 121).

In the apocryphal version in which these words were recorded in Varvara Bakunina's diary, the emperor said to Shishkov, "I have not read many things Russian, but rather a lot that is foreign, but I have never read anything so beautiful as your speech on love for the fatherland" (Bakunina 1885, 404). The emperor's words probably reached the diary's author via several mediating links, and the nature of the transformation clearly shows both the image of the sovereign in social consciousness as well as the reaction of the Petersburg public to the changes taking place. We will never know if the emperor really read Shishkov's "Treatise," which the author had decided to read aloud at a meeting of the "Colloquy of Lovers of the Russian Word" several months earlier, after worrying that his performance would be taken "as a bold attempt to rouse national pride without permission of the government" (Shishkov 1870, 117–118). Be that as it may, Alexander did not apprehend Shishkov's idea expressed in the "Treatise" that love for the fatherland was based on using the native tongue.

When N. S. Kiselev and Iu. F. Samarin published Shishkov's memoirs, they drew attention to a difference between the manuscript and the version that the admiral had published in 1831. According to them, "in the printed text the emperor speaks to Shishkov 'on *ty*,'" that is, using the intimate and not the polite form of the pronoun "you" (ibid., 121; cf. Shishkov 1831, 1–2). It was usual for the autocrat to address a subject in this way, and other places in the memoir preserve this form (Shishkov 1870, 249, 259, 262, etc.). At the same time, it is hard to suspect Shishkov of forgetting such a significant detail of their conversation which he himself called "the most important event in my life" (ibid., 118), the more so since the manuscript version was created long before the printed one (Tartakovskii 1980, 49–50). Apparently the audience had taken place in French, in which the etiquette for using second person pronouns significantly differed from the Russian.

It is all the more improbable that the emperor chose Shishkov instead of Karamzin, who was also a candidate (Grot 1867, 118), out of considerations of language and style, as Kiselev and Samarin suggested, referring to the intellectual leader of the "Colloquy"'s "simple, true, sincere, as well as powerful word that inspired heroic exploits" (Shishkov 1870, 124; cf. Lotman i Uspenskii 1996, 420–424, etc.). More likely, on the eve of inevitable war, Alexander wanted to demonstrate to the Russian people that the ideological orientation had changed and that he was now prepared to find support in the social groups and circle of ideas that Shishkov had represented over for an entire decade. S. T. Aksakov, who was an extraordinarily ardent supporter of the new state secretary, claimed that "in Moscow and in the inner provinces of Russia ... everyone was very pleased by Shishkov's appointment" (Aksakov II, 305; cf. Zharinov 1912).

Figure 19 Variants for a medallion commemorating the home guard by A. N. Olenin.

Shishkov wrote the first, trial manifesto in one evening (see Shishkov 1870, 121). "His style is serious, eloquent and strong," wrote V. Bakunina in her diary, "but harsh to many: they are unused to sayings and phrases that are completely Russian" (Bakunina 1885, 394). Despite his lack of experience writing such documents, which made him nervous, Shishkov was able to cope with the new task with the help of those rhetorical and ideological models that he and his associates had been working out since 1806. "The present condition of affairs in Europe," began the manifesto, "demands firm and decisive measures, constant vigilance and a strong home guard which could protect Our Great Empire in a certain and reliable way from all enemy assaults" (Shishkov 1870, 423). Note the use of the word "home guard" (*opolchenie*); in fact, Shishkov was referring to a special levy of recruits for the army. Less than four months later, when it was necessary to summon an actual militia, Shishkov described the difference clearly: "The internal force created today is not a militia or levy of recruits but a temporary force of true sons of Russia that is being set up as a precaution to support the regular troops and for the most reliable safeguarding of the Fatherland" (ibid., 428). Shishkov distinguishes the home guard not only from the regular recruits but also from a militia, while the manifesto of November 30, 1806, to which he was obviously referring, had been called "On the Summoning and Formation of Universal Temporary Militias or Police" (PSZ № 22374). Shishkov was apparently either troubled by the unsuccessful attempt to form a militia in 1806–1807 or he simply did not like the foreign word "militia."

In the first manifesto Shishkov chose the perhaps not fully accurate but emotionally powerful term "opolchenie" because this rhetorical move allowed him to emphasize the universal character of the mobilization and to have Russian society make the necessary historical connection. In the manifesto on the home guard, the associative mechanism was employed in full force:

> Let him [the enemy] meet in every Nobleman a Pozharskii, in every clergyman a Palitsyn, in every citizen a Minin. Most Noble estate! In all ages you have been the savior of the Fatherland; Most Holy Synod and clergy! You have always summoned grace onto Russia's head with your heartfelt prayers; Russian people! Brave descendants of the brave Slavs! You have repeatedly broken the teeth of the lions and tigers who have assailed you; be united, all, and with a cross in your heart and weapon in your hands no human force can overcome you. (Shishkov 1870, 427)

In this patriotic rhetoric, the parallel between the anti-Napoleonic home guard of Moscow and the troops of Minin and Pozharskii that had been worked out five years earlier naturally came to the fore.

The emperor signed the manifestoes "To the First Capital City, Our Moscow" and "On the Summoning of a Home Guard" (zemskoe opolchenie) on one day—July 6. In their texts Shishkov clearly defined the continuity between them: "We have already called out to our First Capital City, Our Moscow, and now we summon all of our subjects, of all conditions, secular and religious" (ibid., 427). Such an order of address, in which "the ancient Capital of Our Ancestors" was preferred not only over Petersburg, but the entire country, was motivated by the fact that Moscow "was always the head of the other Russian cities; ... according to its example, sons of the Fatherland from all other regions have flowed to it, like blood to the heart, in its defense" (ibid., 425). The excess of organicist metaphors that followed from Shishkov's ideas about the state having to form "one body and soul" (Shishkov IV, 184) indicated by lack of mention that this was also a rejection of the Petrine model of statehood. In one of his conversations with the emperor, Shishkov allowed himself to note that the evil undermining

Russian's strength had begun with "the otherwise great Peter I, but in this case who did not foresee the consequences. Together with useful arts and sciences he allowed trivial imitations to enter that disturbed native customs and habits" (Shishkov 1870, 160). Petersburg did not have the right to be either the "heart" or the "head" of Russia. The disease that was threatening the national body demanded consolidation around historical holy places. "We Ourselves do not hesitate to stand among our people in this Capital and in other places of our Realm to summon and guide all of our home guards," it said in the manifesto addressed to Moscow (ibid., 425).

Alexander mastered the art of subordinating his actions to the "general will," as he understood it, but only gradually. The first symptoms of this new attitude were manifested in the appointment of Shishkov and Rostopchin—whom he found profoundly unappealing—to important positions. Then, pressured by Shishkov and Minister of Police Balashov, he agreed to leave the army and go to Moscow despite his own desire to remain. This decision, as Richard Wortman has demonstrated, testified to the fact that the autocrat, despite "his most personal inclinations," took upon himself "the role of national leader who mobilized all the estates of the realm in the cause of defending the empire" (Wortman 1994, 217). The culmination of this autocratic self-abnegation was the appointment of M. I. Kutuzov, whom the emperor hated, as commanding general. "When Rostopchin reported to me in his letter of September 5 that all Moscow wants Kutuzov to command the army,... my choice had to fall on the one whom general opinion designated," the emperor wrote to his sister Ekaterina Pavlovna (Nikolai Mikhailovich 1910, 87–88). The choices of "all Moscow" and "general opinion" were essentially identical, and the "first capital city" became a symbol of national unity. It was not by accident that Sergei Glinka compared the emperor's arrival in Moscow to the election of Mikhail Romanov as ruler of the nation (Glinka 1814; cf. Wortman 1994, 219).

In the official announcements on the surrender of Moscow and the enemy's departure from it, no analogies with the events of 1612 were drawn (Shishkov 1870, 157–159, 438–442), even though the parallel was strongly present in the minds of contemporaries. It sounded in Ivan Kovan'ko's "Soldier's Song," which had been published in the first issue of the journal *Son of the Fatherland* and had attained extraordinary popularity:

> Хоть Москва в руках французов,
> Это, право, не беда—
> Наш фельдмаршал князь Кутузов
> Их на смерть привел туда.
>
> Вспомним, братцы, что поляки
> Встарь бывали тоже в ней,
> Но не жирны кулебяки—
> Ели кошек да мышей.
>
> Напоследок мертвечину
> Земляков пришлось им жрать,
> А потом пред русским спину
> В крюк по-польски изгибать.
>
> Побывать в столице слава,
> Но умеем мы отмщать.
> Знает крепко то Варшава,
> И Париж то будет знать.
>   (Kovan'ko 1812; cf. Grech 1930, 304–305)

(Although Moscow's in French hands / This, truly, is no misfortune—/ Our field-marshal Kutuzov / Led them there to die. // Remember, brothers, that the Poles / Also visited Moscow / But it wasn't rich pastries that they ate / But cats and mice. // At last they were forced / To scarf down dead countrymen, / And then bend their backs in Polish fashion / Before the Russians. … // It may be glorious to visit the capital / But we know how to take revenge, / Warsaw knows that very well / And Paris will know it too.)

At the end of 1812 D. P. Troshchinskii consoled Kutuzov about the fact that he had been forced to abandon the capital: "Of course you regret that you were not able to stand up for the first capital city of ours. But who can fight against fate? … Pozharskii was [also] unable to defend the mother of Russian cities; he threw out an enemy that was a hundred times weaker than the one that now flees from your sight. Destiny has compared you to that great man; both of you will remain in the memory of posterity as benefactors of the fatherland. Moscow fell, but, supporting itself on her, Russia came through" (SbRIO III, 14–15). Thanking his correspondent, Kutuzov answered: "It was comforting to me to read in your friendly letter that Pozharskii drove the enemy out of Moscow and didn't let it get established there" (ibid., 16). Kutuzov wrote this phrase in his own hand at the end of the copyist's version of the letter.

Together with this, the manifestoes' descriptions of the French army's brutality in the occupied city markedly duplicated formulas that had been created earlier to depict the horrors of the Polish occupation. In the celebrated "News from Moscow of October 17," which contemporaries considered Shishkov's best publicistic work,[1] he emphasized that "surveying all of the horrors [of the French presence] as a whole, we cannot say that we are conducting war with a [normal] enemy" (Shishkov 1870, 438). The behavior of the French army was juxtaposed to "the image of war between powers that maintain the honor of their names" (ibid., 439), and as examples of these he cited England, Sweden, and, naturally, Russia. In just the same way in 1807, V. M. Severgin, in listing the violence that the Swedes had committed in Russia, noted: "But these evils I would call virtues in comparison to the unspeakable horrors of the Polish troops" (Severgin 1807, 9). It is not impossible that this historical parallel led Shishkov to insist that the Moscow fire had been perpetrated by the enemy, like that of two hundred years before (on contemporaries' views of the reasons for the Moscow fire, see Tartakovskii 1973; cf. Zharinov 1912a). The monstrous immorality of the Polish and French interventionists predetermined their blasphemous hatred toward the capital of ancient Russian piety.

∞ 2 ∞

Battle with this kind of enemy required the full concentration of all national forces. In the first manifesto about the levy of recruits, Shishkov wrote about the necessity "to protect Our Great Empire from all powerful enemy assaults on it" (Shishkon 1870, 423). Then in the manifesto about the home guard, he proclaimed that these "new forces, … bringing new horror to the enemy, constitutes the second line of defense of the homes, wives and children of each and everyone" (ibid., 426–427). This rather elementary metaphor would probably not be worth mentioning if the motif of separating the opposing sides by an

---

1 In the words of D. N. Bludov, who had no liking for Shishkov, "to arouse his eloquence it was necessary for Moscow to burn down" (Grech 1930, 351).

impermeable barrier had not taken on such special significance in Shishkov's writing. In the "News from Moscow," the issue comes up with the choice that will face Russia after the occupiers' excesses in the first capital city: "… [W]e must necessarily choose between two things: either continue to feel a partiality for this dishonorable people, and be its dishonorable slaves; or, cutting all moral connections with it, return to the purity and virtue of our [traditional] ways, and be in name and soul brave and Orthodox Russians. We must decide once and for all between good and evil, and erect a wall so that evil will not touch us" (ibid., 442).

In one of the notes to his translation of *A Short and Just Tale of Napoleon Bonaparte's Ruinous Works* by the German publicist E. M. Arndt, Shishkov wrote that Napoleon had gotten hope for success from "the French language, books, theater, teachers, educators, merchants and all sorts of *dear* (milye) seducers and traitors who had so long ago settled in it [Russia] and who tried to eradicate almost all Russian habits and customs," as well as from "the perverted Sarmatians who thought that it would be better to be slaves of that hellish monster than brothers to their countrymen, and from the Russians in lands adjacent [to Poland] who could not help being partially infected by this plague." However, "as soon as the *revolutionary monster* (chudovishche) approached" "the heart of Russia" and "stirred up its blood, and then such a fiery lava streamed from it that no one could withstand it: … forces and weapons and schemes and temptations all burned up. That is how blessed Russia revealed itself! Be always thus, my most precious Fatherland! Erect an insuperable wall between French depravity and your virtue" (Arndt 1814, 46n).

For Shishkov the issue here was not about rhetorical effects. The image of a wall that was necessary to erect between good and evil also defined his political views. In his *Memoirs* he expressed doubts about the necessity of the European campaign. "Why continue it [the war] when it is done?" he asked Kutuzov in December 1812 (Shishkov 1870, 167). In the manifesto about the French invasion of June 13, he had put the following words into Alexander's mouth: "I will not lay down arms while a single enemy remains in my realm" (ibid., 425). Now that mission had been fulfilled, and any other war goals were deeply foreign to Shishkov. However, if at first Shishkov only made up his mind to voice his doubts about a European campaign to Kutuzov, who may have had some sympathy for him,[2] the idea of taking the war directly onto the enemy's territory so distressed him that he decided to speak directly to the emperor. On November 6, 1813, he wrote an almost hysterical letter to Alexander imploring him not to cross the Rhine and not to continue the war in France. In his words, "the safest and most necessary protection" for Russia was "curing internal wounds and restoring our disturbed forces" (Shishkov 1870, 239). At the same time, a war to liberate Germany could still be beneficial insofar as "first, the powers of the untamable and impudent enemy have been weakened; second, the barrier between him and us has been restored; third, it is noble and worthy of honor and glory to snatch an innocent victim out of the clutches of a fierce predator" (ibid., 239–240). But to send the army into France was senseless and risky. A month earlier Shishkov had concluded his Leipzig manifesto with the words: "We are on the shore of the Rhine and Europe has been liberated" (ibid., 234). France, cursed by God, was not included as part of Europe and did not need liberation, and it was quite acceptable to leave it under Napoleon's sway.

Upon receiving Shishkov's memorandum, at first Alexander decided to somewhat soothe his state secretary, who was quite sick at the time. "I am very pleased with your paper and read it through more than once; there is much truth in it, and although I will not follow your advice, in many things I agree with you," he told Shishkov (ibid., 245). However, a month later during one of his "gracious" conversations he conjectured that Shishkov "was not so much sick in body as in his thoughts" (ibid., 249). This declaration was a clear indication that his state secretary was not long for the job.

The fierce intensity of anti-Napoleonic rhetoric has long been noted as a special feature of the publicism and literature produced during the war. In the words of A. V. Predtechenskii,

> It seems that there was no single poem, no single ode, no single work of prose in which Napoleon was forgotten, and of course, it was not to put in a good word about him. Such epithets as "the Attila of the nineteenth century," "predator," "outcast," "monster," "most vile hypocrite and deceiver," "bloody

---

2   According to a persistent tradition, Kutuzov allegedly told the Emperor: "Your promise is fulfilled; not one armed enemy remains on Russian soil; now only the second part of your vow remains—to lay down your arms" (Shil'der III, 137). However, Soviet historians consistently denied the truth of this account (see, e.g., Okun' 1947, 282–286).

and vengeful," "immortal Kashchei" and "Zmei Gorynich" [villains of Russian folklore], "the greatest murderer," "universal scourge," "horror personified," "hell in the flesh," "cannibal," and a multitude of others of this kind abundantly adorned the works of poets and prose writers who commented on the events of 1812–1814. (Predtechenskii 1950, 224; cf. Kazakov 1970)

On this background the restraint with which Shishkov speaks about the French emperor is noteworthy. In the manifestoes of 1812, Shishkov mentions Napoleon extremely rarely, preferring the collective forms "enemy" and "foe" that signify France just as much as its leader, as well as the country in general. There is not the slightest doubt that Shishkov related to Napoleon with not even the slightest bit more sympathy than any of his countrymen. However, he was not so much interested in Napoleon as in the French as a whole. As he exclaimed in the "News from Moscow":

> Could he [Napoleon] have been able to inspire millions of hearts with the spirit of frenzy and lawlessness if they themselves were not corrupt and did not breathe depravity? Although, of course, in any, even a pious people, there may be deviants; however, when almost every single person in the entire army acts as deviants, robbers, arsonists, rapists, offenders of humanity, desecrators of what is sacred—then it is impossible that among such people there were good morals and manners (nravy). (Shishkov 1870, 441)

In 1814, when the Russian troops were already located in France, Shishkov, extremely annoyed by the indulgent tone the commander of allied forces K.-F. Schwarzenberg assumed toward the French, wrote a project for an address to them that was not meant for publication or to be shown to the emperor, but for that reason expressed the author's thoughts with special clarity:

> Wiping you from the face of the earth would not sufficiently satisfy justice. In vain will you try to accuse Napoleon alone of all these cruelties. No! Even before him you demonstrated to what degree of depravity and ferociousness atheism (bezverie) had brought your way of living (nravy); sown among you long ago it has grown, spread and matured; having taken control of you it vomited your teachers and heroes out of the depths of hell—your Marats and Robespierres, and finally it sent you Napoleon. You chose them to rule over you because you saw in them the most vicious possible minds, the cruelest hearts. (Ibid., 271)

The idea formulated here that the French had chosen their revolutionary leaders, and especially Napoleon, is extremely important. Shishkov repeats it several times, including in a published manifesto: "A people, ... having trampled faith, the throne, laws and humanity, falls into discord, anarchy, ferociousness, steals, punishes, torments its very self and ... chooses as its leader, then tsar, a commoner, a foreigner" (ibid., 472). From this perspective the favorite idea of a significant number of Russian and European publicists that Napoleon was a usurper of the French throne played no role. The French emperor emerges as having been just as purposefully chosen by his people as once the Russians had called the blessed dynasty of the Romanovs to the throne. A nation that observes divine order elects an anointed one to the throne with a single will, creating the basis for a great dynasty, while a nation that lives according to the dictates of the devil places "above itself a tsar, or, more justly, ataman, born as a commoner on Corsica, who surpasses everyone ... in dishonor, cunning and malice" (ibid., 270).

Therefore, according to Shishkov, the Russian army should in no case enter France. It may have been possible to end the war with Napoleon, but the metaphysical "struggle between godlessness and piety, between vice and virtue" should not and could not be halted (ibid., 441–442). But it was necessary to continue this struggle within Russia, eradicating the French infection that had penetrated deeply.

In 1813 Shishkov had a violent quarrel with Kutuzov ("Out of respect I will not call him by name," he wrote in his memoirs; ibid., 177), who believed that in order to improve the mores of Russian society it was necessary to preserve the French theater in Petersburg and the traditions of secular education for children of the nobility. "Why not then [build the theater] on the ashes of Moscow," wrote the furious Shishkov. "My soul turned from such thoughts with disgust, and it seemed that if she[3] too were infected with them I would rip her out of my very self" (ibid., 177–178). The linguistic structure of this utterance is itself highly symptomatic. The penetration of alien influence into the people's body, "the secret attempt to beguile minds, to charm hearts" was for Shishkov "a surer means than swords and cannon" to defeat another people (Shishkov IV, 171). He cites with great approval a fragment from F. N. Glinka's

---

3   In Russian, the soul (dusha) is a feminine noun. (Translator's note)

Figure 20 Portrait of A. S. Shishkov. Lithograph by P. F. Borel' after the painting by George Dawe.

Letters of a Russian Officer where he speaks about the dangers that French prisoners pose for Russian ways (see ibid., 177).

Moreover, Shishkov's extremely militarist rhetoric contrasted with his natural geniality as a person. He was not at all inclined to persecute anybody. This task fell to Rostopchin, who in 1806 had demanded that Alexander "cure Russia of infection" by kicking all French people out of the country without exception, and when he became commander of Moscow in 1812, he immediately began to draw up lists of foreigners to be deported (Shchukin II, 67–68; cf. Ogloblin 1901; Mel'gunov 1923, 140–146). After Moscow's liberation his main concern was that insignificant part of the population that had remained in the city and that could have been exposed to foreign infection. As A. G. Tartakovskii writes, "all those inhabitants who had remained in Moscow during the period of occupation ... fell under police surveillance; each of them was considered politically unreliable and subjected to nonstop police surveillance" (Tartakovskii 1973, 261).

In a letter to Alexander in December, Rostopchin shared his characteristic concerns with the emperor concerning the mood in Moscow: "Every fainthearted nobleman, every merchant who escaped the capital and every transient priest considers himself—this is no joke—a Pozharskii, Minin or Palitsyn, because one contributed several peasants, and another several pennies, to save all of their property. In a mass the Russians are awesome and unconquerable, but as individuals extremely negligible" (Shil'der 1893, 187). Polemically turning Shishkov's lines from the manifesto on the home guard inside out, Rostopchin characteristically juxtaposes the united, mobilized people to their individual representatives. At the same time Rostopchin wrote to the sovereign asking that insofar as "Bonaparte has evidently slipped away from us, would it not be wise to think about measures to fight against your enemies within the state?" (ibid.). He gave a description of these enemies in letters of September 24, 1813, and January 19, 1814:

> It is necessary to take measures right now to extirpate the new evil that the presence of captured Frenchmen—generals and officers—represents for our inner provinces. They have penetrated into private homes and spread very dangerous views. ... The mania for the French has not passed in Russia, and their current situation evokes more and more sympathy for them on the part of fools and nobles. ... Since 1812 could not cure them of this stupid partiality for this accursed breed, we must seriously begin the destruction of these ecstatic devotees, and there are many of them in all social classes, especially among school-age youth. (Ibid., 200, 204)

The measures Rostopchin proposed would have extended the regime of national mobilization that had been worked out for the war for an unlimited period. It was necessary for the national body to finally be purged of the inner contagion and be securely isolated from the incursion of alien elements.

∞ **3** ∞

Understandably, such an isolationist policy was hardly acceptable to all of Russian society. For Alexander himself, the liberation of Russia from the invaders was, in essence, only a necessary step in the realization of a far more broad-scale plan. On December 12, 1812, when celebrating his birthday in Vilnius, he told the gathered generals and officers, "Gentlemen, we have not only saved Russia, we have saved Europe" (Shil'der III, 134). He was not willing by far to be content with a national war within the borders of the state. He was talking about a universal historical and even eschatological confrontation that would completely alter the way the world was set up.

N. K. Shil'der noted that Shishkov's and Rostopchin's appointments "had resulted from the extraordinary conditions of 1812 and certainly did not correspond to the emperor's personal plans, and seemed to constitute a concession to public opinion; it is unsurprising that once peace was concluded they simultaneously received new assignments" (ibid., 259–260). In Shishkov's memoirs it says that, when one of his friends had suggested the admiral as a member of the State Council in 1810, Alexander had answered, "it would be better if I agreed not to rule" (Shishkov 1870, 115). The dismissal of the two ideologues occurred on August 30, 1814, but attempts to take the monopoly on the official view of the causes, course, and goals of the war out of their hands had begun much earlier, in the final months of 1812. At first these attempts were connected with the transfer of the war outside of Russia and the necessity of organizing anti-Napoleonic propaganda that was aimed at European—first of all German—readers (see Sirotkin 198a; Shtein 1905, 886). Simultaneously the ideological product designed for internal consumption was gradually changing.

A substantive watershed in these changes was the parallel publication in the *Son of the Fatherland* (1813, ch. VII, № 32) and *Readings in the Colloquy of Lovers of the Russian Word* (1813, vyp. 13) of Archimandrite Filaret's "Essay (rassuzhdenie) on the Moral Reasons for Our Unprecedented Successes in the War with the French of 1812." The publication of the "Essay" in both outlets had been preceded by A. N. Olenin's "Letter to Archimandrite Filaret," which encouraged the addressee to write this work. Olenin wrote:

> Forgive me that I am bothering you and writing about the same subject about which I troubled you orally. But what can I do? I dream about this day and night and I continually hear in my ears the echoes of the beautiful expressions in the speeches or discussions you have composed *on the moral reasons for our unprecedented success in the current war* ... that was waged against us by almost all of Europe under the leadership of the eternally impudent, cruel and godless French.
>
> In my opinion, there has not been a more fitting opportunity for the eloquent pen of a religious figure to boldly assume the role of a secular writer. And indeed for whom then, if not a servant of the Holy Altar, is it fit to prove that the events of the current war and the unprecedented achievements of the Russian people has its start and finish in their limitless faith in

God, in natural, simple morality, not spoiled by false reasonings, and in loyalty to the Tsar, not due to philosophizing but according to God's law and love for the Fatherland. (Olenin 1813, 219–220)

This letter was written on January 5, 1813, five days after the Russian troops crossed the Niemen, initiating the European campaign. At this time Olenin, in his capacity of senior state-secretary, took Shishkov's place in Petersburg while Shishkov was accompanying the emperor. During the short period between Speranskii's removal and Shishkov's appointment, it had also been Olenin who had carried out the responsibilities of state secretary. When Alexander appointed Shishkov to the post, Varvara Bakunina had written in her diary, "Olenin, who had worked in all kinds of ways to replace the State Secretary, and who let everyone know that he himself would receive the post, wrote to Shishkov that he would have been insulted by any other choice, and that he recognized him as more worthy than himself, and added: 'Do not take this for a Judas's kiss'" (Bakunina 1885, 405).

Thus the campaign to undercut Shishkov's position was instigated by his own deputy, which was a time-honored bureaucratic tradition. However, in this case there were profound intellectual differences involved. Olenin was not at all a run-of-the-mill bureaucrat. For almost a decade he had been the ideologue and inspiration of a literary and artistic salon whose program consisted to a large degree in developing the cultural dimension of Catherine II's "Greek Project." An admirer of Winckelmann and Herder and former member of the Derzhavin-L'vov circle, Olenin shared a common interest with the Shishkovites in the problem of nationality and the desire to contrast national originality to an ideal of universalist culture, which in his case was oriented on French models. He saw the roots of Russian nationality not in the Church Slavonic linguistic domain or in folklore, national traditions and rituals (see Al'tshuller 1984), but in the historical ties between Russia and ancient Greece, and he perceived a direct succession from classical Greek to modern Russian culture.

The idea of constructing Russian national culture on the basis of the Greek inheritance had been advanced with great energy in Catherine II's "Beginning of Oleg's Reign" and in N. A. L'vov's preface to I. I. Prach's *Collection of Russian Folk Songs*. It also inspired Derzhavin's Anacreontic poems and especially the illustrations for them that were done under Olenin's direction, and it defined the work of writers in the Alexandrine epoch who were close to Olenin.[4] Within this sphere of ideas were: V. A. Ozerov's dramaturgy; the translation of the *Iliad* in hexameter that N. I. Gnedich was working on; and I. M. Murav'ev- Apostol's *Letters from Moscow to Nizhnii Novgorod* that was published in the *Son of the Fatherland* in the years during and right after the war.

In the second half of the 1800s, the Olenin and Shishkov circles lived through several rather sharp literary clashes. In 1807 Shishkov and Derzhavin, who were close at that time, initiated attacks on "Dimitrii Donskoi" by Ozerov, a playwright sponsored by the Olenin circle, and rumor placed responsibility for the failure of Ozerov's "Poliksena" in 1809 on A. A. Shakhovskoi, who had left the Olenin circle and allied with the Shishkovites (see Medvedeva 1960; Al'tshuller 1984, 147–157; Gordin 1991). Then the members of the Russian Academy rejected Krylov's candidacy; Krylov was an undisputed authority in the Olenin circle, but, as Mark Al'tshuller writes, the Academy members "demonstratively gave preference and juxtaposed the rejected fable writer" to S. A. Shirinskii-Shikhmatov, who was elected a member (Al'tshuller 1975, 163).[5] Later, in 1815, V. A. Zhukovskii, who often visited Olenin, wrote that "His home is a place where authors gather, over whom he wants to be dictator. ... Here they disparage Shishkov, and if they don't disparage Karamzin then they at least dispute those who praise him" (Zhukovskii 1904, 13).

The intense rivalry between Olenin and Shishkov by no means contradicted Olenin's, Krylov's, and to some degree Gnedich's membership in the "Colloquy." In forming the "Colloquy," Shishkov's goal had been to attract all of the even somewhat noticeable literary and government figures, so that the list of its honored members included Karamzin, Ozerov, Uvarov and even Speranskii. On the other hand, Olenin's position in the "Colloquy" was rather

---

4   On the political and cultural orientation of the Olenin circle, see Maiofis 1998; on the circle's aesthetic program, see Tomashevskii 1948, viii, xxiv-xxvii; Gillel'son 1974, 4–37; and Kukulevich 1939, who writes that "The conception of classical style (classical topoi) formed in A. N. Olenin's circle for works with national content ... arose as a result of the interaction of Winckelmann's neoclassicism and nationality in the spirit of Herder" (312).

5   Al'tshuller's insistence that the positions of Olenin and Shishkov were identical (Ibid, 173–183; cf. Al'tshuller 1987, 98–103, etc.) cannot be accepted in our opinion, and contradicts the facts that he himself relates. O. A. Proskurin, in our view, analyzes the history of these literary relations more accurately, although he rejects the existence of an "Olenin circle" as a special "literary grouping that worked out its aesthetic program [and] that occupied its own special position" without sufficient basis (Proskurin 1987, 72–76, 65).

ambiguous. We have no information at all on his participation in its work in the first years of the organization's existence, until the spring of 1813, when he addressed himself to Shishkov, who was still attached to the emperor, with a letter, fragments of which were first published by Al'tshuller:

> Fate has again pleased to assign me a place in which I am called on to represent your person. Gracious sir, guess what place—the Colloquy of Lovers of the Russian Word! In your absence the first group [of which Shishkov was its chair and Olenin a member] is orphaned. Its turn is coming, and they appointed me caretaker. So this is what moves me to trouble you with a request ... Would you not be able to present something in the "Colloquy" for the first group—are not there any of your works that could be read in public? (Al'tshuller 1975, 173–174)

The meeting Olenin was writing about took place on May 20.[6] Shishkov's works were not read at it, but on the other hand the public that attended heard Olenin's letter to Filaret and the latter's "Answer to a Letter in Which it was Proposed that an Essay be Written [or: That I Write a Letter] on the Moral Reasons for Our Unprecedented Successes In the Current War." Besides this, S. S. Uvarov's "Letter to N. I. Gnedich on the Greek Hexameter," a programmatic work of the Olenin circle, was also read, as well as Gnedich's response and his hexameter translation of Book 4 of the *Iliad* that illustrated the basic ideas of Uvarov's letter. If we add to this several fables by Krylov and a passage from a translation of Racine's "Iphegenia" by M. E. Lobanov, "one of the habitués of Olenin's house" (see Timofeev 1983, 99), we may say that the meeting led by the first group of the "Colloquy" that took place in the absence of its chair turned into a special benefit for Olenin and his allies.

∽ 4 ∽

In expressing the desire that "the eloquent pen of a religious figure boldly assume the role of a secular writer," Olenin was making a particularly subtle move. Providentialist interpretations of the recent events were at that time a commonplace and reflected the emperor's own position. "And so in this great matter we recognize God's wisdom (promysl)," wrote Shishkov in the

---

6 Al'tshuller assigns the general date of 1813 to this letter, but considering the date of the meeting we may date it more precisely.

manifesto of December 25, 1812 (Shishkov 1870, 172). During the entire European campaign, Shishkov occupied himself looking in holy books for "various descriptions and expressions that correspond to our present war" (ibid., 252; for what he found, see ibid., 252–257). However, it was far more natural for an authoritative figure from the church to interpret God's purposes and manifestations. With his request Olenin addressed the most striking and popular of such figures.

In the memoirs of a contemporary seminary student, Filaret, "an all-powerful archimandrite, a renowned marvel of intellect and learning," at that time

Figure 21   Portrait of Archimandrite Filaret (Drozdov). Gravure by J. Brian.

stood "on a height that was the more unattainable the less his rank in the hierarchy corresponded to his actual influence" (Giliarov-Platonov II, 74). The young rector of the St. Petersburg Spiritual Academy was the rising star of the Russian church. At the dawn of his career he had been patronized by the celebrated Russian preacher, Moscow Metropolitan Platon, who said of the developing pastor, "I write like a human being, but he writes like an angel," and who predicted that in time Filaret would occupy his pulpit (Ponomarev 1867/1868, № 12, 518). Called to Petersburg, Filaret attracted general attention with his sermons in the Alexander Nevskii Lavra, and among his regular audience members were Olenin, A. N. Golitsyn, A. S. Sturdza (Stourdza), and A. I. Turgenev (Chistovich 1897, 54). In 1811 by personal order of Alexander, Filaret was asked to serve at the dedication of the Kazan Cathedral. At the end of that year his father, the priest Mikhail Drozdov of Kolomenskoe, was on recommendation of the Ober-procuror of the Synod Prince A. N. Golitsyn awarded with a kamelaukion and pectoral cross "as a mark of the Monarch's special favor toward his son, who had commended himself so well in the capacity of preacher of God's word" (Sukhomlinov 1868, 17). In the same year, 1811, Filaret became close with Golitsyn, whom he called "a true zealot of the faith and the church," and who presented him with "Fénelon's religious works" (Steletskii 1901, 55). In September 1812, when the French army was in Moscow, Filaret wrote to his family that "Amid the general upset one person amazed me with his generosity of spirit. While many people were abandoning their homes, Prince Aleksandr Nikolaevich set up a church in his" (Filaret 1882, 166–167).

Golitsyn's church, built during the most difficult months of the war, was meant to as it were resurrect the spirit of original Christianity. Derzhavin compared the services in Golitsyn's church with "the shade of Tabor" and a secret temple "of the first Christians" (Derzhavin III, 170). One of the constant attendees of the church that had been created for an extremely narrow circle of people was Alexander I, for whom Golitsyn was one of the main spiritual pastors in those years. In the autumn of 1812 in this select company, Filaret began to present his sermons that aroused huge interest in the highest Petersburg society (see Korsunskii 1885; cf. Florovskii 1937, 166–184). In the service on the consecration of the cathedral, he connected current events with the inner consecration of those who were praying, something that—in the words of Filaret's biographer I. N. Korsunskii—"was one of the central questions of mysticism" (Korsunskii 1885, 398; for a comparison of Filaret's sermons of this period with those of the French mystic Jean Philippe Dutoit, see Galakhov 1875, 165–175).

"Christians! *You are the living church of God!*," Filaret preached. "… Curiosity to see the consecration of the visible temple would be in vain if at the same moment we did not think about *the consecration of our inner invisible temple*. … The image of inner consecration is represented in the image of external consecration" (Filaret 1812, 2–3). Among the congregants of Golitsyn's home church Filaret's sermon had such success that, in violation of church traditions, they asked him to repeat it (see Korsunskii 1885, 398). Later he did not include this sermon in his collected works, explaining that "I clarified the significance of diverse objects and rituals incorporated into the order of consecration of temples,… according to my own considerations, arbitrarily, if you please—hypothetically" (see Ponomarev 1867/1868, № 4, 135).

The view of the ideal church that Filaret's sermon expressed contradicted the entire structure of Shishkov's thought. Shishkov considered ancestral faith the most important component of love for the fatherland, thus putting the historical, ritual side of Orthodoxy in first place. This was all the more natural for Shishkov and his followers because love for the fatherland itself took on the character of a ritual cult for them.

> Ограда царств необорима,
> О ты, к Отечеству любовь,
> Достойна быть боготворима,

(Invincible defense of kingdoms, / Oh, you, love for Fatherland, / Worthy to be deified).

Thus began Shirinskii-Shikhmatov's poem "Pozharskii, Minin, Germogen, or Russia Saved." As Stefano Garzonio discovered, when he prepared his poetry for (an unpublished) re-issuing in 1834, Shikhmatov, who had already taken monastic vows, changed the problematical word "bogotvorima" (deified or worshipped) to the more cautious "sacredly honored" (sviashchenno-chtima) (Garzonio 1994, 73).

Shishkov's "Treatise on Love for the Fatherland," in which this cult reached its culmination, was recited with resounding success in the "Colloquy" on

December 15, 1811. Ten days later in his "Sermon on Christ's Birth," Filaret developed the idea that Christ's Kingdom was not of this world, and thus, intentionally or not, he unambiguously refuted Shishkov: "Only defenseless wanderers find Bethel and Bethlehem—the house of God and the house of the Bread of Life. Only voluntary exiles of the earth are accepted as citizens of heaven. One who desires to be a receptacle for the Son of God must have one's fatherland in God alone, and, for all one's regard for the earthly fatherland, which by the way is perfectly natural and just, one should consider it only an antechamber to heaven (predgradie nebesnogo)" (Filaret 1994, 43). D. I. Khvostov, who was present at the session when Shishkov read his "Treatise," subjected it to criticism that partly anticipated Filatet's: "On December 16 there was a reading by Shishkov of his 'Speech on Love for the Fatherland,'" he wrote in his diary. "The public was satisfied with it, the members of the Colloquy were wild about it, but really the speech is poor. The examples are puerile, the proofs weak, somehow [having to do with] faith, upbringing, and language. Faith is love for the Celestial Power, and whether it instills patriotism in us, I don't know. History often demonstrates the opposite." Later Khvostov added a sarcastic postscript to this entry: "Be that as it may, this love for the fatherland got the author promoted to state secretary" (Khvostov 1938, 378). Shishkov even had to face criticism that his patriotic feelings were un-Christian. "Many protest against this dictum ["Great is the Russian God"], seeing something pagan in it, saying that God is one for all peoples, so how can one say *the Russian God*?" he wrote in the notes to Arndt's *Short and Just Tale*. "But these protests are unjust. Here the Russian God does not signify a special divinity that the Russians have, but one and the same God [who confers] great grace on the Russians" (Arndt 1814, 51n).

In the "Essay on the Moral Reasons for Our Unprecedented Successes in the War with the French of 1812" that he read in the Colloquy, Filaret repeated many of the rhetorical moves that had been employed in Shishkov's manifestoes. Thus he fully reproduced the metaphors characteristic of the Shishkov circle relative to the moral infection that the French brought with themselves to Russia: "Did he [Napoleon] not strive to organize within our very own borders an unseen advance guard, sending crowds of revolutionary scum who carried infection in the wake of orphaned sons of the French kingdom who were running to us to escape that very infection which was consuming their homeland? And the sons of the North, just as alien to base suspicion as susceptible to deviousness, sometimes accepted them into their unsuspecting homes, like a snake into their bosoms" (Filaret 1822, 172). Just as familiar to those who heard the "Essay" was Filaret's providentialist interpretation of recent events and the conviction that the European catastrophe had only been the fulfillment of God's unfathomable plan that had at first been hidden from mortal eyes (ibid., 183–185).

At the same time, a whole series of thoughts that Filaret expressed sharply distinguish his position from the Shishskovite one. The most profound differences emerge when Filaret speaks of the place that Russia occupies in the world and in Europe, as well as his ideas concerning Russia's divine predestination. "What is the state?" he asked. His first definition was: "A certain district in the general domain of the Almighty, externally separate but linked to the unity of the whole by an unseen power" (ibid., 177). Here the notion that was arguably central to Shishkov's world view as expressed in his manifestoes—that the national body had to be walled off in isolation from alien peoples—was rejected. For Filaret the separate existence ("otdelennost'") of any state was an external attribute of political reality that only thinly covered over the inner unity of God's world order. Filaret underscored this inner unity with his second definition, when he noted the functional nature of the separation of mankind into state formations: "What is the state? A great family of people which because of its increasing numbers and the differentiation of clans could not be controlled as it was at the beginning by a single and natural father, and so it recognizes a Sovereign to rule over it in this capacity who is chosen by God and the law" (ibid., 178). Translating this argument from the metaphysical into the historical sphere, Filaret again postulates the original unity of humanity in which various peoples are likened to different families within the bounds of one state.

While the metaphor of the state-family may differ from that of the state-organism, it does not essentially contradict it; a family may also be understood as an organic whole. Thus Shishkov, who constantly resorted to personalizing formulas (e.g., "The Sovereign and fatherland are the head and body," "The troops, grandees, nobles, clergy, merchants, peasants ... made up a single soul"; Shishkov 1870, 142, 171), at times used the family metaphor himself (e.g., "On the one hand, landowners, out of paternal concern for them [their peasants] as for their own offspring, and [the peasants] on the other hand, like ardent householders, filled with [a sense of] filial responsibility and duty, bring themselves to that happy condition in which well-behaved and successful families thrive." Ibid., 307). In this light it is important that the third and last definition that Filaret gives for a state emphasizes the conscious moral choice made by citizens who take upon themselves the corresponding civic obligations: "What is the state? A union of free moral beings who join together and sacrifice part of their freedom for the preservation and support of morality through the general powers of the law, which is a necessary condition of their being" (Filaret 1822, 179). Here too the view of the state is universalist. The moral law is one for all peoples and monarchs, only some of them "enter the universal order of His rule ... through devotion and virtue," while others, on the contrary, "get together only out of fear and are motivated only by personal interest," "bring society closer to failure," and are ultimately "struck down by justice as an unacceptable part of God's domain" (ibid., 177–179). It was precisely this moral participation of Alexander's subjects in a "union of love" with their sovereign, their adherence to a single moral law, that enabled them to preserve national unity even "when the voice of the laws was almost inaudible amid the noise of battle" (ibid., 182). This unity was guaranteed not so much by the organic strength of the national body as by the free moral choice of Russia's inhabitants, including the enserfed peasants: "… A multitude of free hands abandoned their scales, pens, and other peaceful tools and reached for swords; free sacrifices for the needs of warfare were not only made generously by free people, but also by those who themselves could be sacrificed by others" (ibid., 181). In Filaret's "Essay," the words "free" and "freedom" occur nine times, while, for comparison, in the entire corpus of Shishkov's manifestoes, about seven times larger in size, they occur only eleven times, and of these, eight refer to European peoples that Napoleon conquered. "We have already saved [them], glorified our fatherland, and returned Europe its freedom and independence" (Shishkov 1870, 258)—this usage is typical of the rhetoric of Shishkov's manifestoes.

As state secretary, Shishkov was obliged to extol the Russian army's European campaign and not raise doubts about his own sincere pride in its successes. But, as noted, for him the campaign of liberating Europe only supplemented and highlighted the war's main task—to save Russia from the enemy and to guarantee its safety. In Filaret's conception these two tasks were reversed.

The expulsion of the French from Russia only served as the first step in realizing its universal historical mission—to confirm the Christian order throughout Europe. He concluded his essay:

> Today, errant peoples, know the path to the wellbeing you desire that you lost in vain fantasies! The divine scourge has struck Europe so that its blows would be heard at all ends of the universe. Heed the voice of the One Who Punishes and turn to Him, so that He be your Savior.
>
> Today, Russia, blessed by God, know your greatness and do not slumber—preserve the basis on which that greatness was achieved!
>
> And You,... Who, firm in the truth, saved Your realm and with goodness in might is saving other realms. *Rejoice in His strength and be joyful for His salvation!* (Filaret 1822, 184–185)

Figure 22 Medallion commemorating the expulsion of the enemy from Russia in 1812 by A. N. Olenin.

In the first half of 1813, the doctrine of national messianism was only briefly sketched out. After a year, however, in his "Sermon on the Day of the Triumphant Coronation (venchanie na tsarstvo) and Holy Anointing of the Pious Sovereign Emperor Aleksander Pavlovich," Filaret could formulate it with exhaustive fullness and specificity:

> There is only one true—because natural—route to national power, the route to social good and to the salvation of suffering humanity. If the Tsar and people have the blessing of Providence such that their strength revealed in saving themselves from danger, extends to the salvation of other peoples that suffer under a heavy and unjust yoke, then their happiness is not deceptive and their joy is fulfilled. If God not only manifests His salvation for us, but through us, then we are not only an object but an active instrument of His plan. ... The Russian Tsar *delights in Your strength* and for Your [sending] *saving* [*grace*], first onto us, then through us and now for the entire Christian race, he *rejoices*. (Filaret 1873, 195, 197)

This Christian universalism, based on the sense of a special providential mission for Russia and its emperor, came to replace Shishkov's isolationism as imperial state ideology. This kind of rhetoric attained special intensity in the framework of the popular apocalyptic interpretation of recent events. In one of his most celebrated sermons, the "Sermon on the Voice Crying in the Wilderness," delivered in Prince Golitsyn's home church, Filaret said:

> Do we not already hear the end of the great universal sermon—this Gospel will be brought to all creation and then the end will come. In this gloomy midnight You alone see if it is already time for the cry: *Behold, the bridegroom cometh; go ye out to meet him!*...
> But if someone does not yet hear, or does not recognize the voice of God in the exploits of his own life; yet at least he will not shut his ears and heart to the destinies of those universal voices which suddenly stun tribes and peoples, astonish the eyes, unsettle heaven and earth. ... We will not speak about the blows with which He *shakes* the entire great *desert* of Western Christianity. Do you not hear that *voice* that thundered not long ago and that has still not abated within the borders of our land, in the ruins, in the barren desert of the great city? (Filaret 1814, 14–17)

On June 16, 1813, Filaret returned the proofs of the journal *Readings in the Colloquy of Lovers of the Russian Word*, along with the text of his "Essay," to S. P.

Potemkin. "Having read the notebook and having found it correct, I return it to Your Highness," he wrote in the accompanying letter. "I only have doubts about the two last words, that is, the name of the writer, but if the Colloquy wants them to be there, I cannot keep water in a sieve" (Filaret 1883, 45). "To keep water in a sieve" was completely impossible. Filaret's influence and fame continued to grow. On June 29, 1813, after the sermon he delivered over M. I. Kutuzov's coffin in the Kazan Cathedral, he was awarded the Order of Equiapostolic Prince Vladimir in the second degree. "This decoration is unparalleled in our time, all the more so in those years," wrote S. Ponomarev in 1867 (Ponomarev 1867/1868, № 12, 528). Yet D. I. Khvostov, who had been so critical of Shishkov's "Speech on Love for the Fatherland," also remained dissatisfied with this sermon:

> They say that Filaret, the well-known preacher, was sent the Order of Vladimir second degree. A great distinction. [Was it] really for his sermon at Pr[ince] Kutuzov-Smolenskii's grave? A work of oratory is a very secondary type of creation, and hundreds of priests in Russia could write something similar. It does not live up to its content and is unworthy of the leader about whom it preaches. Why the comparison with [Judah] Maccabee? It is indecent if only for the reason that after Maccabee's death, the kingdom of Judea fell. (Khvostov 1938, 392)

Khvostov's grumbling, however, could not halt the ideological changes either in 1811 or in 1813. It was Filaret and no other who was entrusted with composing a commemorative service for the holiday "of saving the Church and Russian State from the Invasion of the Gauls and with them the twelve nations" which, by the *ukase* of December 25, 1812, was ordered to be celebrated on Christmas day (PSZ № 25669). The order of service included: verses from the fourth book of Kings (2 Kings in the Western Bible) about the sign given to Hezekiah (2 Kings 19: 20–22, 27–28); the famous passage from Revelations about the horseman on a white horse (Rev 19: 11–16); the visions of the Babylonian king from the Book of Isaiah; and the hymns "Glory to God in the Highest," "We Praise You God," and "In the Bethlehem Manger" (Izhe vo iasliakh Vifleemskikh) (see Dobronravov 1913). As Georgii Florovskii noted, "this was a service for the salvation of the whole world" (Florovskii 1937, 583). Alexander I's new political course had received eloquent ideological and ritual formulation. Now he needed new bards.

CHAPTER 8

Holy Alliances:

V. A. Zhukovskii's Epistle "To Emperor Alexander" and Christian Universalism

∾ **1** ∾

The period of the war with Napoleon and the first postwar years saw the appearance of a new state poet, arguably the last one in the history of the empire, but undoubtedly the last to be equally accepted both by state and society. With the publication of "The Singer in the Camp of Russian Warriors," in the December 1812, issue of *Herald of Europe*, V. A. Zhukovskii's name outgrew literary circles to reach a national audience, after which followed the poet's recognition at court. The success of "The Singer" is all the more striking against the background of Derzhavin's unsuccessful attempt to treat the great events of 1812—his "Lyric-Epic Hymn on the Expulsion of the French from the Fatherland" (see Derzhavin III, 137). We do not know the exact date of the rough draft in which Derzhavin expressed the intention to pass on his "decaying lyre" (vetkhaia lira) "as a legacy to Zhukovskii" (ibid., 449), but some time on the threshold between 1812 and 1813, this intention was accomplished. In February 1813 "The Singer" earned approval through the court of the Dowager Empress Maria Fedorovna, who—in the absence of Alexander, who was away with the army, and who in any case had little interest in literary affairs—provided ideological leadership for the literary process. On May 8 the empress presented the poet with a ring and ordered that a separate edition of the poem be published at her cost (Dmitriev 1871, 417–421).

Zhukovskii himself, despite the persistence of the humility topos in his works ("my weak gift," "unknown singer," "timid strings," etc.), rather quickly acquired a sense of his providential mission. "Send me a copy, and everything good [that has been written] on the occasion of current victories," he wrote to A. I. Turgenev on April 9, 1813, after the separate edition of "The Singer" had come out. "I also want to write something, the more so since I have the right to do so, because I foretold them: many places from my song were simply prophetic and happened à la lettre" (Zhukovskii 1895, 98–99). However, the victories of Russian arms remained unsung by him. In May 1814 after receiving news of the taking of Paris, he was in distress over his lack of creative production that had been caused by grievous personal circumstances:

> You order me to write. Priceless friend, my soul takes fire at the great things that are happening before our eyes. My heart contracts when recalling our Sovereign and that divine role that he is now playing in the sight of the entire world. Russia has never been so exalted. What a wonderful greatness! But as if on purpose my imagination is having a dry spell. Thoughts awaken in my head, but when I take up the pen I feel paralysis and I can only pity myself. I cannot describe this condition to you. It is not grief—no! Grief is also life, but this is some kind of dead aridity. Everything seems empty, and life—even more empty. Such a state is worse than death, and perhaps only Napoleon's could be even worse. (Ibid., 119)

Zhukovskii's writer's block was all the harder for him because he felt both prepared and obligated to give poetic expression to Russia's greatest victory. Moreover he almost immediately knew what literary form this would take. "However, despite my paralysis, I sometimes have thoughts about writing an epistle to our Mark Aurelius. What an enchanting character. And what pages for history does 1814 have in store! Brother, brother! It would be happiness whatever I could write!" he complained in the same letter (ibid., 120). In the fall of 1814 work on an epistle to Alexander was his main creative occupation. "*Between us:* I would like to write an Epistle to the Sovereign. Will it be accepted, and is it not too late?" the poet asked the same Turgenev in October (ibid., 125). Also at that time, in listing his future projects in a letter to Masha

Protasova, he included a single original poetic undertaking—the "Epistle to the Sovereign" (Zhukovskii 1907, 46).

In October Zhukovskii finally experienced the long-desired creative surge. On the twentieth he reported to Turgenev that he had finished the plan for the epistle: "The plan is done, it seems, well, and this is the most important thing for me. It is *written*, so I need not fear that ideas written down in a moment of heat will depart my brain in a moment of coldness" (Zhukovskii 1895, 126; various fragments of the plan are published and analyzed by: Poplavskaia 1983, 105–115; Iankushevich 1985, 104–108; Iezuitova 1989, 153–154). On November 8 the poet reported to his correspondent that "not one line [of the epistle] is written yet," because he wanted "to finish many trivial tasks to take on one important one without any distraction." Now when the preliminary plan was done, Zhukovskii prepared "to add his name to a monument to Alexander." Work on the epistle now went quickly. As I. A. Poplavskaia has shown, the main part of the text was written between November 13 and 23 (Zhukovskii I, 722). "You are waiting for the plan of my Epistle to the Sovereign," the poet wrote Turgenev on December 1, "but I am sending you the completed work" (Zhukovskii 1895, 130).

Zhukovskii asked Turgenev that, before presenting the epistle to the empress, he should read it to K. N. Batiushkov, D. N. Bludiov, S. S. Uvarov and D. V. Dashkov. This request was fulfilled, and the poet's friends responded to his new creation with delight. "Your work is enchanting, everything in it is noble, both its thoughts and feelings. It is full of life and poetry—in a word, you are equal to your subject, and what a subject," Batiushkov enthused. He, together with N. I. Gnedich and A. F. Voeikov, made a series of minor criticisms, most of which Zhukovskii took into account when editing the poem (Batiushkov II, 1989, 317–318). "Wonderful! Wonderful! Lofty feelings, profound and powerful thoughts, bold and noble praise, the language of a poet. ... Turgenev and I are thinking of the best way to present your beautiful work to the Sovereign Empress," Uvarov wrote to Zhukovskii on December 20 (Uvarov 1871, 0163).

This presentation took place on the thirtieth before the grand princes and princesses and Maria Fedorovna's secretary, the poet Iu. A. Neledinskii-Meletskii. Turgenev read the epistle while the empress followed the text in a copy she held in her hands. As Turgenev reported to Zhukovskii, the grand princes interrupted the reading with cries of "Beautiful! Excellent! *C'est sublime*" and expressed the desire that the epistle be translated into English and German, the languages of Russia's allies. The tongue of defeated France apparently seemed unworthy for singing the praises of their lawfully-crowned brother. However, Turgenev expressed doubts about the prospects for such translations: "For that you would need another Zhukovskii, and he belongs to Russia alone; only Russia has an Alexander and a Zhukovskii. ... I am sure that Alexander with his soul that is insensible to honors will feel the force of his genius and will render justice to himself and to the age that produced this genius" (Zhukovskii 1864, 885–887).

The dowager empress expressed the desire to familiarize herself with everything that came from Zhukovskii's pen, and also to receive a copy of the epistle to send to Alexander at the Congress of Vienna. On September 4, 1815, Zhukovskii arrived in Petersburg from Derpt and was received by the empress and grand princes at court, where he himself read "The Singer in the Camp of Russian Warriors." At the conclusion of the meeting, Neledinskii-Meletskii recited the epistle "To Emperor Alexander," which had become Zhukovskii's calling-card. Zhukovskii was branded as a state poet, and he himself was quite eager to accept this status. A year later, in October 1816, when Prince Golitsyn presented the emperor with a copy of Zhukovskii's newly published *Poems*, the poet wrote to Turgenev, "The Sovereign's attention is a sacred matter—I can also have a right to it if I will be a Russian poet in the noble sense of the name. And I will! Poetry ... must have influence on the soul of the entire people, and it will have this positive influence if the poet turns his gift to this end. Poetry belongs to national education" (Zhukovskii 1895, 163). The emperor fully appreciated Zhukovskii's writing and his intentions. The poet was awarded a pension of 4000 rubles in 1816 and, a short time later, the position of teacher of Russian to the Grand Princess Aleksandra Fedorovna, wife of the future Emperor Nicholas I. Zhukovskii could not have become more "official."

∽ **2** ∽

Recognition came to Zhukovskii against the background of the complete destruction of his hopes for personal happiness. His joining Moscow's home guard on August 12, 1812, occurred a few days after E. A. Protasova refused him entry to her house because of what she felt were improper hints at his feelings for her daughter. The *ukase* awarding Zhukovskii a mention in December 1816 came only a little before Masha Protasova's wedding to Dr. Moyer on

January 14, 1817. Over the course of four and a half years, Zhukovskii first gained and then lost his hopes for the happy arrangement of his fate. In these years the political storms and personal drama merged in his poetry, mutually embellishing each other. Evidently, the personal tone that was unthinkable for traditional official battle poetry was what guaranteed "The Singer" its resounding success.

> А мы?.. Доверенность к Творцу!
> Что б ни было — Незримой
> Ведет нас к лучшему концу
> Стезей непостижимой.

(And us?.. [Have] confidence in the Creator! / Whatever comes—the Unseen One / Will lead us to the best end [could also mean: "a better end"] / By an inscrutable path.)

These providential formulas easily fit into the official position on the ongoing military actions: misfortunes and military setbacks, including the surrender of Moscow, were only part of God's unknowable design, hidden for a time from mortal eyes, but ultimately directed toward the greater glory of the Russian Empire. "The Singer" had been written when these were still only poetic hopes and it was published when they had begun to come true. In 1815, when they were fated to be totally fulfilled, Batiushkov repeated Zhukovskii's formulas once again:

> Мой дух! доверенность к Творцу!
> Мужайся; будь в терпеньи камень.
> Не он ль к лучшему концу
> Меня провел сквозь браный пламень?
> (Batiushkov I, 165)

(My spirit! [Have] confidence in the Creator! / Have courage; be patient like a stone. / Was it not for the best end /He led me through the flame of war?)

The word combination "confidence in the Creator" (or more precisely, its prose equivalent, "confidence in Providence") had a long history from Zhukovskii's lips. Back in 1803 after the death of his friend and spiritual mentor Andrei Turgenev, he had tried to console Turgenev's father: "However it may be, as Karamzin says, and every good person should say: [have] confidence in the Creator! " (Zhukovskii 1895, 10). Zhukovskii clearly indicates the source of his frame of mind, but in borrowing Karamzin's words he—perhaps not fully consciously—subtly shifts the meaning in ways that are extremely suggestive. Zhukovskii was citing Karamzin's fictional correspondence published in 1795 between Melodor and Filaret, names that in Greek mean "giver of songs" and "truth-lover," i.e., a poet and a philosopher. The philosopher Filaret, consoling his friend who has become disillusioned with humanity and the meaning of life after the bloody disturbances of the French Revolution, wrote:

> Why not have that same confidence in Providence that two people may have in one another? ... I have confidence in the All-High and I am tranquil. No! The lamp of learning will not die out on the earthly sphere. ... Enlightenment is always beneficial; enlightenment leads to virtue, proving to us the close union of the personal and the general good, revealing a never-ending source of happiness in our own breasts; ... in enlightenment alone we find the salvific antidote for all human misfortunes. (Karamzin II, 186, 188)

To Karamzin, confidence in Providence is—despite all possible reservations— the conviction that the supreme power arranges the world for the best, both for an individual and for humanity. For Zhukovskii, it is hope for the immortality of the soul. For both Zhukovskii and Batiushkov, the Creator leads those who have trust in Him "to a better [or: the best] end"—victory and miraculous deliverance on the field of battle. But in the broader context of both poems, the "better end" is synonymous with "a better world," to which, in Zhukovskii "the son of combat" flies "on wings of lightning," while in Batiushkov, a "better life" comes when, having shed "earthly raiments," the poet "quenches the desire for love" "with a stream of heavenly rewards."

Zhukovskii's correspondence with Masha Protasova in 1814–1815 literally abounds with similar phrases. The poet describes a vision of future happiness that came to him: "I seem to see through some sort of fog: calmness, spiritual tranquility, confidence in Providence" (Zhukovskii 1883, 207). "Confidence in Providence has awakened in me," he notes in his diary for his beloved his impression from reading "Our Father." "You and Providence—in both of you is my true happiness. I give you over to its protection, and I myself give my word to give myself over to it with perfect tranquility," he writes to Masha, and in answer she nevertheless reproaches him for "little confidence in Providence" and wishes him "more confidence in God and the carefree [feeling] of a child" (Zhukovskii 1907, 32–37). This list could be continued.

Placing oneself unconditionally into the hands of Providence demands the inevitable relinquishing of one's individual will and desires. The single action worthy of a person is to reject the notion that one is capable of influencing one's life and the course of events and obligated to do so; one must instead meet any manifestation of higher will with the necessary acceptance. Another constant refrain in the letters of Zhukovskii and Masha is the line from Zhukovskii's recently written poem "Teon and Eshkin"—"everything in life is the means for [something] great"—which they occasionally cite, replacing the epithet "great" with "beautiful" (ibid., 59, 65, 70; cf. Zhukovskii 1895, 156). "You will not get far with Stoicism! Woe to him who depends on himself in anything,… and here only virtue *ne pas avoir d'excés: resignation parfait à la volonté de Dieu* (may not be excessive: perfect resignation to God's will)," wrote Masha to A. P. Elagina on April 25, 1815 (Zhukovskii 1904, 144).

It was just this "perfect resignation of oneself to God's will" that becomes the central feature ascribed to the addressee of the epistle "To Emperor Alexander." All of the appearances of the sovereign in the poem are marked by descriptions of prayers and by the corresponding rhetorical formulas that express the hero's supreme degree of humility before Providence, which deserves particular reverence in someone with such unlimited power:

> Смиренно приступив к сосуду примиренья,
> В себе весь свой народ Ты в руку Провиденья,
> С спокойной на Него надеждой положил —
>   [коронация Александра]
>
> И в грозный между тем полки слиянии строй,
> На все готовые, с покорной тишиной
> На твой смотрели взор и ждали мановенья.
> А Ты?.. Ты от небес молил благословенья…
> И ангел их, гремя, на щит Твой низлетел,…
> И Ты средь плесков сих — не гордый победитель,

Chapter 8: Holy Alliances

Но воли Промысла смиренный совершитель. ...
                    [начало европейского похода]

На страшном месте том смиренный вождь царей
Пред миротворною святыней алтарей
Велит своим полкам склонить знамена мщенья...
            [молебен в Париже на месте казни Людовика XVI]

И се!.. приникнувший к престола ступеням
Во прах пред божеством свою бросает славу!..
О Вечный! осени смиренного державу;
            [возвращение Александра в Петербург]

Склоняю, Царь земли, колена пред тобой,
Бесстрашный под твоей незримою рукой,
Твоих намерений над ними [подданными]
    совершитель...
                        [молитва Александра]

(Zhukovskii I, 367–376; on the same prayers in the "Prayer of the Russian People" of 1815, the prototype of the future hymn, see Kiseleva 1998)
(Humbly approaching the vessel of reconciliation, / You have placed yourself with all Your people / Within you in the hand of Providence, with tranquil hope in Him -

[Alexander's coronation]

And meanwhile the regiments merged together into awesome ranks, / Ready for anything and in humble silence, / Looked at your expression and awaited a signal. / And You?.. You were praying for heaven's blessing / And their angel, roaring, flew down to your shield ... / And you among these bursts of applause are no proud conqueror / But the humble executor of the will of Providence...

[the beginning of the European campaign]

On that terrible place the humble leader of tsars, / Before the sacred altar of reconciliation, / Orders his regiments to lower the banners of vengeance...

[prayers in Paris in the place of Louis XVI's execution]

> And that one! .. Bending down to the steps of the altar / Casts his glory into the dust before the deity! / Oh, Eternal One! Protect the dominion of the humble;
>
> [Alexander's return to Petersburg]
>
> I bend my knee before you, Tsar over the earth; / Under your unseen hand I am fearless, / Executor of your intentions for them [my subjects].)
>
> [Alexander's prayer]

One should note that the accent on humility and submission to Providence, which reached an apogee in this epistle, fully corresponded to official propaganda. Thus Archimandrite Filaret, whose spiritual eloquence had a huge influence on Zhukovskii, delivered his "Sermon on the Day of the Triumphant Coronation to the Kingdom and Holy Anointment of the Most Pious Sovereign Emperor Aleksandr Pavlovich" at the same time Zhukovskii was beginning to contemplate his epistle to the emperor. Here it said in part:

> At that very time when our Most Pious Autocrat wants to give worthy praise to his victorious troops he sings David's hymn: not to us, Lord, *but to Your name give glory*. ... [He] does not only profess what is, but also senses and predicts the future influence of Providence on his actions. God alone, he says, rules everyone, it is He that accomplishes this matter, so that the great matter of saving shattered kingdoms and groaning peoples and of pacifying the world is accomplished. (Filaret 1873, 195–196)

In this sermon Filaret refers to Alexander's well-known manifestoes and *ukases* that themselves contain abundant formulas of ritual self-abnegation. On June 30, 1814, the emperor declined a petition from the Synod, Senate and State Council that they be allowed to erect a monument to him and that he be granted the appellation "Blessed." Alexander explained that all of his soul's "thoughts and efforts" consisted in seeking divine and human blessing, but nevertheless he emphasized that "I do not permit Myself, as person, the presumption to think that I have already achieved that and can accept and bear that title. All the more so ... since I have always and everywhere encouraged My subjects to modesty and a humble spirit..." (PSZ № 25629).

Richard Wortman has collected a broad range of materials which testify that this whole rhetorical arsenal was not formal, but that it reflected the emperor's deep psychological mindset (Wortman 1994, 221–231). Alexander not

Chapter 8: Holy Alliances

Figure 23 Prayer of Thanksgiving in Paris, 1814. Gravure by I. V. Cheskii.

only "took every opportunity to display self-effacement in his work to effect the designs of God" (ibid., 224), but he also incessantly tried to assimilate the "technology" of this self-effacement. According to Golitsyn's testimony, at one of the meetings of the war council in 1814 in France, Alexander, as he said himself, felt "an overpowering desire to turn the matter over to God's will."

> "I strongly desired to pray," continued the emperor, "and to pour out the heavy doubts and vacillations of my soul before the Lord. The council continued to work, but I left it for a while and hurried into my own room; there my legs bent at the knee by themselves and I poured out my whole heart before God." After long and energetic prayers, Alexander finally heard God's word. "A sweet world in my thoughts, penetrated with calm, a firm decisiveness of will and a kind of radiant clarity of purpose—all this was given me then in this joyful and certain injunction." (Bartenev 1886, 95)

In this way, and despite the opinion of the majority of his generals, the decision was made to march on Paris. In these memoirs it is also related how, after the French were driven from Russia, Alexander cut off his generals who had ascribed the victory "to the unmatched courage of the glorious Russian army and the just as immoveable will of their powerful ruler and commander." The emperor objected that, in his words, "the Lord Jesus is the only Conqueror and Liberator of the motherland from the fierce enemy invasion" (ibid., 91).

The heavy labor of deciphering the preordained will of Providence demanded helpers. Over the course of his entire life Alexander sought spiritual advisers and surrounded himself with mystics and visionaries who helped him determine the necessary condition of the spirit.[1] Soon after taking Paris, on July 10, 1814, his meeting with the most celebrated European mystic Johann Heinrich Jung (Stilling) occurred. Alexander was more or less familiar with Stilling's works, about which he had written to Ekaterina Pavlovna in the note "On Mystical Literature" (Nikolai Mikhailovich 1910, 288). In the beginning of the nineteenth century, Stilling's autobiography, which told of the endless and beneficent interventions of Providence in the author's fate, was known all over Europe. One section of the book concluded with the assertion that it describes not "Stilling's whole life in general [the autobiography was written in the third

---

1   The legend originating from Alexander himself that his religious awakening was connected with the events of 1812 was decisively disputed by G. Florovskii (1937, 130).

person], but only the history of how he was guided by Providence" (Jung-Stilling II, 175).

With Jung-Stilling Alexander discussed the religious situation in Russia, the position of Christians in the Ottoman Empire, and also the question of which confession best corresponds to the spirit of true Christianity. However, Alexander wanted most of all to find out from his conversation partner what this true Christianity consists of. In Jung-Stilling's words, he told Alexander the main things were "perfect abnegation (abandon parfait), constant concentration (receuillement continuel), and heartfelt prayer (oraison de coeur)." "'Yes,' answered the emperor, 'that's exactly what I practice.' 'But how does Your Excellency manage to maintain this state amid so many activities?' 'I am sometimes able to reach it,' said the emperor, 'but I must admit that it is becoming harder and harder'" (Ley 1975, 88). Stilling's list of Christian virtues was probably already familiar to Alexander. On December 22, 1814, about the time Zhukovskii's epistle was being read by his friends in Petersburg, in a letter to F. M. Tseier Speranskii named "prayer, humility and renunciation" as the feelings that are "most significant for piety" (Speranskii 1870b, 175). Living in the country far from court news, Speranskii could hardly have known about Alexander's latest mystical conversations; however, he himself had had many such talks with him three or four years earlier. Similarly, while working on the epistle, Zhukovskii almost certainly did not know about the lessons that the emperor had received from the famed mystic.[2] Even so, he was still able to represent Alexander's Christian ideal accurately. Under his pen the emperor appeared just the way Jung-Stilling had described the ideal Christian: someone who completely casts off worldly strivings, continually concentrates on understanding divine predestination, and who turns to the creator with words of heartfelt prayer.

❧ 3 ☙

In Zhukovskii's epistle Alexander is shown conversing alone with God, without the clergy. Even in his frequent descriptions of church rituals, the poet does not

---

2   Theoretically, information about such an important conversation could have reached the poet, if we take into account his close relationship with A. I. Turgenev, Turgenev's with Golitsyn, and Golitsyn's with Alexander. However, in the second half of 1814 Zhukovskii was far from Petersburg, and hardly anyone would have dared trust such stories to writing.

mention any religious figures even once, each time choosing—perhaps not fully consciously—grammatical constructions that create the feeling that the holy rite is taking place by itself:

> Когда ж священный храм при громах растворился —
> О, сколь пленителен Ты нам тогда явился,…
>
> И погрузился крест при громах в древни воды!
>
> И се!.. подъемлется спасения сосуд…
> И звучно грянуло: воскреснул Искупитель!
>
> Россия, Он грядет; уже алтарь горит,
> Уже Его принять отверзлись двери храма,
> Уж благодарное куренье фимиама,
> С сердцами за него взлетело к небесам!
> (Zhukovskii I, 367; 373–375)

(When the holy temple opened to the sound of thunder—/ Oh, how enthralling You appeared to us,… // And to the sound of thunder the cross was plunged in the ancient waters! // And so!… the vessel of salvation will rise up… / And it resounded loudly: the Redeemer has been resurrected! // Russia, He will come; the altar already burns, / The doors of the temple have already opened to receive Him, / Already the grateful smoke of incense / Has flown up to the heavens with our hearts after it!)

This consistent way of describing church services came from the epistle's basic artistic conception; in Zhukovskii the tsar communes directly with God, so there is no room for mediators. However, this scenario is also founded on a whole series of biographical, ideological and historical presuppositions.

"Why should a person dressed in a cassock and called a protopope have more influence on you than our common good, than the sight of your children, than your own reason?," wrote Zhukovskii with poorly-motivated irritation to A. P. Kireevskaia in the summer of 1813; Kireevskaia had intended to invite a clergyman to console her after the death of her husband. Zhukovskii's none-too-tender attitude toward the church hierarchy was

Figure 24 Portrait of V. A. Zhukovskii. Gravure by A. A. Florov from the original by P. F. Sokolov.

additionally complicated in these years by the fact that, in his opinion, wrongly-interpreted church rules stood in his path to happiness. Ekaterina Afanas'eva Protasova—Zhukovskii's half-sister—had refused to permit Zhukovskii's marriage with his niece, her daughter, on the basis of her religious convictions. Zhukovskii's letters to Turgenev of the period were full of sarcastic comments on cassocks and those who wear them. In one of them Zhukovskii wrote that "Nature and God" did not oppose his marriage to Masha and that

Ekaterina Afanas'eva was "acting out of some sort of cruel and fanatical motives" (Zhukovskii 1895, 139). Zhukovskii hoped to overcome these motives and prejudices by attracting authority figures to his side; he also insisted that technically, according to the official register of births, he was not considered the Protasovs' relative: "The written law opposes marriages between relatives, but in nature relatives do not exist. ... The law does not call me her brother, consequently I recognize a single law of nature, and it is not against me. The Lutheran and Roman Catholic religions also allow marriages between relatives" (ibid.).[3]

Zhukovskii juxtaposed ecclesiastical formalism to living, personally experienced faith that told him that the feelings he shared with Masha were preordained by Providence. After leaving the home guard in February 1813 or 1814, he went to I. V. Lopukhin in the country to make his emotions and hopes known to him. The poet counted on the fact that the support of Lopukhin, who enjoyed great moral authority, would help him overcome Ekaterina Afanas'eva's opposition:

> I didn't pray, but felt that God, hidden beyond that clear sky, saw me, and this feeling was stronger than any prayer. ... How sweet and invigorating is the idea of God, when one imagines oneself in His presence together with her. ... To this moment I have often noticed in myself some kind of detachment from religion—I never rejected it, but it seemed to be the cause of all of the losses in my life and I did not separate it from the prejudice which deprived me of everything! But superstition is not religion. And now in this light I see that it is essential for true happiness! And this will be a gift from my Masha. ... How can I not consider her the means, chosen by Providence, to grant me the way to be worthy of citizenship in the City of God!

---

3   Protasova herself argued that for Zhukovskii "everything in the Christian law that did not profit him he considered a prejudice" (Zhukovskii 1904, 289). On his part, Zhukovskii denied that his sister had true Christian feelings: "Christianity (in her words) forces her to refuse us our happiness, but she doesn't have [the features] that constitute the character of a Christian woman" (Zhukovskii 1895, 137). Most later biographers have agreed with his assessment. K. K. Zeidlits (1883, 60) called Protasova's views "outward formalism," and in P. A. Viskovatov's opinion, "she believed in various prejudices and saw religiosity in external ritualism" (Viskovatov 1883, 187). However, A. E. Gruzinskii's point of view also seems quite reasonable—that "it is hard to consider E. A. Protasova a formalist on this question. The proponents of the marriage posed the question in far more *formal* terms ... when they based their argument on the fact that there was no kinship between Zhukovskii and Masha *according to the books*" (Zhukovskii 1904, III).

Zhukovskii returned to this feeling that he had experienced on the road to Lopukhin again on the return trip: "This living feeling did not deceive me; I am sure that this is God's voice, [and] Ivan Vladimirovich approved of my intentions" (Zhukovskii 1883, 209).

The impossibility of marrying Masha Protasova in no way made the existence of their heavenly union less real. At the start of 1814 Zhukovskii exchanged rings with Masha and wrote in his diary which was meant for her: "We will become betrothed in the name of God for the sake of virtue, of a good life, which will pass if not together, then at least *in the identical way* and for *one* [*goal*]. We cannot be together, ... but one roof or one sky—is it not all the same?" (Zhukovskii 1907, 6). At the end of 1815, when the impossibility of being with Masha had become clear, he wrote to her in the same diary: "Let us forget about the distance that separates us from that boundary beyond which our motherland begins, from that future, in which we will be together and inseparable. ... And our identical life here is a preparation for eternity" (ibid., 70). The similarity of the lives of the lovers, betrothed by Providence, was to be assured by reading the very same passages from Holy Writ and from religious writers and moralists, above all their favorite Fénelon ("You have your Fénelon, whom you can understand," writes Zhukovskii to Masha in the spring of 1815—Zhukovskii 1883a, 671; cf. 668). It was also ensured by attempts to keep parallel diaries that were meant for each other. This spiritual union was not to be destroyed by Masha's marriage, which Zhukovskii ultimately accepted. The poet planned to establish with Masha and her husband "a close triumvirate whose goal was general happiness" (Veselovskii 1904, 206). Even Masha's death hardly seemed to change anything in this special psychological condition that enriched Zhukovskii by means of "comradeship with a heavenly being"; the very thought of his lost beloved became "a religion" for the poet (ibid., 237; Vinitskii 1998, 55–91).

In the words of the author of one of the best books on the mystical roots of the Holy Alliance, E. Mühlenbeck, "in the milieu of German sectarians there existed the practice ... of entering into mystical marriages that was invented by Swedenborg and popularized by Jung-Stilling's novel. Two people came together spiritually for common prayers. ... Sometimes people could enter into such marriages even if they were already married, or persons of one sex. Some people had several spiritual husbands or wives. Others gave special significance to earthly betrothals, seeing them as the antechamber to marriage in the other world" (Mühlenbeck 1887, 157).

The similarity of the poet's spiritual drama to this kind of psychological and mystical experience is obvious; Florovskii wrote long ago about the German Pietist roots of Zhukovskii's religiosity (Florovskii 1937, 129). It is indicative that spiritual illumination came to the poet while on the road to Lopukhin, the most important Russian mystic and author of the popular tract *Some Features of the Inner Church* (1789–1791). According to Lopukhin, the "inner church" was a union of the select who had been enlightened by the light of divine wisdom. The varying degree of communion with this light determined each member's position within the fellowship. As for traditional church rituals, they were assigned a purely supplementary, although important role—they were "to prepare [people for] the most correct and efficacious organization of spiritual exercises for the inner service of God" (Lopukhin 1997, 89). According to Lopukhin, the "inner church" was a kind of ideal Masonic order. Zhukovskii's membership in Masonry remains a rather debated question (see Lotman 1960), but the ideal of a close union of souls that understand one another was always important for him. Even in "The Singer in the Camp of Russian Warriors" the very choice of metaphors for toasts in honor of military camaraderie refers to this kind of human relations:

> Святому братству сей фиал
>   От верных братий круга!
> Блажен, кому Создатель дал
>   Усладу жизни, друга;
> С ним счастье вдвое; в скорбный час
>   Он сердцу утешенье,
> Он наша совесть; он для нас
>   Второе Провиденье.
>
> (Zhukovskii I, 237)

([Raise] this flask to sacred brotherhood / From the circle of loyal brothers! / Blessed [be] the one to whom the Creator gave / The joy of life, a friend; / With him happiness is doubled; in an hour of grief / He is consolation for the heart, / He is our conscience; for us he is / A second Providence.)

At times Zhukovskii saw the prototype of such fraternal association in idyllic provincial existence in the circle of friends and family, at times in the court at Pavlovsk, to which he addressed his collections *Für Wenige* (For the Few), and at other times in the union of poets. Zhukovskii instilled the same ideal in Masha, whose motto was "Activité dans un petit cercle" (Activity in a small circle) (see Petukhov 1903, 98).

"You, me, and Batiushkov should make an alliance for life and death. Poetry—the goal and means; to glory—honor; to hell with the praise of babblers; to friendship—everything!," he wrote to Viazemskii on November 10, 1814, the day he began working on the epistle "To Emperor Alexander" (Arzamas I, 228). According to Oleg Proskurin, who published this letter, under the text "a picture of a torch with three tongues of flame" was drawn (ibid., 527). And in February of that year, possibly under the fresh impression of the visit to Lopukhin, he wrote to Voeikov:

> Without creating parties, we should be crowded into a little circle: Viazemskii, Batiushkov, me, you, Uvarov, Pleshcheev, and Turgenev should be under one banner—of simplicity and good taste. I forgot a very, very important person: Dashkov. Embrace him like a brother for me. Let Karamzin and Dmitriev be the ministers of enlightenment in our republic, and our pope—Filaret. ... Brother, brother! Imagine our Surinam life, imagine our tight union, our tranquility, based on spiritual calm and illumined by spiritual joys. ... (Ibid., 220)

The reference in this context to the Orthodox hierarch as the "pope" of a literary republic or perhaps of a Masonic order might seem unexpected, unless we take into consideration the special place Filaret occupied in Zhukovskii's life and that of his close associates. It was Filaret who, in answer to A. I. Turgenev's question, declared that he did not see any obstacles to Zhukovskii marrying Masha (see Zeidlits 1883, 60). But it was even more important that Filaret, rising star of the Orthodox Church, was at this time not only sympathetic to reigning mystical moods but in many ways helped define them.

As I. N. Korsunskii writes, by 1814 "Filaret had reached the acme of his fame as a preacher in Petersburg" (Korsunskii 1885, 460). On May 18, 1814, the day the manifesto on peace with France was proclaimed, he delivered his "Sermon on the Day of the Holy Spirit's Descent" in Golitsyn's house church. He declared that "God *gives* the Holy Spirit to anyone who is disposed to *accept* Him," and he also subjected the acting hierarchy—to which he belonged—to criticism of a kind that was almost unthinkable on the lips of a man of the church:

> And so, believe not us, whom, of course, as punishment for our unworthy service to the word God no longer places as your guides to faith and as nourishers of love, but puts us before you for only disgrace and condemnation, so that in this sacred place there is not so much the Word of God, living and real, which judges the heartfelt thoughts and designs of those listening, as much as the cold consideration of those listening that judges and condemns dead human words; [but] believe the chosen instruments, the envoys and heralds of the Holy Spirit. (Filaret 1814a)

Filaret excluded this whole fragment from his sermon in its following republications, up to and including the phrase "dead human words." Probably the juxtaposition of chosen instruments of the Holy Spirit to preachers who are unworthy to serve the word seemed inadmissible to him. Aleksandr Sturdza, who was his close associate, even thought that the future metropolitan was then being "shaken by the suggestions of many various spirits that were transgressing ancient Orthodoxy" (Nevodchikov 1868, 6). However, such ideas were completely in accord with the religious ideals of Alexander and Golitsyn.

As Florovskii wrote, "the second decade of the new century in Russia proceeded under the sign of the Bible Society," which had been founded on the emperor's initiative in December 1812 simultaneously with the final expulsion of the French from Russia (Florovskii 1937, 147). In the Report of the Bible Society for 1815, its president, Golitsyn, wrote that the emperor "enlivens the Society's activity *with the promptings of his own heart*. He himself is *removing the stamp of incomprehensible speech* that to this day has barred the way to Jesus's Gospel for many Russians, and he is revealing this book to the most undeveloped of the people (ot samykh mladentsev naroda) from whom not its goal but solely *the gloom of time* has hidden it" (Pypin 2000, 56). By *"the stamp of incomprehensible speech"* and *"the gloom of time,"* both Golitsyn and Alexander meant the Church Slavonic language in which the Bible was traditionally published, and which in their opinion was not understood by the majority of people in the empire.

One of the several directors of the Bible Society was S. S. Uvarov, and one of its two secretaries was A. I. Turgenev. Filaret took part in the society's work from the moment it was created, and in 1814 became one of its directors. Having become one of its vice-presidents, he headed the work of translating the Bible into Russian and for many years remained one of the main supporters of this idea. This led to numerous conflicts with the more conservatively-oriented members of the hierarchy, as well as with A. S. Shishkov and his followers (see Chistovich 1899; Pypin 2000, 20–303; on the linguistic and cultural significance of the polemics around the Bible translation, see Proskurin 1996).

Possibly, two years before work began on the Society's Russian translation of the Bible, a similar idea had occurred to Zhukovskii. Listing the main projects he planned to complete for Masha in 1814, together with the "Epistle to the Emperor," he included in one point his intention "to translate the Bible" (Zhukovskii 1907, 46). Perhaps he meant the poem "La Bible" by the French poet L. de Fontanes that he had translated that very year (Zhukovskii I, 331–333). However, in the context of the main goal of the Bible Society, his precise phrase indicates a far more ambitions idea that Zhukovskii partially realized in the 1840s and 50s when he translated the entire New Testament (Ianushkevich 1992, 287).

Among the poet's exalted outpourings of those years, the fervent confessions that he made to Aleksandr Turgenev especially stand out. "Be my genius-leader," Zhukovskii addresses him in the poem "On a day of happiness to remember you" (V den' schast'ia vspomnit' o tebe) (Zhukovskii 1895, 110; in the printed version this line sounded a bit more moderate: "Be my companion-leader"). In another letter to him he calls him "guardian angel" (ibid., 111). Such ardent feelings were inspired by various things, including Turgenev's attempts to help Zhukovskii in his love drama and the memory of Aleksandr's prematurely deceased brother Andrei, who had been the poet's elder friend and mentor. But the fact that in this small circle, Turgenev served as representative of the Bible Society, of Prince Golitsyn, and in some sense of the emperor himself, also could have played a significant role.[4]

---

4   On the very same paper as Zhukovskii, Voeikov wrote to Turgenev, pathetically exclaiming, "Is it possible that in the nineteenth century and during Alexander's reign, and while the

4

Alexander's spiritual experience of those years was first of all a search for mystical partners and the formation of a complex system of spiritual alliances. According to Princess S. S. Meshcherskaia, who was close to the emperor, she and Alexander "gave each other their word to begin reading the Bible on the same day and to read a page from the Old Testament every morning, so as to always be reading the very same chapters, whatever distances may have separated them." The emperor frequently wrote to the princess about "what impressions the reading of this or that place in Holy Writ has made on him" (Grellet de Mobillier 1874, 3–4). Possibly, the princess didn't realize that he had taken a similar vow together with Golitsyn and also with the well-known Mason R. A. Koshelev. In 1821, Koshelev reminded the emperor "about the union all three of them had entered into before the face of the living God" and how Alexander himself had placed Koshelev "at the top of this triangle" (Nikolai Mikhailovich I, 553). Still another triangle of the same type arose in 1814, when, as in the first instance, Alexander inserted himself into an already existing mystical pair.

During the emperor's conversation with Jung-Stilling, they had begun speaking about Empress Elizaveta Alekseevna's maid of honor Roksandra Strudza, with whom both men had established unusually confidential relations. Shtilling admitted to Alexander that "he had entered into an eternal union (alliance éternelle) with her to live for the Lord. 'We will also create such a union,' the emperor said, and embraced Jung" (Ley 1975, 88). On the same day Alexander spoke about this with Strudza, who left her recollections of this conversation: "'This morning I saw Jung-Stilling,' said the emperor. 'We had an explanation with him, as we could, in German and in French, however, I understood that you have entered into an indissoluble union with him in the name of love and mercy. I asked him to accept me as a third, and we shook each other's hands. Do you also agree?' 'But this union already exists, Sovereign!' 'Is it true?'—and at this he took me gently by the hand, and I could feel that tears were pouring out of my eyes" (Edling

---

benevolent Prince Golitsyn as well as you keep the holy swords sheathed and do not allow fanatics to shed their brothers' blood, tears of innocent sufferers must flow and two angels [Zhukovskii and Masha] must be sacrificed to the devil of superstition?" (Ibid).

199, 198). The Swiss researcher Francis Ley, author of the monograph *Alexander and His Holy Alliance,* called the association of the philosopher, maid of honor, and emperor "a mystical trinitarian pact" (Ley 1975, 89).

Without a doubt, this definition also fully applies to the Holy Alliance itself. The rulers who signed this pact bound themselves to be guided in their politics by the Christian commandments, "which was by no means limited to applying them to their private lives alone, but on the contrary, they had to govern the will of the tsars and to guide them in all of their actions." They declared themselves and their subjects "members of a single Christian people (nation chrétienne)," whose autocrat "is no other than ... Jesus Christ," "insofar as in him are attained the treasures of love, conduct, and wisdom" (VPR VIII, 518). Both the lexicon and argumentation of this international agreement fully coincide with those which were used when the mystical *ménage à trois* was created between Alexander, R. Strudza, and Jung-Stilling. [5]

A year earlier Jung-Stilling had already foretold the basic parameters of the Holy Alliance, having written about the symbolic significance of the allies' victory over Napoleon:

> You will search in vain in history for three monarchs who were filled with the fear of God to such an extent, all three true Christians, united among themselves by fraternal love. ... What strikes me most of all is that our liberators represent the three basic confessions into which the Christian world is divided. The emperor of France is the greatest of the Roman Catholics, Emperor Alexander is first among the Christians of the Greek confession, and King Friedrich-Wilhelm is the most outstanding of the Protestants. As if the Lord desired that the entire Christian world and its most respected leaders would conquer the constitutional idol. (Ley 1975, 90)

This type of ecumenical program was also the basis of the Bible Society. In his reports Golitsyn expressed both pride that "all Christian confessions are united together in it" (Pypin 2000, 79) and the hope that its "activity opens up the beautiful dawn of a betrothal day for Christians and [the possibility]

---

5   It is extremely tempting to imagine that—in keeping with Golitsyn's language—the three mystical unions described above were connected among themselves by the presence of the Russian Emperor in each, like three triangles coming together at the top. The resulting geometrical figure—a pyramid—was one of the main Masonic symbols.

Figure 25 Medallion commemorating the Triple Alliance by A. N. Olenin.

of a time when there will be one pastor and one united congregation, that is, when there will be one divine Christian religion for all confessions of a diverse Christian configuration" (Strelletskii 1901, 163).[6]

---

6 In this connection the hypotheses that Alexander and Golitsyn planned "the evangelization" of Russia (see, for example, Etkind 1996) or that Alexander intended to convert his empire to Catholicism before his death (Dmitrieva 1996, 94–95), which is based on a Jesuit legend long proved wrong by S. P. Mel'gunov (1923, 105–109), do not seem convincing. The "conversions" about which Etkind and Dmitrieva write would have been very modest compared to the messianic-eschatological synthesis which Alexander was contemplating.

It is known that Alexander did not like to recall the Fatherland War (the Russian name for Napoleon's invasion), did not visit its memorable places, and did not commemorate its great events, although as his biographer Nikolai Mikhailovich notes, "he did travel to Wagram and to Waterloo" (Nikolai Mikhailovich I, 212; cf. Shil'der IV, 50; Wortman 1994, 231). Of course, biographical considerations played a part here: the emperor's role in the events of 1812 was mostly passive, while the European campaign was in many ways his personal triumph. Nevertheless, ideological considerations determined these preferences to a great extent. A war for liberating the fatherland from an invasion corresponded to the emperor's ideas about his predestination and the destiny of his country far less than a war for saving humanity and establishing the universal Kingdom of Christ. When the Russian monarch wrote to his Austrian colleague that the agreement that they were about to sign "crowns the salvific mission of our union" (VPR VIII, 516), the word "salvific" was to be taken literally. The union under the leadership of Alexander was to assume the function of Christ.

Zhukovskii's epistle was written more than nine months before the Holy Alliance was concluded. Still ahead were the fruitless negotiations at the Congress of Vienna, Napoleon's escape from Elba, the Hundred Days, Waterloo, the imprisonment of the emperor on the island of St. Helena, the signing of the peace and the allied courts' sojourn in Paris. Nevertheless, the general conceptual and metaphorical schemes realized in this act and in Alexander's later politics are fully present here. First and foremost the inner proportions of the text attract one's attention. Of the 486 lines of the epistle less than ten percent, or 40 odd lines, are devoted to 1812 and only one to the Battle of Borodino. At the same time, the burning of Moscow is interpreted providentially—it is a "fire of freedom" in which the chains that Napoleon imposed on Europe are consumed:

> Пылает!., цепи в прах! Воскресните народы!
> Ваш стыд и плен Москва, обрушась, погребла,
> И в пепле мщения свобода ожила!

(It blazes!., chains into dust! Revive (lit., resurrect), peoples! /Moscow, collapsing, you have buried your shame and imprisonment / And from the ashes freedom awakened revenge!)

The political providentialism of Zhukovskii's interpretation corresponded to Alexander's own personal providential view of the Moscow fire as told to Pastor Eilert: "The fire of Moscow illuminated my soul and filled my heart with such warm faith as I have not felt since then. Then I knew God" (Shil'der III, 117).

In the epistle the culminating point in the description of the military campaign is the Russian army's crossing of the Niemen River; Zhukovskii dedicates about thirty lines to Alexander's decision to continue the war in Europe. It is precisely at this moment that the Russian emperor acquires the right to the title "Blessed" and assumes a divine nature:

> И руку Ты простер, и двинулися рати!
> Как к возвестителю небесной благодати,
> Во сретенье Тебе народы потекли,
> И вайями Твой путь смиренный облекли.
> (Zhukovskii I, 371)

(And you stretched out your arm, and the armies set off! / As to the one who announces heavenly grace, / The peoples flowed to You in greeting / And strew Your humble path with palms.)

These "palms" (vaia) are the palm branches with which people greeted Christ upon his entry into Jerusalem. The Russian emperor entering Europe is thus directly likened to the Savior.

Just as once during the Russo-Turkish War of 1768–1774 King Leonid arrived from the north to the Spartans, making Greeks into Greeks once again, now the Russian Hermann returns the defeated Teutons to life:

> Как всколебалися тевтонов племена!
> К ним Герман с норда нес свободы знамена —
> И всё помчалось в строй под знамена свободы;
> В одну слиялись грудь воскресшие народы,
> И всех царей рука, наш царь, в руке твоей.
> (Ibid., 372)

(How the Teutonic tribes began to move! / Hermann brought the banners of freedom to them from the north / And everything rushed into formation under the banners of freedom; / The resurrected peoples merged into one breast / And the might of all tsars is in your hand, our tsar.)

This all-European—and, given the political map of the time, world-wide—character of Russia's predestination and its emperor becomes the leitmotif of the epistle. Depicting the emperor's touching farewell to the dying "leader-starets" Kutuzov, Zhukovskii supplements this picture with a just as touching description of the death of J. V. M. Morreau, the French general who fell fighting in the allied army. The significant space dedicated to Morreau in the text of the epistle symbolizes the expiation of the sins of France, which, forgiven by the magnanimous victor, offers its repentance on the site of Louis XVI's execution:

> И чуждый вождь — увы! — судьба его щадила,
> Чтоб первой жертвой он на битве правды пал —
> Наш царь, узнав тебя, на смерть он не роптал;
> Ты руку падшему, как брат, простер средь боя;
> И сердцу верному венчанного героя,
> Смягчившего слезой его с концом борьбу,
> Он смело завещал отечества судьбу. … (Ibid.)

(And the foreign leader, alas, was preserved by fate / Only so he would fall as first victim in the struggle for truth—/ Our Tsar, recognizing You, did not grumble at death; / Amid the battle you stretched out your hand to the fallen man like a brother; / And to the faithful heart of the crowned hero / Who eased his last minutes with a tear / He [Morreau] boldly bequeathed the fate of his fatherland.)

The high honors that the allied monarchs rendered to Morreau aroused Shishkov's profound dissatisfaction, as he wrote in his memoirs:

> Of course, Morreau was a skilled and brave warrior. With Napoleon he shared his people's admiration and fame, and was probably also seeking supreme power; and, perhaps, if he had attained it, being a person of better morals, he would not have been such a bloodthirsty monster trying to get power; however, together with him he led the revolutionary troops, and if he had now turned against him, that was not because he wanted to see his fatherland ruled as before by the heirs of legitimate sovereigns (since he had

no such desire earlier), but only because he had been insulted and held a personal grudge. Thus it seems to me it was not proper for the two autocratic heads of state to immediately gallop up to him, as to some creature who was better than anyone else or heaven-sent. Our leaders who were immeasurably more glorious than he—Rumiantsev, Suvorov, Kutuzov—were never shown this kind of honor. If not yours, then the people's pride should not have permitted this. (Shishkov 1870, 210)

Neither Shishkov nor Zhukovskii could have known, of course, that for Alexander himself both Morreau's celebratory meeting and farewell were strictly formal gestures. As far as Jung-Stilling's recommended "complete abnegation" is concerned, the emperor outdid anything either the skeptical memoirist or the ecstatic poet could have imagined. "They wrongly thought that if Morreau was with us, everything was decided," Alexander wrote to Golitsyn from Teplitz after the general's death. "Only God and not Morreau or anyone else can bring this matter to a good end. ... I believe in Him more strongly than all the Morreaus on earth" (Nikolai Mikhailovich, 144).

More than twenty lines in the epistle are dedicated to the "battle of the peoples"—the Battle of Leipzig. In the original plan of the epistle Zhukovskii wrote, "Here the argument for freedom should be decided, [with] all of the peoples on earth present. The forefathers of all peoples watch—Hermes [Zhukovskii apparently meant Germann], Peter, Gustav" (Ianushkevich 1985, 105). In the final text, however, the forefathers who inspire their nations are replaced by "the shades of all ages ... above the luminous head of the tsars' leader." Alexander, "the young Agamemnon of the union of avengers," represents all of humanity before God:

> Я зрю Тебя, племен несметных повелитель.
> Сей окруженного всемирной тишиной,
> Над полвселснною парящего душой,
> Где все Твое, где Ты над всех судьбою властен,
> Где Ты один всех благ, один всех бед причастен.
> (Zhukovskii I, 376)

(I see You, commander of numberless tribes, / The one who is surrounded by universal calm, / Soaring in spirit above the universe, / Where everything is Yours, where You have power over everyone's fate, / Where You alone are privy to all good things and alone to all misfortunes.)

As is clear from the published fragments of the plan, Zhukovskii was going to include the "Council of Tsars," the Congress of Vienna, in the epistle (see Iezuitova 1989, 153–154).[7] However, by the time he completed work on the epistle, the congress had still not finished and its results remained unclear. Therefore the chronological and thematic culmination for the poet became the emperor's arrival in Petersburg in 1814, before his departure for Vienna. The epistle is crowned by a huge description—taking up more than a quarter of the text—of the mystical betrothal of tsar and people before the face of the Almighty. The ruler of the world, Alexander, swears to make "his throne" "an altar of love" for his people. In its turn, the people "raises its hand" to "the sacred hand" of the monarch:

> Как пред ужасною святыней алтаря,
> Обет наш перед ней: все в жертву за Царя!
> (Ibid., 378)

(Before the terrifying sacred altar, / [We make] our promise: Everything in sacrifice for the Tsar!)

Only divine rule can be a holy "mirror" of Alexander's rule which is wholly directed toward the other world and eternal bliss. "Everything here be for good, /As all is for the good there," the Russian tsar prays in the epistle "To Emperor Alexander" (ibid.). The poem written at the same time, "Prayer of the Russian People," the prototype for the future state hymn, is crowned with the lines:

> Жизнь наднебесная,
> Сердцу известная,
> Сердцу сияй!

---

7   It is difficult to agree with the researcher when she proposes that the original plan was changed because Zhukovskii was dissatisfied with "advancing the person of the tsar to the first place … [since] he had not played the first role by far in destroying Napoleon" (Ibid). It would hardly be possible to advance the tsar to first place more strongly than in the final text.

(Heavenly life, / Known to the heart, / Shine to the heart!)⁸

The marriage of the ideal tsar with the ideal people can be realized in the same place where the marriage of Zhukovskii and Masha Protasova occurred—in heaven.

∞ 5 ∞

Zhukovskii's success was universal and unconditional only for a short time. On September 23, 1815, came the premiere of A. A. Shakhovskoi's "Lipetsk Spa" (Lipetskie vody), in which the author of the epistle "To Emperor Alexander" became the butt of cruel mockery.⁹ And in the next year Zhukovskii was subject to attack from another social flank—by P. A. Katenin and A. S. Griboedov. This historical and literary collision was first comprehensively analyzed in Iu. N. Tynianov's classic work, "The Archaists and Pushkin." As Tynianov wrote, "in 1815/1816 a ferocious war was waged against Zhukovskii, and the first shot was fired by the elder archaist Shakhovskoi, ... but it was the young archaists Katenin and Griboedov who clarify the true meaning of the battle, its deep basis" (Tynianov 1968, 36). Together with these open "anti-Zhukovskian" attacks, Tynianov examines the hidden criticism of the poet in the correspondence of the members of Arzamas themselves. "It seems at times," he notes, "that he dissatisfied 'his own' even more than their enemies" (ibid., 38). In A. S. Nemzer's observation, by the end of the 1810s, Zhukovskii "was alone in literature and he understood this" (Nemzer 1987, 191).

In Tynianov's interpretation, the agreement between literary folk who were far apart in their political views is connected with the autonomous nature of literary and linguistic development in relation to ideological and social factors. The mechanisms of literary similarities and ideological differences lie on different planes and their zones of action do not impede each another. Still, at least in the given case there is no need to resort to the theory of "the immanence of the literary series." Alexander's popularity, that in the second half of

---

8   On the meaning of these lines, see Kisileva 1998.
9   In his work A. S. Nemzer shows that Zhukovskii first stung his opponent in his epistles to P. A. Viazemskii and V. L. Pushkin (see Nemzer 1987, 168–176). Nonetheless, the experienced polemicist Shakhovskoi was by no means only moved by the personal offense. He did not recognize the right of an author of sentimental ballads to hold the position of state poet.

1814 had reached beyond the clouds, plummeted. Dissatisfaction came not only from Shishkov's circle that he had summoned in Russia's moment of need and then excluded from the country's ideological leadership, but also from among young freethinkers who brought from Germany not visions of a future Christian kingdom but fashionable ideas about national revival. For both groups, cosmopolitan mysticism and mawkish visionary fancies—on the part of both Alexander and the most famous singer of his reign—looked more and more like an affront to Russia's national interests and dignity.

CHAPTER 9

"Star of the East":
The Holy Alliance and European Mysticism

Translation by
Daniel Schlaffy*

∽ 1 ∽

The Petersburg audience that applauded and booed the premiere of "Lipetsk Spa" on September 23, 1815, did not yet know that nine days earlier a document had been signed in Paris that for almost a decade was destined to define the fate of Russia, and in many ways, that of all Europe. The document creating the Holy Alliance, described by the French publicist Abbé Dominique de Pradt as "the apocalypse of diplomacy" (Edling 1999, 223), is one of the most enigmatic treaties in the history of international relations. No wonder that time and again researchers have scrutinized both the preparations for and the conclusion of the treaty (See Mühlenbeck 1887; Nadler I-V; Presniakov 1923; Shebunin 1925; Bühler 1929; Dorland 1939; Geiger 1954; Ley 1975; Martin 1997; for a concise selection of documents, see Bertier de Sauvigny 1972).[1]

We can assume that the basic factual picture of the events has been clear for a long time. The memoirs of participants and witnesses (see Empaytaz 1828,

---

* First published in *Kritika: Explorations in Russian and Euroasian History* 4 (2) (2013): 279–312.
1 Also quite valuable is A. N. Shebunin's unpublished monograph, *Vokrug Sviashchennogo soiuza* (OR RNB, f. 849, № 110–11), based on a wide range of archival documents (cf. Sirotkin 1975, 118).

36–38; SbRIO III, 201; Edling 1999, 221–224; Metternich 1880, 209–212) paint a sufficiently complete and consistent picture. The finishing touch was added in 1928, when Werner Näf published and analyzed the text of the initial draft of the treaty, composed by Alexander I with remarks by the Austrian Emperor Franz (Näf 1928, 34–39; cf. Ley 1975, 149–155; for a Russian translation, see VPR VIII, 504–5, 518). The Russian emperor personally wrote the first draft of the treaty, which was edited by State Secretary Ioannes Kapodistrias and his assistant, A. S. Sturdza (see Sturdza 1864, 69; SbRIO III, 201; Liamina 1999). It was reviewed in Baroness Juliette von Krüdener's mystical circle, which Alexander frequented in the summer and fall of 1815; and then transmitted to his allies, the Austrian emperor and the Prussian king. Both sovereigns found the treaty's apocalyptic-messianic rhetoric quite disconcerting, and they were totally unreceptive to Alexander's vision of a foreordained union of their peoples and armies in a single Christian power. Prince Klemens von Metternich, the real director of Austrian foreign policy, was even more skeptical toward the project. In light of Russia's preeminent military and diplomatic authority after the victory over Napoleon, however, the monarchs of Austria and Prussia decided not to deny their august ally the fulfillment of his cherished aspirations. After Alexander agreed to remove the more radical formulas from the text, the treaty was signed on September 14 (26), the feast of the Exaltation of the Cross and the day before the anniversary of the coronation of the Russian emperor. Both of Alexander's allies presumed that they had signed some kind of confidential declaration of intentions. Nevertheless, three months later the Treaty of the Holy Alliance was promulgated by Alexander in St. Petersburg, together with the corresponding manifesto.

Even if the course and sequence of the key events in the history of the treaty are sufficiently well-known and do not require special discussion, issues concerning the meaning and purpose of this peculiar diplomatic relic and its political, philosophical, and ideological sources are much less clear. What goals was the Russian emperor pursuing? He literally forced his allies to sign an act quite contrary to all of their preconceptions about the structure of relations between states and then, breaking all existing promises, publicized it. This question disturbed diplomats of the 1810s and continues to trouble historians until the present day.

Almost all those who have tried to reconstruct the history of these dramatic months touch upon the relations between Alexander and Baroness Krüdener in some way. They met on June 4 (16), 1815, in the German city of Heilbrunn. Afterwards the baroness followed the sovereign by imperial invitation to Paris, where the almost daily meetings between the emperor and the prophetess continued right up to the signing of the treaty and Alexander's departure for the homeland. As a rule, this dramatic and well-documented episode is used either to support or to refute the theory that the baroness had a profound influence on the plan for the Holy Alliance. Many at the time believed this theory, which undoubtedly had its origins in Krüdener's own assertions. The Leipzig pastor Wilhelm Traugott Krug, who visited Krüdener in 1818, wrote that he asked her "about the Holy Alliance, for which you, Frau von Krüdener, have been identified as the real inspiration. She only half agreed with this and said 'the Holy Alliance was the direct work of the Lord. He chose me as His instrument. Thanks to Him I accomplished this great work'" (Krug 1818, 6–7). On the contrary, Sophie de Tisenhaus, Comtesse de Choiseul-Gouffier, who knew Alexander well, wrote: "I do not know on what basis the authors of

Figure 26 Portrait of Baroness von Krüdener. Gravure by J. Pfenninger.

two histories of the Emperor Alexander ascribed the idea of the Holy Alliance and universal peace to the excited imagination of Frau Krüdener. This noble project could have sprung only from the heart of Emperor Alexander" (Choiseul-Gouffier 1999, 302). Historians also hold quite opposite views. We can say that among the authors we have noted, Eugène Mühlenbeck and Francis Ley consider Krüdener's role very significant while V. K. Nadler and Arthur Dorland categorically reject it.

There probably is no answer to the question as posed in this form. It is almost impossible to draw a clear distinction in the full spectrum of Alexander's mystical notions between impulses from meetings with the baroness and impressions he derived from other sources. However, some aspects of the celebrated encounters between the emperor and the prophetess, which have not yet been elucidated completely, can offer us important insight into a whole complex of ideologies reflected in the text of the Holy Alliance treaty and in many of the emperor's political decisions.

∽ **2** ∽

One of the first accounts of the June 4, 1815, meeting came from Empress Elizaveta Alekseevna's maid of honor, Roksandra Sturdza, who at that period was close to both participants. For some time she had been in regular correspondence with Baroness Krüdener and as described in the preceding chapter was bonded to the sovereign in a special mystical union. It was Sturdza who showed Alexander Krüdener's letter, which could have been interpreted as an obscure prediction of Napoleon's flight from the island of St. Helena (Elding 1999, 217). This letter impelled the emperor to seek the baroness's acquaintance, even more eagerly after the prophecy was fulfilled.

As Sturdza wrote in her memoirs, on that day Alexander

> was weighed down by boredom, fatigue, and grief. His soul was given over to self-introspection. "Finally I breathed more freely," he said ... "and my first act was to open the book I always have with me. But my perception was clouded, and I could not comprehend the meaning of what I had read. My thoughts were disconnected and my heart constricted. I put the book aside and thought how comforted I would be in such a moment to converse with a sympathetic being. I remembered you, what you told me about Madame Krüdener, and the wish I expressed to make her acquaintance. Where could she be now, I asked myself, and where could I meet with her? Just as I was

> thinking about this, I heard a knock at my door. It was Prince [P. M.] Volkonskii. His face expressed impatience. He told me that he had no intention of disturbing me at this hour, but that he could not get rid of a woman who insisted on seeing me. Then he named Madame Krüdener. Can you imagine my surprise? I wondered if I were delirious. Such an unexpected answer to my musings could not be accidental. I caught sight of her, and she, literally looking into my soul, turned to me with powerful words of consolation, calming my troubled thoughts, which had tortured me for so long. Her appearance was a blessing to me, and I promised myself I would continue a relationship so dear to me." (Ibid., 221)

Certainly, for a real mystic like Emperor Alexander there are no accidental coincidences. Besides, Frau Krüdener's appearance with her daughter in his study at that hour was not completely accidental. She knew from Roksandra Sturdza of Alexander's growing interest in her, persistently tried to run into him in those weeks, and arrived in Heilbronn hoping to find him there (Ley 1994, 281–299; on Krüdener, see Knapton 1939; Pypin 2000, 304–397). The episode just described, more than almost any other, confirms the extraordinary powers of persuasion that all memoirists noted in Krüdener. Convincing the adjutant general to report to the emperor in the middle of the night that two unknown women wanted to see him was a rhetorical triumph, in many respects much more striking than those that her many readers and followers have described.

According to the mystical practices of the time, just as Providence guided its chosen ones in life, it did more than send them the necessary companions and spiritual teachers at the proper moment. More often and more infallibly it opened sacred books before them to the proper pages, as if Providence were pointing to the necessary prophecies. According to Prince Golitsyn, sometime in September 1812, in the most critical period of the war, a Bible he gave to the emperor accidentally fell open to Psalm 90 [Psalm 91 in Protestant translations]:

> A thousand shall fall at thy side and ten thousand at thy right hand, but it shall not come nigh thee. Only with thine eyes shalt thou behold and see the reward of the wicked. Because thou hast made the LORD, which is my refuge, even the most High, thy habitation. There shall no evil befall thee, neither shall any plague come nigh thy dwelling. For he shall give his angels charge over thee, to keep thee in all thy ways. They shall bear thee up in their

> hands, lest thou dash thy foot against a stone. Thou shalt tread upon the lion and adder: the young lion and the dragon shalt thou trample under feet. [Ps. 91: 7–13 King James Version]

Alexander read this, shaken to the core by how closely the words of the psalm corresponded to his thoughts and his situation. A few days later, the emperor attended a solemn prayer service and unexpectedly heard the priest read that very psalm. After this, his confusion gave way to a firm belief in the providential nature of what had occurred (Grellet de Mobilier 1874, 22–24).

It is impossible to say how closely the above account corresponds to the actual course of events. More importantly, it echoes a specific type of mystical reflection on the ways of Providence and the means by which it reveals itself to mortal eyes. Baroness Krüdener's companion and follower Pastor Empaytaz recorded in his memoirs how Alexander applied verses he read from Psalms 35 and 37 to current events (Empaytaz 1828, 22–24). Alexander's letters to Golitsyn are filled with similar interpretations and applications (see Nikolai Mikhailovich I: 548–559 and passim). In J. H. Jung-Stilling's memoirs, this technique for discerning divine plans is mentioned so frequently that the author felt compelled to raise a special caution, lest readers be led into temptation: "Opening up the Bible [at random] to gain knowledge of the Divine will or of the future is an abuse of Sacred Scripture. This is a kind of divination forbidden to a Christian. If it is done to comfort oneself with the word of God, then it should be done with complete composure and submission of self to the will of God" (Jung-Stilling II, 238).[2] The meaning of this not completely transparent passage is that such knowledge is totally accessible to the author, who is endowed with direct mystic intuition and who is able "to correlate events of the present time with biblical prophecies" (Jung-Stilling II, 232), but is not granted to ordinary man.

It is precisely in the account of the emperor's encounter with Baroness Krüdener that mention of a book which he opened but was unable to understand precedes her appearance in his house. The phrase that Roksandra Sturdza attributed to the emperor, "the book which I always have with me," suggests the Bible, which he read daily according to a prearranged schedule. Eugène

---

2   The practice of opening the Bible to a "random page" to seek the intentions of Providence was taught in particular by the famous mystic Abbé Fournier to the founder of Martinism, Robert Martinez de Pascually (see Viatte I, 45).

Mühlenbeck claims that on that day the emperor read Psalm 20 and quotes a lengthy extract from it (Mühlenbeck 1887, 223). N. A. Troitskii writes in a recently published book, however, that the baroness entered when Alexander read the apocalyptic prophecy about "a woman clothed in the sun" (Rev 12: 1; Troitskii 1994, 284). But the book Alexander was concerned with that night was not the Bible.

I. N. Bartenev quotes Golitsyn, the closest confidant of the emperor, in his memoirs:

> Undoubtedly, Krüdener, who was living in the faith, strengthened the Sovereign's awakening faith by her impartial and mature advice. She resolutely directed Alexander's will towards ever greater self-surrender and prayer and probably at the same time revealed to him the secret of that prayer of the spirit which God has decreed that all who dwell here below might attain, but unfortunately is destined only for a few of the elect.
>
> The following episode demonstrates that Krüdener had spiritual conversations with Alexander. At the time R. A. Koshelev gave the Sovereign a book popular then, *The Cloud over the Sanctuary, or That Which Prideful Philosophy Cannot Imagine*, which the late Aleksandr Fedorovich Labzin had translated from German. Although Alexander read the book, he was completely unable to understand its content. According to Alexander's precise testimony, when Krüdener was summoned, she was able to interpret and explain the hitherto difficult and incomprehensible passages of the work to him. (Bartnev 1886, 93–94)

It is impossible to determine from Golitsyn's statement whether he is referring specifically to the encounter between the emperor and the Baroness that interests us or to one of their later conversations. However, an entry in Krüdener's daughter Juliette's diary resolves the issue. The first person to publish the diary was the Swiss historian Francis Ley, a distant descendant of the Krüdener family and keeper of the family archive. Juliette Krüdener's testimony basically confirms evidence from other sources, except for a few details. She writes, for example, that when the baroness gave Prince P. M. Volkonskii a letter for the emperor, Alexander ordered his overnight guests summoned as soon as he received it. She recalled:

> We found Alexander alone. He was somewhat embarrassed when he saw us. I was completely composed. I want to relate the whole discussion. We were struck by what dear Alexander told us, that when he arrived at Heilbronn, he

remembered his conversation with Mademoiselle Sturdza and thought that Madame Krüdener should be somewhere nearby. He also wanted to write to the margravine. When he received maman's letter, which apparently had a great impact on him, he had just finished reading a passage from Eckartshausen which spoke of *the economy of grace for that Church of which he hitherto had had no idea* (l'économie de la grâce pour cette Église dont il n'a encore aucune idée). He accepted everything that maman disclosed to him "with true humility," convinced that the Lord helps him whom He calls, but was not convinced that he in particular had been chosen *to accomplish this great work* (pas convaincu de son élection particulière pour opérer cette grande oeuvre). (Ley 1994, 289–290; Krüdener 1998, 129)[3]

Thus it is clear not only which book the emperor was reading before the baroness appeared, but also what constituted the source of his bewilderment and anxiety. That makes it all the more important to understand this forgotten yet historically extremely important mystical work.

∞ 3 ∞

The Cloud over the Sanctuary (*Die Wolke über dem Heiligtum*) was one of Karl von Eckartshausen's last works (see Faivre 1969; cf. Viatte II, 41–51). It appeared in 1802, one year before his death, and was translated into Russian only two years later by Labzin in 1804. *The Cloud* was something of a culmination of Eckartshausen's philosophical legacy. It is almost totally devoted to the problem of the interior church, which was the mystic's constant preoccupation and central to European mysticism as a whole at the end of the eighteenth and beginning of the nineteenth centuries. As he began to read, Alexander must have realized that true faith was hidden by external senses from ordinary mortals. To know God, man had "to uncover inner feeling in himself" (Eckartshausen 1804, 21), something fully accessible only to members of the "Lightbearing Divine society, which is diffused throughout the whole world, but which is guided by a single truth and linked by a single spirit" (ibid., 25). This society "has existed since the first day of the world's existence" and appears as an "inner assembly" and "great Temple for the rebirth of mankind," with "Christ Himself" as its head (ibid., 25–26). If God has ruled the society directly

---

3   There is no indication of the source of the italics in the quotations, which were published in Ley's monographs from material from the personal archive. It is possible the historian was responsible for them.

throughout its entire history, then "its first Deputy" has been "the best man of that time. ... He does not know all his members, but if, by Divine intention, it becomes necessary for him to recognize them, at that very minute he will find them in the world, ready to assist in achieving the preordained goal" (ibid., 47). The "lightbearing" society is divided into three levels. At the first level, "inspiration," allegiance is manifested in "moral goodness," and at the second, "enlightenment," with the achievement of "enlightened understanding," that is, immersion in the world of mystical composition. At the third level, "vision," "faith progresses to contemplation"; that is, man attains the facility of sensible communion with higher powers (ibid., 41; cf. Faivre 1969, 336).

An essential feature of the lightbearing society is that its members have no "distinguishing external characteristics. ... If those who really are fellow members need to assemble, they unerringly will find and recognize each other, and there will be no deception. No member will be able to choose another, for this election will be revealed to the spirit of all" (ibid., 48). This revelation distinguishes the membership of the lightbearing society from, for example, Masonic lodges, where it is precisely the ritual of initiation and reception of new brethren that plays an organizational role. According to Eckartshausen, election, separating the devotees from other mortals, was achieved at inception and it needed only to be discerned. "God and nature," he wrote, "hold no mysteries for their progeny. The mystery lies only in our infirmity, our inability to bear the light. ... Our infirmity is the cloud which covers the sanctuary. ... Sons of the truth! There is but one order, one brotherhood, one likeminded union of the followers of the light, through which the light can be attained" (ibid., 51, 59). Hence people endowed with the gift of penetrating the cloud covering the sanctuary truly are destined for a providential role. In the author's words, "all the original knowledge of the human race is preserved in this society. ... It is the society whose fellow members constitute the Theocratic (ruled by God) government, which some day will be the center of the whole world's governments" (ibid., 50). Here the author presents an eschatological perspective, in which the members of the lightbearing society dispersed across the globe unite to establish a mystical theocracy to direct the world order.

The notion that a special fellowship of dedicated souls existed in the world was not invented by Eckartshausen but was common to all mystical savants of the time. It was developed, in particular, in the book by I. V. Lopukhin *Some*

Features of the Inner Church, probably the only eighteenth-century book by a Russian author that acquired international prominence. Eckartshausen heartily endorsed this work, a few days before his death writing a letter to the author where he called *Some Features* "a precious book, replete with true wisdom" (Lopukhin 1990, 39; cf. Faivre 1969, 178–179, 222–225 and passim). At the end of the first decade of the nineteenth century, the public had access to this testimonial, both in the widely circulated manuscript text of Lopukhin's *Notes* and in the foreword to the 1810 French edition of the book (see Lopukhin 1810).

Alexander was quite familiar with these ideas. His note "On Mystical Literature," meant for Grand Princess Ekaterina Pavlovna, probably written in the first half of 1812, presents a fairly detailed account of the basic doctrine of the interior church. The emperor wrote that "the origin of the so-called mystical societies is hidden in the distant past" and dates from the mysteries of ancient religions. One of their essential elements was that not everyone was able "to see the light" of truth, to experience divine love, and to recognize the "outpouring or revelation of the deity" in his works in nature. In Alexander's words:

> The Christian religion established the bond between ancient and contemporary societies. At its inception it was nothing but a secret society. No one was admitted to the church of Jerusalem without trial and purification. The policy of rulers converted this secret knowledge into a public religion. But while policy revealed the rites, it was unable to divulge the secrets. Hence, today as always, there is an external Church and an interior Church. (Nikolai Mikhailovich 1910, 286–287)

Unlike ordinary theological works intended for the external church, books addressed to the inner church constitute a body of "Secret or Mystical Theology," which in turn is divided into three levels. The first consists of works "whose principal subject is the theory of this doctrine or of its first abstract principles." Since these authors were "enlightened people, but not Angels … among their truths one encounters a multitude of different systems, more or less bold and sometimes completely strange." Authors of the second level of works treat "not so much … theory as practical moral learning." According to the emperor's classification, Eckartshausen belonged in this group. Finally, the third, "most trustworthy and most reliable category" was made up "of those … who are concerned solely with moral education, pointing out the practical path validated by experience, but not going into any kind of theories" (ibid., 286–287).

It does not follow from the extensive list of mystical authors the emperor inserted in the memorandum that he personally was acquainted with their works. Thus, A. E. Presniakov convincingly proposes that Speranskii's lessons were reflected here, while George Florovskii points to R. A. Koshelev (see Presniakov 1923, 76; Florovskii 1937, 130). Still, it is quite plausible that in 1815 Alexander could have been sufficiently familiar with Eckartshausen's work, which appeared in Russian as early as 1804 and which dealt with themes that so concerned him. Besides, mystical reading of this type envisioned returning again and again to the same texts, seeking new and even more hidden profundities. Alexander's words set down by Roksandra Sturdza about "the book I always have with me" probably were not a chance remark by the memoirist; instead, they indicate that when Baroness Krüdener arrived, Alexander was rereading a work with which he already was familiar and turned to the prophetess asking her to interpret a passage that long had been a source of anxiety.

The passage that disturbed the emperor spoke "of the end times and of grace preserved in that Church of which he hitherto has no concept" (Ley 1994, 289–290). Like many other mystical works, *The Cloud over the Sanctuary* is full of repetitions, so it is impossible to be absolutely certain to which passage Juliette Krüdener referred. Even so, it can be suggested with a certain measure of caution that she had the following episode in mind:

> Since the Disciples of the Lord could not understand the great mystery of the new and ultimate Covenant, Christ deferred it to the future last days, now drawing nigh, saying "on that day (on which I will announce my mystery to you), you shall know that I am in the Father, and you in me, and I in all of you" (Jn 17: 22–23). This Covenant is called the Covenant (union) of peace. Then the Divine law shall be imparted to the innermost recess of our heart, and all of us shall recognize the Lord and shall become His people and He our God. (Eckartshausen 1804, 102)

It is easy to see that the issue is how the apostles will acquire an understanding of divine Providence and divine grace (l'économie de la grâce). Eckartshausen refers to the chapter from the Gospel according to John, which gives Jesus's prayer for his chosen disciples. ("I pray not for the world, but for them which thou hast given me," John 17: 9). This is preceded by a description of the bewilderment of the apostles, unable to understand the prophecy about the time when the spirit of truth will descend (John 16: 17–18).

Just as the "disciples of the Lord" initially did not understand the essence of what was preached to them, the emperor, according to the unanimous testimony of Roksandra Sturdza, Aleksandr Golitsyn, and Juliette Krüdener, was unable to understand the sense of Eckartshausen's prophecies immediately. In the German mystic's opinion, eschatological events were imminent: "Everything already has been prepared for God's essential assembly and for union with Him, which even here is possible" (Eckartshausen 1804, 102). The last days, in the opinion of Eckartshausen and other celebrated mystics of that epoch, were supposed to begin as early as the first decades of the nineteenth century (see Faivre 1969, 514–20; for Jung-Stilling's calculations, see Jung-Stilling 1815, xiii–xv).

We recall that the lightbearing society was divided into three levels, depending on the degree to which its members had achieved higher perfection. In exactly the same way mystical science was supposed to enlighten the world in three stages, "*first*, to regenerate man individually, or precursors from the Elect; *then*, regenerate many men; and *finally*, all mankind" (Eckartshausen 1804, 102). Apparently, the historic moment which Europe was experiencing corresponded to the second stage in this eschatological plan; it fell to the scattered members of the interior church to recognize each other and begin the task of regenerating "many men." Here if the "precursors of the Elect" were monarchs, their duty was to accomplish the genuine enlightenment of their own peoples.

Thus the emperor's bewilderment at Eckartshausen's pages becomes more understandable. It seemed that too much of his extraordinary and awful fate pointed unambiguously to his providential election, but at the same time an explicit awareness of such a destiny and the inner conviction that he belonged to the society of lightbearers constantly eluded him. As Juliette Krüdener wrote, Alexander was not convinced that "*precisely he was chosen to accomplish this great task*," or, to translate the French literally, "in his special election" (Ley 1994, 290; Krüdener 1998, 129).

A translation problem emerging in the above citation from *The Cloud over the Sanctuary* is extremely revealing. Speaking of the mystery of the new and ultimate Covenant which the apostles could not understand, Eckartshausen, in Labzin's rendering, indicates that "this Covenant is called the Covenant (union) of peace."[4] The translator needed the parentheses to convey the full sense of the

---

4   Labzin uses the words "zavet" and "soiuz," translated here as "covenant" and "union." (Translator's note).

German "Bund," almost inevitably lost in choosing any Russian term. The general consensus among German mystics was that the first union ("alter Bund") concluded by God with Abraham and the second ("neuer Bund") with the disciples of Jesus now was replaced by the "holy union" ("heiliger Bund") (Mühlenbeck 1887, 251). The same connection between the concepts of "covenant" and "union" exists in French, which was the primary medium by which the emperor became acquainted with the sacred books. There the corresponding biblical term is rendered as "alliance." The semantic structure both of the French "alliance" and the German "Bund" convey fully the biblical concept of covenant, which, strictly speaking, represents the union between God and his people. In a letter written in 1815, Baroness Krüdener cited the book of Ezekiel (37: 26), saying that God concludes a covenant with Israel, "a Covenant [Alliance] of peace, and it shall be an everlasting covenant with them" (Ley 1994, 282). Thus, the new covenant instituted by Jesus signified a change in the terms of this union:

> If the first covenant had been faultless, there should have been no need to seek a place for another one. But the prophet reproached them, saying, "Behold, the days are coming, says the Lord, when I shall make a new covenant with the house of Israel and with the house of Judah, not that covenant I made with their fathers at that time when I took them by the hand in order to lead them out of the land of Egypt." ... In saying "new" he showed the obsolescence of the former one, but what is decaying and growing old is near its end [Heb. 8: 7–9, 13].

The advent of apocalyptic times required yet another renewal of the covenant, or, in other words, conclusion of a new union of peace.

∞ 4 ∞

Two aspects of the draft treaty proposed by Alexander provoked dissatisfaction among the sovereign's allies. First, they were able to remove from the text extreme expressions of the coming unity whereby subjects of the three powers were to "see each other as fellow-countrymen," and their armies as "part of one army." In place of the reference to "a single people designated a Christian nation," the Austrian emperor and the Prussian king preferred the somewhat less binding expression, "a single Christian people," and instead of "three sectors of this one people," characterized their powers as "three branches of a single family" (VPR VIII, 504–505). A second feature of the Russian emperor's draft, perhaps even less acceptable to the allies, was its zeal for totally altering the entire system of international relations. A directive in the draft stated that "the form of mutual relations previously established by the powers must change completely and it is absolutely necessary to strive to replace it with an order based on the supreme truths inspired by the eternal law of the Divine Savior" (ibid., 504). In the final text, after radical reworking, this passage was shortened considerably and recast as a much more neutral aspiration that "the form of mutual relations as presented be subject to the supreme truths inspired by the eternal law of the Divine Savior" (ibid., 518).

Franz and Friedrich Wilhelm also were troubled by the assertion in the preamble of the draft that the sovereigns adhering to the treaty intended "in the future to be guided by no other principles whatsoever except the precepts of this holy faith … which are by no means restricted to applications just in private life, as they hitherto have been, but on the contrary, are to rule the will of the monarchs directly and govern all their actions." Next to the words "in the future" and "as they hitherto have been," the Austrian emperor noted emphatically "bleibt aus" – "omit" (ibid., 503–504; for more detail, see Näf 1928, 39–52; Ley 1975, 149–156). Thus criticism of the existing system was suppressed, and the passage as a whole acquired a descriptive character.

Meanwhile, Alexander considered the prospect of general and total renewal particularly important. After the universal historical combat between good and evil and on the threshold of the advent of the end times, everything had to change, both for tsars and for peoples. On August 29 (September 10), two weeks before the text of the Holy Alliance was signed, there was a massive parade of the Russian army in the town of Vertus, near Paris, determined, as Alexander later told Golitsyn, "according to a special secret revelation," which also dictated the scenario of the celebrations (Bartenev 1886, 100). The following day, all who took part in the parade, more than 150,000 men, again were led onto the field for a thanksgiving service on the occasion of the Russian emperor's name-day. "The revelation … judged it necessary that the Russian army be divided into seven squares," Golitsyn related. "The prayer service was conducted in the central, that is, the fourth square with the tsar's entire staff and all our Russian generals. Divine services also were held in the other squares" (ibid.). Baroness Krüdener alluded to these "seven altars" on which "the blood of the covenant (l'alliance) called for divine mercy" in one of her last letters to Alexander (Ley 1994, 407; on the parade, see Shil'der III, 340–344).

Undoubtedly these seven altars were ordered to symbolize the seven churches whom Jesus addresses in the first three chapters of the Apocalypse, promising "grace ... and peace from him which is, and which was, and which is to come, and from the seven spirits which are before his throne" (Rev 1: 4). Golitsyn recalled that Alexander was so taken with the Apocalypse "that, in the Sovereign's own words, he could not read it enough" (Bartenev 1886, 88). Jung-Stilling, in his enormously popular interpretation of the Apocalypse, called it "the manifesto of the King of Kings to his subjects from those times until the last day." In Jung-Stilling's words, the seven spirits mentioned in the verse cited earlier "stood before the throne of Jehovah" and are transfigured "in the Old Covenant by the seven-branched lampstand standing in the tabernacle, and later in the Temple before the Holy of Holies" (Jung-Stilling 1815, 4–5). It was with just such a "seven-branched lampstand" that the seven squares of the Russian army offered praise to the Lord for the victory they had won. The Christian Russian forces were equated with the new Israel.

According to Jung-Stilling, the seven churches alluded to the diversity of historical Christianity (ibid., 11). The emperor himself and "the tsar's entire staff" prayed in the fourth square, which was located not just in the geometric center, but which also, according to the Apocalypse, corresponded to the Church of Thyatira. In the Apocalypse, denunciation of many of its members who are condemned to terrible punishments is followed with the promise of blessings to "the rest in Thyatira, as many as have not this doctrine and which have not known the depths of Satan, as they speak; I will put upon you none other burden. ... And he that overcometh and keepeth my works unto the end, to him will I give power over the nations. And he shall rule them with a rod of iron; as the vessels of a potter shall they be broken to shivers: even as I received of my Father. And I will give him the morning star" (Rev. 2: 24, 26–28).

Alexander could not fail to see an obvious prophecy of his own destiny in the reference to the "victor" to whom "power over the nations" ("pouvoir sur les nations" in the French translation) was given. Note that Jung-Stilling perceived the Church of Thyatira as the Moravian Brethren (Jung-Stilling 1815, 34–40), whom the emperor visited during his European journey and about whom he questioned the German mystic in detail when they met in person (see Geiger 1954, 283–297, 333–334; Ley 1975, 63–76).

Baroness Krüdener, who accompanied Alexander to Paris, was with the Russian emperor throughout the entire ceremony and so was in the group that reviewed the parade and offered prayers in the central square. Undoubtedly she became the official interpreter of the symbolism of the celebration. Her brochure, *The Camp at Vertus*, written literally during the very days Alexander was considering the text of the Holy Alliance treaty with his allies, was published in an enormous number of copies, and, by imperial order, was immediately translated into Russian. In a note to the Russian edition, the translator explained that "the word 'vertus' means virtue [dobrodetel'], which is why when the sovereign emperor came to review the army in Vertus, the French said 'Alexander set out for his own domains'" (Krüdener 1815, 3). The French title of Krüdener's brochure, *Le Camp de Vertus*, theoretically also could have been translated as *The Field of Virtue* (Pole dobrodeteli) (Krüdener 1815a). In the baroness's account, the military parade assumed features of a cosmic drama, signifying the advent of the eschatological age. "We were witnesses to one of those grandiose spectacles where Heaven and earth converge. … Who dares depict the history of our times? What Tacitus ventures to concern himself with events which like the legendary Sphinx devour those who fail to guess the meaning of the riddle?" (Krüdener 1815, 4). The parade not only indicated symbolically the hidden meaning of the upheavals that had totally altered Europe and the world, but also was itself transformed into a kind of mystery, which only the elect could interpret.

As Eckartshausen wrote, "[M]ysteries … hold the promise of secrets which were and always will be the heritage of just a few men, secrets which neither are sold nor proclaimed openly from the pulpit, secrets accessible only to the heart striving for Wisdom and Love, and in which wisdom and love already have been awakened" (Eckartshausen 1804, 54). "In the last times everything hidden shall be revealed," however, and mankind already is approaching "that time when the great Veil concealing the Holy of Holies shall be drawn back" (ibid., 73, 57). Baroness Krüdener would not go beyond vague hints about the hidden meaning of the drama that was being played out: "Thus all who either delight in penetrating this great secret, which still is veiled, like Isis, or fear lest its cover be rent, experience either hope or fear from this epoch.

This solemn spectacle, where so many great Sovereigns have bowed before the Tsar of Tsars, already appears as if it were leading the universe into different times and as if it were a living prelude to that sacred history, which should regenerate all" (Krüdener 1815, 10).

The essence of Krüdener's interpretation was that present occurrences were absolutely unprecedented: "Who could doubt that there were great inspirations here, and who did not say with the Apostle that *the old has passed away and all things are made new!* And who would not wish for something new amidst such destruction" (Krüdener 1815, 9). The verse cited from Paul's Second Letter to the Corinthians [2 Cor 5: 17] in French translation sounds even more precise: "Le monde ancien s'en est allé, un monde nouveau est déjà né" (The old world has passed, and a new world has already been born). Thus the definitive victory over Napoleon that renewed the entire world profoundly and completely was symbolically equated with the birth of Christ. The grandiose prayer service on the field near Vertus became the first testimony to the significance of what had occurred. Signing the treaty creating the Holy Alliance two weeks later was interpreted by its authors and ideologues as an act of worship to the infant Jesus.

According to the memoirs of Baroness Krüdener's companion, Pastor Henri-Louis Empaytaz:

> A few days before his departure from Paris, [Alexander] said to us, "I am leaving France, but before my departure I want to render in a public act the homage which we owe to God the Father, Son, and Holy Spirit for the protection He has granted us and invite the peoples to obey the Gospel (inviter les peuples à se ranger sous l'obéissance de l'Évangile). I have brought the draft of this treaty to you and I urge you to read it carefully. If there are any expressions in it of which you disapprove, inform me about this. I want the emperor of Austria and the king of Prussia to join me in this act of worship so that we, like the Magi of the East, recognize the higher power of God the Savior (afin qu'on nous voie, comme les mages d'Orient, reconnâitre la suprême autorité du Dieu Saveur)." (Empaytaz 1828, 40–41; Ley 1975,146–47)

The comparison of the monarchs entering into the alliance with the Magi worshipping the infant Jesus was reinforced further by the fact that, according to early Christian tradition, there were three magi who were Eastern kings (see Averintsev 1980). In the same way, the text of the treaty is associated

Figure 27 Mother of God (1814-1815). Icon based on a passage from Revelations by V. L. Borovikovskii.

with the gifts brought by the magi to the cradle of Jesus and with the act of worship itself.

On Christmas Eve Catholics and Protestants mark the feast of the three magi. In the nineteenth century, Alexander's birthday fell precisely on this date, according to the Western calendar (December 12 according to the Russian). Three years in a row, from 1812 to 1814, the emperor celebrated his birthday in the company of Western Christians—in Vilnius, Karlsruhe, and Vienna—when most of the population of these cities recalled the magi and prepared for Christmas. Such a coincidence, of course, could not but be noticed by Alexander, who sought hidden omens everywhere and who anxiously followed the mysticism of the calendar.

The thematic complex linked to the Nativity played an extraordinary role in European mysticism. In the words of A. D. Galakhov, the Nativity became the favorite subject of mystical literature, because "the incarnation of God in the soul" provided it with material for secret comparisons and a secret parallel with what the French preacher Du Toit called "the transformation of fallen man into a new creation" (Galakhov 1875, 104). The doctrine of inner rebirth or regeneration (régénération) was a central element of mystical study of the person. *The Cloud over the Sanctuary* presented this parallel very forcefully:

> In us, everything is unclean, everything is covered by a web of vanity, everything sullied by the filth of sensuality. Our will is an ox harnessed in a yoke of passions. Our intellect is a donkey, obstinate in its opinions, prejudices, and stupidities. In this transitory and disintegrating hovel, the abode of brute passions, Christ is born in us through faith. The simplicity of our soul creates a pastoral situation, for it brings Him the first sacrifices, then the three main powers of our royal dignity: Intellect, Will, and Action prostrate themselves before Him and bring Him the gifts of truth, wisdom, and love. (Eckartshausen 1804, 140)

God's awakening in the soul of man corresponds to the birth of Christ in the cradle of Bethlehem, and man's inner acknowledgment of the dominion of Jesus to the gifts of the magi, the three kings of the East, who once had been given the morning star as a sign of the Nativity. Juliette Krüdener's diary entry for September 23, 1815, describes the emperor's first appearance in the prophetess's home after he learned his allies were prepared to sign the treaty, "Alexander remarked that if he had not been prepared by this act, he could not have understood 'the adoration of the magi.' ... Alexander was unusually candid, talked about the king [Louis XVIII], the need for inner regeneration, reading Sacred Scripture, his own life, making use of time, and trust in God" (Ley 1994, 318).

Long before, Alexander had compared the victory over Napoleon with the new birth of Christ. As early as the Christmas of 1812, he issued a manifesto in which he ordered the day commemorated as the feast "of the deliverance of the Church and the Russian realm from the invasion of the French and the twelve tribes with them" (PSZ № 25669). At the same time, he signed a decree to begin construction of the Cathedral of Christ the Savior in Moscow (PSZ № 25296), as if summoning all the emperor's subjects to worship Jesus. The actual consecration of the new cathedral to Christ testified to the supraconfessional character of the future temple (see Florovskii 1937, 134; for the text of the *ukase*, see PSZ, № 25296; on the plan, see Witberg 1954; Medvedkova 1993). Now, relying on the spiritual and intellectual support of West European mystics, he urged his august allies and their peoples to the same kind of worship.

БОЖІЕЮ МИЛОСТІЮ
МЫ АЛЕКСАНДРЪ ПЕРВЫЙ
ИМПЕРАТОРЪ и САМОДЕРЖЕЦЪ
ВСЕРОССІЙСКІЙ,

и прочая, и прочая, и прочая.

Объявляемъ всенародно!

Познавъ изъ опытовъ и бѣдственныхъ для всего Свѣта послѣдствій, что ходъ прежнихъ политическихъ въ Европѣ между Державами соотношеній, не имѣлъ основаніемъ тѣхъ истинныхъ началъ, на коихъ премудрость Божія въ откровеніи Своемъ утвердила покой и благоденствіе народовъ, приступили МЫ, совокупно съ Ихъ Величествами Австрійскимъ Императоромъ Францомъ Первымъ и Королемъ Прусскимъ Фредерикомъ Вильгельмомъ, къ постановленію между НАМИ союза (приглашая къ тому и прочія Христіанскія Державы), въ которомъ обязуемся МЫ взаимно, какъ между СОБОЮ, такъ и въ отношеніи къ подданнымъ НАШИМЪ, принять единственнымъ ведущимъ къ оному средствомъ правило, почерпнутое изъ словесъ и ученія Спасителя Нашего Іисуса Христа, благовѣствующаго людямъ жить, аки братіямъ, не во враждѣ и злобѣ, но въ мирѣ и любви. МЫ желаемъ и молимъ Всевышняго о ниспослании благодати своей, да утвердится Священный союзъ сей между всѣми Державами, къ общему ихъ благу, и да не дерзнетъ никто, единодушіемъ всѣхъ прочихъ воспящаемый, отпасть отъ онаго. Сего ради, прилагая при семъ списокъ съ сего союза, ПОВЕЛѢВАЕМЪ обнародовать оный и прочитать въ Церквахъ.

Санктпетербургъ. Въ день Рождества Спасителя Нашего. Декабря 25го 1815 года.

На подлинномъ подписано собственною ЕГО ИМ-ПЕРАТОРСКАГО ВЕЛИ-ЧЕСТВА рукою тако:

АЛЕКСАНДРЪ.

Печатанъ въ Санктпетербургѣ при Сенатѣ Декабря дня 1816 года.

Figure 28 The manifesto of December 25, 1815.

Insofar as the Russian emperor felt himself to be God's chosen one, called to bring Christian enlightenment to the world, he could not be satisfied with the compromises reached with his allies, above all with their demand that the treaty of the Holy Alliance be kept confidential. His goal was that the magi's act of worship, performed by the three monarchs, at the same time be revealed to all as testimony to the advent of new times and as an example for general emulation. On Christmas, December 25, 1815, also the date commemorating Russia's liberation from the French, Alexander published the text of the treaty. Moreover, he accompanied this publication with a manifesto that included the provisions he had been forced to exclude from the draft. First and foremost among these was the concept that, after the conclusion of the treaty, the basis of international policy would be subject to complete change:

> We have understood from the consequences of trials and tribulations for the entire World that the conduct of previous political relations between the Powers in Europe was not founded on those true principles on which Divine wisdom in its revelation secured the tranquility and prosperity of peoples. Hence We, united with Their Majesties the Austrian Emperor Franz the First and the Prussian King Friedrich Wilhelm, undertook to establish an alliance between Us (inviting the other Christian powers to join us). In this We mutually pledge ourselves, both between us and in relation to Our subjects, to take as the only means leading to this the rule drawn from the teaching of Our Savior Jesus Christ, proclaiming to people that they should live as brothers, not in enmity and malice, but in peace and love. We hope and pray to The Most High to send down his grace and that this Holy alliance be securely established between all Powers for their general welfare. Also, let no one, obstructing the unanimity of all the others, dare stand aside from it. To this end, enclosing herewith a copy of this alliance, We order it promulgated and read in the Churches.
>
> St. Petersburg. On the day of the Nativity of Our Savior.
>
> December 25, 1815. (PSZ № 26045)

In concluding the Holy Alliance treaty, Alexander hardly could have expected to find fellow brethren of the interior church in his allies and the other monarchs invited to subscribe to the text. The knowledgeable Roksandra Sturdza asserted that the crowned heads of Europe signed the document either "not understanding it and not taking the time to familiarize themselves with its significance," or wholly in a spirit of "resentful indignation." In her opinion, Alexander "knew people too well to delude himself in this respect, but he thought that it ought to be proclaimed in Europe from the mouths of its sovereigns for all to hear that Europe was turning away from the impiety which had characterized the recent past in order openly to confess its faith in Christ" (Edling 1999, 223–224).

News that the documents had been made public in St. Petersburg caused consternation in the capitals of Europe. An epoch in which policy was supposed to be based directly upon the teachings of the Gospel started with an unprecedented breach of agreements that had been concluded and promises that had been made. The allies, as Metternich's closest associate, Friedrich Gentz, wrote in a dispatch from Vienna to St. Petersburg, "were shocked and confused" (Ley 1975, 165). Alexander achieved his purpose, however, by demonstrating his dissatisfaction with traditional secret diplomacy and revealing the coming of the new times to the whole world.

∽ **5** ∽

"True religion, like the ark of the covenant (l'arche d'alliance) between God and his creation, embraces the horizon of the inhabited world with new love," asserted A. S. Sturdza in his "Meditation on the Act of Fraternal and Christian Union," in preparation for publicizing the ideas of the finalized agreement (Stourdza 1815, 4). "Our dear Sovereign, subjected to ordeals and turning toward faith, felt the need to loudly proclaim through the Holy Alliance the inception of the Kingdom of Christ, whose only authorized representatives the first three kings of Europe had declared themselves to be. It is impossible to look at the act of Holy Alliance otherwise than as a manifesto preparing the way for the kingdom of the Savior," Golitsyn wrote in 1820 to Baron Berkheim, Krüdener's son-in-law (Shebunin, manuscript, № 110, 196). Of course, both Golistyn and Sturdza belonged to those closest to Alexander and were familiar with his most intimate thoughts first-hand. However, other sensitive and sympathetic contemporaries also caught the gist of the emperor's designs.

Even before New Year's the news made it to Speranskii's Penza estate. By this time his exile had ended, but he had still not returned to government service and retained the status of a statesman in partial disgrace. The published agreement aroused his warmest approval. He wrote to his friend F. I. Tseier on December 31, 1815:

> At last a ray of light has illuminated my spirit and dispersed all my doubts. I mean the manifesto of December 25. I may finally give myself up fully to the direction of my thoughts; I may dare to state my excitement, and to converse with the Sovereign about a subject worthy of his attention. ... Do you remember our discussion last summer in the Velikopol'skii garden, when, speaking of the spirit that should guide monarchs in their actions at the Congress of Vienna, I had the faintheartedness to despair? But is this a phantom? Do I correctly understand the true meaning given to this act? Woe to them who would be so brazen as to play with the very most holy names and objects. No; the spirit of darkness could again extinguish this manifestation of grace, as has often happened, but now this light is still pure and acts in all fullness. (Korf 1867, 445–446)

And indeed on September 6, Speranskii addressed a letter directly to the emperor:

> The truths described in the manifesto of December 25 in the act of alliance places on all of Your subjects a new obligation of unlimited trust and openness. More than many others I must feel and fulfill this obligation. ... Can I, should I now be silent when I see indubitable marks of true, heartfelt and not cerebral, grace that illuminates your heart. Let not Your modesty be offended by this statement! Christ's grace is given without merit and may be admitted without flattery. (Ibid., 447)

In full agreement with Alexander's own view of his role, Speranskii emphasized that the act of Holy Alliance was not a "personal action" by the rulers who signed it but "a pure outpouring of the most abundant Christian grace for which they were favored to be the vehicles." The direct intervention of grace into the course of the historical process also established "a new political right" based on two fundamental principles. In the first place, "the goal of human societies is to guide people into union with Christ," and secondly, "Jesus Christ is and should be the head of all Christian societies. The true rules for their governance cannot be taken from anywhere but from His rules and teaching" (ibid., 448–449). Thus the single task of an earthly state turned out to be preparing nations either for a universal Christian republic or straightaway for the start of a chiliastic Divine Kingdom on earth. Speranskii explained the nature and character of the future theocracy to the same F. I. Tseier in a letter of January 22:

> People err when they assert that the spirit of God's kingdom is incompatible with the principles of political societies. Is not rulership (derzhavstvo) a kind of priesthood (sviashchenstvo)?... What is the anointment of Sovereigns?... Can one doubt the reality of the outpouring of the Holy Spirit onto the anointed person, if only that person is capable of receiving it?... I do not know even one question of state that could not be reduced to the spirit of the Gospels. Everything down to taxation can be worked out in this spirit and under its guidance. Did not the *Jiménezes*, St. Bernards, St. Louises, Alfreds all draw abundantly from this source? (Speranskii 1870b, 188–189)

Inspired by the Holy Alliance, Speranskii was ready to see the monarchs who headed it as the direct recipients of grace, summoned to embody the utopia of the kingdom of the gospels and to implement it in practical measures and state structures.

Still, in a letter to a close friend who considered Speranskii his "spiritual father" (ibid., 192), the former state secretary made so bold as to also express some criticisms of the new document. Speranskii probably did not exclude the possibility that his correspondence was being monitored, and may have even thought that his ideas would make it all the way to the royal addressee. "It is true that the expressions of the act of alliance are insufficiently clear," he wrote. "Thus, for example, one cannot call Jesus Christ the head of everyone, even infected members; because He is the head of a single body which is His Church; a kingdom is not the Church of the truly faithful; but why nitpick at the form, ignoring the spirit and general direction of this act?" (ibid., 189). Despite all polite provisos, the differences between Speranskii and Alexander were quite serious. Speranskii fully shared Alexander's conviction, reflected in his note "On Mystical Literature," concerning the existence of the "Church of the truly faithful" that was under the direct authority of Christ. His deputies on earth might be anointed monarchs if they comprehend their divine mission and prove worthy. At the same time the former state secretary was not ready to indiscriminately consider all powers as part of the "Church of the faithful," even if they were in care of the most devout monarchs. Speranskii's references to historical analogies show that while he considered the idea of Christian politics proclaimed in the manifesto a new thing for the contemporary world, he nevertheless did not find it completely unprecedented. Having been separated from the sovereign during several extremely eventful years, he joyfully recognized echoes of old conversations in the new public documents but remained deaf to ideas from different sources that had influenced Alexander after his removal from office. He accepted the mystical spirit of the act of union with sincere enthusiasm, but did not see, or did not want to see, its eschatological dimension. Yet the eschatological pathos of the agreement he had written was especially important for the emperor. The end days were imminent, and the truth would cease being the possession of a narrow circle of the select and bring many people—and then everybody—along. As Eckartshausen prophesied, the epoch when the society of lightbearers were to proclaim their existence in everyone's hearing and its members would recognize one another were rapidly approaching. It was for this very reason that on the day of Orthodox Christmas Alexander spoke to his people, and, as he could not have helped realize, to all of the peoples of Europe, over the heads and despite the wishes of his allied monarchs.

The new ideological conception's nodes of meaning, which the state secretary who knew the emperor so well ascribed to "insufficient precision," were, however, fully clear to the poet. Apparently, Zhukovskii had thought of a continuation of "The Singer in the Camp of Russian Warriors" even before the start of active work on the epistle "To Emperor Alexander." In the words of the author, it was supposed "to present the singer of Russian warriors returning to the Motherland and singing a song of liberation in the Kremlin ... on the very day that Russia, triumphant, is bending her knee with gratitude before Providence, which through her had saved all the peoples of Europe and [brought] all the benefits of freedom and enlightenment" (Zhukovskii 1902 II, 143). This explanation was given in the separate edition of the poem "The Singer in the Kremlin" that came out in 1816 with a note that "these verses were written at the end of 1814." They were probably composed for the second anniversary gala celebration of the liberation of Russia from the French, in which the emperor might have participated had the Congress of Vienna successfully finished its work. However, the Congress's deliberations dragged on and then were completely interrupted by the news of Napoleon's escape from Elba. On March 4, 1815, Zhukovskii reported to A. I. Turgenev that he intended to publish a booklet "under the title 'The Singer in the Kremlin' (it is almost finished and only requires corrections), with the addition of other lyric poems" (Zhukovskii 1895, 142). Making corrections continued for almost a year. The publication of the Christmas manifesto of 1815 and the Holy Alliance pact probably served as the culminating stroke that helped Zhukovskii finalize the poem's definitive configuration.

Like "The Singer in the Camp of Russian Warriors," "The Singer in the Kremlin" is composed of a series of poetic panegyrics that the singer recites and which an attentive chorus echoes. In the poem's last fragment, the singer's words sound like a direct response to the text of the manifesto and treaty:

> О совершись, святой завет!
>   В одну семью, народы!
> Цари! в един отцов совет!
>   Будь сила щит свободы!
> Дух благодати, пронесись
>   Над мирною вселенной
> И вся земля совокупись
>   В единый град нетленной!

(Oh come to pass, holy behest [sviatoi zavet]! / Into one family, peoples! / Tsars! Into one council of fathers! / Strength, be shield of freedom! // Spirit of grace, be carried / Over the peaceful universe / And [let] the whole earth come together / Into a single imperishable city!)

Zhukovskii accurately feels the eschatological overtones of the ratified agreement. Hence the interpretation of coming days as the realization of the "holy behest" (i.e., alliance). Like Speranskii, Zhukovskii sees in the union that had been concluded the action of the spirit of grace, but, unlike him, he understands that the issue does not so much concern a new political organization of earthly states as it does "a single imperishable city," whose outlines one may discern beyond the curtain of the ages:

> Ты, мудрость смертных, усмирись
>   Пред мудростию Бога
> И в мраке жизни озарись
>   К небесному дорога.
> Будь вера твердый якорь нам
>   Средь волн безвестных рока
> И ты в нерукотворный храм
>   Свети, звезда востока.

(You, mortals' wisdom, be humbled / Before God's wisdom / And in the murk of life illumine / The path to heaven. / Faith, be a steady anchor for us / Amid the unknown waves of fate / And you, star of the East, / Shine into the temple not made by mortal hands.)

Zhukovskii could hardly have been informed of the emperor's statements in which he compared the concluded act with Christ's Nativity, and he and his allies with the magi. Nevertheless he accurately grasped the symbolic significance of the date the imperial manifesto was published. "The star of the East" by which the three magi—or to translate the French formula more literally, the three king-sorcerers—found the infant Jesus again lit up the sky above the earth, and the three allied monarchs bowed to the "temple not made by mortal hands," the new manger of Bethlehem.

In the final lines of the poem the singer and the people merge in one surge of rapture, one act of reverence to this sign that has now become visible:

> Свети, свети, звезда небес,
>   К ней взоры, к ней желанья,
> К ней, к ней за тайну их завес
>   Земные упованья.
> Там все, что здесь пленяло нас
>   Явлением мгновенным,
> Что взял у жизни смертный час,
>   Воскреснет обновленным!
> Рука с рукой! вождю вослед!
>   В одну, друзья, дорогу
> И с нами в братском хоре, свет,
>   Пой: слава в вышних Богу!

(Shine, shine, star in the heavens, / To it our gazes, to it our desires, / To it, to it, behind the mystery of their veils, / Our earthly hopes [are directed]. / There everything that captivated us here / [Seems but] a momentary occurrence, / What the hour of death takes from life / Is resurrected, renewed! / Hand in hand! Follow the leader! / To one road, friends / And together with us in our fraternal chorus, world [or: light], / Sing glory to God in the highest!)

The celebration of the great national victory on the ruins of the ancient capital is crowned by a nationwide apotheosis of the future resurrection of the dead, promised by the new Nativity. The voices of all peoples of the world merge in this "fraternal chorus."

∞ **6** ∞

In the brochure *The Camp at Vertus*, Baroness Krüdener wrote that the meaning of contemporary events "eludes the understanding of those who do not have the living God to interpret them and who remain forever orphaned and enveloped in the darkness of perplexity. ... But among those in exile, also in this land of captivity, there always remained a holy race, there always was a people pleasing to God. These, those people of all ages, were the only ones who carried out that great work of the Creator" (Krüdener 1815, 5). In using the words "race" (race) and "people" (peuple), the baroness did not have in mind the subjects of one or another monarch, and even less an ethnic group. This "chosen people, children of promise" consisted of "men of great enlightenment, placed at the top of the ladder." They alone are able "to view this epoch in the light with which the majesty of the Sacred Scriptures has illumined them" (ibid., 5, 10).

In essence, this is the same society of lightbearers that Eckartshausen had described, a mystical union of the initiated, comprising a single nation. In another place, the baroness uses the word "people" in the more traditional sense when speaking of the subjects of the Russian empire as "simple-hearted peoples (peuples), who have not yet drunk from the cup of all the abominations, and who have not yet fallen away from the God who saves them" (ibid., 6). "Simple-hearted peoples" could be the instrument of providence as long as they are not ruled by the false enlightenment that had ruined debauched peoples, above all, the French. These are identical with the inhabitants of Thyatira who "did not know the satanic depths." Their historical role is determined by having at their head a monarch associated with true enlightenment, whose attributes are "rule over the nations," "iron rod," and "morning star," or, as Krüdener expressed this concept, "a man of great judgments, predestined to this before all ages" (ibid.). Thus Alexander stood simultaneously at the head of two peoples entrusted to him by God: the people of his own empire and "the chosen people of the reborn."

The baroness called Alexander "the Lord's chosen one" (l'élu du Seigneur) in a letter of May 17, 1815, to Roksandra Sturdza (Ley 1994, 288). At the time of her first conversation with the emperor on June 4, she was prepared to dispel

Alexander's doubts about his "special election." On June 23 Krüdener wrote to the emperor about "those who should comprise the small number of *members of that Church which Christ chose for himself in order to renew the world* and rule by means of it for the next thousand years." "*You are one of these Chosen Ones,*" she addressed Alexander, "and Your heart already has been prepared by great sacrifices. If You, Sire, had not been able to respond to these great plans, the Lord would not have called you to his service and would not have made you the victor over the dragon (Antichrist) and *the leader of peoples*" (Nikolai Mikhailovich II, 216). For Krüdener, the church of the reborn (régénérés) existed as a concrete historical institution, at the given moment more or less corresponding to the circle of her devotees and persons aroused by her preaching. Thus she actively sought to enlist Alexander's closest associates as members of this church. On June 22 she "spoke fervently" to Karl Freiherr vom Stein and Kapodistrias of "the need to be reborn" (Ley 1994, 296). As early as March 1815, before the meeting with the emperor, the baroness's daughter noted her mother's prophecy about the Russian sovereign's coming mission in her diary: "Maman thinks that Alexander will leave his country, that he will be lifted up by the Lord into a lofty school of trials, and then the people of God will join him, after which he will return to Russia" (ibid., 286). Like the new Moses, Alexander was supposed to lead the "chosen people" into the Promised Land, which, according to Baroness Krüdener, was located in the southern provinces of the Russian Empire.

In his memoirs on Alexander, Pastor Empaytaz included a letter which the emperor wrote to him from Baden on October 6, 1815. Thanking his correspondent for his spiritual counsels, the emperor wrote that his soul "rejoices in that which belongs to the nation (nation) unknown to the world, but whose triumph is approaching swiftly" (Empaytaz 1840, 47). Apparently, in publishing the letter, the memoirist simply did not notice the polite but inflexible refusal under the veil of genteel deference so characteristic of the emperor. Alexander sincerely wished to believe in his divine predestination, and so received the fervent addresses of his confidante gratefully and trustingly. He envisioned the structure of the interior church completely differently, however. He regarded it as a secret fellowship of the elect. Its members could belong to different Christian confessions, live in various countries, and have no idea of each other's existence, but they should be able to discern that they were alike by a special mystical sense. On this issue, Alexander clearly was much more akin to Eckartshausen, who wrote that the elect "belong to no sect and no society other than the grand and authentic society of all the lightbearers" (Eckartshausen 1804, 65). This was the hitherto unknown people which the whole world was soon destined to recognize.

Even at the time of the first encounter between the emperor and the baroness, her daughter thought to remark that Alexander was "less interested" in what "maman" said about the "Church of our times" than what "pertained to the way of the Christian, to prayer, and to holiness" (Ley 1994,290; Krüdener 1998, 130). Distinct disagreements became apparent exactly two months later, on September 4, a week before the prayer service at Vertus. "Alexander came," Juliette Krüdener wrote in her diary. "*We had a conversation about the Church*. I spoke with him without any fear and told him that *I felt that he had not yet committed himself to this work*. He told us that *he thought that it was not true, for example, that the church consisted of a few individuals*, and that it should be established *in a specific country; he thought that it would exist everywhere*" (Ley 1994, 307; Krüdener 1998, 133). This is why the baroness's missionary activity put Alexander on his guard. According to Juliette Krüdener, when Stein discussed her mother's ideas with Alexander "concerning the church," he was afraid that the baroness was too "open with others on this issue" (ibid.).

As Eckartshausen wrote, man "henceforth should know and be instructed in everything that pertains to regeneration: … [F]irst, a Teacher and Mentor is necessary, but to know him, one must believe in Him, for what is the use of a Teacher if the pupil does not believe in him" (Eckartshausen 1804, 135). The general regeneration was approaching, but meanwhile Alexander, as A. N. Pypin noted long ago, very quickly lost faith in Madame Krüdener. The scholar refers to the testimony of Princess Meshcherskaia, who cited the sovereign's "own words": "The emperor spoke of his unexpected encounter with Frau Krüdener at the very minute when in his mind he hoped God would send him a person who would help him understand God's sacred will correctly. Then he continued: 'For some time I have thought that it was precisely she whom God had chosen to this end, but *I very quickly* saw that this light was nothing but an *ignis fatuus* [will-o'-the-wisp]'" (Pypin 2000, 365). In 1818, Alexander spoke to Countess S. I. Sollogub about the "simplicity" of Christianity and about "unsettled souls who lose themselves in subtleties they themselves do not understand.

For example, Madame Krüdener," he added, "might have had good intentions, but caused irreparable harm" (Posnikova 1867, 1038–1039).

For a time Krüdener was able to help Alexander overcome his doubts and become convinced of his election and his membership in the society of lightbearers. As his belief in his special predestination increased, however, it enabled the emperor to reject the baroness's claim to spiritual leadership. In the words of Eckartshausen himself, "in the end times, everything hidden shall become manifest, but it also is prophesied that in these times many false prophets shall arise, and the precept is given to the faithful not to believe in every spirit, but to test the spirits to see whether they are of God"(1 John 4: 1; Eckartshausen 1804, 73). Krüdener's teaching envisioned Alexander's role as leading the exodus of the baroness's followers out of Europe and bestowing upon them a place for the coming chiliastic kingdom in the confines of his own empire (see Ley 1994, 347–385). This could only clash with the sentiments of the sovereign, whose eschatological expectations, in large part with the assistance of Krüdener herself, had been raised to the highest level.

∞ 7 ∞

Roksandra Sturdza wrote in her memoirs that the Holy Alliance was "the realization of the grandiose concept of Henry IV and Charles Irénée Castel, the Abbé de Saint-Pierre" (Edling 1999, 223). Undoubtedly the emperor himself had a similar view, for as the Austrian diplomat Friedrich von Gentz put it, he saw "himself as the founder of a European federation and wanted to be regarded as its leader." As Gentz noted in 1818, "over a period of two years he did not write a single memoir or a single diplomatic note in which this system was not presented as the glory of the age and the salvation of the world" (Nikolai Mikhailovich I, 219–220).

Creating this kind of European federation, or Christian republic, with Russia playing an active role, was a goal of Catherine II's policy as early as the 1770s and constituted one of the significant bases of the "Greek Project." It is not surprising that the treaty of the Holy Alliance, suffused with religious rhetoric, was perceived by European public opinion as an anti-Turkish declaration. Gentz, troubled by the publication of the treaty, wrote in one of his dispatches:

> The first instinct of almost everyone who learned of the treaty's existence was to regard as it as the portent of a project directed against Turkey. They said that since Christianity was the principal subject and sacramental word (le mot sacramental) of this document, then clearly it did not prohibit military action against unbelievers, and that Emperor Alexander's secret intention was to bind the leading Christian powers by a solemn oath and then to propose a new crusade to them. (Ley 1975, 180)

Similar interpretations of the emperor's Christian sentiments were shared not only by such staunch opponents of the liberation of Greece as Metternich and Gentz, but also by passionate advocates of the Greek cause. Roksandra Sturdza recalled how as early as 1814, despite the opposition of the Austrian court, she had induced Alexander to visit a church of the Turkish Greeks in Vienna. The Russian sovereign's visit was, in her words, "a minute of happiness for the unfortunate Greeks, and in their imagination they envisioned their august protector in the Church of Saint Sophia" (Edling 1999, 203).

Grecophile sentiments also were common in Baroness Krüdener's inner circle. Her son-in-law F. Berckheim recalled that on one occasion he read "ancient prophecies" to Alexander, "contained in collections of works of alchemy, where the ruler of a certain northern monarchy was proclaimed, who would gather the people around him who were the most like him in piety." As Berckheim reported later, this prophecy came from Madame Jeanne Marie Bouvier de la Motte Guyon, who supposedly predicted that "this chosen monarch would be a Russian, that he would become the head of a universal church, and that his capital would be either Constantinople or Jerusalem" (Shebunin, manuscript, № 110, 120). Apparently, from the very beginning Alexander regarded these prophecies warily, since he did not share his grandmother's expansionist plans (Arsh 1976, 236–38 and passim). By March 1816, he instructed his envoy in London, Count Kh. A. Lieven, to explain to the English cabinet that the treaty as approved "contains no hostile intentions towards peoples who are not fortunate enough to be Christians," and that his intention was to provide the same explanations to the Ottoman Porte (Shil'der III, 553). In his view, there was no special place assigned to a Christian republic of Greece. The emperor put his hopes in the universal Church, hence Russia's historical ties to Byzantine Orthodoxy, so essential to any design for a

"Greek Project," became less important to him. What is more, the classical connotations of Catherine's plans, which a significant number of those who shared the emperor's apocalyptic sentiments still found attractive, held no fascination whatever for him.

Alexandros Ypsilantis's uprising in 1821 posed a choice for Alexander (Fadeev 1958; Dostian 1972, 196–331; Arsh 1976; Prousis 1994, 6–54, which also contains a short bibliography, 185–186). It seems that he made a decision without particular difficulty. On February 24, 1821, he wrote from the Congress of Laibach to Golitsyn, who on the whole was sympathetic to the Greek liberation:

> There is no doubt that the summons for this revolt was given by the same central governing committee (comité central directeur) from Paris in order to create a diversion on behalf of Naples[5] and to prevent us from destroying one of these synagogues of Satan, established with its only goal to preach and disseminate its anti-Christian teaching. Ypsilantis himself writes in a letter addressed to me that he belongs to a secret society founded for the liberation and rebirth of Greece. But all these secret societies are affiliated with the central committee in Paris. The revolution in Piedmont has the same goal—to establish one more center to preach the same doctrine and paralyze the influence of the Christian authorities who profess the Holy Alliance. (Nikolai Mikhailovich I, 219–220)

Ten days earlier, Alexander, referring to "reliable evidence" at his disposal, tried to convince the same correspondent of the existence of a general conspiracy of "revolutionary liberals, radical levelers, and Carbonari" who "communicate and agree with each other," and that this conspiracy was based "on the so-called philosophy of Voltaire and those like him" (ibid., 546). About this time the emperor sent a letter to Princess Meshcherskaia in which he informed his correspondent that the sovereigns assembled in Laibach were seeking means for battle with "*the Empire of Evil*, which is expanding ... with the help of all the occult means which its directing satanic spirit employs" (ibid., 251).

Like V. P. Petrov ten years earlier, Alexander regarded an international conspiracy with its center in Paris as the principal threat to the coming Christian republic. In the opinion of V. G. Sirotkin, "the basic premise set forth in the treaty creating the Holy Alliance about the reasons for the emergence of the

---

5 A revolution was taking place there at this time.

'revolutionary spirit' was the same as before; it is the conspiracy of Masons and Jacobins, who were not destroyed and continue to sow intrigues." As the historian puts it, "these old ideas of the Abbé Augustin Barruel were modernized by the Paris jurist Nicholas Bergasse," who wrote to Alexander about the existence of the "principal center" of revolutionary propaganda in France. He also wrote about "the Bavarian philosopher and mystic, Franz von Baader," who in a brochure published in 1815, *On the Necessity Prompted by the French Revolution of Establishing a New and Closer Bond between Religion and Politics*, proposed measures for the struggle with the worldwide conspiracy quite similar to the sentiments of the Russian emperor at the time (Sirotkin 1981, 45; cf. Baader 1987). In 1814, that is, a year before publication, Baader sent the text of his work to the Russian and Austrian monarchs in Vienna (Sirotkin 1981, 46; Ley 1975, 125–126).

The various appropriations of Barruel's framework were by no means solely the work of two publicists, however; rather, they were common to all mystical thought of the epoch. In his autobiography Jung-Stilling wrote that Abbé Barruel "in the main is correct, erring only in details" (Jung-Stilling II, 218). Six years before the appearance of *Memoirs of the History of Jacobinism*, Eckartshausen published a multivolume work on magic in which he pointed to secret societies in particular as the principal danger to the political and social order. "Everything that assumes the mask of secrecy is in the highest degree suspect," he wrote, and declared that societies spawning "vain enthusiasts," "nurturing imposters," or even worse, adopting political goals, were to be avoided (Eckartshausen I, 387; II, 215–223).

By analogy with the inner church, or "society of lightbearers," thinkers with a mystical orientation developed their concept of a conspiracy of the powers of darkness, nefariously opposing the accomplishment of the divine plan and willingly or unwillingly carrying out the designs of the devil. With the advent of the end times, the struggle between good and evil inevitably assumed an eschatological character. "To submit to the spirit of evil," Alexander wrote in 1815 to Frédéric-César La Harpe, who had advised him to make peace with Napoleon, "means to strengthen his power, to give him the means to establish a tyranny in an even more terrible form than the first time. One must have courage to do battle with him, and, with the help of Divine Providence, unity, and perseverance, we will achieve a favorable outcome" (Shil'der III, 327).

For those with such views, the French Revolution and the Napoleonic empire were a kind of open revelation of the Antichrist to mankind. Overthrown and on the brink of final defeat, the agents of darkness had to operate especially craftily and cunningly. Naturally, the blacker and more malevolent the true goals of the conspirators, the more they had to camouflage their actions with noble and virtuous slogans. To withstand them required insight and resolution, which the Lord alone could provide to his chosen ones. Such a perception of the world, which Alexander had formulated even before the war and which took definite shape during the campaigns of 1812–15, provided a set standard for interpreting the revolutionary wave between the end of the 1810s and the beginning of the 1820s, from the upheavals in Naples and Piedmont to the mutiny in the Semenovskii Regiment, in which the emperor persistently tried to discern signs of a widespread conspiracy (see Shil'der IV, 179 and passim). For him the Greek uprising was one more testimony to the diabolical cunning of the spirit of evil. Neither the execution of the Greek patriarch, nor the massacres of Greeks in Constantinople in April 1821, nor the pressure of public opinion in his own land, where demands to support the Greeks as fellow Orthodox Christians had a major impact (see, for example, Fadeev 1964, 41–52), persuaded the emperor to alter his point of view. At the end of 1821, he ordered Baroness Krüdener exiled from St. Petersburg, where she had come to preach the coming mystical triumph of the Russian tsar in the walls of the Church of Saint Sophia (see Ley 1994, 404–409).

The two basic ideological models of Russian policy created in the 1770s, the "Greek Project" and the theory of a worldwide conspiracy, came into irreconcilable conflict, and the conspiracy theory was the total and unquestioned victor. Much later, Aleksandr Sturdza, an ardent Greek patriot and partisan of Russian intervention in Greek affairs, wrote that the July 1830 Revolution in France "vindicated the emperor's foresight" (Sturdza 1864, 104; cf. 98–99). In 1822, at the time of the Congress of Verona, Alexander discussed these questions with François René de Chateaubriand, who in February 1823 quoted Alexander's words in his speech in the French Chamber of Deputies and later included them in his memoirs:

> "Suppose," Alexander asked, "that as our enemies maintain, alliance is only a word advanced to cloak ambition? That might have been valid in the old

order of things, but is it possible to speak of private interests today when the whole civilized world is in mortal danger?

"An English, French, Russian, Prussian, or Austrian policy can no longer exist, for there is only a common policy that must be shared by peoples and sovereigns for the benefit of all. I ought to have been the first to demonstrate my devotion to the principles upon which I based the alliance, and a case presented itself: the Greek uprising. Nothing, it would seem, would be more in my interests, the interests of my people, and in accord with the opinion of my country than a religious war against Turkey, but I perceived the sign of revolution in the upheavals occurring in the Peloponnese. And so I stayed on the sidelines. ... No, I never will break with the monarchs to whom I am bound. Sovereigns should be permitted to conclude open alliances in order to oppose secret societies." (Chateaubriand 1840, 96–98; cf. Nikolai Mikhailovich I, 295–296)[6]

In the letter to Meshcherskaia cited above, Alexander stressed that effective methods to combat satanic intrigues are, "alas, beyond meager human strength." "Only the Savior, with the power of his Divine word," the emperor explained, "can give us the necessary means" (Nikolai Mikhailovich I, 251). And if a member of the "society of lightbearers" needed mystical intuition and spiritual support to be aware of his election and recognize his comrades, then the same degree of perceptive intervention was necessary for him to discover the enemy and expose his schemes. By 1818–19, the emperor had concluded that mystical associations of a pious tendency might be an effective means to combat subversive forces. In these years he openly protected E. F. Tatarinova's "spiritual union," hoping with its help, as he himself said, "to root out heresies, both the Skoptsy and the Masons" (Tolstoi 1872, 224; cf. Dubrovin 1895/1896; Etkind 1997) and to defeat the "Carbonari," who now are "spreading in the West" and "already have penetrated" to its "seat of power" (Kossovich 1872, 1233).

In 1822, however, Alexander decided that all secret societies, without exception, ought to be banned categorically, above all, it seems, Masonic lodges (see Lebedev 1912; Serkov 2000, 242–244). A signed statement was obtained from Tatarinova that her meetings would be discontinued, and in 1825, after the collapse of the Russian Bible Society and the dismissal of Aleksandr

---

6 Here we are not considering the influence of Austrian diplomacy and Metternich on the development of the Greek crisis, which is extremely important for the political history of the conflict but not directly relevant to our topic (see Bertier de Sauvigny 1960; Bertier de Sauvigny 1972, etc.)

Golitsyn, she, in effect, was exiled from St. Petersburg. In the last year of his life, Alexander also apparently began to be disillusioned with the ideas of the Holy Alliance. The light of the "star of the East," sent from above to guide the chosen one on the path of spiritual revelation, turned out to be just the next "will-o'-the-wisp."

∞ **8** ∞

Faith in the existence of a universal conspiracy run by a secret committee in Paris was one of the extremely few mythologems that united the partisans of mystical universalism that, for many years, surrounded Alexander with the national isolationists of Shishkov's orientation. "From both sides the arguments and even the entire phraseology were absolutely identical," noted Pypin, concerning the accusations of participating in a Masonic conspiracy and aiding the Antichrist which were traded by the leader of the mystical sect, Esaul Kotel'nikov from the Don, and his persecutors from the conservatively-oriented Orthodox hierarchs, first of all Archimandrite Fotii (Pypin 2000, 448). This kind of similarity in many ways facilitated Alexander's falling under Fotii's influence toward the end of his life (see ibid., 190–287; Chistovich 1899; Kondakov 1998; Gordin 1999, etc.). Sensing the growing dissatisfaction and again becoming disillusioned with his former spiritual guides, the emperor tried to step in the water in the same place for a second time, to repeat the move that he had made with such success in 1812. In the place of Golitsyn as minister of popular enlightenment he again appointed Shishkov. However, this time the superannuated admiral was not to get a chance to influence the empire's ideological course. The new reign that began with the tragic events of December 14, 1825, demanded other people and other programs.

CHAPTER 10

The Cherished Triad:

S. S. Uvarov's Memorandum of 1832 and the Development of the Doctrine "Orthodoxy—Autocracy—Nationality"

∞ 1 ∞

A new phase of ideological production began in the early 1830s, which was a turning point in the Russian Empire's foreign and domestic policies. The Peace of Adrianople with Turkey in 1829 had put an end, at least for a time, to Russian striving for dominance over the Orthodox East and the unification of the peoples of this faith under its aegis. The new Emperor Nikolai Pavlovich (henceforth referred to as Nicholas I) fully shared his elder brother's skepticism toward the grandiose notions of their grandmother (see, e.g., Lincoln 1989, 118). However, educated Russian society still cherished the dream of Russia's historical destiny of restoring Greece and therefore had been disillusioned by the lack of mention of Greece and the Orthodox faith in the imperial manifesto that had declared war (see, e.g., Benkendorf 1929, 157–158; cf. Fadeev 1958; Prousis 1994). Now, if the Slavic question remained on the agenda, it had been shifted from the realm of real politics into that of hypothetical schemes, while the Greek question was taken off of the table completely. This was even more the case after the assassination in 1831 of Ioannis Capodistria, the first president of Greece and former Russian state secretary for foreign affairs (see Woodhouse 1973).

Having rejected expansionist plans in the East, the Russian autocracy also adopted a more cautious policy in the West. This path was more likely intended to curtail the influx of foreign influences into Russia than to aggressively pursue its own agenda beyond Russia's borders. When he received word of the revolutions in France and Belgium in 1830, Nicholas I considered the possibility of military intervention in Europe, but the Polish uprising forced him to completely reject such an idea and to preserve the status quo (Shil'der 1903 II, 284–320).

Thus the section of the Holy Alliance's legacy that was based on collective armed defense of existing monarchial regimes was ideologically repudiated, at least until 1848. The moderate isolationism that came to the fore in Nicholas I's foreign policy, however, was by no means connected to a focus on long-awaited internal reforms. On the contrary, under the impact of the same complex of historical events—the July Revolution in France, the Polish revolt, the cholera riots of the summer of 1831—the emperor discarded the reformist plans of the first five years of his reign, in which he had "revived" Russia "with war, hopes, and labors." Even the highly modest recommendations of the "December 6 Commission," which were the culmination of these efforts, were as it turned out essentially shelved (see Kizivetter 1912, 410–502; Lincoln 1989, 92–98).

The rejection of reforms did not mean that the emperor no longer believed in their necessity. In the early 1830s Nicholaevan politics took on its classical form, whose essence the autocrat expressed aphoristically in 1842; while putting the brakes on yet another project for gradual reform, he declared, "There is no doubt that serfdom in its present situation is an evil, the most palpable and obvious to everyone, but to touch on it *now* would be an even more ruinous matter" (Mironenko 1990, 187). This formula is endlessly fruitful and may be applied to many sides of Russian state life: an obvious political evil may not be corrected out of the fear of shaking the very foundations of the existing power. Nicholas I preferred to trust the recommendations of his elder brother the Tsesarevich Konstantin Pavlovich, who wrote to him that "old age (drevnost') is the most reliable protection for government regulations," advising him to leave reform "to the judgment of time" (SbRIO XC, 77).

In implementing this strategic turn in politics, the emperor undoubtedly felt the need for a system of gradual and organic development that, at the same time, occurs under government control. Necessary changes were postponed to

Figure 29 Portrait of S. S. Uvarov. Lithograph by M. Mukhin.

some vague future, but their reliability and solidity would be guaranteed by the very course of events. Thus the responsibility for them was transferred from the authorities to the movement of history; the purely conservative functions of maintaining the state's stability and preserving the fundamental bases of the political order were left to the government.

S. S. Uvarov, who was appointed deputy minister of popular education in early 1832, was able to present the emperor with an outline for this kind of system. His triad of "Orthodoxy—Autocracy—Nationality," which A. N. Pypin aptly labeled the "theory of official nationalism" (Pypin I, 380), was fated to be empire's state ideology for many decades (on Uvarov and his political philosophy, see Davydov 1856; Schmid 1888; Pypin I; Shpet 1989; Koyré 1929; Durylin 1932; Riazanovskii 1967; Whittaker 1999; Gordin 1989; Kazakov 1989; Tsimbaev 1989; Isambaeva 1990; Shevchenko 1991; Kachalov 1992; Egorov 1996; Shevchenko 1997). The unusually large historical significance of this ideological system lies in characteristic contradiction to the extremely limited circle of sources on whose basis one may try to reconstruct its initial form. Uvarov did not leave any kind of developed exposition of his own political philosophy. The preamble to the first issue of the *Journal of the Ministry of Popular Education*; a circular published on his appointment to the post of minister; several paragraphs from reports on his inspection of Moscow University and documents concerning the activities of the Ministry of Popular Education during his decade-long work there; and two or three oral comments recorded in the diaries of M. P. Pogodin and A. V. Nikoitenko—until very recently this has exhausted the entire corpus of sources (Uvarov 1875; Uvarov, "Ot redaktsii" 1834; Uvarov, "Tsirkuliarnoe" 1834; Uvarov 1864, 2–4; Nikitenko I, 174; Barsukov IX, 235–237).[1]

This kind of practice is quite usual. Having armed itself with an ideological doctrine, the state authorities do not usually put much energy into clarifying its content, preferring a multitude of tautological restatements over interpretation. Thus the institutions of power leave themselves sufficient room for maneuvering when it comes to deciding whether or not any particular manifestation of social life fits its parameters. Furthermore, and in contrast to their opponents, the authorities often make it seem that they do not require particular theoretical explication of their principles insofar as they have the possibility of realizing them in practice, at least ideally. Consequently, and in reference to "Orthodoxy—Autocracy—Nationality," the document that would offer the best explanation would be one that had preceded its imperial approbation; that

---

1   In the single existing monograph on the theory of official nationalism there is little on Uvarov in distinction from the more prolific Pogodin and Shevyrev (see Riazanovskii 1967), and the single biography of Uvarov says relatively little about his intellectual legacy, but much about his practical activities as minister and his contribution to Russia's educational system (see Whittaker 1999). Even in an article especially dedicated to Uvarov's ideology (Whittaker 1978) the analysis is based primarily on his "liberal" period, most fully expressed in his 1818 speech at Petersburg Pedagogical University (on this see also Pugachev 1964; Isambaeva 1990).

is, in which its author would have been compelled to defend and explain his views. Hence a valuable addition to the known corpus of sources is the report Uvarov gave to Nicholas I, "On Some General Principles that Can Serve as Guide in Administering the Ministry of Popular Enlightenment" that was published by M. M. Shevchenko (see Uvarov 1995). Together with the familiar formulations that were later repeated in the corresponding reports and circulars, it contains a whole series of propositions that let us connect the triad to the time and conditions of their creation. However, this document—as is revealed by Uvarov's note on the copyist's text discovered by Shevchenko—was presented to the emperor on November 19, 1833 (ibid., 70). This was eight months after the start of Uvarov's term as minister, and almost eleven months before the earliest known references to the triad, to be found in a report on his inspection of Moscow University written in December 1832 (Uvarov 1875, 511). Here Uvarov was undoubtedly presenting ideas to the emperor that he had already approved. Shevchenko reported that he was not able to find a signature on this report, and one might have concluded that such a document did not exist. Uvarov wrote most of his works in French, and they were later translated and edited by his assistants; indeed we found a rough draft of Uvarov's letter, in French, in the same archival fond as the document that Shevchenko located (OPI GIM, f. 17, op. 1, № 98, 16–22 ob.). It is a little more protracted and significantly less official than the final version, and differs from it in various important details. Moreover, the draft was written in March 1832, more than a year and a half before the final report was presented to the emperor. We published this document in 1997 (see Uvarov 1997; it will be cited from here on without further references). On its basis we will attempt to reconstruct Uvarov's project for Russia.

This is the earliest known mention of the triad. Uvarov had just received the position of assistant minister and the assignment to inspect Moscow University. Considering the advanced age and weak health of the minister, Count K. A. Liven, this assignment indicated the emperor's intention to give the ministerial chair to Uvarov if he successfully carried out his mission (see Rozhdestvenskii 1902, 170–223). The newly-appointed assistant minister sent the emperor a memorandum in which he described his "most vital need to open [his] heart" to the monarch, "to throw [himself] to His feet [with] a confession faith" and to lay out his guiding principles. These words were not merely dutiful formulas or ritual flattery, to which Uvarov was more than inclined. A professional careerist and experienced administrator, he was nonetheless inspired by an exceptionally ambitious project to gradually change the citizens of the empire via the institutions of the Ministry of Popular Enlightenment and thus to mold Russia's future. "Either the Ministry of Popular Enlightenment represents nothing or it represents the soul of the administrative corps," he wrote to Nicholas I, clearly unconcerned that his explicit claim to be ideological leader for the entire government apparatus might upset his addressee.[2] Uvarov achieved his goal: the emperor handed him a mandate to carry out his designs.

The fate of the triad was not the only thing that testified to this approval. After a year and a half in the report "On Some General Principles," and ten years later in the report "A Decade of the Ministry of Popular Enlightenment," Uvarov repeated almost word for word several fragments from the letter, including its most important ones. The sentiments expressed in the letter became official doctrine. Uvarov had correctly understood the emperor's cherished aspirations and subtly grasped the current needs of government politics. In Uvarov's opinion, Russia could count on recovery since the religious, political and moral ideals that the supreme power wanted to spread still retained palpable force. Nevertheless, decisive and well-considered actions by the government were required because these ideals had been "dissipated by premature and superficial civilization, fantasy systems, and reckless undertakings; they are disconnected, not unified into a whole, without a center, and, moreover, over the course of thirty years have had to withstand the assault of people and events."

Uvarov's chronology is remarkable. The reference to thirty years unambiguously described the first years of Alexander's reign, which was thus being rejected from start to finish, with all of its hopes, disillusionments, victories, failures, and efforts at change, and in which Uvarov himself had actively participated. To characterize the political style of Alexander and his close associates, Uvarov conceived the formula "administrative Saint-Simonism," which is worthy of adoption by history textbooks. Uvarov's definition does not so much indicate the visionary scope of the innovations of the Alexandrine era as it does

---

2   N. I. Kazakov's assertions that Uvarov's triad was exclusively intended for departmental use in the Ministry of Popular Enlightenment (Kazakov 1989), challenged by V. A. Mil'china and A. L. Ospovat (1995, 21), thus seem baseless.

their utopian fervor, as well as their armchair activism, based on the conviction that any problem may be solved with the help of abstract schemes, paper projects, and bureaucratic measures.[3] In this sense Arakcheev's military colonies truly differed little from Saint-Simon's phalansteries. By connecting the discredited administrative style with the name of the celebrated utopian thinker, among the last heirs to eighteenth-century theoretical rationalism, Uvarov signaled that he himself intended to follow a totally different intellectual path.

∞ **2** ∞

In the memorandum only one name is mentioned, and its choice and the very way it is cited deserve thoughtful consideration. Discussing the worldwide consequences of the July Revolution in Paris, Uvarov exclaimed, "Did not one of the authors of the July Revolution, Mr. Guizot, a man of conscience and talent, not recently proclaim from the tribune: 'Society no longer has any political, moral or religious convictions'? This wail of despair, involuntarily bursting from all well-intentioned people of Europe, whatever views they may hold, serves as the single creed (simvol very) that still unites them in today's conditions."

Uvarov wrote his letter in March, and thus was responding to the latest events in Paris. On February 18, 1832, the French Chamber of Deputies was discussing the question of state subsidies for Catholic seminaries. The radical deputy Odilon Barrot, who demanded that such subsidies be sharply curtailed, accused the parliamentary majority—which was by no means disposed in favor of the Catholics, but which had opposed the demand for cuts for political considerations—of having no firm principles. François Guizpot's speech in response, according to the Parisian newspaper "Journal des debats," had imparted "greatness and sublimity" to parliamentary discussions "which it so often lacks" (Journal des debats, 1832, February 17). Guizot declared:

> Recall, gentlemen, what our worthy colleague Odilon Barrot recently said— he complained bitterly about our lack of firm principles, and said, as far as I remember, that for many minds there is already no longer any good or evil,

---

3   Oleg Proskurin has observed in conversation with the author that the combination of utopianism and castles in the air, together with a high degree of bureaucratic efficiency, was the characteristic feature of the bureaucrat of the Alexandrine era. The model here is Speranskii. Uvarov himself also belonged to this type of government functionary.

neither truth or falsehood, that people move about without knowing themselves what feeling is guiding them.

Mr. Odilon Barrot is correct, and I consider this evil as serious as he, but I think that he did not explain this in full. The issue is not merely that our political and moral convictions are unstable and impermanent but also that they contradict convictions that are far more definite, ... be they shut off in a narrow circle and belonging to a small number of people, but on the other hand more passionate, and, I do not fear to say, more fanatical, than those which we profess. ... We are forced to deal both with revolutionary ideas that are still trying to devour society as well as with old counter-revolutionary beliefs that are by no means as weak as we might think at times, but still full of energy and danger. What can we with our moderate views, I ask you, oppose to these two hostile parties whose convictions are filled with fanaticism and therefore unworthy of our trust?

Love for order, which in our day in France truly makes up a universal desire, and the well-known moral instinct for decency and justice. These are our two single strengths, two single beliefs: with love for order and the instinct of a decent person we enter into battle with the dual fanaticisms, revolutionary and counter-revolutionary. (Guizot I, 386–387)

Uvarov interpreted Guizot's speech quite freely, as it by no means represents "a wail of despair." The French orator's partial agreement with the accusations of a lack of firm principles was merely a rhetorical move to contrast the instinctively correct moral feeling of the majority with the infatuated adherence of both left and right doctrinaires to their wild theories. Uvarov, however, was attracted by Guizot's apologia for the golden mean and used his polemical concession to construct his own political model. "There is a huge distance between the old prejudices which do not recognize anything that did not exist at least a half a century ago and the new ones, who ruthlessly destroy everything that they come to replace, furiously attacking the remnants of the past. [But] there is also firm soil, a reliable support, a basis which cannot let you down," he wrote to the emperor in the memorandum. In Europe, according to Uvarov, "well-intentioned" people occupy a similarly reasonable position, but shocked by the dramatic course of historical events and having lost their orientation, their "creed" inevitably became "a wail of despair."

We have no information about what the imperial addressee of Uvarov's letter thought of Guizot's speech. On the one hand, the emperor, enraged and frightened by the July Revolution, would not have sympathized with one of its leaders, but on the other, Guizot had done much to keep popular discontent within legal limits. Especially important for Russia, he categorically opposed French interference in the Polish crisis, which the Parisian radicals insisted on (ibid., 330–336). Furthermore, we don't know if the mention of Guizot was preserved in the final text, which might have diverged from the draft. In any case, in ascribing despair over the events taking place in his country to one of the French political leaders, Uvarov made Guizot and his ideas politically palatable for his correspondent. This kind of rhetorical device strongly recalls the condescending intonation of Soviet propaganda in relation to progressive figures of the West. As the narrative goes, these were people of "conscience and talent," who while incapable of true understanding of historical dialectics were nevertheless able to attack the evils of the capitalist system sincerely and profoundly. To use a later expression, it was important for Uvarov "to push Guizot through" (that is, through the censorship) in order to endorse his conception of French civilization.

Uvarov, who always followed the cultural and political life of Paris with great interest, must have already been long familiar with Guizot's career, which revealed unexpected parallels with his own. In 1811, when Uvarov had begun his service in the Ministry of Popular Enlightenment, Guizot had founded the journal "Annals of Education," in which he laid out his views on creating a national educational system. In 1816 he had published a treatise, co-authored with P.-P. Royer-Collard, who later became an important figure in post-July France, in which they spoke of the duty of the state to take charge of education and to realize national principles through educational institutions (see Johnson 1963, 110–113). This idea Uvarov promoted strongly. By strange coincidence, in one year, 1821, both Guizot and Uvarov had been removed from educational activity due to their excessive liberalism. Guizot's return to a university professorship in 1828 had been a personal and political triumph. At about that time he delivered his lectures on the history of European civilization and especially in France, to great success. These two courses were published in 1828 and 1829 as separate volumes and, together with much else, contained a general theory of civilization that at the time represented the last word in European historical science.

Following Guizot's example, Uvarov founded the *Journal of the Ministry of Popular Enlightenment*, in 1834. This publication became the transmitter of the new official policy. Its very first issue featured the introductory lecture from *The History of Civilization in Europe* in which the basic theoretical ideas for both courses were laid out. According to Guizot, it was the development and perfection of civilization that was the key to mankind's progress, because civilization was handed down from generation to generation and thus constituted "the destiny of the human race" (Guizot 1834, 432). Civilization of this or that people combines in itself "the development of social activity and the development of private activity" (ibid., 441); on the one hand, "its establishments, trade, industry, wars, all of the particulars of government," and on the other, "religion ... the sciences, literature, the arts" (ibid., 432–433). Its presence is revealed "everywhere where the external position of a person is extended, enlivened, improved, everywhere that the inner nature of a person reveals its splendor and greatness" (ibid., 41). At the same time, while belonging to one people, civilization is also the property of all humanity. For Guizot the existence of one single European civilization is obvious, and he tried to embrace it in one general conception; it goes without saying that, from his perspective, France had the uncontested leading role in this civilization.

In the Russian translation that appeared in the *Journal of the Ministry of Popular Enlightenment*, Guizot's key concept of "civilization" is translated as "civic education" (grazhdanskoe obrazovanie). The publication itself bore the title "The First Lecture of Mr. Guizot from the Course of Lectures He Read On the History of European Civic Education." The issue here was not finding a Russian equivalent. The word "tsivilizatsiia" (civilization) was fairly common at the time and even frequently occurs in the text. At times the translator resorted to using both terms, e.g., "From ancient times and in many countries they use the word *civilization, civil education*" (ibid., 434; the original has only "civilisation"). In one place, an incorrectly chosen pronoun, it seems, indicates incomplete editing: "the existence of European civilization is obvious; a kind of unity is clearly revealed in the civil education of various states of Europe; it [sic][4] follows from almost identical facts" (ibid., 428).

The journal's editors evidently divided the main category of Guizot's historiosophy into two parts, relatively speaking, into "bad" civilization and

---

4 The feminine pronoun that would grammatically refer back to "tsivilizatsiia" is evidently in error, as the expected referent, "unity," is neuter.

"good" civil education.[5] In his memorandum Uvarov sharply delineated what he understood by the word "civilization." He emphasized that the events of 1830 "had done away with" the idea of social progress that inspired the French historian and had taken unaware "those who believed in the future of peoples most strongly of all" and caused them to doubt "if that which they call civilization is really the path to social good." The rhetoric suggested that even the author of the concept of European civilization should at least to some extent reassess his former views.

The terminological operation performed on Guizot's first lecture turned out to be uncommonly productive. The word "civilization" took on the meaning of social experience that was unacceptable for Russia. "We are forced to use the name *Europe* for something that should never have had any other name than its own: Civilization," is the way F. I. Tituchev (II, 57) later formulated this position. The authorities used this to their advantage, categorizing this term as falling in the sphere of "civil education."

It is very likely that Uvarov personally edited the translation. Publication of the *Journal of the Ministry of Popular Enlightenment* was the most important element of the new minister's plan for spreading his doctrine. As Uvarov instructed his readers in the forward to the first issue, "The Ministry considers its primary and holy duty to give ... a useful direction for readers of our Journal and to satisfy the just desire of true sons of the Fatherland to know how they can better facilitate the lofty objectives of the Father of Russia" (Uvarov 1834, VII). The coincidence of mentioning Guizot in the letter to the emperor and the appearance of his lecture in the first issue of his journal was hardly accidental. Two notes to the lecture demonstrate that Uvarov took part in preparing

---

5   In a letter to the author of January 6, 1998, Z. Bauman wrote: "[I have] one note concerning the dual Russian translation of "civilization." It follows from your research that Uvarov drank his fill of German milk and even looked at the Germans through French eyes. Before he happened to read Guizot, the image of the process Guizot was writing about had already formed in his mind as Bildung, and this concept is best translated into Russian as *obrazovanie* (education). By the way, in Guizot's time 'civilization' was similar in spirit to 'education.' This concept (like the concept of culture) was born in the late eighteenth century to describe not a condition but an activity, task, creation, reworking, formation. It was only after many years that civilization, like culture, was considered something finished (something like 'developed socialism') and they forgot the initial idea of the concept. Hence in explaining what the matter was about, Uvarov (or the translator), it seems, was correct." Cf. Fevr 1991, 270–281.

this publication. In both cases the commentator's dissatisfaction is caused by similar passages. Guizot's statement that traces of French civilization "are visible in all of the monuments of European literature" was accompanied by the important proviso: "Everywhere the action of this influence is decreasing. Now every people is creating its own literature just as the civil education of every people must be achieved to meet its own requirements" (Guizot 1834, 440). An even more irritated response was provoked by Guizot's assertion that "there is practically no great idea and no great principle of civil education that France has not spread everywhere." In the editors' opinion, most likely directly Uvarov's,

> the author has been carried away by the one-sidedness characteristic of French writers. This will continue until that time when France ceases to regard itself as the focus of global enlightenment. But was it so long ago that France itself became familiar with the country nearest to it, Germany, and was she in a condition to make use of the fruits of its all-encompassing learning? After this it is unforgivable for us Russians to take the opinions of French writers as the single standard. We have before our eyes all of the countries of Europe, including our very own Fatherland that is so little known by foreigners, but nevertheless acquiring more and more influence on their fate. The civil education of the Slavic peoples was not part of Mr. Guizot's plan at all. ... For a true, complete picture, of course, we will have to wait for a long time for a skilled artist who must necessarily know all of Europe. (Ibid., 430)

The reference to France's acquaintance with Germany's "all-encompassing learning" refers to Madame de Staël's *On Germany* that came out in 1811. The goal of this book had been to acquaint what, in the author's opinion, was egocentric French culture with the treasures of the German soul. Uvarov had known Madame de Staël in Vienna in 1807–1809 at the time she was beginning to work on her book (see Durylin 1939). But the most important aspect of these two notes lies elsewhere. Guizot's Francocentric view of European civilization is contrasted here to the notion of Europe as the amalgamation of national cultural worlds. Russia and the Slavic peoples as a whole only appear in this argument after Germany. Putting his main emphasis on Russian nationality, Uvarov unavoidably had to turn to those thinkers who were first to consciously challenge France's cultural hegemony.

∽ **3**⁶ ∽

The connection of Uvarov's triad with the political theory of German Romanticism was first explored more than seventy years ago by Gustav Shpet who, very generally and in many ways by guesswork, indicated the dependence of Uvarov's ideas on the Romantics, and in particular on the "state doctrine" of the German historian Heinrich Luden (Shpet 1989, 245–246; cf. Luden 1811). And indeed, in the very broad circle of sources for Uvarov's doctrine, which encompasses a wide spectrum of European anti-revolutionary philosophy from Joseph de Maistre to Burke and Karamzin, the political doctrine of German Romantics plays a leading role.

Uvarov's main source was evidently the books and lectures of Friedrich Schlegel. Uvarov lived in Vienna from 1807 to mid-1809, at the same time as Schlegel. He became acquainted with his brother, August Schlegel, who accompanied Madame de Staël and was her consultant in writing *On Germany*. Fifteen years later, in 1823, August wrote to Uvarov, who had by that time become president of the Imperial Academy of Sciences: "Your Excellency once deigned to encourage my scholarly efforts with the attention with which you favored me with in Vienna, when I had the honor of being acquainted with you" (OPI GIM, f. 17, op. 1, № 86, 293). In his Vienna diary, large portions of which were published by S. N. Durylin, Uvarov wrote, "I have heard that Madame de Staël has earnestly extolled Mr. F. Schlegel's intellect, but I do not know him well enough to be convinced of the justice of this praise. The exterior of a German writer is so hard to penetrate that one must be very convinced of the benefits to try and pierce it" (Durylin 1939, 236).

The guarded nature of this comment does not contradict the intense interest with which Uvarov followed the work of the German thinker. It was precisely in 1808 that Schlegel's book *On the Language and Wisdom of the Indians* came out; in it the author demonstrated that Indian history, mythology, language, and literature not only lay at the basis of all European culture, but also infinitely surpassed all of Europe's achievements in its inner perfection (see Schlegel 1808; cf. Schwab 1950; Wilson 1964). Uvarov sent a copy of this book to Karamzin in Petersburg and recommended it to Zhukovskii (see Gillel'son

---

6   For a more detailed discussion of the ideas in this section, see Zorin 1996.

1969, 51). More importantly, he himself was deeply taken by the idea of developing Eastern studies, which from the start took on a distinct political coloration. One year after returning to Petersburg, he proposed "A Project for an Asian Academy," which served as the basis of his career in scholarship. Extensively citing Schlegel's work, Uvarov planned to turn the Russian capital into an international center of Oriental studies. In the project he not only based his ideas on the geographical position and political interests of Russia, but also on the necessity of returning modern civilization to its genuine roots (see, e.g., Riazanovskii 1960; Whittaker 1978).

Nine years later Uvarov wrote to Speranskii, "The establishment and spread of *Eastern languages* should also help spread healthy ideas about Asia in its relationship to Russia. Here ... is a new source of national politics that should save us from premature decrepitude and from European contagion" (Uvarov 1896, 158). Friedrich Schlegel was among the European luminaries who received the projects' plans, and he responded sympathetically. He answered Uvarov in April 1811, "The plan fully accords to the greatness of the capital of the Russian Empire as well as to the many supplementary means that you have at your disposal. If such an undertaking actually comes into being, it would allow us to hope for the embodiment of everything that for the time being is impossible to realize in any of the remaining capitals on the European continent" (OPI GIM, f. 17, op. 1, № 86, 298–299 verso). He clearly fully approved of the project's political direction.

Schlegel promised Uvarov to help propagate his idea in Austria and Germany. Soon Schlegel sent Uvarov his "Course of Lectures on Most Recent History," delivered in Vienna in 1810 and published a year later. "Of course, in these lectures I mostly oriented myself towards my German audience. But I hope that this work will not be totally devoid of general interest for all enlightened peoples. I would be very happy if this attempt attracted the attention of such an enlightened expert of the sciences and history [as you are]," he wrote in an accompanying letter (ibid., 300). Here the German philosopher's political philosophy was developed on the basis of extremely wide-ranging historical material. Uvarov also sent this book to Karamzin, presuming that the work of his German colleague would be useful for the historiographer, who was laboring at the time on his *History of the Russian State*. Karamzin was skeptical towards Schlegel's work, however, seeing in his nationalistic imaginings a pursuit "of the phantom of new ideas" and "historical mysticism" (Gillel'son 1969, 52).

Uvarov, like Karamzin, was an educated conservative and at this time belonged to the same wing of Russian social thought. The enthusiasm that Schlegel's "historical mysticism" inspired in him reflected an important generational break in the development of Russian conservatism. This break had incalculable influence on the formation of national consciousness, and, in the future, on the entire spirit of official Russian imperial ideology. As often happens, chance biographical factors here turned out to be inseparable from deep historical processes. The time in which Uvarov and Schlegel came together was a very unique period in Austrian history. The atmosphere of these months was greatly determined by the expectation of a military clash with Napoleon. The anti-Napoleonic coalition that had come together in Vienna at that time bizarrely united almost totally opposing forces: remnants of the French ancient régime, the aristocratic emigration, and young German nationalists. Uvarov himself later wrote about the fact that "this crusade united all of the independent salons and all of the peoples that were not drawn into the orbit of the great captain," and that these allies were not welded together "by any common creed apart from [the desire of] bringing down the imperial tyranny [of Napoleon]" (Uvarov 1848, 96–97).

Due to his philosophical system, Schlegel was the natural leader of this strange alliance. He had been invited to Vienna by I.-F. Stadion, the head of the hawks at the Austrian court, to give a course of public lectures on history that was meant to help cultivate national self-consciousness on the part of the German public. These public lectures, which were the basis for the book he sent to Uvarov, did not take place in Vienna in 1809 due to the war; instead, they were delivered the year after the defeat. With the start of military action Schlegel received the position of court secretary and was attached to army headquarters. There, he published the newspaper "Österreichische Zeitung" and published proclamations in which he tried to convince the Germans that Austria was waging war on their behalf and that only thanks to Austria would Germany obtain independence and freedom (Langsam 1936, 40–64).

At the heart of Schlegel's political views of these years lay the conception of the nation as an integral personality, a unity based on blood relations and secured by common customs and language. In his *Philosophical Lectures of*

1804–1806, which presented the fullest and most detailed exposition of his system, he says:

> The notion of the nation presumes that all of its members compose a single personality. For this to be possible, they must all have the same origin. The older, purer and less mixed with other races, the more a nation will have common customs. And the more of these common customs and the more attachment to them it manifests, the greater the degree to which a nation will be formed from this race. In this connection language has supreme importance because it serves as unconditional proof of common origins and binds the nation with the most vital and natural links. Together with the commonality of customs, language is the strongest and most reliable guarantee that the nation will live for many centuries in indissoluble unity. (Schlegel II, 357–358)

Schlegel divided the ethnos ("race") into a natural community and a "nation" that arises on the basis of an ethnos as a political formation. This collective personality should also develop into a state. Schlegel's ideal of a national state was the medieval limited monarchy in which the unity of the national organism was guaranteed by its division into corporations. In the philosopher's opinion, the national rebirth and unification of Germany should occur around Austria, which had best preserved medieval state institutions: the ancient aristocracy, the dynasty of Hapsburgs, and the Catholic Church. In 1803, at the dawn of his interest in national ideas, he complained in his *Journey to France* that the world capital of Catholicism was located in Italy and not in Germany. Now he was ready to reconcile himself to this insofar as he saw the Hapsburgs as the natural leaders of the Catholic world (ibid.; cf. Meineke 1970). These ideas obviously depend on Herder's philosophy, on the one hand, and on Rousseau and the ideologists of the French Revolution, on the other. In distinction from Herder, Schlegel shifts the emphasis in the concept of the "nation" from cultural and religious factors to political ones. On the contrary, Schlegel also parted company from the French in that he saw the nation not as participants in a social contract, but as the product of organic development. Accordingly, he understood the state in natural-historical terms as the spontaneous expression of a people's history.

At this period Schlegel's interpretation of the national state was quite unusual. In the Europe of the early nineteenth century, this idea was primarily associated with liberal thought and served as a fighting slogan for destroying or reforming the dynastic limited monarchial regimes that predominated. Understanding the nation as the basis for the state system helped with the demand to end class distinctions, the formation of popular representative institutions, and so on. One of the most noted reformers of the time, the Prussian statesman H.-F. Stein, wrote at the end of 1812, "At this moment of great changes I do not care at all about any dynasty. My desire is that Germany become great and strong, and acquire its freedom, independence, and nationality (Nationalität)" (Stein III, 818).

This was also the time when Stein, with the help of the Russian court, was trying to unify all forces in Germany in order to promote a spirit of nationalism and anti-French attitudes among Germans. Uvarov also played a certain role in these plans. From his time in Vienna he had preserved profound support for a German national revival; Stein even found it necessary to give him lessons in Russian patriotism. In September 1812, almost immediately after the Battle of Borodino, Stein wrote with some surprise to his wife in Vienna from Petersburg, "Uvarov just returned to the city from his village near Moscow. As always, he is amicable, obliging, helpful, and very much sympathizes with Germany, but he doesn't like it here and I try to reconcile him with his motherland insofar

Figure 30 Portrait of Karl Freiherr vom Stein. Sketch by S. S. Uvarov.

as, for the time being, he has to remain here and live among his countrymen, and insofar as he can be of use to his motherland with his knowledge and his most highly creditable way of thinking" (ibid., 751).

These sentiments were not a momentary flirtation for Uvarov. In practically all of his letters to Stein from 1812–1814, one can trace his profound worry over Germany's future and his hope that "the precious flower of nationality (Nationalität) and freedom must rise up from within itself" (OPI GIM, f. 17, op. 1, № 86, prilozh. 1). At the end of 1813, after the Battle of Leipzig, Uvarov criticized the policy of the Austrian court and at the same time wrote to Stein, "The spectacle of Prussia may serve to console us for everything. This people should become the first in Europe. It is a complete and universal renaissance. I am convinced that it will produce results that are great in all respects. One can't praise a people enough that awakens in this way" (ibid.). Against this background, Uvarov's pessimism about contemporary Russian reality is especially striking:

> I will not hide from you that a trip abroad is my greatest wish, which I have cherished for a long period of time. Everything makes me prize this idea, not only those real torments connected with the work I am now occupied with; I find this work itself more and more *thankless* or, more accurately, more and more *hopeless*. ... This is demeaning and almost useless labor. When I think about all of the failures in my life, the idea occurs to me that I will never put down roots here and will always remain an *exotic* plant; against my will I come to the thought that I should have been born your *fellow countryman*, or perhaps Your *son*—but this is a dream, I renounce it and want to renounce it. (Ibid., 12 verso, 18 verso)[7]

Quite an unusual psychological picture arises before us: a young Russian nobleman and bureaucrat of very high rank, a man of letters who speaks, thinks, and writes primarily in French, who, at the same time, considers himself a German nationalist. In Vienna Uvarov came into contact with the most popular and forward-looking ideology of his day and was completely captivated by it. Furthermore, having obtained it from German sources, he considers the only suitable place for its embodiment to be Germany for the foreseeable future. As

---

7   Two of the surviving eight letters from Uvarov to Stein have been partially published in: Peretts III, 692, 697; Uvarov 1871a.

appropriate for someone of his circle and upbringing, he was likely convinced that Russia was not ready for it, and even the "grand spectacle that the Russian nation demonstrated to the world and to posterity"—as Schlegel wrote to him in January, 1813, (OPI GIM, f. 17, op. 1, № 86, 301 verso)—could not persuade him otherwise. The combination of aristocratic and national spirit that Uvarov had assimilated from Schlegel made Germany seem far more natural a field for his ideas than his own native land.

Yet as an outsider to German nationalistic issues, Uvarov perceived quite dissimilar and in some cases even opposing phenomena as compatible. For him, ideas of "freedom of the press and trade, enlightenment in its true sense, a tolerant spirit of rule, the elimination of obsolete forms" as well as "hatred for despotism and a broadminded (liberal'nyi) taste for the Beautiful and True," about which Uvarov wrote Stein (ibid., prilozh. 17 verso), easily got along with Schlegel's imperial conception. He was so blind to the differences between the political programs, or, more broadly speaking, between the nationalisms of Schlegel and Stein, that he confidently recommended Schlegel to Stein as the leading organizer of the anti-Napoleonic front of German intellectuals who could "be of great service" organizing education in Prussia (ibid., prilozh. 2). Despite Uvarov's expectation that Stein would like his plan, Stein was by no means enthralled by the proposal, and, it seems, did not even consider it necessary to respond.

Still, Schlegel and Stein's political projects did have one common feature at this stage—neither led to any appreciable results. The campaign of 1809, in which Schlegel was the main ideologist, ended in failure. It was not able to convince public opinion in the German principalities that the Austrian Empire stood for pan-German interests, and no one followed Schlegel and Stadion except the rebellious Colonel Schiel. Neither did Stein's intention to create a federation of German states under Prussia's patronage come to pass after the Napoleonic wars. The allied rulers rejected the national principle of state building, casting its lot in favor of legitimism. Metternich, who took the reins of Austrian politics into his hands, and who had tremendous influence on European life, sharply rejected nationalist ideas, seeing them as a threat to the principles on which any empire was built. That Stein's reforms provided the basis for Prussia's rapid development as well as, ultimately, the nucleus for Germany's unification, was something that, naturally, Uvarov could not have foreseen.

The further course of European history, the rebellions and other shocks of the late 1810s and 20s, and the interventions of the Holy Alliance all testified that the principles of legitimacy and nationalism were coming into ever greater conflict. These historical cataclysms are what Uvarov has in mind when he characterizes events since his retirement from the Ministry of Popular Enlightenment in 1821 as being "of huge importance" but as having "utterly ruinous influence on the development of enlightenment in our Fatherland ... and even more so in all of the countries of Europe." The revolutions of 1830 decisively forced those loyal to the old order into a completely defensive position. In this situation such a committed supporter of historical compromise as Uvarov hardly had any other choice but to turn his gaze to Russia. In many respects Russia could seem an even more fitting place than Germany to realize a nationalist-imperial utopia. Indeed it had a unified state, and the center of the reigning religion was located within the empire, thus freeing a proponent of the idea of a national religion from the difficulties that Schlegel faced. True, the concept of nationality ("narodnost'") still required definition and development, but it was this very circumstance that could be remedied with the help of a well-regulated system of education.

∞ 4 ∞

"Our common duty consists in accomplishing the people's education in accord with the Supreme objective of the Most August Monarch, in the combined spirit of Orthodoxy, Autocracy, and Nationality," Uvarov wrote in a circular that was distributed to school districts (okrugi) on March 21, 1833, in connection with his appointment as minister of popular education (Uvarov, "Tsirkuliarnoe" 1834, il). Naturally, Orthodoxy headed the list. Thus in his memorandum to the emperor, Uvarov had begun his description of the triad with a discussion of its religious component:

> Without a people's religion, the people, like an individual person, are doomed to destruction; to deprive them of faith is to remove their heart, their blood, their insides; this means to put them on the lowest level of the physical and moral order, this means to betray them. Even national pride rebels against such an idea; a person who is devoted to the Fatherland will just as little agree with the loss of one tenet of the reigning church as he would to stealing one of the pearls from the crown of Monomakh.

This passage apparently seemed so successful to Uvarov that he included it almost without change in his report "On Some General Principles" (Uvarov 1995, 71) a year and a half later and again eleven years later in his review of the ministry's activities under his leadership (Uvarov 1864, 32). But even the strongest expressions that the author used could not hide his obvious confessional indifference. Despite the rhetorical emphasis, Uvarov intentionally does not mention the divine nature of Orthodoxy; Orthodoxy is significant for him not for its truth but for its tradition. His characteristic comparison to the crown of Monomakh clearly suggests his—perhaps only half-conscious—desire to legitimize the church through the symbolism of state power and national history.

An examination of the French original reveals an even more expressive picture. Orthodoxy is not mentioned *even once*. French offered at least three usual ways to refer to Russia's religion and church: "orthodoxie," "église grecque," and "chrétienneté orientale." Uvarov, however, consistently uses the formulas "religion nationale" and "église dominante." The phrase "religion nationale" is used in listing the elements of the triad itself. Where "Orthodoxy" figures in the triad in the Russian version of the report "On Some General Principles," the corresponding place in the French has "love for the Faith of our ancestors" (Uvarov 1995, 71). It seems clear that it is decidedly all the same to Uvarov what precise faith and which church is meant, as long as they are rooted in national history and the state's political structure. Uvarov's own personal religiosity also seems to have had certain provisions. M. D. Buturlin cited with indignation one of his French witticisms about the clergy that made the rounds of St. Petersburg: "That caste is just like a sheet of paper thrown on the ground—however much it is trampled one is unable to crush it" (Buturlin 1901, 411; Buturlin cites it in Russian). We may surmise that Uvarov assigned Orthodoxy a functional role as a religious principle, insofar as it was subordinated to the state principle of Autocracy. However, Autocracy is treated in the memorandum to a great extent in a similar way.

Back in 1814 in his brochure *Alexander and Bonaparte*, Uvarov had expressed the unfulfilled hope that on the ruins of Napoleon's empire, kings and nations would perform "a mutual sacrifice of autocracy and popular anarchy" (Uvarov 1814, 14). In an 1818 speech at the Petersburg Pedagogical Institute's gala meeting—which had no small public resonance—he sympathetically referred to Thomas Erskin, who called political freedom "God's ultimate and most beautiful gift" (Uvarov 1818, 41; cf. Pugachev 1967, 43–44). Of course, these hopes relate to the period of Uvarov's liberalism. The petulant N. I. Grech even wrote that for his speech in the Pedagogical Institute, Uvarov "would later have had himself imprisoned in the fortress" (Grech 1903, 365). But even in the 1830s, already under the new emperor, Uvarov's apologia for autocracy suggests a characteristic uncertainty:

> The strength of autocratic power represents the necessary condition for the existence of the Empire in its current form. Let political dreamers (I will not speak of sworn enemies of this order) who are off their heads due to false notions, who think up schemes about how things should be in the ideal, be shocked by appearances, enflamed by theories, animated by words; we can answer them that they do not know the country and are mistaken about its position, its needs, its desires. ... If it accepted the chimaera of limited monarchy, equal rights for all estates, national representation in the European manner, and a pseudo-constitutional form of rule, the colossus would not last two weeks, and what's more, it would collapse even before these false transformations would be completed. (cf. Uvarov 1995; Uvarov 1864, 33)

In this letter Uvarov did not simply address an absolute ruler. He wrote to a monarch who deeply believed in his divine anointment. But still Uvarov said not a word about the providential nature of Russian autocracy or about its absolute merits. Autocracy was merely "the necessary condition for the existence of the Empire," and what is more, "in its current form"—at least not excluding the suggestion that sometime in the future an autocratic monarch would no longer be needed in Russia. Imperial power is legitimized here not by divine sanction but by the "conditions," "needs" and "desires" of the country; that is, it represents primarily "Russian power," just as Orthodoxy is interpreted primarily as Russia's faith. Thus the two first members of the triad appear as kinds of attributes of national existence and national history, and thus are rooted in the third member—the notorious concept of "Nationality" (narodnost'—on the early history of the concept see Azadovskii I, 190–200; Lotman and Uspenskii 1996, 506–508, 555–556).[8]

---

8 Translator's Note: The precise meaning of the Russian the word "*narodnost*," from *narod*, people or nation, was hotly debated by Russian intellectuals during the nineteenth century, and this and the adjectival form *narodnyi* may be translated, depending on the context, as referring to "the people," "the folk," "the nation," or as "popular." There also are many places, however, where more than one of these meanings might be applicable.

If, according to Uvarov, autocracy was a "conservative principle," nationality presumes neither "*movement backward*" nor "*immobility*"; "the state organization must and should develop like the human body," and it is precisely this principle of nationality that guarantees the continuity of this development, at the same time allowing it to preserve the "main elements" that are inherent to the national personality. The responsibility for supporting and spreading this principle lies with the government and "in particular" on the system of popular education that it creates. Uvarov had already been casting about for such an evolutionary metaphor in his speech of 1818: "In this case the theory of government resembles the theory of education. That which can perpetuate physical or moral infancy is not worthy of praise; that government is most wise that can facilitate transitions from one age to another and, while submitting to the law of necessity, grows and matures together with the people or with the individual" (Uvarov 1818, 52). Now Uvarov tried to fill this scheme with concrete content. In the more or less distant future the development of Russian nationality would unavoidably have to create the necessary state institutions. Therefore the corresponding governing bodies—first and foremost, the ministry of popular enlightenment, under the watchful eye of its newly-appointed leader—had to establish control over the direction of this evolution. Uvarov fully understood the complexities connected with introducing such a contemporary and two-edged category as nationality as the basis for the empire's state ideology. As an observer of the national revolutions in Europe, he recognized that historically the principles of autocracy and nationalism could clash; however, he presumed that "whatever these quarrels (altercations) might be that had to be overcome, they lived a common life and could enter into alliance and conquer together." And in his memorandum he undertook to sketch out a strategy for this future victory in Russia.

5

In creating his tripartite formula, Uvarov could not help recalling F. Schlegel's well-known patriotic triad—common descent ("race"), customs, and language—as well as that of Shishkov—faith, education, and language. Both of these constructions had been created at about the same time, on the basis of the same Rousseauian—Herderian tradition, and in comparable circumstances; both Schlegel and Shishkov stood on the threshold of a decisive military clash of their peoples and empires with Napoleonic France and were trying to promote a nationalist version of traditional values. The disagreement between the two authors on the first plank of their triads was mostly due to specific political circumstances. A strong emphasis on faith was just as unacceptable in Germany, which was divided into Catholic and Protestant regions, as the demand for common descent would have been in the Russian Empire. From time to time nationalistically-oriented thinkers might dream of converting national and religious minorities to Orthodoxy, but they could not expect them to blend into one "race" with the Slavic majority. The second elements in both formulas were considerably closer to one another. "Customs" and "education" are closely related notions, especially if one agrees with Rousseau's conception of national upbringing that consists in cultivating folk traditions. Still, the difference between the German and Russian thinkers' approach is obvious. Shishkov, who was in many ways a man of the eighteenth century, believed in the limitless power of education and that it could transform individuals into members of the national body, or, on the contrary, cast them out. In contrast, the Romantic Schlegel trusted in the completely supra-personal and unconscious mechanism of tradition. However, the main difference between the two triads was in the subject being defined. While Schlegel was listing elements that ensured unity of the German nation, Shishkov was talking about the forces that could make inhabitants of his country feel themselves part of the state organism. Shishkov's mission was to indicate the natural sources of patriotic feeling. For this reason his speech in the "Colloquy," in which he laid out his understanding of the basic pillars of national existence, was entitled "Treatise on Love for the Fatherland."

Schlegel's understanding of the nation as the basis for an ideal empire was unacceptable for Shishkov not only because of national and confessional problems.[9] The category of nationality in its Romantic recension could not even be applied to the properly Great Russian part of the population. The social and cultural division that separated the highest and lowest estates in the first half of the nineteenth century was insuperable. To find any common customs, say, among the Russian nobility and peasantry, was truly impossible. The issue was no more encouraging as concerned language; suffice it to say that the very

---

9   On the policies that Uvarov proposed implementing that concerned non-Slavic and Orthodox ethnic and religious groups, see Uvarov 1864, 35–70; cf. Whittaker 1999, 215–240.

document that declared nationality the foundation of Russian statehood was written in French. As for ancestry, the great majority of ancient Russian aristocrats traced their genealogy back to Germanic, Lithuanian, and Tatar stock. There was nothing at all unusual in this; in traditional societies the elite often insisted on their foreign extraction in order to justify a way of life that differed from that of the rest of society. Thus in France, for example, the ideologist of noble privilege A. de Boulainville insisted on the German pedigree of the French aristocracy, so that his radical opponent from the third estate, the Abbé Sieyès, could propose that all aristocrats take themselves off to the Teutonic forests (Greenfeld 1992, 170–172).

Nevertheless, almost everywhere ideas of national unity were directed at breaking down the class divisions that threatened the national organism's integrity. In the final analysis, the issue had to do with transforming traditional

Figure 31 Monument to Ivan Susanin by V. I. Demut-Malinovskii (1838). Drawing by V. M. Vasnetsov.

imperial structures into institutions of the national state. It is precisely in this sense that nationality was understood in Decembrist and quasi-Decembrist circles in the later 1810s and early 1820s; the same applies to the Slavophiles in the 1830s-1850s, right up until the era of the Great Reforms (see Syroechkovskii 1954; Tsimbaev 1986; Egorov 1991). Uvarov advocated the same slogan in order to preserve the existing order of things indefinitely. This kind of change in mission demanded a profound rethinking of the very category of nationality, and in his memorandum such a reconsideration was realized with exceptional inventiveness and even a distinctive elegance. Unable to base his understanding of nationality on objective factors, Uvarov decisively shifts his focus onto subjective ones. His argumentation belongs completely to the sphere of historical emotions and national psychology. Russia "still retains religious convictions, political convictions, moral convictions in her breast [which constitute] the single pledge of her happiness, the remnants of her nationality, the precious and final guarantees of its political future." In the words of the author of the memorandum, "several years of special studies" (it is hard to say from the known facts of Uvarov's biography what exactly these were) allowed him to "assert that the three great linchpins of religion, autocracy, and nationality constitute the cherished legacy of our fatherland." Thus the basis for nationality turns out to be convictions. Simply put, a Russian is someone who believes in his church and his sovereign.

Having defined Orthodoxy and autocracy in terms of nationality, Uvarov now defines nationality in terms of Orthodoxy and autocracy. In formal logic this kind of maneuver is called a vicious circle, but ideology is built on qualitatively different laws, and this risky rhetorical pirouette turns out to be the weight-bearing element of the entire new official construction. This line of reasoning had serious long-term consequences for Russian state ideology. If only those Russians who profess "the national religion" may be members of the reigning church, then Old Believers and sectarians among the lower levels of society are excluded as well as converted Catholics, deists, and skeptics in the higher ones. In exactly the same way, if nationality necessarily presumes acceptance of autocracy, any constitutionalist or republican automatically forgoes the right to be a Russian. This approach is uncannily similar to the model of the "Soviet person" developed by the communist regime, as someone to whom a strictly prearranged set of views and convictions is ascribed. A "non-Soviet person" in this ideological system cannot be considered part of "the people" and is declared to be a "renegade" (otshchepenets). In the early nineteenth century the term used for this phenomenon was "izverg" (monster or outcast).

This parallel forces us to look again at Shishkov's conception of the people's body. Long before Uvarov, Shishkov had been interested not so much in the objective criteria of a nation's unity as in the ideological instruments capable of unifying that people in a general burst of enthusiasm that would transcend class and other barriers. To many contemporaries of Uvarov and Shishkov, as to subsequent researchers, it has seemed that their ideological constructions had a direct link. For example, D. N. Sverbeev (1871, 178), wrote that

> Shishkov did not define for himself the three main ideas of his whole life, even less put them into words, but he, nevertheless, so to speak unconsciously, was first to embody in himself the three-part Russian creed "Orthodoxy—Autocracy—Nationality," which then became both the program for Emperor Nicholas I' reign and Count Uvarov's motto, and, finally, the banner of the late Slavophiles.

However, beyond the external resemblance, the two ideological systems hide much more profound differences. Shishkov and his like-minded colleagues were promoting a program for national mobilization. Designed for a period of military action, it did not propose anything for peacetime except maintaining the regime of mobilization with all of its excesses indefinitely. The issue concerned the total isolation of Russia, a "wall" that had to be erected between piety and depravity and a struggle against hostile influences and all those who would give in to it and cease being part of the people's body. As noted, it was no accident that with the end of the war, both Shishkov and Rostopchin were removed from their posts.

In contrast, Uvarov was active not in the pre-war but in the post-war situation, and he needed to craft an ideological strategy for peaceful evolutionary development. At the same time, he by no means strove to unconditionally isolate Russia from the West. Uvarov scrutinized and reinterpreted Guizot's parliamentary speech so passionately and subjectively precisely because it would help him tackle his main task. The issue was to create an ideological system that would preserve the possibility of Russia belonging to European civilization, outside of which Uvarov neither conceived of himself nor of his work as minister of popular enlightenment. At the same time, such a system would protect the country from that civilization by means of an impermeable barrier. In Uvarov's formulation the dilemma consisted of "how to march in step with Europe and not move away from our own place,... what art we must master in order to take from enlightenment only what is necessary for a great empire and to firmly reject that which contains the seeds of disorder and shocks?" For many decades the Russian authorities would ask themselves how to appropriate the achievements of Western civilization and not the system of social values that had given rise to them.

Uvarov was also completely lacking in Shishkov's missionary zeal. He by no means desired a fundamental break with the upper classes' education and lifestyle, including the use of the French language that had so infuriated Shishkov. He simply desired the establishment of Orthodoxy and autocracy as objects of obligatory veneration for all subjects of the Russian Empire. As M. M. Shevchenko justly remarked, in his formula "Uvarov essentially paraphrased the ancient military motto 'For Faith, Tsar and Fatherland!'" (Shevchenko 1997, 105). However, the very nature of the paraphrase reveals the kernel of Uvarov's approach. The concrete, emotionally palpable patriotic symbols for which a soldier must go into battle are here replaced with the historical institutions of national existence and abstract principles. The task of the entire system of popular education became the clarification and affirmation of these principles and these institutions, as Uvarov wrote, "not in the form of panegyric speeches to the government, which it does not need, but as the conclusions of reason, as incontestable fact, as political dogma that guarantees the tranquility of the state and which is the birthright of one and all." Thus the ideological guarantee of state politics was translated from a "hot" register into a "cold" one, transforming mobilizational slogans into a program of routine bureaucratic and educational work. The memorandum also interpreted the sources of danger that were menacing the empire as well as the measures proposed to eliminate them in an analogous way.

6

Uvarov began his letter to the emperor with recollections of his previous career in the Ministry of Popular Education. In 1811, thanks to his marriage to the daughter of the then minister, Count A. K. Razumovskii, he received the brilliant appointment (for a twenty-five-year-old) to the post of administrator of the St. Petersburg educational district. In this position he showed himself to be energetic and able (see Whittaker 1999; cf. Shpet 1989), about which Nicholas I was naturally well-informed. The emperor also knew about the reasons for Uvarov's departure in 1821 that provided the basis for somewhat paradoxical parallels with the circumstances of his new appointment.

Uvarov was to begin his new responsibilities by making an inspection of Moscow University. The review of this institution of higher learning that had given serious grounds for suspicion—there had recently been arrests from among the students—clearly suggested a forthcoming change of government course (see Herzen VIII, 135–148). In recent history this situation had a well-examined precedent. In 1819 the task of carrying out an inspection of Kazan University had been entrusted to M. L. Magnitskii. The result was not only the decimation of the university but the start of repressions throughout Russia's educational system, which did not spare Uvarov's beloved St. Petersburg University. On the initiative of Magnitskii's henchman, D. P. Runich, its leading professors were ousted—K. I. Arsen'ev, A. I. Galich, and E. Raupakh. Uvarov unsuccessfully tried to oppose these persecutions and was forced to retire (see Sukhomlinov II, 382–386; Whittaker 1999, 88–99), although several of the fired professors were quickly accepted into military educational institutions under the administration of Grand Prince Nikolai Pavlovich. The future emperor did not conceal his dislike for Magnitskii and Runich, to whom he once ironically asked to accept his gratitude for their concern with the cadres of the Engineering School (Grech 1930, 381; sf. Shil'der 1903 II, 60–62). As N. I. Grech wrote, banishing Magnitskii from Petersburg was "the single matter that Nikolai Pavlovich permitted himself [to get involved with] before he ascended to the throne" (Grech 1930, 383–384).

In 1831, a year before Uvarov's memorandum, Magnitskii tried to escape his political disfavor. Together with the well-known mystic of the Alexandrine era, Andrei Golitsyn, he submitted two closely connected denunciations to Nicholas I that allegedly exposed a global conspiracy of the Illuminati. In their opinion, this conspiracy was coordinated from abroad and had sunk deep roots in Russia (see Shil'der 1898/1899; for more detail, see Gordin 1999). They declared Speranskii—once a patron and friend of Magnitskii, who had at that time been leading the effort to compile a law code for the Russian Empire—the inspiration for and organizer of the Illuminati's activity in Russia. The immediate cause for the denunciations was probably the newly-minted proposals of the commission of December 6 (see Gordin 1999, 252–255). However, Golitsyn and Magnitskii wrote about affairs of twenty years prior. Apparently the two disgraced bureaucrats wanted to attract attention to themselves by demonstrating that they were conversant with past events. In one denunciation it said that Speranskii "was accepted to a high rank of Illuminism" during the Erfurt Congress and that "Weishaupt was ordered by Napoleon to pay attention to state secretary Speranskii" (Shil'der 1898/1899, № 12, 524, 534). In 1831, after the Polish uprising that echoed the July Revolution in France, the Polish question again became topical. In Magnitskii's words, "the hurried and unripe Polish revolt at the very beginning of a great rebellion that apparently was supposed to embrace Europe again is a clear sign" of the activity "of the all-destructive union of the Illuminati" (ibid., № 1, 87). However, here too the informers' argument was based on peripeties of a bygone era.

Magnitskii asserted that among Speranskii's papers were "especially important constitutional projects for Russia and especially one, written in Czartoryski's hand, as well as an introduction to the extensive and grand work that Speranskii wrote while returning from Erfurt where he had been with the sovereign and from where, it seems, he came back with *various* foreign impressions" (ibid., № 1, 82). The connections between the Illuminati and the Poles were proved by the fact that "their first action" in 1794 was the liberation of Tadeusz Kościuszko, who led the uprising against Russia. Moreover, their weapon within Russia already in the nineteenth century was the lodge of the Polish aristocrat Tadeusz Grabianka. The lodge counted members such as Speranskii and F. P. Lubianovskii and influenced the emperor through his favorite M. A. Naryshkina, who was Polish by birth (ibid., № 2, 292–293, 298). Magnitskii and Golitsyn calculated that the emperor, whose reign had begun with the revolt on Senate Square and who five years later faced revolutions in France and Belgium, the Polish uprising, and student conspiracies, could hardly remain deaf to this sort of warning. They therefore revived the old constructions of Abbé Barruel that had been so effective in 1812 for denouncing Speranskii, and again in 1824 when Fotii was able to unseat Aleksandr Golitsyn. Curiously, Magnitskii, who had been sent into exile on account of the first intrigue was, like Andrei Golitsyn, an active participant in the second one. Neither Nicholas I nor Uvarov was immune to ideas about a multi-pronged conspiracy coordinated from abroad. However, the mythology of an eschatological clash between good and evil, so natural in the overwrought atmosphere of Alexandrine mysticism, did not arouse anything in either man except irritation and repulsion. In Uvarov's memorandum the carriers of the revolutionary spirit were not the prevailing servants of "Satan's synagogue" but "minds dimmed by false ideas and prejudices worthy of pity." Uvarov clearly distinguished between "the sworn enemies of the empire," with whom one could only handle with repressive measures, and "political dreamers" who were "confused by false notions" and whom the authorities could still return to the lap of national life.

Uvarov's triad was designed to perform this task, as it represented, in B. A. Uspenskii's persuasive hypothesis, a polemical reversal of the most famous tripartite political formula, the French Revolutionary slogan "Liberty, Equality, Fraternity" (Uspenskii 1999). If in Barruel's scheme "Liberty" corresponded to the conspiracy by "sophists of atheism," for Uvarov "Orthodoxy" was called on to oppose it. The answer to the conspiracy on the part of "sophists of rebellion" that preached "Equality" became "Autocracy." Against the conspiracy of "the sophists of anarchy" that challenged the foundations of society and patriotic feeling, "Nationality" was put forward as a replacement for "Fraternity," which was equally objectionable for a Russian monarchist due to its cosmopolitan and Masonic implications (see Ozouff 1988).

After a short investigation that established the complete falsity of their accusations (see Gordon 1999), both Golitsyn and Magnitskii were sent into exile. Uvarov was left to decide how to battle freethinking and the revolutionary threat. In the start of 1832 he found himself in the situation that Magnitskii had been in thirty years earlier—he was expected to come up with a complex of measures that would eliminate the rabble-rousing that had infiltrated higher education. However, the role of fanatical obscurantist did not at all appeal to him; thus, he needed to be assured once again that the emperor did not expect anything of this kind from him and had not chosen him to carry out a pogrom in Russia's oldest university in the fashion of his unfortunate predecessor. "It is precisely in the sphere of popular education that we need first of all to revive faith in monarchist and national principles, and to restore it without shocks, without haste, without violence. Enough ruins surround us—[we are] able to destroy, but what have we built"? he wrote to Nicholas I in his memorandum.

"Ruins" was not merely a metaphor here; Magnitskii had proposed that they not limit the punishment of Kazan University to a purge but give it over for "public destruction" (Zagoskin II, 309).

In the report on his inspection, Uvarov recommended that they fight "against the influence of so-called *European ideas*" not by the use of repression but by instilling young people "with a penchant for other concepts, other occupations and principles, increasing where we can the number of *intellectual levees*" that could direct the energy of the young generation's minds into a channel the government needed (Uvarov 1875, 517). In the late 1810s Uvarov proposed that the study of the East could save Russia from the "European infection." Now he had in mind constructing "intellectual levees" (umstvennye plotiny) capable of changing the natural flow of ideas, "inculcating into young people the desire to become better acquainted with the fatherland's history, paying greater attention to our nationality in all of its diverse manifestations." "It is unquestionable," he continued, "that this kind of affinity for works that are continuing, substantial, inoffensive, will serve as a kind of support against the influence of so-called *European ideas*" (ibid.). Encouraging study and research in the field of Russian history was basically the only positive proposal that Uvarov was able to put forward. The past was ordained to replace the empire's perilous and uncertain future, and Russian history, with its deeply rooted institutions of Orthodoxy and autocracy, was to become the single repository of nationality and the ultimate alternative to Europeanization.

7

In suggesting that loyalty to the church and to the throne were the main features of Russian nationality, Uvarov was forced to presume that these feelings unite "the incalculable majority" of his countrymen (Uvarov 1995, 71), at the same time as

> the senseless passion for innovations without restraint or reasonable plan, [and leading] to unexpected destructive consequences, characterizes an extremely insignificant circle of people in Russia and serves as the credo for a school that is so weak that it not only cannot increase the number of its adherents but loses several of them daily. One may assert there is no doctrine less popular in Russia, because there is no system that would offend so many

ideas, be hostile to so many interests, be so fruitless and surrounded by mistrust to any greater extent.

In such a situation and social dynamic it would seem that the government had nothing to worry about. Nonetheless Uvarov prepared for a difficult struggle, the prospectives for which he was by no means inclined to be optimistic. Despite what he said, literally two paragraphs previously, among the factors that threatened the final victory of his mission was "the universal state of people's minds, and, in particular, that of the generation that is graduating today from our bad schools and for whose moral neglect we, perhaps, should reproach ourselves, a lost generation, if not an antagonistic one, a generation of ignoble beliefs, bereft of enlightenment, grown old before it had a chance to enter life, withered away by ignorance and fashionable sophisms, whose future will bring no benefit to the Fatherland."

Defeatist notes resound in Uvarov's letter. His mission as he himself conceived it was, on the one hand, rooted in the nature of national existence, and on the other—infinitely lonely and Sisiphean. Uvarov wrote that he would defend the "breach" which the emperor had commanded him to fill "until the last," but expressed misgivings that he would be "overcome by the force of circumstances." An influential statesman summoned to formulate and implement a new system of state consciousness, he felt himself, as before, an "exotic flower" unable to put down roots in his native soil, as he had characterized himself eighteen years earlier in the letter to Stein. This situation seems quite paradoxical. Given the Russians' love for the native principles of national life that Uvarov postulated, where could that generation—whose disposition was described in terms that today almost seem like quotations from Lermontov's poem "Thought" (Duma), written six years later—have come from, and why did the task of raising future generations in the spirit of Russian nationality seem so dangerous and unattainable to the future minister?

Of course, a significant measure of the responsibility for such a situation predates Uvarov. Rather, it lies with the state's ideological apparatus, whose permissiveness and lack of well-considered policy had allowed the evil to penetrate so deeply. Yet the main reason for the spread of anti-national tendencies lies elsewhere. The very metaphor of "intellectual levees" suggests that Uvarov was trying to partition off a current of thought that he himself felt was natural.

In his opinion, Russia had for the moment "avoided the humiliation" like that which Europe suffered after the July Revolution. But the very phrase "has not arrived at that point of disgrace" (n'a pas arrivé à ce point de degradation) indicates that he clearly discerned an analogous evolution for Russia. Also very pessimistic were Uvarov's sense of the fragility of the Russian government's mode of being and his above-cited assertion that if reforms began, the empire would not be able to last even two weeks (cf. Shevchenko 1997, 105). Apparently, while Uvarov saw the European path of development as ruinous for Russia, he simply could not envisage any alternative.

As one of the most authoritative scholars of nationalism, Benedict Anderson, has written, in Russia, "'official nationalism'—[the] willed merger of nation and dynastic empire— ... developed *after*, and *in reaction to*, the popular national movements proliferating in Europe since the 1820s. ... It was only that a certain inventive legerdemain was required to permit the empire to appear attractive in national drag" (Anderson 1994, 68–87). Consequently, in historical practice the experience of Western nation-states inevitably served as the measure for any realization of this very "nationalism." The intellectual drama of Russian state nationalism consisted in the following: the key notion of "nationality" or "nationalism" (nationalité, Volkstum) had been developed by Western European social thinkers to legitimize the new social order that was replacing the traditional confessional and dynastic principles of the state system; but Uvarov's triad declared that precisely those institutions that nationalism had been summoned to destroy were the cornerstones of Russian nationality—the reigning church and imperial absolutism. In fulfilling the Russian monarchy's political mandates, Uvarov attempted to unite the contradictory demands of the time and to preserve the existing order, but his European education proved stronger than the traditionalism he had adopted. Nationalism thus predominated over both Orthodoxy and autocracy, turning them into ethnographically ornamental components of national history.

Works Cited

Adrianova-Peretts 1 – Русское народное поэтическое творчество. Т. I: Очерки по истории русского народного поэтического творчества X – начала XVIII веков / Под ред. В.П. Адриановой-Перетц и др. М.; Л., 1953.

Aksakov II – *Аксаков С. Т.* Собрание сочинений. В 4 т. Т. II. М., 1955.

Aleksandr 1902 – Рескрипт Александра I графу Ростопчину по поводу письма его о слухах и беспорядках в провинции // РС. 1902. № 9.

Althusser 1969 – Althusser, L. *For Marx*. London: Allen Lane, 1969.

Althusser 1971 – Althusser, L. "Ideology and Ideological State Apparatuses." In *Lenin and Philosophy*. Ed. L. Althusser. London: New Left Books, 1971.

Al'tshuller 1975 – *Альтшуллер М. Г.* Крылов в литературных объединениях 1800-1810-х годов // Иван Андреевич Крылов: Проблемы творчества / Под ред. И.З. Сермана. Л., 1975.

Al'tshuller 1984 – *Альтшуллер М. Г.* Предтечи славянофильства в русской литературе. (Общество «Беседа любителей русского слова»). Ann Arbor, 1984.

Anderson 1989 – Anderson, M.S. *The Rise of Modern Diplomacy, 1450-1919*. London: Longman, 1989.

Anderson 1994 – *Imagined Communities: Reflections on the Origin and Spread of Nationalism.* London: Verso, 1994.

Arnaud 1992 – Arnaud, C. *Chamfort: A Biography.* Chicago: U. of Chicago Press, 1992.

Arndt 1814 – – [Арндт Э -М.] Краткая и справедливая повесть о пагубных Наполеона Бонапарта промыслах, о войнах его с Гишпаниею и Россиею, о истреблении войск его и о важности нынешней войны. Книжка в утешение и наставление немецкому народу сочиненная. СПб., 1814.

Arned III – Arneth, A. *Maria Theresia Und Joseph II: III.* Wien: C. Gerold's Sohn, 1868.

Arsh 1970 – *Арш Г.Л.* Этеристское движение в России: Освободительная борьба греческого народа в начале XIX в. и русско-греческие связи. М., 1970.

Arsh 1976 – *Арш Г.Л.* И. Каподистриа и греческое национально-освободительное движение 1809–1822 гг. М., 1976.

Arzamas I – «Арзамас»: Сб.: В 2 кн. Кн. I / Под общей ред. В.Э. Вацуро и А.Л. Осповата. М., 1994.

Averintsev 1980 – *Аверинцев С.С.* Волхвы // Мифы народов мира: Энциклопедия. Т. 1: А-К / Под ред. С.А. Токарева. М., 1980.

Azadovskii I – *Азадовский М. К.* История русской фольклористики. Т. I. М., 1958.

Baader 1987 – Baader, F.X. von. *Samtliche Werke. Bd. 6: Gesammelte Schriften zur Sozietatsphilosophie.* Bd. 2. Aalen: Scientia-Verl., 1987.

Bakunina 1885 – Двенадцатый год в записках Варвары Ивановны Бакуниной // РС. 1885. № 9.

Bakunina 1967 – Bakounine, T. *Répertoire Biographique Des Francs-Maçons Russes, 18. Et 19. Siècles.* Paris: Inst. d.'Études Slaves de l'Univ, 1967.

Barruel I-IV – Barruel, A. *Mémoires pour servir à l'Histoire du Jacobinisme.* Vol. I-IV. London, 1797-1798.

Barruel 1805/1809 I-XII – [Баррюэль О.] Волтерианцы, или История о якобинцах, открывающая все противу христианские злоумышления и таинства масонских лож, имеющих влияние на все европейские державы. Ч. I-XII. М., 1805-1809.

Barruel 1806/1808 I-VI – [Баррюэль О.] Записки о якобинцах, открывающие все противухристианские злоумышления и таинства масопских лож, имеющих влияние на все европейские державы. Т. I-VI. М., 1806-1808.

Barskov 1915 – *Барсков Я.Л.* Переписка московских масонов XVIII века. 1780-1792. Пг., 1915.

Barsukov 1873 – *Барсуков А.* Князь Григорий Григорьевич Орлов. (1734-1783) // РА. 1873. Кн. I.

Barsukov IX – *Барсуков Н.П.* Жизнь и труды М.П. Погодина. Кн. IX. М., 1894.

Bartenev 1886 – Рассказы князя А.Н. Голицына. Из записок Ю.Н. Бартенева // РА. 1886. № 3.

Bartenev 1892 – *Бартенев П. Б. [Бартенев П.И.]* [Примеч. к: Сперанский. I. Пермское письмо Сперанского к Александру Павловичу. II. Оправдательная записка / Публ. Н.К. Шильдера // РА. 1892. № 1.

Bartlett 1981 – Bartlett, R.P. "Catherine II, Voltaire and Henry IV of France," *SGECRN* 1981: 9.

Barton 1969 – Barton, P. F., and I. A. Fessler. *Ignatius Aurelius Fessler: Vom Barockkatholizismus Zur Erweckungsbewegung*. Wien: Böhlau, 1969.

Batalden 1982 – Batalden S.-K. *Catherine II's Greek Prelate: Eugenious Voulgaris in Russia. 1771-1806*. New York: Columbia UP, 1982.

Batiushkov I-II – *Батюшков К. Н.* Соч.: В 2 т. / сост., подгот. текста, коммент. В. Кошелева, А. Зорина. М., 1989.

Bauman 1999 – Bauman, Z. *In Search of Politics*. Stanford: Stanford UP, 1999.

Benkendorf 1929 – Гр. А. Х. Бенкендорф о России в 1827-1830 гг. (Ежегодные отчеты III отделения и корпуса жандармов) / Предисл. и публ. А. Сергеева // Красный архив. 1929. Т. 6 (37).

Bertier de Sauvigny 1960 – "La Sainte-Alliance et l'alliance dans les conceptions de Metternich." *Revue Historique* 223(2): 1960. 249-274.

Bertier de Sauvigny 1972 – *La Sainte Alliance. Textes choisis et présentés par G. Bertier de Sauvigny*. Paris: Armand Colin, 1972.

Bershtein 1992 – Bershtein, E. "The Solemn Ode in the Age of Catherine: Its Poetics and Social Function." In *Poetics of the Text. Essays to Celebrate Twenty Years of the Neo-Formalist Circle*. Ed. J. Andrew. Atlanta: Rodopi, 1992.

Bestuzhev-Riumin 1859 – *Бестужев-Рюмин А.Д.* Краткое описание происшествиям в столице Москве в 1812 году. / Сообщ. В. Чарыков // ЧОИДР. 1859. Кн. II. Отд. V.

Bethea 1996 – *Бетеа Д.* Юрий Лотман в 1980-е годы: Код и его отношение к литературной биографии // НЛО. 1996. № 19.

Bieberstein 1976 – Bieberstein, J. R. *Die These von der Verschworung 1776-1945: Philosophen, Freimaurer, Juden, Liberale and Sozialisten als Verschworer gegen die Sozialordnung*.Frankfurt: Peter Lang, 1976.

Bobrov 1798 – *Бобров С.* Таврида, или Мой летний день в Таврическом Херсонисе. Лиро-эпическое песнотворение. Николаев, 1798.

Bobrov 1806 – *С. Б-в [Бобров С.С.]* Патриоты и герои везде, всегда и bо всяком // Лицей. 1806. Ч. 2. № 3.

Bogdanovich II – *[Богданович М. И.]* История царствования императора Александра I и России в его время. Т. II. СПб., 1869.

Bochkarev 1959 – *Бочкарев В.А.* Русская историческая драматургия начала XIX века (1800-1815 гг.). Куйбышев, 1959.

Boutaric I – Boutaric, M. E. *Correspondance secrète inédites de Louis XV*. Vol. I. Paris, 1866.

Brenner 1947 – Brenner, C.D. *A Bibliographical List of Plays of the French Language, 1700-1789*. Berkeley: U. of California Press, 1947.

Brikner 1891 – *Брикнер А.* Г. А. Потемкин. СПб., 1891.

Broglie I-II – Broglie, A. *The King's Secret: Being the Secret Correspondence of Louis XV with his Diplomatic Agents from 1752 to 1774*. Vol. I-II. New York: Cassell, Petter, & Galpin, 1879.

Bray 1902 – Петербург в конце XVIII и в начале XIX века. (По бумагам графа Франца-Габриэля де Брэ) // PC. 1902. № 4.

Bulgakov 1792 – *[Булгаков Я. И.]* Записки о нынешнем возмущении Польши. СПб., 1792.

Bulgakov 1867 – Выдержки из записок Александра Яковлевича Булгакова / Сообщ. Н.С. Киселев // РА. 1867.

Busanovв 1992 – *Бусанов А.В.* Русская история в памяти крестьян XIX века и национальное самосознание. М., 1992.

Butterfield 1968 – Butterfield, H. "The Balance of Power." In *Diplomatic Investigations: Essays in the Theory of International Politics*. Eds. Herbert Butterfield and Martin Wight. Cambridge, Mass.: Harvard UP, 1968

Bühler 1929 – Bühler, F. *Die geistigen Wurzeln der heiligen Allianz*. Freiburg im Breisgau, 1929.

Buturlin 1901 – Записки графа М.Д. Бутурлина // РА. 1901. № 11.

Bychkov 1872 – В память графа М.М. Сперанского. Т. II / Под ред, А.Ф. Бычкова. СПб., 1872.

Bychkov 1902 – Ссылка Сперанского в 1812 году. (Из бумаг академика А.Ф. Бычкова) / Сообщ. И.А. Бычков // РС. 1902. № 4.

Bychkov 1902а – Пребывание Сперанского в Нижнем Новгороде и Перми. (Из бумаг академика А.Ф. Бычкова) / Сообщ. И.А. Бычков // РС. 1902. № 5.

Campe 1798 – Campe, J.H. *Wörterbuch für Erklarung und Verdeutschung der unserer Sprache aufgedrungenen fremden Ausdrücke*. Braunschweig, 1798.

Campe I-II – Детская библиотека, изданная на немецком языке г. Кампе. Ч. I-II. СПб., 1783-1785.

Chamfort 1789 [*Шамфор С.Р. Н. де*] Возвращенное благодеяние, комедия в одном действии. М., 1789.

Chartorizhskii I-II – Мемуары князя Адама Чарторижского и его переписка с императором Александром I / Ред. и вступ. статья А. Кизеветтера. Т. I. М., 1912. Т. II. М., 1913.

Chateaubriand 1840 – Chateaubriand, F. de. *Congrès du Vérone*. Paris, 1841.

Chevalier 1939 – Chevalier, A. *Claude-Carloman de Rulhière premier histories de la Pologne: Sa vie et son oeuvre historique d'aprés des documents inédits*. Paris, 1939.

Chibiriaev 1989 – Чибиряев С.А. Великий русский реформатор. М., 1989.

Chistovich 1894 – Чистович И.А. Руководящие деятели духовного просвещения в России в первой половине XIX текущего столетия. СПб., 1894.

Chistovich 1899 – Чистович И.А. История перевода Библии на русский язык / 2-е изд. СПб., 1899.

Choiseul-Gouffier 1999 – Шуазель-Гуфье С. Исторические мемуары об императоре Александре и его дворе // Державный сфинкс / Сост. А. Либерман, В. Наумов, С. Шокарев. М., 1999.

Cross 1971 – Cross, A.G. "British Freemasons in Russia during the Reign of Catherine the Great." *Oxford Slavonic Papers* IV: 1971.

Cross 1976 – *Кросс А.Г.* Василий Петров В Англии (1772-1774) II XVIII век. Сб. 11: Н.И. Новиков и общественно-литературное движение его времени. Л., 1976.

Cross 1977 – Cross, A. G. "The Duchess of Kingston in Russia." *History Today* 27(6): 1977.

Cross 1990 – Cross, A.G. "Catherine's 'Oleg': A Bicentennial Visitation." *SGECRN* 18: 1990..

Cross 1996 – *Кросс Э. Г.* У темзских берегов. Россияне в Британии в XVIII веке. СПб., 1996.

Dälmen 1977 – Dälmen, R. van. *Der Geheimbund der Illuminaten*. Stuttgart, 1977.

Danilevskii 1980 – *Данилевский Р. Ю.* И. Г. Гердер и сравнительное изучение литератур в России // Русская культура XVIII века и западноевропейские литературы: Сб. статей. Л., 1980.

Davydov 1856 – [*Давыдов И.И.*] Записки председательствующего о занятиях второго отделения академии в истекающем 1855 году. (Читано 3-го декабря 1855) // Известия Императорской академии наук по отделению русского языка и словесности. 1856. № V. Л. 1-4.

Deforneau 1965 – Deforneau, M. "Complot maçonnique et complot jésuitique." *Annales historiques de la Révolution française*. 180: 1965

Derzhavin I, III, IV, VI – Сочинения Державина / С объяснительными примеч. Я. Грота. Т. I, III, IV, VI. СПб., 1864-1871.

Dmitriev 1871 – Письма И.И. Дмитриева к В.А. Жуковскому // РА. 1871.

Dmitriev 1986 – *Дмитриев И. И.* Сочинения / Сост. и коммент. А. М. Пескова и И.З. Сурат. М., 1986.

Dmitriev 1998 – *Дмитриев М.А.* Главы из воспоминаний моей жизни / Подгот. текста и примеч. К.Г. Боленко, Е.А. Ляминой и Т.Ф. Нешумовой. М., 1998.

Dmitrieva 1996 – *Дмитриева Е. Е.* Обращение в католичество в России в XIX в. (историко-культурный контекст) // Arbor mundi. 1996. Вып. 4.

Dobronravov 1913 – *Добронравов Г.* Последование молебного пения, деваемого в день Рождества Христова в воспоминание избавления церкви и державы Российской от нашествия галлов и с ними двадесяти язык // Московские церковные ведомости. 1913. N 29-31.

Domashnev 1769 – *Домашнев С.* Ода победоносной Екатерине Второй... на одержанные славным оружием ее многократные над турками победы и на взятие Хотина под предводительством генерала князя Голицына. [СПб., 1769].

Domashnev 1770 – *Домашнев С.* Ода победоносной Екатерине Второй... На одержанную славным ее оружием совершенную над турецким флотом победу, произошедшую между острова Сцио и Чесменской пристани, под предводительством морских и сухопутных ее сил генерала графа Орлова в июне месяце, 1770 года. СПб., [1770].

Dorland 1939 – Dorland, A.G. "The Origins of the Treaty of Holy Alliance of 1815." *Transactions of the Royal Society of Canada* 23: 1939.

Dostian 1972 – *Достян И. С.* Россия и балканский вопрос. Из истории русско-балканских политических связей в первой трети XIX в. М., 1972.

Dovnar-Zapol'skii 1905 – *Довнар-Запольский М.В.* Политические идеалы М.М. Сперанского. [М.,] 1905.

Droz 1961 – Droz, J. "La légende du complot illuminists et les origins du romantisme politique en Allemagne." *Revue historique* 226: 1961.

Druzhinina 1955 – *Дружинина Е.И.* Кючук-Кайнарджкйский мир 1774 года (его подготовка и заключение). М., 1955.

Druzhinina 1959 – *Дружинина Е.И.* Северное Причерноморье в 1775-1800 гг. М., 1959.

Dubrovin 1885-1889 – *Дубровин Н.* Присоединение Крыма к России. Рескрипты, письма, реляции и донесения. Т. 1-IV. СПб., 1885-1889.

Dubrovin 1895 – *Дубровин Н.Ф.* Наполеон I в современной ему русской литературе // Русский вестник. 1895. № 2, 4, 6, 7.

Dubrovin 1895/1896 – *Дубровин Н.Ф.* Наши мистики-сектанты: Е.Ф. Татаринова и А.П. Дубовицкий // РС. 1895. № 10-12; 1896. №1-2.

Durylin 1932 – *Дурылин С.* Русские писатели у Гете в Веймаре // Литературное наследство. [Т.] 4/6. М., 1932.

Durylin 1939 – *Дурылин С.* Госпожа де Сталь и ее русские отношения // Литературное наследство. Т. 33/34. М., 1939.

Dusi 1844 – *Дуси Г.* Записка об амазонской роте // Москвитянин. 1844. № 1.

Eagleton 1991 – Eagleton, T. *Ideology. An Introduction*. New York: Verso, 1991.

Eagleton 1994 – Eagleton, T. *Mapping Ideology*. London: Longman, 1994.

Eckartshausen 1804 – Эккартсгаузен К. Облако над святилищем, или Нечто такое, о чем гордая философия и грезить не смеет. СПб., 1804.

Eckartshausen I-II – Eckartshausen, K. *Aufschlüsse zur Magic*. Bd. I-II. Münich, 1791.

Edling 1999 – Эдлинг Р.С. Записки // Державный сфинкс / Сост. А. Либерман, В. Наумов, С. Шокарев. М., 1999.

Edwards 1977 – Edwards, D.V. "Count Joseph de Maistre and Russian Educational Policy." *Slavic Review* 36: 1977.

Egorov 1991 – Егоров Б.Ф. Эволюция национализма у славянофилов // Вопросы литературы. 1991. № 7.

Egorov 1996 – Егоров Б.Ф. Очерки по русской культуре XIX века // Из истории русской культуры. Т. V (XIX век). М., 1996.

Ekaterina 1808 – Высочайшие собственноручные письма и повеления блаженной и вечной славы достойной памяти государыни императрицы Екатерины Великой к покойному генералу Петру Дмитриевичу Еропкину и всеподданейшие донесения в трех отделениях, собранные и с высочайшего дозволения в печать и зданные колежским советником Яковом Ростом. М., 1808.

Ekaterina 1871 – Высочайшие рескрипты императрицы Екатерины II с министерская переписка по делам Крымским. Из семейного архива графа Виктора Никитича. Панина. Ч. 1 // ЧОИДР. 1871. Кн. IV. Отд. II.

Ekaterina 1874 – Рескрипты Екатерины Второй князю Потемкину / Сообщ. Ф.А. Бюлер; предисл. Е. Белова // РА. 1874. № 8.

Ekaterina 1889 – Письма императрицы Екатерины II к Якову Александровичу Брюсу, во время путешествия ее величества в южные губернии в 1787 году. СПб., 1889.

Ekaterina 1971 – *Documents of Catherine the Great: The Correspondence with Voltaire and the Instruction of 1767 in the English text of 1768*. Ed. W. F. Reddaway. New York: Russell & Russell, 1971.

Ekaterina VIII – Сочинения императрицы Екатерины II / На основании подлинных рукописей и с примеч. А.Н. Пыпина. Т. VIII. СПб., 1901.

Ekaterina i Potemkin 1997 – Екатерина II и Г.А. Потемкин. Личная переписка. 1769-1791 / Изд. подгот. В.С. Лопатин. М., 1997.

Ekaterina Pavlovna 1888 – Письма великой княгини Екатерины Павловны / Читано в заседании Тверской ученой архивной комиссии 13 апреля 1888 года членом комиссии Е.А. Пушкиным. Тверь, 1888.

El'chaninov 1906 – *Ельчанинов А.* Мистицизм М.М. Сперанского // Богословский вестник. 1906. № 1-2.

Empaytaz 1828 – E.H.L. [Empaytaz H.-L.] *Notice sur Alexandre, Empereur de Russie*. Geneva, 1828.

Empaytaz 1840 – E.H.L. [Empaytaz H.-L.] *Notice sur Alexandre, Empereur de Russie*. Paris, 1840.

Engel'gardt 1997 – *Энгельгардт Л.Н.* Записки / Подгот. текста, сост. и примеч. И.И. Федюкина. М., 1997.

Epstein 1966 – Epstein, K. *The Origins of German Conservatism*. Princeton: Princeton UP, 1966.

Ermolov 1895 – Памфлет Г.П. Ермолова на графа М.М. Сперанского / С предисл. Е.И. Соколова. М., 1895.

Etkind 1996 – *Эткинд А.* «Умирающий Сфинкс»: Круг Голицына-Лабзина и петербургский период русской мистической традиции // Studia Slavica Finlandesia. T. XIII. Helsinki, 1996.

Etkind 1997 – *Эткинд А.* Примечания // *Радлова А.* Богородицын корабль. Крылатый гость. Повесть о Татариновой / Публ., предисл. и примеч. А. Эткинда. М., 1997.

Evgenii 1775 – *Евгений (Булгарис)*. Победная песнь на заключение торжественного мира... всероссийского самодержицею Екатериною Второю с Оттоманскою Портою, по одержании над нею многочисленных побед на земли и на море. [М.,] 1775.

Fadeev 1958 – *Фадеев А.В.* Россия и восточный кризис 20-х годов XIX века. М., 1958.

Fadeev 1964 – *Фадеев А.В.* Греческое национально-освободительное движения и русское общество первых десятилетий XIX века // Новая и новейшая история. 1964. № 3.

Faivre 1969 – Faivre, A. *Ekartshausen et la théosophie chrétienne*. Paris, 1969.

Faivre 1991 – *Февр Л.* Цивилизация: Эволюция слова и группы идей // *Февр Л.* Бои за историю / Отв. ред. А.Я. Гурев М., 1991.

Fateev n.d. – *Фатеев А.Н.* Потемкин-Таврический. Прага, б.д.

Fateev 1940 – Fateev, A. "La disgrace d'un Homme d'Etat." *Записки русского научно- исследовательского объединения в Праге*. Т. X. Прага, 1940.

Filaret 1812 – *Филарет (Дроздов)*. Слово по освящении храма во имя святой живоначалъной Троицы, в доме князя Александра Николаевича Голицына, 1 октября. СПб., 1812.

Filaret 1814 – *Филарет (Дроздов)*. Слово на воспоминание произшествий 1812 года, говоренное в 1814 году, о гласе вопиющего в пустыне, говоренное в церкви святой живоначалъной Троицы, что в доме г. синод. обер-прокурора князя А.Н. Голицына, генваря 18 дня. СПб, 1814.

Filaret 1814a – *Филарет (Дроздов)*. Слово на день сошествия Святого духа, говоренное в церкви живоначалной Троицы, что в доме г. синод. обер-прокурора князя А.Н. Голицына, мая 18 дня. Из слов: исполнится духом. СПб., 1814.

Filaret 1822 – *Филарет (Дроздов)*. Рассуждение о нравственных причинах неимоверных успехов наших в войне с Французами 1812 года // Собрание образцовых русских сочинений и переводов в прозе / Изд. Обществом любителей Отечественной Словесности. 2-е изд., испр., умнож.... Ч. II. СПб., 1822.

Filaret 1873 – Сочинения Филарета митрополита московского и коломенского. Слова и речи. Т. I. М., 1873.

Filaret 1882 – Письма к родным митрополита Московского Филарета (в мире Василия Михайловича Дроздова) к родным от 1800-го до 1866 года. М., 1882.

Filaret 1883 – Филарет, митрополит московский, и архимандрит Иннокентий в письмах к графу С.П. Потемкину за 1812-1848 гг. / Предисл. и примеч. Н.И. Барсова // РС. 1883. № 4.

Filaret 1994 – Филарета митрополита Московского и Коломенского творения / Сост. и вступ. статья М. Козлова. М., 1994.

Fisher 1970 – Fisher, A. W. *The Russian Annexation of Crimea*. Cambridge: Cambridge UP, 1970.

Florovskii 1937 – *Флоровский Г.* Пути русского богословия. Paris, 1937.

Flynn 1970 – Flynn, J. "The Role of Jesuits in the Politics of Russian Education." *Catholic Historical Review* 56: 1970.

Fomenko 1999 – *Фоменко И.Ю.* Кирьяк // Словарь русских писателей XVIII века. Вып. 2 (К-П). СПб., 1999.

Freidin and Bonnet 1995 – Freidin, G. and V. Bonnet. "Televorot: The Role of Television Coverage in Russia's August 1991 Coup." In *Soviet Hieroglyphics: Visual Culture in Late Twentieth-Century Russia*. Ed. N. Condee. Bloomington, 1995.

Galakhov 1875 – *Галахов А.* Обзор мистической литературы в царствование Александра I // ЖМНП. 1875. № 11.

Gardner 1971 – Gardner, B. *The East India Company: A History*. London, 1971.

Gardzonio 1994 – *Гардзонио С.* Автографы поэтов-шишковистов в книгах РГБ // Маргиналии русских писателей XVIII века. СПб., 1994.

Gasparov 1984 – *Гаспаров М.Л.* Очерк истории русского стиха: Метрика. Ритмика. Рифма. Строфика. М., 1984.

Gauenshil'd 1902 – М.М. Сперанский (по Гауеншильду) / Сообщ. В.А. Бильбасов // РС. 1902. № 5.

Geertz 1973 – Geertz, C. *The Interpretation of Cultures: Selected Essays*. New York: Basic Books, 1973.

Geertz 1983 – Geertz, C. *Local Knowledge*. New York: Basic Books, 1983.

Geertz 1998 – *Гирц К.* Идеология как культурная система // НЛО. 1998. № 29.

Geiger 1954 – Geiger, M. *Aufklarung and Erweckung*. Zurich, 1954.

Giliarov-Platonov II – *Гиляров-Платонов Н.* Из пережитого. Автобиографические воспоминания. Ч. II. М., 1886 [на обложке «1887»].

Gillel'son 1969 – *Гиллельсон М. И.* Письма Н.М. Карамзина к С.С. Уварову // XVIII век. Сб. 8: Державин и Карамзин в литературном движении XVIII – начала XIX века. Л., 1969.

Gillel'son 1974 – *Гиллельсон М. И.* Молодой Пушкин и арзамасское братство. Л., 1974.

Girard 2000 – *Жирар Р.* Священное и насилие. М., 2000.

Glinka 1807 – *Глинка С.* Пожарский и Минин, или Пожертвования Россиян. М., 1807.

Glinka 1812 – [*Глинка С. Н.*] Неизменность Французского злоумышления против России // Русский вестник. 1812. Кн. IX.

Glinka 1814 – [*Глинка С.Н.*] Воспоминания о московских происшествиях в достопамятный 1812 год, от 11 июля до изгнания врагов из древней русской столицы // Русский вестник. 1814. Кн. IX.

Glinka 1836 – Записки о 1812 годе Сергея Глинки, первого ратника московского ополчения. СПб., 1836.

Glushkovskii 1940 – *Глушковский А.П.* Воспоминания балетмейстера / Публ. и вступ. статья Ю.И. Слонимского; подгот. текста и комментарии А.Г. Мовшензона и А. А. Степанова; общ. ред. П.А. Гусева. М.; Л., 1940.

Gogol' I – *Гоголь Н.В.* Полн. собр. соч. Т. I. [М.,] 1940.

Golikov II – *Голиков И.* Дополнение к Деяниям Петра Великого. Т. 11. М., 1790.

Gordin 1989 – *Гордин Я.* Право на поединок. Роман в документах и рассуждениях. Л., 1989.

Gordin 1991 – *Гордин М.* Владислав Озеров. Л., 1991.

Gordin 1999 – *Гордин Я.А.* Мистики и охранители. дело о масонском заговоре. СПб., 1999.

Grech 1930 – *Греч Н.И.* Записки о моей жизни. Под ред. Иванова-Разумника и Д.М. Пинеса. М.; Л., 1930.

Greenfeld 1992 – *Nationalism: Five Roads to Modernity.* Cambridge, Mass: Harvard UP, 1992.

Grellet de Mobillier 1874 – [*Грелле де Мобилье Э.*] Записки квакера о пребывании в России. 1818-1819 / Сообщ. И. Т. Осиних // РС. 1874. № 1.

Griffiths 1970 – Griffiths, D.M. "The Rise and Fall of the Northern System: Court Politics and Foreign Policy in the First Half of Catherine II's Reign." *Canadian Slavic Studies* 4(3): 1970.

Grimstead 1969 – Grimstead, P. K. *The Foreign Ministers of Alexander I: Political Attitudes and the Conduct of Russian Diplomacy.* Berkeley: The U. of California Press, 1969.

Grizhbek 1995 – *Гржибек П.* Бахтинская семиотика и московско-тартусская школа // Лотмановский сборник. [Вып.] 1. М., 1995.

Grot 1867 – *Грот Я. К.* Очерк деятельности и личности Карамзина // Сборник статей, читанных в Отделении Языка и словесности Императорской Академии наук. 1867. Т. I. № 10.

Grot 1997 – *Грот Я. К.* Жизнь Державина. М., 1997.

Guizot 1834 – Первая лекция г-на Гизо из читанного им курса истории европейского гражданского образования // ЖМНП. 1834. Ч. I. № 3.

Guizot I – Guizot, F. *Histoire parlementaire de France.* Vol. I. Paris, 1864.

Gukovskii 1927 – *Гуковский Г.* Из истории русской оды XVIII века (Опыт истолкования пародии) // Поэтика: Временник Отдела словесных искусств Государственного института истории искусств. [Вып.] III. Л., 1927.

Gukovskii 1995 – *Гуковский Г.А.* Пушкин и русские романтики. М., 1995.

Harris I – Harris, J. *Diaries and Correspondence.* Vol. I. New York, 1970.

Hertzen I, VIII – *Герцен А.И.* Собр. соч.: В 30 т. Т. I. М., 1954. Т. VIII. М., 1956.

Hösch 1964 – Hösch, E. "Das sogenannte 'griechische Project' Katharinas II: Ideologie and Wirklichkeit der russischen Orientpolitik in der zweiten Hälfte des 18. Jahrhunderts." *Jahrbiicher für Geshichte Osteuropas.* 1964. Bd. XII.

Ianushevich 1985 – *Янушкевич А.С.* Этапы и проблемы творческой эволюции В.А. Жуковского. Томск, 1985.

Ianushevich 1992 – *Янушкевич А.С.* Жуковский // Русские писатели 1800-1917: Биографический словарь. Т. 2: Г-К. М., 1992.

Iezuitova 1989 – *Иезуитова Р.В.* Жуковский и его время. М., 1989.

Ikonnikov 1873 – *Иконников В. С.* Граф Н.С. Мордвинов. Историческая монография, составленная по печатным и рукописным источникам. СПб., 1873.

Isambaeva 1990 – *Исамбаева Л.М.* Общественно-политические взгляды С.С. Уварова в 1810-е годы // Вестник МГУ. Сер. 8. История. 1990. № 6.

Istoricheskaia kartina 1808 – Историческая и политическая картина 1807 года // Политический, статистический и географический журнал. 1808. Ч. I. Кн. II. Февраль.

Ivanov 1973 – *Иванов В.В.* Значение идей М.М. Бахтина о знаке, высказывании и диалоге для современной семиотики // Ученые записки Тартуского гос. ун-та. Вып. 308: Труды по знаковым системам. [Вып.] VI: Сборник научных статей в честь Михаила Михайловича Бахтина (к 75-летию со дня рождения). Тарту, 1973.

Ivanov 1997 – Иванов О.А. Тайны старой Москвы. документальные очерки по материалам Тайной экспедиции, III Отделения Собственной Его Величества канцелярии, а также секретной канцелярии московских генерал-губернаторов. М., 1997.

Jacob 1991 – Jacob, M.S. *Living the Enlightenment: Freemasonry and Politics in Eighteenth- Century Europe.* New York: Oxford UP, 1991.

Jameson 1981 – Jameson, F. *The Political Unconscious: Narrative as a Socially Symbolic Act.* Ithaca: Cornell UP, 1981.

Jonson 1963 – Jonson, D. *Guizot: Aspects of French History, 1787-1874.* Toronto: U. of Toronto Press, 1963.

Jung-Stilling 1815 – [Юнг-Штиллинг Г.И.] Победная песнь христианина. СПб., 1815.

Jung-Stilling II – [Юнг-Штиллинг Г.И.] Жизнь Генриха Штиллинга. Истинная повесть. Ч. II. СПб., 1816.

Kachalov 1992 – Качалов И.Л. О теории официальной народности. К проблеме авторства // Вестник Белгородского университета. Серия 3. 1992. № 3.

Kaliagin 1973 – Калягин В.А. Политические взгляды М.М. Сперанского. Саратов, 1973.

Kapterev 1885 – Каптерев Н. Характер отношения России к православному Востоку в XVI и XVII столетиях. М., 1885.

Karamzin 1991 – Карамзин Н.М. Записка о древней и новой России в ее политическом и гражданском отношениях / Предисл., подгот. текста и примеч. Ю.Спиваровара. М., 1991.

Karamzin II – Карамзин Н.М. Соч.: В 2 т. Т. 2 / Сост. Г.П. Макогоненко, коммент. Ю.М. Лотмана, Г.П. Макогоненко. Л., 1984.

Kates 1995 – Kates, G. *Monsieur d'Eon is a Woman. A Tale of Political Intrigue and Sexual Masquerade.* New York: Basic Books, 1995.

Katetov 1889 – Катетов И. Граф Михаил Михайлович Сперанский как религиозный мыслитель. М., 1889.

Kazakov 1970 – Казаков Н.И. Наполеон глазами его русских современников // Новая и новейшая история. 1970. № 3-4.

Kazakov 1989 – Казаков Н.И. Об одной идеологической формуле николаевской эпохи // Контекст-1989. М., 1989.

Kendall 1981 – Kendall, G. "Ideology. An Essay in Definition." *Philosophy Today* 25: 1981.

Kheraskov 1769 – *Херасков М.* Ода Российскому храброму воинству, при объявлении войны противу Оттоманской Порты. М., [1769].

Kheraskov 1770 – *Херасков М.* Ода... Екатерине Алексеевне... на торжественную победу при городе Чесме над турецким флотом. М:, 1770.

Kheraskov 1773 – *Херасков М.М.* Ода на торжественное бракосочетание... великого князя Павла Петровича и... великой княгини Натальи Алексеевны 1773 года, сентября 29 дня. СПб., [1773].

Kheraskov 1774 – Ода... Екатерине Алексеевне,... которою приносит при заключении с Оттоманскою Партой торжественного мира все-подданейшее поздравление Михайла Херасков. СПб., [1774].

Kheraskov 1785 – *Х[ерасков] М.* Владимир возрожденный, эпическая поэма. М., 1785.

Kheraskov 1787 – [*Херасков М.М.*] Щастливая Москва или 25 летний юбилей. Пролог представленный 1787 года, июня 28 дня, в день всерадостного на престол вступления Екатерины II. [М.,] 1787.

Kheraskov 1961 – *Херасков М.М.* Избранные произведения / Вступ. статья, подгот. текста и примеч. А.В. Западова. Л., 1961.

Khodasevich 1988 – *Ходасевич В.* Державин / Вступ. статья, сост. и коммент. А.Л. Зорина. М., 1988.

Khrapovitskii 1874 – Дневник А.В. Храповицкого. 1782-1793 / Статья и указ. Н. Барсукова. СПб., 1874.

Khvostov 1938 – *Хвостов Д.И.* Записки о словесности / Публ. А.В. Западова // Литературный архив. Т. 1. М.; Л., 1938.

Kizivetter 1912 – *Кизеветтер А.А.* Исторические очерки. М., 1912.

Kizivetter 1915 – *Кизеветтер А.* Ф.В. Ростопчин // *Кизеветтер А.И.* Исторические отклики. М., 1915.

Kir'iak 1867 – *Кирьяк Т.* Потемкинский праздник 1791 года (Письмо в Москву) / Сообщ. А.И. Долгоруков // РА. 1867.

Kisileva 1981 – *Киселева Л.Н.* Система взглядов С.Н. Глинки (1807-1812 гг.) // Ученые записки Тартуского гос. ун-та. Вып. 513. Труды по русской и славянской филологии. [Т.] XXXII: Проблемы литературной типологии и исторической преемственности. Тарту, 1981.

Kisileva 1983 – *Киселева Л.Н.* К языковой позиции «старших архаистов» (С.Н. Глинка, Е.И. Станевич) // Ученые записки Тартуского гос. ун-та. Вып. 620. Труды по русской и славянской филологии. Литературоведение: Типология литературных взаимодействий Тарту, 1983.

Kisileva 1997 – *Киселева Л.Н.* Становление русской национальной мифологии в николаевскую эпоху (сусанинский сюжет) // Лотмановский сборник. [Вып.] 2. М., 1997.

Kisileva 1998 – *Киселева Л.Н.* Карамзинисты – творцы официальной идеологии заметки о российском гимне) // Тыняновский сборник. Вып.10: Шестые – Седьмые – Восьмые Тыняновские чтения. М., 1998.

Kliuchevskii 1993 – *Ключевский В.О.* О русской истории / Под ред. В.И. Буганова. М., 1993.

Knapton 1939 – Knapton, E.J. *The Lady of The Holy Alliance*. New York: Columbia UP, 1939.

Kochetkova 1999 – *Кочеткова Н.Д.* Петров // Словарь русских писателей XVIII века. Вып. 2 (К-П). СПб., 1999.

Kochubinskii 1899 – *Кочубинский А.* Граф Андрей Иванович Остерман и раздел Турции. Из истории восточного вопроса. Война пяти лет (1735-1739). Одесса, 1899.

Kondakov 1998 – *Кондаков Ю.Е.* Духовно-религиозная политика Александра I и русская православная оппозиция. СПб., 1998.

König 1954 – König, H. *Schriften Zur Nationalerziehung in Deutschland Am Ende Des 18. Jahrhunderts*. Berlin: Volk u. Wissen, 1954.

Kopanev 2000 – Kopanev N. "Les travaux de J.-J. Rousseau en Russie en 1758-1765, d'après la correspondance de Marc-Michel Rey et G. Fr. Miller." *J.-J. Rousseau, politique et nation. II-e Colloque international de Montmorency: 27 septembre - 4 octobre 1995*. Paris, 2000.

Korf 1867 – Из бумаг [М.А. Корфа] о графе Сперанском, в дополнение. к его «Жизни», изданной в 1861 году / Сообщ. М.А. Корф // РА. 1867.

Korf 1902 – Деятели и участники в падении Сперанского. Неизданная глава из «Жизни графа Сперанского» барона М.А. Корфа. (Из бумаг академика А.Ф. Бычкова) / Сообщ. И.А. Бычков // РС. 1902. № 3.

Korf I-II – *Корф М.* Жизнь графа Сперанского. Т. I-II. СПб., 1861.

Korsunskii 1885 – *Корсунский И.* Проповеднический период деятельности Филарета (Дроздова), впоследствии митрополита московского // Вера и разум. 1885. Ч. II.

Koshanskii 1807 – *Кошанский [Н. Ф.]* Памятник Минину и Пожарскому, назначенный в Москве // Журнал изящны искусств. 1807. Кн. II

Kossovich 1872 – Иоаннов [*Коссович К.А.*] Дополнительные сведения о Татариновой и о членах ее духовного союза // РА. 1872. № 12.

Kostrov 1972 – *Костров Е.И.* Екатерине Великой [посвящение перевода «Илиады»] // Поэты XVIII века. Т. II / Сост. Г.П. Макогоненко и И.З. Сермана; подгот. текста и примеч. Г.С. Татищевой. Л., 1972.

Kostrov I – Полное собрание всех сочинений и переводов в стихах г. Кострова. Ч. I. М., 1802.

Kovalenskaia 1938 – *Коваленская Н.* Мартос. М.; Л., 1938.

Kovan'ko 1812 – *Кованько Ив.* Солдатская песня // Сын отечества. 1812. Ч. I. No 1.

Kozel'skii I – Сочинения Федора Козельского. Ч. I. [СПб.,] 1778.

Koyré 1929 – Koyré, A. *La philosophie et le problème nationale en Russie au début de XIX siècle.* Paris: Champion, 1929.

Kriukovskii 1964 – *Крюковский М. В.* Пожарский // Стихотворная трагедия конца XVIII - начала XIX в. / Вступ. статья, подгот. текста и примеч. В.А. Бочкарева. М.; Л., 1964.

Kroll 1964 – Kroll, G. "Preface." In C. W. Glück, *Iphigenie auf Taurus. Klavierauszug.* Kassel: Burenreiter, 1964.

Krüdener 1815 – *Крюденер Б.-Ю.* Лагерь при Вертю. СПб., 1815.

Krüdener 1815a – Krüdener, B. *Champs de Vertu.* St. Petersburg, 1815.

Krüdener 1998 – Баронесса Крюденер. Неизданные автобиографические тексты / Вступ. статья, сост., публ. и примеч. Е.П. Гречаной. М., 1998.

Krug 1818 – Krug, W. T. *Gesprach unter vier Augen mit Frau von Krüdener.* Leipzig, 1818.

Kukulevich 1939 – *Кукулевич А.М.* Русская идиллия Н.И. Гнедича «Рыбаки» // Ученые записки ЛГУ. Вып. 3. Л., 1939.

Kurganov 1769 – *Н. К. [Курганов Н.Г.]* Российская универсальная грамматика или всеобщее письмословие, предлагающее легчайший способ основательного учения русскому языку с седмью присовокуплениями разно учебных и полезнозабавных вещей. СПб., 1769.

Lakoff and Johnson 1980 – Lakoff, G., and M. Johnson. *Metaphors We Live By*. Chicago: University of Chicago Press, 1980.

Lakoff and Johnson 1987 – *Лаков Дж., Джонсон М.* Метафоры, которыми мы живем // Язык и моделирование социального взаимодействия: Сб. статей / Сост. В.М. Сергеев и П.Б. Паршин; общ. ред. В.В. Петрова. М., 1987.

Lakoff and Johnson 1990 – *Лакофф Д., Джонсон М.* Метафоры, которыми мы живем // Теория метафоры / Вступ. статья и сост. Н.Д. Арутюновой; общ. ред. Н.Д. Арутюновой и М.А. Журинской. М., 1990.

Landa 1975 – *Ланда С. С.* «Дух революционных преобразований...»: Из истории формирования идеологии и политической организации декабристов: 1816-1825 гг. М., 1975.

Langsam 1936 – Langsam, C. W. *Napoleonic Wars and the Rise of German Nationalism in Austria*. New York: Columbia UP, 1936.

Larrain 1979 – Larrain, J. *The Concept of Ideology*. London: Hutchinson, 1979.

Lebedev 1912 – *Лебедев А.А.* К закрытию масонских лож в России // РС. 1912. № 3.

Le Forestier 1970 – Le Forestier, R., and A. Faivre. *La Franc-Maçonnerie Templière Et Occultiste Aux Xviiie Et Xixe Siècles*. Paris: Aubier-Montaigne, 1970.

Le Forestier 1974 – Le Forestier, R. *Les Illuminés De Bavière Et La Franc-Maçonnerie Allemande*. Genève: Slatkine-Megariotis Reprints, 1974.

Lentin 1974 – *Voltaire and Catherine the Great; Selected Correspondence*. Trans. and ed. by A. Lentin. Cambridge: Oriental Research Partners, 1974.

Leshchilovskaia 1998 – Век Екатерины II: Россия и Балканы / Отв. ред. И.И. Лещиловская. М., 1998.

Ley 1975 – Ley, F., P. Pascal, and G. Bidaut. *Alexandre I Et Sa Sainte-Alliance: 1811-1825, Avec Des Documents Inédits*. Paris: Fischbacher, 1975.

Ley 1994 – Ley, F., and J. Gaulmier. *Madame De Krüdener, 1764-1824: Romantisme Et Sainte-Alliance*. Paris: Champion, 1994.

Liamina 1999 – *Лямина Е.* Новая Европа: мнение «деятельного очевидца». А.С. Стурдза в политическом процессе 1810-х годов // Россия / Russia. Вып. 3 [11]: Культурные практики в идеологической перспективе: Россия, XVIII – начало XIX века. М, 1999.

Ligne 1989 –Ligne, C. J., and A. Payne. *Mémoires, Lettres Et Pensées*. Paris: Editions François Bourin, 1989.

Lincoln 1989 – Lincoln,W. B. *Nicholas I: Emperor and Autocrat of All the Russias*. De Kalb, Ill: Northern Illinois UP, 1989.

Łojek 1970 – Łojek J. "Catherine II's Armed Intervention in Poland: Origins of the Political Decisions at the Russian Court in 1791 and 1792." *Canadian Slavic Studies* 4(3): 1970.

Łojek 1986 – Łojek, J. *Geneza i obalenie konstytutcji 3 Maja. Polityka zagrniczna Rzeczypospolitei 1787-1792*. Lublin: Wydawn, Lubelskie, 1986.

Lomonosov 1986 – Ломоносов М.В. Избранные произведения / Сост. и примеч. А.А. Морозова; подгот. текста М П. Лепехина и А.А. Морозова. Л., 1986.

Longinov 1860 – Лонгинов М. Один из магиков XVIII века // Русский вестник. 1860. № 8. Кн. II.

Lopatin 1992 – Лопатин В.С. Потемкин и Суворов. М., 1992.

Lopukhin 1810 – [Lopouhin L V.] *Quelques traits de l'église intërieure, de l'unique chemin, qui mène à la vérité, et diverses routes qui conduisent a l'erreur et à la perdition*. М., 1810.

Lopukhin 1870 – Письма И.В. Лопухина к М.М. Сперанскому // РА. 1870.

Lopukhin 1990 – Россия XVIII столетия в изданиях Вольной русской типографии А.Н. Герцена и Н.П. Огарева. Записки сенатора И.В. Лопухина. [Лондон, 1859]. Репринтное воспроизведение. М., 1990.

Lopukhin 1997 – Масонские труды И.В. Лопухина. СПб., 1997.

Lord 1915 – Lord, R.H. *The Second Partition of Poland: A Study in Diplomatic History*. Cambridge, Mass: Harvard UP, 1915.

Lord 1924/1925 – Lord, R.H. "The Third Partition." *SEER* III: 1924/1925.

Lotman 1960 – Лотман Ю.М. Историко-литературные заметки. [III] Жуковский-масон // Ученые записки Тартуского гос. ун-та. Вып. 98. Труды по русской и славянской филологии. [Т.] III. Тарту, 1969.

Lotman 1969 – Лотман Ю.М. Руссо и русская культура XVIII начала XIX века // см. Rousseau 1969.

Lotman 1992 – Лопман Ю.М. Руссо и русская культура XVI I I – начала XIX века // *Lotman* Ю.М. Избранные статьи. Т. II. Таллинн, 1992.

Lotman 1997 – Лотман Ю.М. «О древней и новой России в ее политическом и гражданском отношении» Карамзина – памятник русской публицистики начала XIX века // *Лотман Ю.М.* Карамзин. СПб., 1997.

Lotman and Uspenskii 1993 – *Лотман Ю.М., Успенский Б.А.* Отзвуки концепции «Москва – третий Рим» в идеологии Петра Первого. (К проблеме средневековой традиции в культуре барокко) // *Лотман Ю.М.* Избранные статьи. Т. III. Таллинн, 1993.

Lotman and Uspenskii 1996 – *Лотман Ю.М., Успенский Б.А.* Споры о языке в начале XIX в. как факт русской культуры («Происшествие в цар стве теней, или Судьбина российского языка» – неизвестное сочинение Семена Боброва) // *Успенский Б.А.* Избранные труды. Т. II: Язык и культура I, Изд. 2-е, исправ. и доп. М., 1996.

Lotman and Uspenskii 1997 – *Лотман Ю.М., Успенский Б.А.* «Письма русского путешественника» Н.М. Карамзина и их место в развитии русской культуры // *Лотман Ю.М.* Карамзин. СПб., 1997.

Lubianovskii 1872 – Воспоминания Федора Петровича Лубяновского (1777-1834). СПб., 1872.

Luden 1811 – Luden, H. *Handbuch der Staatsweisheit oder die Politik.* Jena, 1811.

Ludolf 1892 – *Гр. де Л[юдольф].* Письма о Крыме // *Русское обозрение.* 1892. № 3.

Lukács 1971 – Lukács, G. *History and Class Consciousness.* London: Merlin, 1971.

L'vov 1810 – *Львов П.* Пожарский и Минин, спасители отечества. СПб., 1810.

L'vov 1994 – *Львов Н.А.* Избранные сочинения / Предисл. Д.С. Лихачева; вступ. статья, сост., подгот. текста и коммент. К.Ю. Лаппо-Данилевского. Кельн; Веймар; Вена; СПб., 1994.

Madariaga 1959/1960 – Madariaga I. de. "The Secret Austro-Russian Treaty of 1781." S *SEER* 18(90); 1959/1960.

Madariaga 1981 – Madariaga I. de. *Russia in the Age of Catherine the Great.* New Haven: Yale UP, 1981.

Madariaga 1983 – Madariaga I. de. "Catherine and the Philosophes." *Russia and the West in the Eighteenth Century.* Newtonville, Mass: Oriental Research Partners, 1983.

Maikov 1770 – *Майков В.* Ода е.и.в. Екатерине Второй... на преславную победу над турецким флотом, в заливе Лаборно при городе Сисме. СПб., [1770].

Maikov 1774 – *Майков В.* Ода е.и.в. великой государыне Екатерине Алексеевне... на заключение вечного мира между Российской империей и Оттоманской Портою июля дня, 1774 года. 016., [1774].

Maikov 1966 – *Майков В.И.* Избранные произведения / Вступ. статья, подгот. текста и примеч. А.В. Западова. М.; Л., 1966.

Maiofis 1996 – *Майофис М.* Музыкальный и идеологический контекст драмы Екатерины «Начальное управление Олега» // Русская филология. Вып. 7. Тарту, 1996.

Maiofis 1998 – *Майофис М.Л.* Русский филэллинизм: литературные кружки Г.Р. Державина и А.Н. Оленина. М., 1998 [дипломная работа, кафедра истории русской литературы РГГУ].

Maistre 1871 – Письма из Петербурга в Италию графа Жозефа де Местра // РА. 1871. № 6.

Maistre 1995 – *Местр Ж. де.* Петербургские письма 1803-1817 / Сост., пер., предисл. и коммент. Д.В. Соловьева. СПб., 1995.

Maistre VIII, XI, XII – Maistre, J. de. *Oeuvres complètes*. Vol. VIII, XI, XII. Geneva: Slatkine, 1979.

Malmesbury 1970 – Harris, J. *Diaries and Correspondence of James Harris, First Earl of Malmesbury*. Vol. 1. New York: AMS Press, 1970.

Mannheim 1936 – Mannheim, K., L. Wirth, and E. Shils. *Ideology and Utopia; An Introduction to the Sociology of Knowledge*. New York: Harcourt, Brace, and co., 1936.

Manheim 1994 – *Манхейм К.* Диагноз нашего времени. М., 1994.

Mankiev 1770 – [*Манкиев А.И.*] Ядро российской истории, сочиненное ближним стольником и бывшим в Швеции резидентом, князь Андреем Яковлевичем Хилковым, в пользу российского юношества... М., 1770.

Markova 1958 – *Маркова О. Л.* О происхождении так называемого греческого проекта (80-е годы XVIII в.) // История СССР. 1958. № 4.

Martin 1997 – *Romantics, Reformers, Reactionaries: Russian Conservative Thought and Politics in the Reign of Alexander I*. DeKalb, Ill: Northern Illinois UP, 1997.

Martynov 1979 – Martynov, I.F. "Notes on V.P. Petrov and his Stay in England." *SGECRN* 7: 1979.

Martynov 1988 – *Мартынов И.Ф.* Ранние масонские стихи и песни в собрании библиотеки Академии наук СССР. (К истории литературно-общественной полемики 1760-х гг.) // Russia and the World of Eighteeth Century. Columbus, 1988.

Marx and Engels III, XXXIX – *Маркс К., Энгельс Ф.* Сочинения / 2-е изд. Т. 3. М., 1955. Т. 39. М., 1966.

Marx and Engels 1970 – Marx, K., F. Engels. *The German Ideology*. Ed. and intro. C. J. Arthur. London: Lawrence & Wishart, 1970.

McIntosh 1992 – McIntosh, C. *The Rose Cross and the Age of Reason*. New York: E.J. Brill, 1992.

Medvedeva 1960 – *Медведева И.* Владислав Озеров 1/ *Озеров В.А.* Трагедии. Стихотворения / Вступ. статья, подгот. текста и примеч. И.Н. Медведевой. Л., 1960.

Medvedkova 1993 – *Медведкова О.А.* Соломонов храм – дом премудрости: к истории неосуществленного проекта храма Христа Спасителя архитектора А.Л. Витберга // Revue des Etudes slaves. 1993. Т. 65. Fasc. 3.

Meineke 1970 – Meineke, F. *Cosmopolitanism and the Nation State*. Princeton: Princeton UP, 1970.

Mel'gunov 1923 – *Мельгунов С.* Дела и люди александровского времени. [Т.] I. Берлин, 1923.

Metternich 1880 – Metternich, Cl. V. prince de. *Mémoires, documents et écrits divers*. Paris, 1880.

Mil'china and Ospovat 1995 – *Мильчина В.А., Оспонат А.Л.* Петербургский кабинет против маркиза де Кюстина: нереализованный проект С.С. Уварова // НЛО. 1995. N2 13.

Mironenko 1990 – *Мироненко С.В.* Страницы тайной истории самодержавия: Политическая история России первой половины XIX столетия. М., 1990.

Montesquieu 1955 – *Монтескье Ш.* Избр. произведения / Общ. ред и вступ. статья М.П. Баскина. М., 1955.

Mordvinov 1901 – [*Мордвинов Н.С.*] Мнение относительно Крыма // Архив графов Мордвиновых. Т. III. СПб., 1901.

Mornet 1967 – Mornet, D. *Les origines intellectueles de la Rëvolution française.* Paris: A. Colin, 1967.

Morozov 1999 – *Морозов В.И.* Государственно-правовые взгляды М.М. Сперанского. СПб., 1999.

Mournier 1979 – Mournier, J. *La fortune des écrits de J.-J. Rousseau dans les pays de la langue allemande de 1782 à 1783.* Paris: P.U.F., 1979.

Mühlenbeck 1887 – Mühlenbeck, E. *Étude sur les origines de la Sainte Alliance.* Paris: F. Vieweg, 1887.

Murphy 1982 – Murphy, O.T. *Charles Gravier, Comte de Vergennes: French Diplomacy in the Age of Revolution: 1719-1787.* Albany: State University of New York Press, 1982.

Nadler I-V – *Надлер В. К.* Император Александр I и идея Священного союза. Т. I-V. Рига, 1886-1892.

Näf 1928 – Näf, W. *Zur Geschichte der Heiligen Allianz.* Bern: Paul Haupt, 1928.

Namier 1962 – Namier, L. *Crossroads of Power. Essays on Eighteenth-Century England.* New York: Macmillan, 1962.

Nemzer 1987 – *Немзер А.С.* «Сии чудесные виденья...» // *Зорин А.Л., Зубков Н.Н., Немзер А.С.* «Свой подвиг свершив...» М., 1987.

Nevakhovich 1809 – *Невахович Л.* Сульеты, или Спартанцы осьмнадцатого столетия. Историческое представление в пяти действиях. СПб., 1810.

Nevodchikov 1868 – *Неофит [Неводчиков Н.В.]* Знакомство и переписка А. Стурдзы с высокопреосвященным Филаретом, митрополитом Московским. Одесса, 1868.

Nikitenko I – *Никитенко А.В.* Дневник. Т. 1: 1826-1857 / Подгот. текста и примеч. И.Я. Айзенштока. Л., 1955.

Nikolai Mikhailovich 1903 – *Николай Михайлович, вел. кн.* Граф Павел Александрович Строганов (1774-1817). Историческое исследование эпохи императора Александра I. Т. I. СПб., 1903.

Nikolai Mikhailovich 1910 – *Николай Михайлович, вел. кн.* Переписка императора Александра I с сестрой, великой княгиней Екатериной Павловной. СПб., 1910.

Nikolai Mikhailovich 1999 – *Николай Михайлович, вел. кн.* Император Александр I. М., 1999.

Nikolai Mikhailovich I-II – *Николай Михайлович, вел. кн.* Император Александр I. Опыт исторического исследования. Т. I- II. СПб.,1912.

Novyi letopisets 1792 – Русская летопись по Никонову списку, изданная под смотрением Императорской академии наук. Ч. VIII: С 1583 до 1630 года. СПб., 1792.

Obolenskii 1858 – Два письма к императрице Екатерине Великой / Сообщ. М.А. Оболенский // Библиографические записки. 1858. № 17.

Oda 1784 – Ода великой государыне Екатерине II самодержице всероссийской на приобретение Крыма 1784 года. СПб., 1784.

Oginski I – Oginski, M. *Mémoires sur la Pologne et les Polonais*. Vol. I. Paris: Ponthieu, 1826.

Ogloblin 1901 – *Оглоблин Н.Н.* К характеристике русского общества в 1812 году // Чтения в историческом обществе Нестора летописца. 1901. Кн. XV. Вып. 2/3.

Okun' 1947 – *Окунь С.Б.* История СССР: Курс лекций. Т. I: 1796-1825. Л., 1947.

Olenin 1813 – *Оленин А.* Письмо архимандриту Филарету // Сын отечества. 1813. Ч. VII. № XXXII.

Ol'ri 1917 – Из донесений баварского поверенного в делах Ольри в первые годы царствования (1802-1806) императора Александра I / Сообщ. вел. кн. Николай Михайлович // ИВ. 1917. № 2.

Orlov 1870 – Первая мысль о морейской экпедиции графа А.Г. Орлова // Заря. 1870. № 6. Прилож.

Ospovat 1994 – *Осповат А.* К прениям 1830-х гг. о русской столице // Лотмановский сборник. [Вып.] 1. М., 1994.

Ozouff 1988 – Ozouff, M. "Fraternité." In F. Furet and M. Ozouff. *Dictionnaire critique
de la Révolution Française*. Paris: Flammarion, 1988.

Palladoklis 1771 – *Палладоклис А.* Ода А.Г. Орлову. СПб., 1771.

Palladoklis 1771a – *Палладоклис А.* Стихи на платье греческое, в кое Ее Императорское Величество изволили одеваться в маскараде. СПб., 1771.

Palladoklis 1773 – *Палладоклис А.* Истинного государствования подвиг. СПб., 1773.

Palladoklis 1775 – *Палладоклис А.* Каллиопа о преславныж победах е.и.в. . . . Екатерины Алексеевны оружием победоносным над оттоманами. . . СПб., 1775.

Pallas 1883 – Записка академика Н.С. Палласа, князю Потемкину о исследовании берегов Каспийского моря / Сообщ. Н. Муракевич // Записки императорского Одесского общества истории и древностей. Т. XIII. Одесса, 1883.

Panchenko 1983 – *Панченко А.М.* «Потемкинские деревни» как культурный миф // XVIII век. Сб. 14: Русская литература конца XVIII – начала XIX века в общественно- культурном контексте. Л., 1983.

Papernyi 1996 – *Паперный В.* Культура Два. М., 1996.

Pelino 1844 – Абрикосовое дерево, посаженное императрицею Екатериною II. Сообщ. Пелино // Записки императорского Одесского общества истории и древностей. Т. I. Одесса, 1844.

Pertz III – Pertz,G.H. *Das Leben des Ministers Freiherrs von Stein*. Вд. III. Berlin, 1851.

Petrov 1775 – [*Петров В.П.*] Ода е.и.в. Екатерине Второй... на заключение с Оттоманскою Портою мира. [М.,] 1775.

Petrov 1782 – Сочинения В. Петрова. Ч. I. СПб., 1782.

Petrov 1793 – *Петров В.* Ода Екатерине Второй... на присоединение польных областей к России, 1793 года. [СПб., 1793].

Petrov 1811 – Два письма Петрова // Москвитянин. 1841. Ч. I. № 1.

Petrov 1864 – Сборник материалов для истории Императорской санктпетербургской академии художеств за сто лет ее существования / Под ред. П.Н. Петрова. Т. I. СПб., 1864.

Petrov I-II – Сочинения В. Петрова. Т. I-II. СПб., 1811.

Petrov A. 1869 – *Петров А.* Война России с Турцией и польскими конфедератами. 1769- 1774 г. Сост. преимущественно из неизвестных по сие время рукописных материалов. Т. I. СПб., 1869.

Petrov A. I-II – *Петров А.Н.* Вторая Турецкая война в царствование императрицы Екатерины II. 1787-1791 г. Т. I-II. СПб., 1880.

Petukhov 1903 – *Петухов Е.В.* Памяти Н.В. Гоголя и В.А. Жуковского. Юрьев, 1903.

Piatigorsky 1997 – Piatigorsky, A. *Who's Afraid of Freemasons? The Phenomenon of Freemasonry*. London: Harvill Press, 1997.

Picchio 1992 – *Пиккио Р.* «Предисловие о пользе книг церковных» М.В. Ломоносова как манифест русского конфессионального пат- риотизма // Сборник статей к 70- летию проф. Ю.М. Лотмана. Тарту, 1992.

Pipes 1959 – Pipes, R. *Karamzin's Memoir on Ancient and Modern Russia*. Cambridge, Mass.: Harvard UP, 1959.

Pipes 1997 – Pipes, D. *Conspiracy: How the Paranoid Style Flourishes and Where it Comes From*. New York: Free Press, 1997.

Pipes 2000 – *Пайпс Д.* Заговор: объяснение успехов и происхождения «параноидального стиля» // НЛО. 2000. № 41.

Platonov 1913 – *Платонов С.Ф.* Древнерусские сказания и повести о Смутном времени XVII века как исторический источник / 2-е изд. СПб., 1913

Pogodin 1871 – *Погодин М.* Сперанский // РА. 1871. № 7/8.

Pogosian 1997 – *Погосян Е.А.* Традиционная одическая фразеология в творчестве Державина // Лотмановский сборник. [Вып.] 2. М., 1997.

Ponomarev 1867/1868 – *Пономарев С.* Высокопреосвященный Филарет, митрополит московский и коломенский. (Материалы для очерка его жизни и ученой деятельности) // Труды киевской духовной академии. 1867. № 12; 1868. № 4.

Ponomareva 1992 – *Пономарева Т.* Посвятил своему святому // Сборник статей к 70- летию проф. Ю.М. Лотмана. Тарту, 1992.

Poplavskaia 1983 – *Поплавская И.А.* Эволюция жанра послания в творчестве В.А. Жуковского // Художественное творчество и литературный процесс. Вып. V. Томск, 1983.

Popov 1875 – *Попов А.Н.* Москва в 1812 году // РА. 1875. № 8, 10.

Posnikova 1867 – Из семейного архива. II. Письмо М.И. Посниковой к А. И. Архаровой в С. Петербург / Сообщ. А.А. Васильчиков // РА. 1867.

Potemkin 1772 – *Потемкин П.* Россы в архипелаге. СПб., 1772.

Potemkin 1852 – О приватной жизни князя Потемкина, о некоторых чертах его характера и анекдотах. (Из современной рукописи) // Москвитянин. 1852. № 2-3.

Potemkin 1865 – Собственноручные бумаги князя Потемкина-Таврического / Сообщ. А.И. Ставровский, Н.С. Киселев // РА. 1865.

Potemkin 1875 – Письма князю Г.А. Потемкину-Таврическому // Записки императорского Одесского общества истории и древностей. Т. IX. Одесса, 1875.

Potemkin 1879 – Из бумаг князя Г.А. Потемкина-Таврического / Сообщ. А.А. Васильчиков // РА. 1879. № 9.

Potemkin 1991 – О приватной жизни князя Потемкина. Потемкинский праздник. М., 1991.

Predtechenskii 1950 – *Предтеченский А.В.* Отражение войн 1812-1814 гг. в сознании современников // Исторические записки. [Т.] 31. [М.,] 1950.

Predtechenskii 1957 – *Предтеченский А. В.* Очерки общественно-политической истории России в первой четверти XIX века. М.; Л., 1957.

Presniakov 1923 – *Пресняков А.Е.* Идеология Священного союза // Анналы. 1923. № 3.

Proskurin 1987 – *Проскурин О.А.* «Победитель всех Гекторов халдейских»: К.Н. Батюшков в литературной борьбе начала XIX века // Вопросы литературы. 1987. № 6.

Proskurin 1996 – *Проскурин О.* Новый Арзамас – Новый Иерусалим. Литературная игра в культурно-историческом контексте // НЛО. 1996. № 19.

Prousis 1994 – Prousis, T.C. *Russian Society and the Greek Revolution.* DeKalb, Ill: Northern Illinois UP, 1994.

Pugachev 1964 – *Пугачев В.В.* К вопросу о политических взглядах С.С. Уварова в 1810-е годы // Ученые записки Горьковского гос. ун- та им. Н.И. Лобачевского. Сер. историко-филологическая. Вып. 72. Горький, 1964.

Pugachev 1967 – *Пугачев В.В.* Эволюция общественно-политических взглядов Пушкина. (Учебное пособие). Горький, 1967.

Pukhov 1999 – *Пухов В.В.* Лазаревич // Словарь русских писателей XVIII века. Вып. 2 (К- П). СПб., 1999.

Pumpianskii 1983 – *Пумпянский Л.В.* Ломоносов и немецкая школа разума // XVIII век. Сб. 14: Русская литература конца XVIII – начала XIX века в общественно- культурном контексте. Л., 1983.

Putilov 1966 – Исторические песни XVIII века / Изд. подгот. О. Б. Алексеева и др.; под ред. Б.Н. Путилова. М.; Л., 1966.

Pypin 1900 – *Пыпин А.Н.* Общественное движение в России при Александре I / 3-е изд., доп. СПб., 1900

Pypin 1997 – *Пыпин А.Н.* Масонство в России. XVIII и первая четверть XIX в. М., 1997.

Pypin 2000 – Пыпин А.Н. Религиозные движения при Александре I. Исследования и статьи по эпохе Александра I / Предисл. А.Н. Цамутали. СПб., 2000.

Pypin I – Пыпин А.Н. История русской этнографии. Т. I: Общий обзор изучения народности и этнография великорусская. СПб., 1890.

Raeff 1957 – Raeff, M. *Michael Speransky: Statesman of Imperial Russia. 17721839.* The Hague: M. Nijhoff, 1957

Raeff 1972 – Raeff, M. "In the Imperial Manner." I In *Catherine the Great: A Profile.* Ed. M. Raeff. New York: Hill and Wang, 1972.

Ragsdale 1988 – Ragsdale, H. "Evaluating the Tradition of Russian Aggression: Catherine II and the Greek Project." *SEER* 66 (1): 1988.

Rasmussen 1978 – Rasmussen, K. "Catherine II and the Image of Peter I." *Slavic Review* 37(1): 1978.

Rebekkini 1998 – Ребеккини Д. Русские исторические романы 30-х годов XIX в. (Библиографический указатель) // НЛО. 1998. № 34.

Riazanovsky 1960 – Riazanovsky, N. V. "Russia and Asia. Two Nineteenth-Century Views." *California Slavic Studies* 1: 1960.

Riazanovsky 1967 – Riasanovsky, N. V. *Nicholas I and Official Nationality in Russia. 1825-1855.* Berkeley: U. of California Press, 1967.

Richards 1990 – Ричардс А. Философия риторики // Теория метафоры / Вступ. статья и сост. Н.Д. Арутюновой; общ. ред. Н.Д. Арутюновой и М.А. Журинской. М., 1990.

Ricœur 1977 – Ricœur, P. *The Rule of Metaphor: Multi-Disciplinary Studies of the Creation of Meaning in Language.* Toronto: U. of Toronto Press, 1977.

Ricœur 1986 – Ricœur, P. *Lectures on Ideology and Utopia.* Ed. G. H. Taylor. New York: Columbia UP, 1986.

Riquet 1973 – Riquet, M. *Augustin de Barruel: Un Jésuit face aux Jacobins francs-maçons.* Paris, 1973.

Roberts 1972 – Roberts, J.M. *The Mythology of the Secret Societies.* London: Watkins, 1972.

Robison 1797 – Robison, J. *Proofs of a Conspiracy against all the Religions and Governments of Europe, Carried on in the Secret Meetings of Free Masons, Illuminati and Reading Societies.* London: Printed for T. Cadell, 1798.

Robison 1806 – [Робайсон Д.] Доказательства заговора против всех религий и правительств // Московские ученые ведомости. 1806. № 18, 22-24, 26, 27.

Rogov 1997 – *Рогов К.* Декабристы и «немцы» // НЛО. 1997. № 26. \
Rostopchin 1875 – Записка о мартинистах, представленная в 1811 году графом Ростопчиным великой княгине Екатерине Павловне / Сообщ. А.Н. Афанасьев // РА. 1875. М 9.
Rostopchin 1876 – Письмо графа Ф.В. Ростопчина к великой княгине Екатерине Павловне / Сообщ. А.Ф. Ростопчин // РА. 1876. Кн. I.
Rostopchin 1892 – Письма графа Ф.В. Ростопчина к императору Александру Павловичу / Сообщ. А.Ф. Ростопчин // РА. 1892. № 8.
Rostopchin 1905 – Письмо графа Ростопчина к императору Александру I с доносом на Сперанского // РС. 1905. № 5.
Rostopchin 1992 – *Ростопчин Ф.В.* Ох, французы! / Сост., вступ. статья, примеч. Г.Д. Овчинникова. М., 1992.
Rousseau 1969 – *Руссо Ж.* Трактаты / Изд. подгот. В.С. Алексеев-Попов, Ю.М. Лотман, Н.А. Полторацкий, А.Д. Хаютин. М., 1969.
Rousseau 1971 I – Rousseau, J.-J. *The Political Writings.* Ed. C.E. Vanghan. Vol. I. New York: Wiley, 1971.
Rousseau III – Rousseau, J.-J.*Oeuvres completes.* / Ed. B. Gagnebin and M. Raymond. T. III. Paris: Gallimard, 1964.
Roussel I-III – *Politique de tous les Cabinets de l'Europe, pendent les règnes de Louis XV et Louis XVI. Manuscripts trouvés dans le cabinet de Louis XVI.* Ed. P.J.A. Roussel. Vol. I-III. Paris: Buison, 1793.
Rozhdestvenskii 1902 – *Рождественский С.В.* Исторический обзор деятельности Министерства народного просвещения. 1802-1902. СПб., 1902.
Ruban 1784 – *Рубан В.* Стихи На всевожделенное и всерадостнейшее рождение. . . великой княжны Елены Павловны, ко щастию всей России последовавшее Во граде святого Петра декабря 13 дня 1784 года. СПб., 1784.
Saint-Pierre 1986 – Saint-Pierre, abbé de. *Projet pour rendre la paix perpétuelle en Europe.* Paris, 1986.
Samoilov 1867 – *Самойлов А.Н.* Жизнь и деяния генерал-фельдмаршала князя Григория Александровича Потемкина Таврического // РА. 1867.
Sanglen 1883 – Записки Якова Ивановича де Санглена. 1776-1831 гг. / Сообщ. М.И. Богданович // РС. 1883. № 1-3.
Schafhäutl 1979 – Schafhäutl, K.E. von. *Abbé Georg Joseph Vogler.* New York: Georg Olms,, 1979.

Schlegel 1808 – Schlegel F. *Über die Sprache und Weisheit der Indier*. Heidelberg : Mohr und Zimmer,1808.

Schlegel I – Schlegel, F. *Philosophische Vorlesungen aus den Jahre 1804 – bis 1806*. Bd. II. Bonn: Weber, 1846.

Schmid 1888 – Schmid, G. "Goethe und Uwarow und ihr Briefwechsel." *Russische Revue*. Bd. 17. № 2:1888.

Schönle 2001 – Schönle, A. "Garden of the Empire: Catherine's Appropriation of the Crimea." *Slavic Review* 60 (1): 2001.

Schuchard 1992 – Schuchard, M.K. "Blake's 'Mr. Femality': Freemasonry, Espionage, and the Double-Sexed." *Studies in Eighteenth-Century Culture*. 22: 1992.

Schwab 1950 – Schwab, R. *La Renaissance Orientale*. Paris: Payot, 1950.

Ségur 1907 – Пять лет в России при Екатерине Великой. Записки графа Л.Ф. Сегюра // РА. 1907. № 10.

Semeka 1902 – *Семека А*. Русские розенкрейцеры и сочинения императрицы Екатерины II против масонства // ЖМНП. 1902. № 2.

Semevskii 1875 – *Семевский М*. Кн. Григорий Александрович Потемкин-Таврический // РС. 1875. № 4.

Semevskii 1911/1912 – *Семевский В*. Падение Сперанского // Отечественная война и русское общество / Ред. А.К. Дживелегова, С.П. Мельгунова, В.И. Пичета. Т. II. СПб., 1911/1912.

Serkov 2000 – *Серков А.И*. История русского масонства XIX века. СПб., 2000.

Severgin 1807 – [*Севергин В.М.*] Похвальное слово князю Пожарскому и Кузьме Минину. СПб., 1807.

Shaepper-Wimmer 1985 – Shaepper-Wimmer, S. *Augustin Barruel, S.J. (1741-1820): Studien zu Biographie und Werk*. Frankfurt am Main: P. Lang, 1985.

Shakhovskoi 1964 – *Шаховской А.А*. Дебора // Стихотворная трагедия конца XVIII – начала XIX в. / Вступ. статья, подгот. текста и примеч. В.А. Бочкарева. М.; Л., 1964.

Shchukin II, VIII – Бумаги, относящиеся до Отечественной войны 1812 года, собранные и изданные П.И. Щукиным. Ч. II. М., 1892. Ч. VIII. М., 1904.

Shebunin 1925 – *Шебунин А.Н*. Европейская контрреволюция Первой четверти XIX века / С предисл. Я. Захера. Л., 1925.

Shebunin, manuscript – *Шебунин А.Н.* Вокруг Священного союза // ОР РПБ. Ф. 849. № 110-111.

Shevchenko 1991 - *Шевченко М.М.* Правительство, цензура и печать в России в 1848 г. // Вестник МГУ. Сер. 8. История. 1991. No 2.

Shevchenko 1997 – *Шевченко М.М.* Сергей Семенович Уваров // Российские консерваторы. М., 1997.

Shil'der 1893 – Переписка императора Александра Павловича с графом Ф.В. Ростопчиным. 1812-1814 гг. / Сообщ. Н.К. Шильдер 1/ РС. 1893. № 1.

Shil'der 1898/1899 – *Шильдер Н.К.* Два доноса в 1831 году // РС. 1898. № 12. 1899. № 1- 3.

Shil'der 1903 II- *Шильдер Н.К.* Император Николай Первый. Его жизнь и царствование. Т. II. СПб., 1903.

Shil'der I-IV – *Шильдер Н.К.* Император Александр Первый. Его жизнь и царствование. Т. I-IV. СПб., 1897-1898.

Shirinskii-Shikhmatov 1807 – *Шихматов С.* Пожарский, Минин, Гермоген, или Спасенная Россия. Лирическая поэма в трех песнях. СПб., 1807.

Shirinskii-Shikhmatov 1971 – *Ширинский-Шихматов С.А.* Пожарский, Минин, Гермоген, или Спасенная Россия // Поэты 1790-1810-х годов I Вступ. статья и сост. Ю.М. Лотмана; подгот. текста М. Г. Альтшуллера. Л., 1971.

Shishkov 1831 – Краткие записки адмирала А. Шишкова, веденные им во время пребывания его при блаженной памяти государе импера- торе Александре Первом в бывшую с французами в 1812 и последующих годах войну. СПб., 1831.

Shishkov 1870 – Записки, мнения и переписка адмирала А.С. Шишкова / Изд. Н. Киселева и Ю. Самарина. Т. I. Берлин, 1870.

Shishkov II, IV – Собрание сочинений и переводов адмирала Шишкова, Российской императорской академии президента и разных ученых обществ члена. Ч. II. СПб., 1824. Ч. IV. СПб., 1825.

Shliapkin 1885 – *Шляпкин И.А.* Василий Петрович Петров, «карманный стихотворец» Екатерины II. (По новым данным) // ИВ. 1885. № 11.

Shpet 1989 – *Шпет Г. Г.* Сочинения / Под. ред. А.В. Антоновой. М., 1989.

Shtein 1905 – *В.Ш.* [*Штейн В.И.*] Барон фон Штейн. При русской главной квартире. (1812-1815) // ИВ. 1905. № 9.

Sidorova 1952 – Сидорова Л. П. Рукописные замечания современника на первом издании трагедии В.А. Озерова «Димитрий Донской» // Записки Отдела рукописей Государственной библиотеки имени В.И. Ленина. Вып. 18. М., 1952.

Sirotkin 1966 – Сироткин В.Г. Дуэль двух дипломатий. Россия и Франция в 1801-1812 гг. М., 1966.

Sirotkin 1975 – Сироткин В.Г. А.Н. Шебунин – историк общественной мысли и внешней политики России первой четверти XIX в. // История и историки: Историографический ежегодник. 1973. М., 1975.

Sirotkin 1981- Сироткин В.Г. Великая Французская буржуазная революция, Наполеон и самодержавная Россия // История СССР. 1981. № 5.

Sirotkin 1981 а – Сироткин В.Г. Наполеоновская война перьев против России // Новая и новейшая история. 1981. № 3.

Smilianskaia 1995- Смилянская И.М. Восточное Средиземноморье в восприятии россиян и в российской политике (вторая половина XVIII в.) // Восток. 1995. № 5.

Smilianskaia 1996 – Смилянская И.М. Русско-арабские связи в контексте политики Екатерины II в Средиземноморье // Арабский мир в конце XX века: Материалы Первой конференции арабистов Института востоковедения РАН. М., 1996.

Smith 1999 – Smith, D. *Working the Rough Stone: Freemasonry and Society in Eighteenth- Century Russia.* DeKalb, Ill: Northern Illinois UP, 1999.

Sokolovskaia 1915 – Соколовская Т.О. Возрождение масонства при Александре I // Масонство в его прошлом и настоящем / Под ред. С.П. Мельгунова и Н.П. Сидорова. Т. II. М., 1915.

Solov'ev 1863 – Соловьев С. История падения Польши. М., 1863.

Solov'ev XIV – Соловьев С.М. Соч.: В 18 кн. Кн. XIV: *История России с древнейших времен.* Тома 27-28. М., 1994.

Souleyman 1936 – Souleyman, E. V. *The Vision of World Peace in Seventeenth and Eighteenth-Century France.* N ewYork, 1936.

Speranskii 1862 – Дружеские письма графа М.М. Сперанского П.Г. Масальскому, писанные с 1798 по 1819 год, с историческими пояснениями, составленными К. Масальским, и некоторые сочинения первой молодости графа М.М. Сперанского: «Досуги», «Краткий очерк священной истории». СПб., 1862.

Speranskii 1870 – Письма Сперанского к А.А. Стольщину / Публ. Д. Столыпина // РА. 1870.

Speranskii 1870a – Письмо М.М. Сперанского к И.В. Лопухину / Сообщ. А.Ф. Бычков // РА. 1870.

Speranskii 1870b – Письма Сперанского к Ф.И. Цейеру// РА. 1870.

Stankevich I-II – *Станевич Е.* Рассуждение о русском языке. Ч. I-II. СПб., 1808.

Starck 1803 – Starck, J.A. *Der Triumph der Philosophie im XVIII Jahrhundert.* Frankfurt, 1803.

Starobinski 1962 – Starobinski, J. "La pensée politique de Jean-Jacques Rousseau." In *J.-J. Rousseau.* Neuchatel, 1962.

Starobinski 1971- Starobinski, J. *La tranparence et l'obstacle.* Paris, 1971.

Stein III – Stein, H. F. K. *Briefe und amtliche Schriften.* Bd. III: *Brünn und Prag: Die Krise des Jahres 1811 in Moskau und Petersburg. Die grosse Wendung (1809-1812).* Ed. Walther Hubatsch. Stuttgart: Kolhammer, 1961.

Stelletskii 1901 – *Стеллецкий Н.* Князь А.Н. Голицын и его духовно-государственная деятельность. Киев, 1901.

Stevenson 1988 – Stevenson, D. *The Origins of Freemasonry: Scotland's Century. 1590- 1790.* Cambridge: Cambridge UP, 1988.

Stourdza 1815 – *Stourdza A.* "Considération sur l'acte d'alliance fratérnelle et chrétienne du 14/26 Septembre 1815." ОР РНБ. Ф. 849. No 90 [копия А.Н. Шебунина; оригинал см.: РО ИРЛИ. Ф. 288. Оп. 1. № 47].

Stourdza 1864 – *Стурдза А. С.* Воспоминания и жизни и деяниях графа И. А. Каподистрии, правителя Греции. М., 1864.

Stroev 1998 – *Строев А.* «Те, кто поправляет фортуну». Авантюристы Просвещения. М., 1998.

Stroev 2001 – *Строев А.Ф.* Летающий философ (Жан-Жак Руссо глазами Фридриха- Мельхиора Гримма) // НЛО. 2001. № 48.

Sukhomlinov 1868 – *Сухомлинов М.И.* Из бумаг в бозе почившего митрополита Филарета // ЖМНП. 1868. № 1.

Sukhomlinov II – *Сухомлинов М.И.* Исследования и статьи по русской литературе и просвещению. Т. Н. СПб., 1889.

Sully X – записки Максимилиана Бетюна герцога Сюлли, первого министра Генриха IV... Т. X. М., 1776. гг.

Sumarokov II – Полное собрание всех сочинений, в стихах и прозе, покойного действительного статского советника, ордена св. Анны кавалера и Лейпцигского ученого собрания члена, Александра Петровича Сумарокова / Собраны и изданы в удовольствие любителей российской учености Н. Новиковым. Ч. II. М., 1781.

Sverbeev 1870 – *Свербеев Д.* Заметка о смерти Верещагина // РА. 1870. \

Sverbeev 1871- Первая и последняя моя встреча с А.С. Шишковым. (Из записок Д.Н. Свербеева) // РА. 1871. № 1.

Syroechkovskii 1954 – *Сыроечковский Б.Е.* Балканская проблема в политических планах декабристов // Очерки из истории движения декабристов: Сб. статей / Под ред. Н.М. Дружинина, Б Е Сыроечковского. М., 1954.

Tartakovskii 1973 – *Тартаковский А.Г.* Показання очевидцев о пребывании французов в Москве в 1812 г. (К методике источниковедческого анализа) // Источниковедение отечественной истории. Вып. 1. М. 1973.

Tartakovskii 1980 – *Тартаковский А.Г.* 1812 год и русская мемуаристика: Опыт источниковедческого изучения. М., 1980.

Tartakovskii 1996 – *Тартаковский А.Г.* Неразгаданный Барклай. Легенды и быль 1812 года. М., 1996.

Tartakovskii 1997 – *Тартаковский А.Г.* Русская мемуаристика и исорическое сознание XIX века. М., 1997.

Teppe 1950 – Teppe, J. *Chamfort. Sa vie, son oeuvre, sa pensée.* Paris: Pierre Clairac, 1950.

Thompson 1984 – Thompson, J. B. *Studies in the Theory of Ideology.* Berkeley: U. of California Press, 1984.

Timofeev 1983 – *Тимофеев Л. В.* В кругу друзей и муз. Дом А. Н. Оленина. Л., 1983.

Timoshchuk 1893 – *В. В. Т.* [*Тимощук В. В.*] Императрица Екатерина II в Крыму. 1787 г. // РС. 1893. № 11.

Tiutchev II – *Тютчев Ф.И.* Соч.: В 2 т. / Общ. ред. К.В. Пигарева, сост. и подгот. текста Л. Н. Кузиной. Т. II. М., 1980.

Tocqueville 1986 – Tocqueville, A. de. *De la démocratie en Amerique. Souvenirs. L'Ancien régime et la revolution.* Intro. and ed. J.-C. Lamberti and F. Mélonio. Paris: Laffont, 1986.

Todd – *Тодд III У. М.* Литература и общество в эпоху Пушкина. СПб., 1996.

Tolstoi 1872 – *Толстой Ю.* О духовном союзе Е. Ф. Татариновой // Девятнадцатый век. Исторический сборник, издаваемый П. Бартеневым. Кн. I. М., 1872.

Tomashevskii 1948 – *Томашевский Б.* К. Н. Батюшков // Батюшков К. Стихотворения / Вступ. статья, ред. и примеч. Б. Томашевского. [Л.,] 1948.

Tomsinov 1991 – *Томсинов В.А.* Светило русской бюрократии. М., 1991.

Triomphe 1968 – Triomphe, R. *Joseph de Maistre. Étude sur 1a vie et la doctrine d'un materialiste mystique.* Geneva, 1968.

Troitskii 1994 – *Троицкий Н.А.* Александр I и Наполеон. М., 1994.

Tsimbaev 1986 – *Цимбаев Н.И.* Славянофильство. Из истории русской общественно-политической мысли XIX века. М., 1986.

Tsimbaev 1989 – *Цимбаев Н.И.* «Под бременем познанья и сомненья...» (Идейные искания 1830-х годов) // Русское общество 30-х годов XIX века. Люди и идеи. Мемуары современников / Под. ред. И.А. Федосова. М., 1989.

Turgenev 1887 – Записки Александра Михайловича Тургенева // РС. 1887. № 1.

Tynianov 1968 – *Тынянов Ю Н.* Пушкин и его современники / Под ред. В. В. Виноградова. М., 1968.

Ulianitskii 1883 – *Уляницкий В.А.* Дарданеллы, Босфор и Черное море в XVII1 веке. М., 1883.

Uspenskii 1999 – *Успенский Б.А.* Русская интеллигенция как специфический феномен русской культуры // Россия / Russia. Вып. 2 [10]: Русская интеллигенция и западный интеллектуализм: история и типология. М., 1999.

Uvarov 1814 – [Ouvaroff S.S.] *L'empereur Alexandre et Buonaparte.* St. Petersburg, 1814.

Uvarov 1818 – [*Уваров С.С.*] Речь президента Императорской Академии наук, попечителя Петербургского учебного округа в торжественном собрании Главного педагогического института 22 марта 1818 г. СПб., 1818.

Uvarov 1834 – [*Уваров С.С.*] [От редакции] // ЖМНП. 1834. Ч. I. № 1.

Uvarov 1834a – [*Уваров С. С.*] Циркулярное предложение г. управляющего министерством народного просвещения начальствам учебных округов о вступлении в управление министерством // ЖМНП. 1834. ч. I. № 1.

Uvarov 1848 – Ouvaroff, S. *Esquisses politiques et littéraires*. Avec un essai biographique et critique par L. Leduc. Paris 1848.

Uvarov 1864 - Десятилетие Министерства народного просвещения. 1833-1843. Записка, представленная государю императору Николаю Павловичу министром народного просвещения гр. Уваровым в 1843 г. СПб., 1864.

Uvarov 1871 – Письма к В.А. Жуковскому / Сергей Семенович Уваров // РА. 1871.

Uvarov 1871a – Письмо (графа) Сергея Семеновича Уварова к барону Штейну // РА. 1871. № 2.

Uvarov 1875 – [*Уваров С.С.*] Отчет по обозрении московского университета // Сборник постановлений по Министерству народного просвещения. Т. II: Царствование императора Николая I. 1825-1855. Отд. I: 1825-1839 / Изд. 2-е. СПб., 1875.

Uvarov 1896 – Собственноручное письмо С. С. Уварова – М. М. Сперанскому / Сообщ. А.Ф. Бычков // РС. 1896. N° 10.

Uvarov 1995 – Доклады министра народного просвещения С.С. Уварова Николаю I / Публ. М.М. Шевченко // Река времен (Книга истории и культуры). Кн. I. М. 1995.

Uvarov 1997 – *Уваров С.С.* <Письмо Николаю I> / Публ. А.Л. Зорина // НЛО. 1997. № 26.

Varnhagen von Ense 1859 – Граф Ф.В. Ростопчин. (Из воспоминаний Варнгагена-фон- Энзе) // Московские ведомости. 1859. 2 окт. № 234.

Veber 1872 – Записки о Петре Великом и его царствовании Брауншвейгского резидента Вебера / Предисл. и примеч. П.П. Барсова // РА. 1872. № 6.

Vereshchagin 1775 – *Верещагин И.* Ода На торжество заключенного мира, между Россиею и Оттоманскою Портом. [М.,] 1775.

Vernadskii 1999 – *Вернадский Г. В.* Русское масонство в царствован ис Екатерины II / 2-ое изд, испр. и расшир.; под ред. М.В. Рейзина и А.Н. Серкова. СПб., 1999.

Veselovskii 1904 – *Веселовский А.Н.* В. А.Жуковский. Поэзия чувства и «сердечного воображения». СПб., 1904.

Viatte I-II – Viatte. A. *Les sources occultes du Romantisme: Illuminisme – Thëosophie. 1770-1820.* Vol. I-II. Paris: Champion, 1979, 1979.

Viazemskii VII – Полн. собр. соч. князя П.А. Вяземского. Т. VII. СПб., 1882.

Vigel' II, IV – Записки Ф.Ф. Вигеля / Изд. «Русского архива», дополненное с подлинной рукописи. Ч. II, IV. М., 1892.

Vinitskii 1998 – *Виницкий И.Ю.* Нечто о приведениях. Истории о русской литературной мифологии XIX века. М., 1998.

Vinogradov 2000 – Век Екатерины II: Дела балканские / Отв. ред. В. Н. Виноградов. М., 2000.

Viskovatov 1883 – *Висковатов П.А.* Василий Андреевич Жуковский. Столетняя годовщина дня рождения // РС. 1883. № 1.

Vitberg 1954 – Записки А.Л. Витберга // Собрание соч. А.И. Герцена: в 30 т. Т. I. М., 1954.

Voltaire XIII – *Oeuvres complètes de Voltaire.* Vol. XIII. Paris, 1785.

Vries de Gunsburg 1941 – Vries de Gunsburg I. de. *Catherine Pavlovna, Grande Duchesse de Russie. 1788-1819.* Amsterdam: Muelenhoff, 1941.

Waegemans 1992 – Waegemans E. "Un Belge dans les villages de Potemkine. Le Prince de Ligne dans 1a Russie de 1a Grande Catherine." *Nouvelles Annales Prince de Ligne* VII: 1992.

Whittaker 1978 – Whittaker,C.H. "The Ideology of Sergei Uvarov: An Interpretative Essay." *Russian Review* 37(2): 1978.

Whittaker 1978a – Whittaker, C.H. "The Impact of the Oriental Renaissance in Russia: The Case of Sergei Uvarov." *Jahrbücher für Geshichte Ost-Europas.* Bd. XXVI. No. 4.

Whittaker 1999 – *Виттекер Ц.Х.* Граф С.С. Уваров и его время. СПб., 1999.

Wight 1968 – Wight, M. "The Balance of Power." In *Diplomatic Investigations: Essays in the Theory of International Politics.* Ed. H, Butterfield and M. Wight. Cambridge, Mass: Harvard UP 1968.

Wilberger 1976 – Wilberger, C.H. *Voltaire's Russia: Window to the East.* Oxford, 1976.

Wilson 1964 – Wilson, L.A. *A Mythical Image.* Durham, N.C.: Duke UP, 1964.

Wolff 1994 – Wolff, L. *Inventing Eastern Europe: The Map of Civilization on the Mind of the Enlightenment.* tanford: Stanford UP, 1994.

Woodhouse 1973 – Woodhouse, C.M. *Capodistria: The Founder of Greek Independence.* London: Oxford UP, 1973.

Wortman 1994 – Wortman, R. *Scenarios of Power. Myth and Ceremony in the Russian Monarchy*. Vol. I: *From Peter the Great to Death of Nicholas I*. Princeton: Princeton UP, 1994.

Yates 1999 – Йейтс Ф. Розенкрейцерское Просвещение. М., 1999.

Zabarinskii 1936 – *Забаринский П. П.* Первые «огневые машины» в кронштадском порту (К истории введения паровых двигателей в России). М.; Л., 1936.

Zabelin 1848 – Сыскное дело о ссоре межевых судей кн. В. Большого Ромодановского и дворянина Лариона Сумина / Предисл. И. Забелина // ЧОИДР. 1848. № 7.

Zagoskin II – *Загоскин Н.П.* История Императорского казанского университета за первые сто лет его существования. 1804-1904. Т. II. Казань, 1902 [на обложке «1903»]

Zapadov 1976 – *Западов В.А.* К истории правительственных преследований Новикова // XVIII век. Сб. 11: Н.И. Новиков и общественно-литературное движение его времени. Л., 1976.

Zavadski 1993 – Zavadski W.H. *A Man of Honour: Adam Czartoryski as a Statesman of Russia and Poland, 1795-1831*. Oxford: Clarendon Press, 1993.

Zeidlits 1883 – *Зейдлиц К.К.* Жизнь и поэзия Жуковского. По неизданным источникам и личным воспоминаниям. СПб., 1883.

Zemskova 2000 – *Земскова Е.Е.* О роли языка в построении национальной утопии: «онемечивание» Кампе и «корнесловие» Шишкова // Философский век. [Вып.] 12: Российская утопия: От идеального государства к совершенному обществу: Материалы Третьей международной Летней школы по истории идей 9-30 июля 2000 г. СПб., 2000.

Zharinov 1911 – *Жаринов Д.А.* Первые войны с Наполеоном и русское общество // Отечественная война и русское общество / Ред. А.К. Дживелегова, С.П. Мельгунова, В.И. Пичета. Т. I. М., 1911.

Zharinov 1912 – *Жаринов Д.А.* Первые впечатления войны. Манифесты // Отечественная война и русское общество / Ред. А.К. Дживелегова, С.П. Мельгунова, В.И. Пичета. Т. III. СПб., 1912.

Zharinov 1912a – *Жаринов Д.А.* Впечатления от пожара и мнения современников // Отечественная война и русское общество / Ред. А.К. Дживелегова, С.П. Мельгунова, В.И. Пичета. Т. IV. М., 1912.

Zhigarev 1896 – *Жигарев С.* Русская политика в восточном вопросе. (Ее история в XVI- XIX веках, критическая оценка и будущие задачи). Историко-юридические очерки. Т. I-II. М., 1896.

Zhikharev 1955 – *Жихарев С.П.* Записки современника / Ред., статья и коммент. Б.М. Эйхенбаума. М.; Л., 1955.

Zhukov 1866 – *Жуков И.Ф.* Разбор известий и дополнительных сведений о казни купеческого сына Верещагина 2 сентября в Москве // ЧОИДР. 1866. Ч. IV. Отд. V.

Zhukovskaia, manuscript – *Жуковская А.В.* Летопись жизни и творчества В.П. Петрова. Рукопись.

Zhukovskii 1864 – Подлинные черты из жизни В.А. Жуковского // РА. 1864.

Zhukovskii 1883 – Письма В.А. Жуковского / Сообщ. К.К. Зейдлиц // РС. 1883. № 1.

Zhukovskii 1883a – Василий Андреевич Жуковский в его письмах. Второй период / Сообщ. К.К. Зейдлиц // РС. 1883. № 3.

Zhukovskii 1895 – Письма В.А. Жуковского к Александру Ивановичу Тургеневу / Изд. «Русского архива» по подлинникам, хранящимся в Императорской публичной библиотеке. М., 1895.

Zhukovskii 1902 II – Полн. собр. соч. В.А. Жуковского: В 12 т. / Под ред., с биограф. очерком и примеч. А.С. Архангельского. [Т.] II. СПб., 1902.

Zhukovskii 1904 – Уткинский сборник. [Вып.] I: Письма В. А. Жуковского, М.А. Мойер и Е. А. Протасовой / Под ред. А. Е. Грузинского. М., 1904.

Zhukovskii 1907 – Письма-дневники В.А. Жуковского. 1814-1815 / Под ред. П. К. Симони. СПб., 1907.

Zhukovskii I – *Жуковский В.А.* Полное собрание сочинений и писем. Т. 1: Стихотворения 1797-1814 годов / Ред. О.Б. Лебедева и А.С. Янушкевич. М., 1999.

Zimnii pokhod 1807 – Зимний поход русских и французов в 1806 и 1807 годах // Вестник Европы. 1807. Ч. XXXIV. № 13.

Žižek 1999 – *Жижек С.* Возвышенный объект идеологии. М., 1999.

Zorin 1996 – *Зорин А.* Идеология «православия – самодержавия – народности» и ее немецкие источники // В раздумьях о России (XIX век). М., 1996.

Index

A

Aksakov, S. T. 233
Al'tshuller, M.G. 219, 174n6, 247, 247n5, 248, 248n6
Aleksander Pavlovich — see Alexander I.
Alexander I 23, 27, 58–60, 106, 113, 158–160, 162, 173n5, 174n6, 182, 185, 187–193, 199, 200, 202–210, 213, 214, 216, 217, 224, 227, 228, 231–233, 236, 239, 240, 243–246, 250, 254, 256–261, 264–266, 268, 268n1, 269, 275–279, 280n6, 281, 282, 284–287, 289–295, 297–306, 308–312, 315–324, 330
Alexander Nevskii 58
Alexander of Macedon — see Alexander the Great.
Alexander the Great 30, 55–57, 59, 60, 98, 107
Algarotti 35
Althusser, Louis 3, 5n2, 19, 21n5
Anacreon 33
Anderson, Benedict 358
Anderson, M. S. 66
Andropov, Yu. V. 14
Anna Ioannovna, Empress 26
Anna, Greek Princess 96
Arakcheev, A. A. 331
Aristotel 17
Armfel'dt, G. 192, 194, 206
Arndt, E. M. 239
Arsen'ev, K. I. 353
Avraamii (Palitsyn) 170, 235, 244
Avril the Elder, Jean-Jacques 106

B

Baader, Franz von 321
Bakhtin, M. M. 8
Bakunina, T. A. 204n9
Bakunina, V. I. 223, 225, 232, 234, 246
Balashov, A. D. 190, 192, 206–209, 216, 236
Baldan, Grigorii 54
Baldani, G. 102
Barklay de Tolly, M. A. 108n3
Barrot, Odilon 331, 332
Barruel, Augustin 197–200, 200n8, 201–203, 206, 214, 215, 222, 321, 354, 355
Bartenev, I. N. 294
Bartenev, P. I. 207
Basil, the Saint 35
Batalden, Stephen 54
Batiushkov, K. N. 253, 260, 262, 275

400 Index

Bauman, Zygmunt 1, 335n5
Beaumarchais, Pierre-Auguste Caron de 85
Beaunoir, A.-L.-B. 135, 136
Belisarius, 179
Benner, Jean-Henri 218
Bentham, Jeremy 88, 91
Berckheim, F. 319
Bergasse, Nicholas 321
Berkheim, Baron 309
Bezborodko, A. A. 25, 61, 93, 110n4, 126, 142, 143, 151
Bieberstein, J. R. von 199
Blank, I. 113
Blok, A. 108n3
Bludov, D. N. 238n1, 260
Bobrov, S. S. 115, 116, 118, 119, 121, 156n1
Bogdanovich, I. F. 72
Borel', P. F. 243
Borovikovskii, V. L. 214, 305
Boulainville, A. de 349
Branicka, Countess 144
Branicki, F. 138, 139
Breteuil, Baron 82
Brian, J. 249
Broglie, A. de 80, 81, 83
Broglie, Count de 79–81, 84, 85, 86n4, 87
Brompton, Richard 59
Bruce, Ia. A. 111
Budberg, A. Ia. 161
Bulgakov, A. Ia. 224
Bulgakov, Ia. I. 150
Bulgaris, Evgenii 54, 57
Burdaev, P. I. 230
Burke, Edmund 10, 337
Burke, Kenneth 18
Buturlin, M. D. 345

C

Campe, J. H. 166
Capodistria, Ioannis 325
Cassirer, Ernst 17
Catherine II — see Catherine the Great.
Catherine the Great 22–29, 29n3, 30, 30n4, 31–36, 38, 42–50, 56–58, 61, 63–65, 72, 81, 82, 82n3, 83, 89, 90, 92–94, 96, 97, 99–102, 105–108, 108n3, 109–111, 113–115, 120–122, 124, 125, 125n2, 126, 127, –129, 131–134, 137–144, 145n13, 147, 148, 150, 151, 151n15, 152, 180, 191n2, 202, 206, 223, 246, 318, 320
Caulaincourt, Armand de 204
Chamfort, Nicolas 135, 137
Chappe d'Auteroche, Jean 82
Chateaubriand, François René de 322
Cheskii, I. V. 267
Choiseul, Étienne François de 65, 86
Choiseul-Gouffier, Sophie 290
Collot, Marie-Anne 44
Comte de Vergennes 65, 70, 82
Constantine Paleologus 94
Constantine the Great 57, 128
Conti, L.-F. Prince 79, 90
Czartoryski, Adam 162, 163, 173, 207–209, 354

D

D'Alembert, Jan Le Rond 198
Danilov, F. D. 132
Darius, the Persian emperor, 57, 107, 108n3
Dashkov, D. V. 260, 275
Dashkova, Princess 84
Dawe, George 243
Dekhtiarev, S. A. 157
Demosthenes 33, 34
Demut-Malinovskii, V. I. 349
Derzhavin, Gavriil 94, 96, 98, 101, 102, 110, 113, 123, 125, 127–134, 134n7, 136, 137, 142, 145, 146n14, 155–157, 170, 172–180, 183, 183n9, 184, 208, 219–221, 246, 247, 250, 258
Destutt, Antoine Louis Claude 1
Dmitriev, I. I. 145, 189, 228, 275
Dmitriev, M. A. 228, 229
Dmitrieva, E. E. 280n6
Domashnev, Sergei 39, 50, 56
Dorland, Arthur 291
Druzhinina, E. I. 93
Du Toit de Mambrini, M. F. 306
Dubrovin, N. F. 93
Durylin, S. N. 337
Dutoit, Jean Philippe 251

E

Eagleton, Terry 2, 19

Eckartshausen, Karl von 210, 295–299, 303, 312, 315, 317, 318, 321
Eilert, R. F. 282
Ekaterina Alekseevna, Grand Princess 80
Ekaterina I 105
Ekaterina Pavlovna, Grand Princess 191, 192, 205, 214, 217–220, 222, 223, 236, 268, 297
Ekimov, P. E. 33
Elagin, I. P. 90
Elagina, A. P. 264
Elizaveta Alekseevna, Empress 278, 291
Elizaveta Petrovna, Empress 84
Empaytaz, Henri-Louis 293, 304, 316
Engel'gart, L. N. 143
Engels, F. 2, 3
Enghien, Duke of 181
Éon de Beamond, Charles 84, 85, 87, 89–91
Ermolov, G. P. 225
Eropkin, P. D. 114
Erskin, Thomas 345
Etkind, A. M. 280n6
Eugene of Württemberg 109
Eugenius (Bulgaris) 102
Euripides 33, 108, 110
Evgenii (Bolkhovitinov) 219

F

Falconet, E. 44
Falkenstein, Count 106, 107
Fateev, A. N. 143, 145n13
Favier, Jean-Louis 82
Fenelon, 67, 210, 273
Feofilakt (Rusanov) 210, 216
Fessler, I. A. 211–213, 215, 216
Filaret (Drozdov) 22, 214, 232, 245, 248–254, 256, 257, 263, 266, 275–277
Fitzherbert, A. 143
Florov, A. A. 271
Florovskii, George 213, 257, 268n1, 274, 276, 298
Fontanes, L. de 277
Forestier, René de 206n11
Fotii (Spasskii) 324, 354
Fournier 293n2
Franz I, Austrian Emperor 289, 301, 308
Frederick II (Frederick the Great), Prussian King 65, 198

Freiherr vom Stein, Karl 341
Freud, S. 5n2
Friedrich Wilhelm III, Prussian King 279, 301, 308

G

Galakhov, A. D. 305
Galich, A. I. 353
Garzonio, Stefano 251
Gauenshil'd, F. 191, 211, 212, 214, 215
Gavrilov, A. G. 230n17
Gebauer, Ernst 205
Geertz, Clifford 4–13, 17–19, 23
Gentz, Friedrich von 309, 318, 319
Georgel, J. F. 83, 84
Germogen, Patriarch 169, 171
Glinka, F. N. 242
Glinka, M. I. 157
Glinka, S. N. 62, 155, 157, 170, 171, 171n4, 173, 221, 226, 236
Glück, Ch. W. 109
Glushkovskii, A. P. 230
Gnedich, N. I. 247, 248, 260
Goethe, J. W. von 109
Gogol', N. V. 142
Golenishchev-Kutuzov, L. I. 187
Golikov, I. I. 176, 177, 182
Golitsyn, A. B. 353, 354
Golitsyn, A. N. 189, 191, 193, 214, 216, 250, 251, 256, 261, 268, 269, 275–279, 279n5, 280n6, 284, 292–294, 299, 301, 302, 309, 320, 324, 354
Gorchakov, N. P. 157
Goudar, A. 128
Grabianka, Tadeusz 202, 354
Grech, N. I. 158, 187, 346, 353
Griboedov, A. S. 20, 286
Grimm, F. M. 58, 60, 82, 101, 135
Grot, Ia. K. 126, 127, 134, 142, 145, 156, 173n5, 219n14
Gruzinskii, A. E. 272n3
Guillard, N.-F. 109
Guizot, F. 331–335, 335n5, 336, 351
Gur'ianov, I. 134
Gustav II Adolf 284
Gustav III 64, 71, 82
Guyon, J. M. B. de 210, 319

H

Hannibal, I. A. 104
Harris, James 25, 28, 29, 93
Hartley 12
Heber 223
Hennin 83
Henry IV, French King 44, 71, 72, 127, 128, 318
Herder, J. G. 36, 246, 340, 347
Herodotus 107, 108n3
Hesiod, 102
Homer 33, 34, 98–101, 109
Howard, Robert 142

I

Ivan the Terrible 16, 100
Ivanov, I. A. 186

J

Jarre, Jean-Michel 16
Joseph II, Emperor 24, 27–29, 106, 109
Jung (Stilling), J. H. 203, 268, 269, 273, 278, 279, 284, 293, 302, 321
Justi, J. H. G. von 71
Justinian, Greek Emperor 179

K

Kapodistrias, Ioannes 289, 316
Karamzin, N. M. 159, 217, 217n13, 219, 225, 233, 247, 263, 275, 337–339
Karzhavin, Fedor 205, 205n10, 207, 208
Katenin, P. A. 286
Kaunitz, W. A. 83
Kazakov, N. I. 330n2
Kheraskov, M. M. 37, 50–52, 56, 58, 100, 114, 156, 171, 173, 180
Khrapovitskii, A. V. 114, 124, 142, 143n12
Khvostov, D. I. 168, 252, 257
Kingston, E., Duchess of 86
Kir'iak, T. 129–131, 133, 134, 137
Kireevskaia, A. P. 270
Kireevskii, P. V. 178
Kiselev, N. S. 233
Kiseleva, L. N. 62
Kliucharev, F. P. 227
Kliuchevskii, V. O. 30
Kochubei, V. P. 208

Konstantin Pavlovich (Constantine), Grand Prince 25, 27, 28, 58, 59, 94, 106, 109, 121, 127, 128, 326
Korf, M. A. 185–187, 191, 193, 228
Korsunskii, I. N. 250, 275
Kościuszko, Tadeusz 354
Koshelev, R. A. 210, 214, 278, 294, 298
Kostrov, Ermil 94, 99
Kotel'nikov, E. 324
Kovalenskaia, N. N. 156n1
Kovan'ko, Ivan 236
Kozel'skii, Fedor 39
Kriukovskii, M. V. 155, 157, 158, 170, 173, 175, 176, 180, 182
Krüdener, B. Yu. 290–295, 298, 300, 301, 303, 304, 309, 315–319, 322
Krüdener, Juliette 289, 294, 298, 299, 306, 317
Krug, W. T. 290
Krylov, I. A. 247, 248
Kukol'nik, N. V. 157
Kurakin, Aleksandr B. 188, 210
Kurakin, Aleksei B. 156
Kurakina, N. I. 156
Kurganov, N. G. 201
Kutuzov, M. I. 236–239, 240n2, 242, 257, 283, 284

L

L'vov, N. A. 134n7, 142, 246
L'vov, P. Iu. 157, 161, 177
La Harpe, F.-C. 321
La Harpe, J.-F. de 135
Labzin, A. F. 203, 294, 295, 299, 299n4
Lacan, J. 5n2
Lampi the Elder, Johann-Baptist von 123
Lazarev, V. V. 136n8
Le Forestier, René 196
Le Pique, Charles 133
Lenin, V. I. 2, 17, 19n4,
Lentin, A. 30n4
Leonid, Greek King 56, 282
Lermontov, M. Yu. 357
Levi-Strauss, Claud 6, 7
Ley, Francis 279, 291, 294, 295n3
Lieven, Kh. A. 319
Ligne, Ch.-J. de, Prince 109, 110
Liubetskii 207
Liubomirskii, K. 139

Liven, K. A. 329
Lobanov, M. E. 248
Loginov, A. A. 207
Łojek, J. 151n15
Lomonosov, M. V. 28n2, 40, 75, 108
Lopatin, V. S. 124n1, 139, 140, 145n13
Lopukhin, I. V. 159, 202, 203, 209, 210, 272–275, 296
Lord, R. H. 126, 142, 143n12,
Lotman, Iu. M. 6–9, 20, 217n13
Louis XIV 67
Louis XV 64, 79, 81, 83, 84, 86, 87, 90, 91, 190, 210
Louis XVI 70, 81, 85, 86, 227, 283
Lubianovskii, F. P. 186, 202, 203, 354,
Luden, Heinrich 337
Ludolf, Count 111
Lukács, G. 3
Lukin, V. I. 90
Luzhkov, Iu. M. 16
Lycurguses 49

M

Macherey, Pierre 19
Macintosh, Christopher 196
Magnitskii, M. L. 211, 225, 353–356
Maikov, V. I. 49, 50, 91
Maistre, Joseph de 156, 199, 200, 204, 214–216, 218, 337
Mani 199
Mannheim, K. 1, 3, 4, 4n1
Marat, J.-P. 241
Maria Fedorovna, widowed Empress 101, 107, 218, 258, 260, 261
Mark Aurelius 259
Marmontel, J.-F. 180
Martos, I. P. 155, 156, 156n1, 158, 171, 177
Martynov, I. F. 63
Marx, K. 2, 3
Masal'skii, P. G. 208
Masha — see Protasova (Moyer) M. A.
Maxentius 57
Mazepa, 226
Mecou, Andre Joseph 218
Mel'gunov, S. P. 228n16, 280n6
Melodor 263
Menander 33
Mercy-Argenteau, Comte de 83

Meshcherskaia, S. S. 278, 317, 320, 323
Metternich, Klemens von 289, 309, 319, 323n6, 343
Meyer, T. 205
Meys, Ferdinand de 106
Mikhail (Drozdov) 250
Mikhail Fedorovich (Romanov) 155, 168, 175, 176, 176n7, 179n8, 180, 182, 236
Mikhailovski-Danilevskii, A. I. 113
Mil'china, V. A. 330n2
Miltiades 35, 35n5
Minikh, B. K. 26
Minin, Kuz'ma 154n16, 155–158, 160, 168–171, 171n4, 172, 176, 177, 224, 235, 244
Miniszech, Marina 179
Mirabeau 200n8
Mniszech, Marina 173, 174
Montesquieu, Charles S. 164
Mordvinov, N. S. 88, 115–117, 232
Mornet, Daniel 199
Morreau, J. V. M. 283, 284
Mouton 229, 231
Mühlenbeck, Eugène 273, 291, 293–294
Mukhin, M. 327
Murav'ev-Apostol, I. M. 247
Musin-Pushkin, A. S. 84, 89
Mustapha, 33

N

Nadler, V. K. 291
Näf, Werner 289
Napoleon Bonaparte 22, 157–159, 161–163, 167, 169, 172, 181, 183, 193, 194, 204–207, 218, 219, 227–230, 239–242, 244, 245, 252, 254, 258, 259, 279, 281, 283, 285n7, 289, 291, 304, 306, 312, 321, 322, 339, 343, 345, 348, 354
Naryshkin, A. L. 158
Naryshkina, M. A. 173n5, 354
Nassau-Siegen, K.-G. 113
Neledinskii-Meletskii, Iu. A. 260, 261
Nemzer A. S. 286, 286n9
Nessel'rode, K. V. 188, 189, 193, 210
Nevakhovich, L. N. 221–223
Nicephorus, Greek Archbishop 97

Nicholas I 186, 191, 261, 326, 329, 330, 351, 353–354, 355
Nikiforus, Greek Archbishop 29
Nikitenko, A. V. 328
Nikolai Mikhailovich, Grand Prince 23, 210, 281
Nikolai Pavlovich 325, 353
Novikov, N. I. 91, 206
Novosil'tsev, N. N. 189, 190, 204, 204n9

O
Obolenskii, V. P. 176n7, 223
Obreskov 37
Oginski, M. 143
Ol'ri, Bavarian envoy 163, 173n5
Oldenburg, prince of 191, 218, 220
Olenin, A. N. 207, 234, 245–247, 247n4n5, 248–250, 255, 280
Olympiada 55
Omar (or Umar), Caliph 128n3
Orlov, A. G. 31, 35, 42–45, 50, 53, 62
Orlov, G. G. 42
Ospovat, A. L. 330n2
Otman 57
Otrep'ev, G. B. 173
Ozerov, V. A. 157, 158, 170, 171, 178, 247

P
Palitsyn — see Avraamii.
Palladoklis, Antonii 54, 57, 98
Panchenko, A. M. 107, 110n4
Panin, N. I. 26, 29n3, 90, 92, 105, 144
Papernyi, Vladimir 120
Parrot, G.-F. 189
Pascually, Jacques Martinez de 196n5, 293n2
Paul I 23, 58, 63, 101, 107, 109, 116, 143, 202
Pavel Petrovich — see Paul I.
Perets, A. I. 208
Peter I (Peter the Great) 9, 16, 26, 30, 33, 43, 44, 58, 105, 111, 114, 114n5n6, 118, 157, 164, 236, 284
Peter III 80
Peter IV 58
Petrov, Ia. V. 62
Petrov, V. P., painter 115
Petrov, V. P., poet 22, 25, 26, 38, 40–42, 46, 47, 49, 50, 54, 56, 61–65, 65n1, 67–70, 72–79, 81, 83–86, 86n4, 87–91, 95, 101, 104, 111, 112, 121, 127, 133, 145–148, 152, 154
Pfenninger, J. 290
Phidias 32
Phidiases 35, 35n5
Pindar 41, 101
Platon, Moscow Metropolitan 202, 250
Pleshcheev, A. A. 275
Pogodin, M. P. 190, 328, 328n1
Poniatowski, S. — see Stanisław August.
Ponomarev, S. 257
Poplavskaia, I. A. 260
Popov, A . N. 228n16
Potemkin, G. A. 22, 24, 25, 25n1, 26, 29, 30, 35, 36, 54, 60, 61, 64, 77, 90, 93, 95–97, 97n2, 101–107, 109, 110n4, 111, 113–115, 119–124, 124n1, 125, 125n2, 126, 127, 129–131, 133, 133n6, 134, 136–145, 145n13, 146, 146n14, 147, 148, 150–152, 257
Potemkin, P. S. 51, 53, 54
Potemkin, S. P. 259
Pozharskii, Dmitrii 154n16, 155–158, 160, 168–171, 173, 175, 176n7, 177, 179n8, 180–182, 224, 230, 235, 237, 238, 244
Prach, I. I. 246
Pradt, Dominique de 287
Predtechenskii, A. V. 240
Presniakov, A. E. 298
Prigogine, Ilya 7
Proskurin, O. A. 247n5, 275, 331n3
Protasova (Moyer), M. A. 260, 261, 263, 264, 271–273, 275, 277, 278, 286
Protasova, E. A. 261, 271, 272, 272n3
Pumpianskii, L. V. 87
Pushkin V. L. 286n9
Pushkin, A. S. 20
Pypin, A. N. 214, 317, 324, 327

R
Racine, J. 248
Radishchev, A. N. 9
Raupakh, E. 353
Razumovskii, A. K. 212, 216, 352
Réal de Curban, Gaspard de 71
Rebekkini, D. 157n2
Rennenkampf, K. P. 212

Richards, I. A. 18
Ricoeur, Paul 4n1, 8, 15, 18
Robespierre 241
Robison, D. 202
Robison, G. 90
Robison, J. 197
Roode, Theodorus de 51
Rostropovich, F. V. 15, 160, 161, 184, 191, 202, 205, 206, 209, 210, 217, 223, 226–228, 228n16, 229–231, 236, 243–245, 351
Rousseau, J.-J. 6, 7, 72, 72n2, 73, 74, 76–78, 81, 82, 82n3, 91, 163–168, 173, 182, 200, 200n7, 340, 347, 348
Royer-Collard, P.-P. 333
Rozenkampf, G. A. 204, 215
Rulhière, Claude-Carloman de 81, 82
Rumiantsev, N. P. 188, 210
Rumiantsev, P. A. 59, 106, 284
Runich, D. P. 353

S

Saint- Pierre, Charles-Irénée Castel, abbé de 72, 72n2, 78, 318
Samarin, Iu. F. 233
Samoilov, A. N. 26n1, 96, 97, 105
Sanglen, Ia. I. 186, 187, 189–192, 194, 206, 208, 214
Schiel, F. B. 343
Schlegel, A. 337
Schlegel, F. 337–340, 343, 344, 347, 348
Schuchard, M. K. 90
Schwarzenberg, K.-F. 241
Ségur, L. F. 111
Serkov, A. I. 212
Severgin, V. M. 156, 171, 173, 238
Shagin-Girei 93
Shakhovskoi, A. A. 221, 247, 286, 286n9
Shebunin, A. N. 288n1
Shevchenko, M. M. 352, 329
Shevyrev, S. P. 328n1
Shil'der, N. K. 187, 190, 191n1, 200, 245
Shikhmatov — see Shirinskii-Shikhmatov, S. A.
Shirinskii-Shikhmatov, S. A. 155, 157, 169–172, 175, 176, 180, 182, 247, 251,
Shishkov, A. S. 22, 136n8, 157, 163–168, 170, 172, 174, 182–185, 193, 207, 232–236, 238, 238n1, 239–247, 247n5, 248, 249, 251–254, 256, 257, 277, 283, 284, 287, 324, 347, 348, 351, 352
Shklovskii, V. B. 8n3
Shpet, G. G. 337
Shtakel'berg, O. M. 210
Shubin, F. I. 132, 133
Sieyès, E. J. 349
Silov, G. I. 63
Simonini, Captain 199, 200
Sirotkin, V. G.
Sivers, Ia. E. 152
Smith, Douglas 201
Sokolov, P. F. 271
Sollogub, S. I. 317
Solow, Robert 9
Sophocles 32–34
Sopikov, V. S. 136n8
Speranskii, M. M. 22, 23, 184–192, 192n3, 193–195, 204–217, 217n13, 221, 223–226, 228, 231, 232, 246, 247, 269, 298, 309–311, 313, 331, 338, 353, 354
St. Martin, Louis-Claude de 196
Stadion, I.-F. 339
Stäel, G. de 336, 337
Stanisław August Poniatowski, king 83, 138, 151n15
Stankevich, E. 164, 166
Starck, J. A. 197, 201
Starobinski, Jean 165, 167, 200n7
Stein, H.-F.-K. 213, 316, 317, 341, 342, 342n7, 343, 357
Stolberg, Count of 109
Stolypin, A. A. 195
Strabo 102
Stroganov, P. A. 156, 207
Sturdza (Stourdza), A. S. 155, 169n3, 173, 250, 276, 289, 309, 322
Strudza, Roksandra 278, 279, 291–293, 295, 298, 299, 308, 315, 318, 319
Sully, M. de 44, 45, 71, 72, 127
Sumarokov, A. P. 91
Sumin, L. 176n7
Susanin, Ivan 349
Suvorov, A. V. 124, 124n1, 142, 284
Sverbeev, D. N. 230, 351

Sviatoslav, Conte 97, 97n2
Swedenborg, Em. 90, 273

T
Taft, R. A. 12
Talleyrand, Ch. M. 188
Tartakovskii, A. G. 243
Tatarinova, E. F. 323
Tchaikovsky, P. I. 15
Tercier, J.-P. 79, 80, 83
Themistocles 56
Tisenhaus, Sophie de 290
Tituchev, F. I. 335
Todd, William Mills 19
Tolstoy, L. N. 228, 230
Tomsinov, V. A. 192n3
Toqueville, A. de 13
Troitskii, N. A. 294
Troshchinskii, D. P. 237
Trubetskoi, D. T. 173
Tseier, F. I. 309, 310
Tseier, F. M. 269
Tseretelli, Z. K. 16
Turgenev Aleksandr I. 207, 250, 259–261, 269n2, 271, 275, 277, 277n4, 312
Turgenev, Andrei I. 263, 277
Tynianov, Iu. N. 286

U
Ubri, P. Ia. 159
Ugriumov, G. I. 168
Ulianitskii, V. A. 43
Urbi, P. Ia. 162
Uspenskii, B. A. 9, 355
Uvarov, S. S. 22, 23, 247, 248, 260, 275, 277, 325, 327, 328, 328n1, 329, 330, 330n2, 331–333, 335, 335n5, 336–339, 341, 342, 342n7, 343–347, 348n9, 350–358

V
Varnhagen von Ense, 230
Vasnetsov, V. M. 349
Venetsianov, A. G. 227
Vereshchagin, M. N. 228–231
Verevkin, M. I. 44

Vergennes, Ch. G. 65, 70, 82, 83, 86
Viazemskii, P. A. 230, 275, 286n9
Victor Emmanuel, king 200
Vielgorsky, M. 81
Vigel', F. F. 162, 185, 209, 210, 224, 225
Viskovatov, P. A. 272n3
Vladimir St., Chersonese Prince 96, 97, 102, 114, 114n5, 116, 199
Voeikov, A. F. 260, 275, 277n4
Vogler, Georg Joseph 136
Volkonskii, P. M. 292, 294
Voltaire 30, 30n4, 31–38, 42, 44, 45, 47, 50, 54, 66, 81, 133, 198, 203, 320
Vorontsov, M. L. 93

W
Watt, James 90
Weber, K. 118
Weishaupt, Adam 196, 198, 203, 206, 206n11, 212, 214
Winckelmann 36, 246, 247n4
Władysław IV Vasa 174
Wolff, L. 106, 109
Wortman, Richard 123, 236, 266

X
Xerxes 56

Y
Yanaev, G. I. 14
Yeltsin, B. N. 14, 15
Ypsilantis, Alexandros 320

Z
Zagoskin, M. N. 157
Zarutskii I. M. 173, 174
Zeidlits, K. K. 272n3
Zeuxis 32
Zhikharev, S. P. 158, 172
Zhukov, I. F. 230n17
Zhukovskii, V. A. 22, 247, 258–266, 269–272, 272n3, 273–275, 277n4, 278, 281–285, 285n7, 286, 286n9, 312–314, 337
Zimmermann, I. G. 113
Zubov, Platon 125

www.ingramcontent.com/pod-product-compliance
Lightning Source LLC
Chambersburg PA
CBHW051107230426
43667CB00014B/2478